THE NEW CAMBRIDGE COMPANION
TO COLERIDGE

This new collection enables students and general readers to appreciate Coleridge's renewed relevance 250 years after his birth. An indispensable guide to his writing for twenty-first-century readers, it contains new perspectives that reframe his work in relation to slavery, race, war, post-traumatic stress disorder and ecological crisis. Through detailed engagement with Coleridge's pioneering poetry, the reader is invited to explore fundamental questions on themes ranging from nature and trauma to gender and sexuality. Essays by leading Coleridge scholars analyse and render accessible his innovative thinking about dreams, psychoanalysis, genius and symbolism. Coleridge is often a direct and gripping writer, yet he is also elusive and diverse. This Companion's great achievement is to offer a one-volume entry point into his rich and varied world.

Tim Fulford is Professor of English and Director of the Biennial Coleridge Conference. He is the winner of the 2019 Robert Penn Warren/Cleanth Brooks Award for Literary Scholarship.

D0781088

THE NEW CAMBRIDGE
COMPANION TO COLERIDGE

EDITED BY
TIM FULFORD

WITHDRAWN

CAMBRIDGE
UNIVERSITY PRESS

CAMBRIDGE
UNIVERSITY PRESS

University Printing House, Cambridge CB2 8BS, United Kingdom

One Liberty Plaza, 20th Floor, New York, NY 10006, USA

477 Williamstown Road, Port Melbourne, VIC 3207, Australia

314–321, 3rd Floor, Plot 3, Splendor Forum, Jasola District Centre,
New Delhi – 110025, India

103 Penang Road, #05–06/07, Visioncrest Commercial, Singapore 238467

Cambridge University Press is part of the University of Cambridge.

It furthers the University's mission by disseminating knowledge in the pursuit of
education, learning, and research at the highest international levels of excellence.

www.cambridge.org
Information on this title: www.cambridge.org/9781108832229
DOI: 10.1017/9781108935555

First published 2023

A catalogue record for this publication is available from the British Library.

ISBN 978-1-108-83222-9 Hardback
ISBN 978-1-108-94079-5 Paperback

CONTENTS

Notes on Contributors   *page* vii

Chronology   xi

List of Abbreviations   xiv

1   Coleridge at 250: A Poet for the Twenty-First Century   1
     TIM FULFORD

2   Political Coleridge   14
     JACOB LLOYD

3   Coleridge and Collaboration   30
     FELICITY JAMES

4   Nature Lyrics   46
     GREGORY LEADBETTER

5   Coleridge's Ecopoetics   62
     JOANNA E. TAYLOR

6   Gothic Coleridge, Ballad Coleridge   80
     MARGARET RUSSETT

7   Coleridge's Metres   96
     EWAN JAMES JONES

8   Coleridge and the Theatre   111
     MICHAEL GAMER AND JEFFREY N. COX

9   Coleridge the Walker   130
     ALAN VARDY

CONTENTS

10 Notebook Coleridge   144
    THOMAS OWENS

11 Coleridge and Science   161
    KURTIS HESSEL

12 Religious Coleridge   178
    JEFFREY W. BARBEAU

13 Coleridge the Lecturer and Critic   192
    CHARLES W. MAHONEY

14 Coleridge's Philosophies   209
    NICHOLAS HALMI

15 Coleridge's Later Poetry   225
    KAREN SWANN

16 Coleridge and History   243
    TOM DUGGETT

    Further Reading   257
    Index   262

NOTES ON CONTRIBUTORS

JEFFREY W. BARBEAU is Professor of Theology at Wheaton College. He is the author or editor of several books, including *Sara Coleridge: Her Life and Thought* (2014), *Religion in Romantic England: An Anthology of Primary Sources* (2018) and *The Cambridge Companion to British Romanticism and Religion* (2021).

JEFFREY N. COX is Distinguished Professor in English and Humanities at the University of Colorado Boulder. His contributions to studies in Romanticism include *In the Shadows of Romance: Romantic Tragic Drama in Germany, England, and France* (1987), *Poetry and Politics in the Cockney School: Shelley, Keats, Hunt, and Their Circle*, winner of the 2000 South Central Modern Language Association Best Book Award, and *Romanticism in the Shadow of War: The Culture of the Napoleonic War Years* (2014). His latest book, *William Wordsworth, Second Generation Romantic: Contesting Poetry after Waterloo*, appeared in 2021. In 2009, he received the Distinguished Scholar Award from the Keats–Shelley Association of America.

TOM DUGGETT is Senior Associate Professor (Reader) in Romanticism at Xi'an Jiaotong–Liverpool University (XJTLU; Suzhou, China) and Honorary Fellow of the Department of English, University of Liverpool. He is the author of *Gothic Romanticism* (2010), a study of Wordsworth, Coleridge and the ancient constitution, which received the Modern Language Association of America's Prize for Independent Scholars for Distinguished Research in Language and Literature (2012). Tom was a guest editor of the special issue of *The Wordsworth Circle* marking the bicentenary of Wordsworth's *Excursion* and is currently an advisory editor of *Romanticism*. He has also produced a two-volume scholarly edition of Robert Southey's *Sir Thomas More: or, Colloquies on the Progress and Prospects of Society*, published in the Pickering Masters series in 2018.

TIM FULFORD is the author of many books and articles on Coleridge, including *The Late Poetry of the Lake Poets: Romanticism Revised* (2103). He is the co-editor of *The Collected Letters of Sir Humphry Davy* (2020), of *The Collected Letters of Robert Southey* (2009–ongoing) and of the forthcoming *Collected Letters of Thomas Beddoes* (2026). He has also edited the poetry of Robert Southey and Robert Bloomfield.

MICHAEL GAMER is British Academy Professor of English and Drama at Queen Mary University of London and Professor of English and Comparative Literature at the University of Pennsylvania. He is author of *Romanticism and the Gothic* (2000) and *Romanticism, Self-Canonization, and the Business of Poetry* (2017). With Jeffrey Cox he has edited *The Broadview Anthology of Romantic Drama* (2003), with Dahlia Porter *Lyrical Ballads 1798 and 1800* (2008) and with Diego Saglia volume 5 of the *Cultural History of Tragedy: The Age of Empire* (2019). He is currently at work on a four-year research project entitled *Romantic Melodrama: Feeling in Search of Form* and (with Angela Wright) is general editor of the *Cambridge Edition of the Works of Ann Radcliffe* (forthcoming).

NICHOLAS HALMI is Professor of English and Comparative Literature at the University of Oxford and Margaret Candfield Fellow of University College, Oxford. He is the author of *The Genealogy of the Romantic Symbol* (2007), editor of *Wordsworth's Poetry and Prose* (2013) and co-editor of *Coleridge's Poetry and Prose* (2003). He is currently completing a study of historicization and aesthetics in the seventeenth to nineteenth centuries.

KURTIS HESSEL is a teaching assistant professor in the Program for Writing and Rhetoric at the University of Colorado Boulder. His research examines the slow development of intellectual disciplines and the changing relationship between literature and chemistry during the eighteenth and nineteenth centuries. He has published articles in *Studies in Romanticism*, *European Romantic Review*, *Configurations* and *The Coleridge Bulletin*.

FELICITY JAMES is Associate Professor of Eighteenth and Nineteenth Century English Literature at the University of Leicester. Her research focuses on Charles and Mary Lamb and their friendship circle, including Coleridge and Wordsworth, religious Dissent and life writing. Key publications include the forgotten novel of Elizabeth Hays Lanfear, *Fatal Errors; or Poor Mary-Anne: A Tale of the Last Century* (2019), co-edited with Timothy Whelan, *Writing Lives Together: Romantic and Victorian Auto/Biography*, with Julian North (2017), *Religious Dissent and the Aikin–Barbauld Circle, 1740–1860* (2011) and *Charles Lamb, Coleridge and Wordsworth: Reading Friendship in the 1790s* (2008).

EWAN JAMES JONES is Associate Professor in English at the University of Cambridge. He is the author of *Coleridge and the Philosophy of Poetic Form* (2014), in addition to numerous articles on prosody, nineteenth-century verse and computational forms of reading. At the point of writing he is a recipient of a Leverhulme Research Fellowship, through which he is researching poetic and scientific modes of attention.

GREGORY LEADBETTER is Professor of Poetry at Birmingham City University. His research focuses on Romantic poetry and thought, the traditions to which these relate and the history and practice of poetry more generally. His book *Coleridge and the Daemonic Imagination* (2011) won the University English Book Prize 2012. His books of poetry include *Balanuve* (with photographs by Phil Thomson) (2021), *Maskwork* (2020), *The Fetch* (2016) and the pamphlet *The Body in the Well* (2007).

JACOB LLOYD is a tutor and fellow at the Montag Centre for Overseas Studies, Stanford University in Oxford. He completed his DPhil thesis on Coleridge's political poetics at Balliol College, Oxford. He has published several articles on Coleridge's poetry and philosophical thought.

CHARLES W. MAHONEY is Professor of English, and Comparative Literary and Cultural Studies at the University of Connecticut. He is currently preparing an edition of Coleridge's writings on Shakespeare. In 2019, he succeeded Marilyn Gaull as the editor of *The Wordsworth Circle*.

THOMAS OWENS is an assistant professor of English at Stanford University. He specializes in literature of the long nineteenth century and is the author of *Wordsworth, Coleridge, and 'the Language of the Heavens'* (2019).

MARGARET RUSSETT teaches at the University of Southern California and sometimes, when the stars align, at Boğaziçi University in Istanbul. She is the author of two books on Romantic poetry and prose: *De Quincey's Romanticism* (1997) and *Fictions and Fakes* (2006). She has also published numerous essays on gothic fiction and Romantic poetics, with special emphasis on Coleridge and the 'suspension of disbelief'.

KAREN SWANN is the Williams College Morris Professor of Rhetoric, Emerita. She is the author of *Lives of the Dead Poets: Keats, Shelley, Coleridge* (2019), as well as numerous articles on poetry of the Romantic period. She is currently working on a study of John Clare's natural history writing.

JOANNA E. TAYLOR is Lecturer in Nineteenth-Century Literature and Digital Humanities at the University of Manchester. Her research explores intersections between literary geographies, digital cartographies and environmental humanities, the themes of a book, co-authored with Ian Gregory, titled *Deep Mapping the Literary Lake District: A Geographical Text Analysis* (2022).

ALAN VARDY is Professor of English at Hunter College and the Graduate Center, City University of New York. He is the author of 'Coleridge on Broad Stand' in *Romanticism and Victorianism on the Net* (2012) and is currently completing a book entitled *In Transit: Time and Terrain in British Romantic Writing*.

1772	Born at Ottery St Mary, Devon (21 October).
1781	Father dies unexpectedly.
1782	Sent to school at Christ's Hospital, London.
1792	Jesus College, Cambridge.
1793	Attends the trial of William Frend (May); enlists in the army under the pseudonym Silas Tomkyn Comberbache (December).
1794	Returns to Cambridge; collaboration with Robert Southey; plan to emigrate and set up commune (Pantisocracy); publishes jointly written *The Fall of Robespierre*; begins *Religious Musings*.
1795	Political lectures at Bristol in conjunction with Southey; marriage to Sara Fricker, sister of Southey's bride; political pamphleteering in Bristol in conjunction with Thomas Beddoes; publishes *Conciones ad Populum*; assistance from Bristol bookseller Joseph Cottle.
1796	With Beddoes's help establishes a journal, *The Watchman*, and tours the Midlands to promote it. Beddoes procures him a job writing for the national newspaper *The Morning Chronicle*. Publishes *Poems on Various Subjects*. His first child, Hartley, born.
1797	Moves to Nether Stowey, Somerset, near Thomas Poole (January). Invites William and Dorothy Wordsworth to live near him in Somerset (June); 'annus mirabilis' outpouring of 'conversation' poems and ballads begins; writes a play, *Osorio*; publishes *Poems, to Which Are Now Added, Poems by Charles Lamb and Charles Lloyd*. Meets Beddoes's friends Thomas and Josiah Wedgwood.
1798	Meets William Hazlitt (January); accepts offer of annuity from the Wedgwoods, freeing him from the need to earn his living as a Unitarian minister. *Fears in Solitude* published,

including 'Frost at Midnight'; starts writing for *The Morning Post*; collaboration with Wordsworth and anonymous joint publication of *Lyrical Ballads,* including 'The Rime of the Ancyent Marinere'; second son, Berkeley, born in May; visit to Germany with the Wordsworths (September–July 1799).

1799   Attends Göttingen University, studying natural history, philosophy and Biblical criticism. Death of Berkeley (April); goes on walking tour of Harz mountains with fellow students; return to England in July; meets brilliant young chemist Humphry Davy, inhales nitrous oxide at Beddoes's Pneumatic Institution; meets Sara Hutchinson, sister of Wordsworth's future bride (October); working for *The Morning Post.*

1800   Moves to Greta Hall, Keswick, to be near the Wordsworths in Grasmere; second edition of *Lyrical Ballads* published.

1801   Ill and using opium heavily. In London (December–April 1802) writing for newspapers.

1802   Marriage starts to founder as love for Sara Hutchinson develops; goes on solo walking tour of Lake District, describing it in letters to Sara Hutchinson (August). Writes verse 'Letter to Sara', published in redacted version as 'Dejection: An Ode'; birth of daughter, whom he names Sara.

1803   *Poems* (1803); Scottish tour with the Wordsworths ends in separation; opium addiction worsens. Writes 'The Pains of Sleep'. Invites Southey and Southey's wife to share his home, Greta Hall.

1804   Addiction leads to health problems. Goes to Malta for his health; becomes Acting Public Secretary there. Loneliness, longing for Sara Hutchinson; addiction. Turns away from Unitarianism towards Trinitarian Anglicanism.

1806   Returns to England via Sicily, Naples, Rome, Florence; separates from his wife; stays with Wordsworths at Coleorton, Leicestershire, where Wordsworth reads *The Prelude* to him. Experiences jealous anger over Wordsworth's supposed attractiveness to Sara Hutchinson.

1807   Moves between London, Stowey and Bristol.

1808   'Lectures on the Principles of Poetry' at the Royal Institution, invited by Humphry Davy; moves to Allan Bank, Grasmere, to live with the Wordsworths; begins to publish his weekly journal *The Friend*, dictating copy to Sara Hutchinson.

1809–10   Publishes twenty-eight numbers of *The Friend.*

1810	Rift with the Wordsworths caused by his conduct as a house-mate (addiction) and by his resentment of Wordsworth's displeasure at this conduct. Leaves Grasmere, never to return. Platonic affair with Sara Hutchinson also ends.
1811	Writing for *The Courier* newspaper in London. Living in Hammersmith with a Bristol friend, John Morgan, Morgan's wife, Mary, and sister-in-law, Charlotte Brent.
1811–12	Lectures on drama and Shakespeare in London. Quarrel with Wordsworth patched up but intimacy not resumed.
1813	*Remorse* (a revised version of the drama *Osorio*) is performed at Drury Lane. Coleridge in Bristol and Bath, where in December he has an opium-induced crisis. Supports Mary Morgan and Charlotte Brent in lodgings near Bath, John Morgan having escaped to Ireland to avoid arrest for debt.
1814	Lectures in Bristol; cared for there by a Bristol friend, Josiah Wade. Moves with the Morgans to Calne, Wiltshire (December).
1815	Composes *Biographia Literaria* and a new play, *Zapolya*, and collects poems for publication (*Sibylline Leaves*) while in Calne, living with the Morgans. His feelings for Charlotte Brent and return to opium and alcohol use cause tensions.
1816	Leaves Calne for London with the Morgans; further opium crises; moves into the Highgate house of James Gillman, surgeon, who undertakes to treat his opium addiction. Lives with the Gillmans for the rest of his life. Publishes 'Christabel' and 'Kubla Khan' with help from Byron. Publishes *The Statesman's Manual*.
1817	Publishes *Zapolya,* also *Biographia Literaria,* in which he plays down his radical politics and Unitarian religion of the 1790s and early 1800s. Collects poems in *Sibylline Leaves*; lectures on poetry and drama (January–March).
1818	Publishes *The Friend* (3-vol. edition); lectures on literature and philosophy.
1819	Meets Keats; occasional contributions to *Blackwood's*.
1821	Begins philosophical/theological work, *Opus Maximum*.
1823	Sees his daughter Sara for the first time in ten years. Henry Nelson Coleridge begins recording *Table Talk*.
1825	*Aids to Reflection* published.
1828	*Poetical Works* (3 vols). Tours the Rhine with Wordsworth.
1829	*On the Constitution of Church and State*.
1834	Death at Highgate.

ABBREVIATIONS

AR	*Aids to Reflection*, ed. John Beer (Princeton University Press, 1993).
BL	*Biographia Literaria*, ed. James Engell and Walter Jackson Bate, 2 vols (Princeton University Press, 1983).
Church and State	*On the Constitution of the Church and State*, ed. John Colmer (Princeton University Press, 1976).
CL	*The Collected Letters of Samuel Taylor Coleridge*, ed. Earl Leslie Griggs, 6 vols (Oxford University Press, 1956–71).
CLRS	*The Collected Letters of Robert Southey*, gen. ed. Lynda Pratt, Tim Fulford and Ian Packer. Romantic Circles Electronic Edition, 2009–; https://romantic- circles.org/editions/southey_letters
CM	Marginalia, 6 vols, ed. George Whalley and H. J. Jackson (Princeton University Press, 1980–2001).
CN	*The Notebooks of Samuel Taylor Coleridge*, ed. Kathleen Coburn, Merton Christensen and Anthony John Harding, 5 vols (Princeton University Press, 1957–2002).
CPW	*Poetical Works*, ed. J. C. C. Mays, 3 vols (Princeton University Press, 2001).
CU	[Samuel Taylor Coleridge], review of Ann Radcliffe, *The Mysteries of Udolpho*. *The Critical Review*, 2nd series, 11 (August 1794).
DWJ	*Journals of Dorothy Wordsworth: The Alfoxden Journal 1798, The Grasmere Journals, 1800–1803*, ed. Mary Moorman (New York: Oxford University Press, 1971).
EOT	Essays on *HisTimes*, ed. David V. Erdman, 3 vols (Princeton University Press, 1978).
EY	*The Letters of William and Dorothy Wordsworth: The Early Years, 1787–1805*, ed. Ernest de Selincourt, 2nd ed., rev. Chester Shaver (Oxford: Clarendon Press, 1967).
Friend	*The Friend*, ed. Barbara Rooke, 2 vols (Princeton University Press, 1969).
Howe	*William Hazlitt, Complete Works*, ed. P. P. Howe, 21 vols (London and Toronto: J. M. Dent and Sons, 1930–34).

Jackson	J. R. de J. Jackson (ed.), *Samuel Taylor Coleridge: The Critical Heritage*, vol. I, 1794–1834, and vol. II, 1835–1900 (London: Taylor and Francis, 1995–6).
LB	*Lyrical Ballads, and Other Poems, 1797–1799*, ed. James Butler and Karen Green (Ithaca, NY: Cornell University Press, 1992).
Lects 1795	*Lectures 1795: On Politics and Religion*, ed. Lewis Patton and Peter Mann (Princeton University Press, 1971).
Lects 1808–1819	*Lectures 1808–1819: On Literature*, ed. R. A. Foakes, 2 vols (Princeton University Press, 1987).
LL	*The Letters of Charles and Mary Anne Lamb*, ed. Edwin W. Marrs, Jr, 3 vols (Cornell University Press, 1975–8).
LS	*Lay Sermons*, ed. R. J. White (Princeton University Press, 1972)
Misc. C	*Coleridge's Miscellaneous Criticism*, ed. T. M. Raysor (Cambridge, MA: Constable and Co., 1936).
OM	*Opus Maximum*, ed. Thomas McFarland with Nicholas Halmi (Princeton University Press, 2002).
Parrish	Stephen Parrish, *Coleridge's "Dejection:" The Earliest Manuscripts and the Earliest Printings* (New York: Cornell University Press, 1988).
P Lects	*Lectures 1818–1819: On the History of Philosophy*, ed. J. R. de J. Jackson, 2 vols (Princeton University Press, 2000).
PVS	(1796) *Poems on Various Subjects, by S. T. Coleridge* (London: G. G. and J. Robinson and J. Cottle, 1796).
PVS	(1797) *Poems, by S. T. Coleridge, Second Edition. To Which Are Now Added* Poems by Charles Lamb and Charles Lloyd (Bristol: J. Cottle and Robinson, 1797).
SM	*The Statesman's Manual, Lay Sermons*, ed. R. J. White (Princeton University Press, 1993).
Swaab	Peter Swaab, *The Regions of Sara Coleridge's Thought: Selected Literary Criticism* (New York: Palgrave Macmillan, 2012).
SWF	*Shorter Works and Fragments*, ed. H. J. Jackson and J. R. de J. Jackson, 2 vols (Princeton University Press, 1995).
TT	*Table Talk*, ed. Carl Woodring, 2 vols. (Princeton University Press, 1990)
Watchman	*The Watchman*, ed. Lewis Patton (Princeton University Press, 1970)
WL (LY)	*The Letters of William and Dorothy Wordsworth: The Later Years*, ed. Ernest de Selincourt, 2nd ed., rev. Alan G. Hill (Oxford: Clarendon Press, 1978–88).

I

TIM FULFORD

Coleridge at 250

A Poet for the Twenty-First Century

His genius at that time had angelic wings, and fed on manna. He talked on for ever; and you wished him to talk on for ever. His thoughts did not seem to come with labour and effort; but as if borne on the gusts of genius, and as if the wings of his imagination lifted him from off his feet. His voice rolled on the ear like the pealing organ, and its sound alone was the music of thought. His mind was clothed with wings; and raised on them, he lifted philosophy to heaven. In his descriptions, you then saw the progress of human happiness and liberty in bright and never-ending succession, like the steps of Jacob's ladder, with airy shapes ascending and descending, and with the voice of God at the top of the ladder. And shall I, who heard him then, listen to him now? Not I! That spell is broke; that time is gone for ever; that voice is heard no more: but still the recollection comes rushing by with thoughts of long-past years, and rings in my ears with never-dying sound.

(*Hazlitt, Lectures on the English Poets* (1818); Howe v, 167)

To his contemporaries, Coleridge was the most extraordinary man of his age – a genius of unmatched capacity – but one who had failed to deliver the great works that seemed always to be in prospect. In Charles Lamb's words, he was 'an Archangel a little damaged' (Lamb's letter to Wordsworth, 26 April 1816; *LL* III, 215). Published 250 years after his birth, this *Companion to Coleridge* gives today's readers an opportunity to explore why his peers thought him so surpassingly brilliant, and to ask what, in his multifarious and often unfinished works, may excite and astonish us now as his talk did Hazlitt then. In many ways, we are more privileged than those who read and heard Coleridge while he was alive: thanks to the efforts of twentieth-century editors, we can read the intimate and incomplete writings that were not published at the time. Coleridge's notebooks are, collectively, one of the great nineteenth-century texts – a demonstration of the growth of a brilliant, self-reflective mind that is worthy of comparison with Wordsworth's *Prelude*. They possess an immediacy that the literary autobiography that Coleridge did publish – *Biographia Literaria* (1817) – cannot match, even if its commentary on poetry did raise literary criticism to a new level, essentially founding it as an intellectual discipline. Coleridge's marginalia – running to six large volumes and also unavailable to his peers – is an unparalleled record of a writer formulating a new, dialogic discourse by thinking in tandem with the author he is reading. His lectures – political, philosophical and literary – have also been restored to modern readers and reveal him, among other things, as one of Shakespeare's best critics. Even his huge philosophical/theological project – the incomplete *Opus Maximum* – has been rescued from manuscript and published. Unlike Hazlitt, twenty-first-century readers have a vast array of Coleridge's writings, as well as his exhilarating conversation, to explore. This *Companion* aims to guide readers as they thread the labyrinth of Coleridge-in-print, by featuring every major aspect of his oeuvre.

Coleridge, Ecological Destruction and Climate Change

Some aspects stand particularly proud in today's context. In our era of ecological destruction characterized by the pollution of the air with gases, of water with sewage and plastic, and of the earth with toxic chemicals, 'The Rime of the Ancyent Marinere' reads as an all too prescient parable of the destruction of both society and nature by extreme weather events caused by human exploitation of the planet:

> All in a hot and copper sky,
> The bloody Sun, at noon,
> Right up above the mast did stand,
> No bigger than the Moon.
>
> Day after day, day after day,
> We stuck, nor breath nor motion;
> As idle as a painted ship
> Upon a painted ocean.
>
> Water, water, every where,
> And all the boards did shrink;
> Water, water, every where,
> Nor any drop to drink.   (*CPW* I, i, 381; lines 111–22)

A ramped-up logic of deliberate disproportion between cause and effect gives the poem its nightmarish instructiveness: if in the real world climate change is death by a billion cuts – the cumulative result of two centuries of countless unremembered acts of environmental degradation – in the Mariner's world it occurs in response to one thoughtless, casual deed – the killing of a single albatross. 'We receive but what we give' ('Dejection: An Ode'; *CPW* I, ii, 699, line 47), Coleridge wrote, and the Mariner 'gives' violence and receives, in return, a nature so violated and disturbed that it becomes unbearably hostile to human life:

> The very deep did rot: O Christ!
> That ever this should be!
> Yea, slimy things did crawl with legs
> Upon the slimy sea.   (*CPW* I, i, 381; lines 123–26)

Today's toxic algae blooms, lethal to animals, are pre-imagined here in images that attain astonishing graphic power because they are so economically expressed. They are resonant because they are simple, colloquial and stark – unqualified, unadorned, unexplained. Held within the short ballad lines, strongly stressed, they gain a searing intensity by accumulation: one after another strange sight appears, obeying no pattern the Mariner or the reader can understand or predict. The result is haunting to a degree neither Coleridge nor anyone else ever matched again: no other poem in the English language possesses the imagist surreality of 'The Rime'.

Coleridge and Cancel Culture: Trauma, Shame and Guilt

Surreal because what the Mariner perceives is driven by experiences so traumatic in their mixture of fear, guilt and shame that they cannot be spoken directly. He is, he feels, enthralled by feelings he cannot consciously articulate: cursed to silence. His perceptions, and their later telling in the story that his body wrenches out of him, are a form of dream writing, his worst nightmares coming true, as when he sees himself crewing the ship with the zombie men – some of them his own family – whose deaths he feels responsible for:

> The mariners all 'gan work the ropes,
> Where they were wont to do;
> They raised their limbs like lifeless tools –
> We were a ghastly crew.
>
> The body of my brother's son
> Stood by me, knee to knee:
> The body and I pulled at one rope,
> But he said nought to me.   (*CPW* I, i, 396; lines 337–44)

These zombie figures, compelled to work but deprived of free will, have been seen by several critics as dramatizations of Coleridge's horror at slavery, while the Mariner's ship has been compared to a slave ship.[1] Indeed, Coleridge's brother-in-law and collaborator Robert Southey read them this way when he adapted the poem into his 1798 ballad 'The Sailor Who Served in the Slave Trade' – reworking the Mariner's guilt and anguish as results of involvement in torturing a captured African to death.[2]

In 'The Rime of the Ancyent Marinere', guilt and shame also relate to the effects of what today we term 'cancel culture'. The Mariner is blamed for a single, brief, unthinking action that the social group within which he functions retrospectively decides has offended against its approved practices. He is ostracized as a 'Jonah' who brings bad luck and avoided as a pariah who is unclean and must not be touched. Having been made a non-person, he internalizes his shipmates' blaming and cursing as his own guilt and shame; he accepts that the horrors which destroy ship and crew are his fault. Self-disgust overcomes him:

> The many men, so beautiful!
> And they all dead did lie:
> And a thousand thousand slimy things
> Lived on; and so did I.
>
> I looked upon the rotting sea,
> And drew my eyes away;
> I looked upon the rotting deck,
> And there the dead men lay.
>
> I looked to heaven, and tried to pray;
> But or ever a prayer had gusht,
> A wicked whisper came, and made
> My heart as dry as dust.
>
> I closed my lids, and kept them close,
> And the balls like pulses beat;
> For the sky and the sea, and the sea and the sky
> Lay dead like a load on my weary eye,
> And the dead were at my feet.   (CPW I, i, 391; lines 236–52)

In the face of exclusion and rebuke, what began as terror persists as trauma; the Mariner becomes fixated on the dead, obsessively replaying their indictment of him:

> All stood together on the deck,
> For a charnel-dungeon fitter:
> All fixed on me their stony eyes,
> That in the Moon did glitter.
>
> The pang, the curse, with which they died,
> Had never passed away:
> I could not draw my eyes from theirs,
> Nor turn them up to pray.   (CPW I, i, 405; lines 434–41)

Stressed beyond belief, he cannot help himself; mind and body become worn out by his alienation. To the Pilot and Hermit who rescue him, he is a revenant:

> I moved my lips – the Pilot shrieked
> And fell down in a fit;
> The holy Hermit raised his eyes,
> And prayed where he did sit.
>
> I took the oars: the Pilot's boy,
> Who now doth crazy go,
> Laughed loud and long, and all the while
> His eyes went to and fro.
> 'Ha! ha!' quoth he, 'full plain I see,
> The Devil knows how to row.' (*CPW* I, i, 415; lines 560–69)

Memories as vivid as when they were first experienced possess his mind and body until they force their way, distorted, into speech. His act of telling is a symptomatic relief of traumatic energies rather than a chosen communication of information (still less an enlightening or entertaining story).

> Forthwith this frame of mine was wrenched
> With a woful agony,
> Which forced me to begin my tale;
> And then it left me free.
>
> Since then, at an uncertain hour,
> That agony returns:
> And till my ghastly tale is told,
> This heart within me burns.   (*CPW* I, i, 417; lines 578–85)

This 'strange power of speech' (line 587) holds hearers against their will, hypnotizing them – the Wedding Guest is horrified because it, like the Mariner himself, bespeaks the world of the dead and embodies ineffaceable anguish. The Mariner is Life-in-Death, the one zombie of the crew who managed to return to shore.

Coleridge's astonishing narrativization of mental torment, self-blame and self-hatred not only renders what we now call Post-Traumatic Stress Disorder with intense force but also declares the fundamental value, and awful precariousness, of life. The lives of the sailors, the life of the albatross, the lives of the water snakes are revealed as precious in the face of their destruction – when it is too late, or almost too late, to save them. It is by an unconscious act of recognition of life's value, no matter in what form, that the Mariner lifts at least some of his self-hatred. 'I blessed them unaware' (*CPW* I, i, 393; line 285), he says of the water-snakes – an unknowing deed that contrasts with his thoughtless shooting of the albatross. The poem, that is to say, finds a story that dramatizes in extremis what is otherwise taken for granted – the value of life, and of love of life. In this respect it resembles the terrible scenes on the heath between the mad King Lear, Gloucester and Poor Tom.

Coleridge, Confession and Mental Health

Coleridge's capacity to imagine human vulnerability, suffering, guilt and shame so vividly emerged from, and rebounded upon, his own insecure, unreliable, addictive selfhood. Exiled from his family to boarding school after his father's sudden death, Coleridge carried into his adult life a need for a strong, reliable brother-figure (essentially a surrogate father) who would preside over an intimate domestic circle in which he could nestle (essentially a surrogate family). In 1794 he was drawn to Robert Southey and to a scheme to live communally with Southey and others; he, Southey and another friend, Robert Lovell, married three sisters to this end. In Bristol and Somerset, the friendship, the scheme and the marriage frayed as (among other things) Coleridge lacked staying power and others grew to resent his unreliability (and he to resent their disapproval). In 1797 he replaced Southey with Wordsworth and substituted Dorothy Wordsworth (platonically) for his wife. This new domestic circle buoyed him and he produced, over the next year, many of his greatest works. The three travelled to Germany together and then moved to the Lake District. There, in 1802, the domestic community became still more intense as Wordsworth brought Mary Hutchinson into it as his wife. Coleridge, though still married, then fell deeply in love with Mary's sister Sara, as if repeating his 1794 choice of the sister of Southey's fiancée to be his partner. In 1802, though, he was not free to complete the fraternal/sororal circle by marrying, and so Sara remained his platonic muse, placing on her – and on Coleridge himself – an ultimately intolerable emotional load, to the Wordsworths' increasing disapproval and Coleridge's own distress. Neglecting his wife and children, Coleridge had recourse to increasing amounts of opium and, in 1804, left the Lakes for Malta, alone, for the sake of his physical and mental health. He returned in 1806, more deeply addicted, more desperately in love and, because crippled by shame at his own weakness in the face of Wordsworth's strength, still more incapable of completing his projected publications. The once reassuring circle had become poisoned – in Wordsworth's view by Coleridge's drinking and drug-taking, in Coleridge's by Wordsworth's unsympathetic rectitude. Tensions broke in 1810, after which Coleridge never lived with the Wordsworths again. Repeating himself in a minor key, in 1811 Coleridge moved into the domestic circle of an old Bristol friend (John Morgan) and his wife and sister-in-law, an arrangement that enabled him to prepare *Biographia Literaria* and old manuscripts such as 'Kubla Khan', 'Christabel' and *Osorio* for print. His addictions and his developing feelings for the sister-in-law led again to breakdowns in the circle. It was not until 1816, when he went to live in Highgate with a surgeon and his wife, that he found a circle that could support him long-term, albeit at a lower level of emotional involvement. There, his drug habit was stabilized and he was treated as a favoured but supervised son. He stayed in this circle until his death in 1834 and was able to complete and publish some of his writings, though few of them ventured the kinds of emotional and spiritual exposure of his earlier poems.

The exposure of those poems had taken a toll – and takes a toll on the reader. In the 'Dejection' verses that he wrote in the form of a letter to his beloved Sara Hutchinson, Coleridge achieves a searing revelation of his feelings of depression and misery in the face of Sara's absence – an absence that stands for her unavailability. The manuscript poem is confessional to an extraordinary degree: it not only relates several of the tender occasions in their intimate relationship but also reveals, in detail, Coleridge's complex blend of thoughts and feelings – including the startling statement that he has sometimes wished his children had never been born. Exposing not just love and yearning but also shame and guilt, it verges constantly on self-embarrassment and self-pity, but is saved from self-indulgence by Coleridge's determination both to analyse the causes of his mental state and to struggle towards a remedy. What results is a profound and moving memoir-in-verse of how it feels to be depressed and anxious, how those feelings grew in response to irresolvable life situations and how a tentative form of self-therapy might be sketched out. It is by imagining another, not as a prospective partner or possession, but as a person in her own right and with her own relationships, and then by offering this act of imagination to that other – to Sara – that Coleridge begins to lift his self-sealed sadness, just as the Mariner began to escape from feeling cursed when he blessed the water-snakes. The poem ends with Coleridge offering this act of imagination to Sara, its addressee, as his blessing: as he thinks of her he has become sufficiently restored, active and altruistic to give a gift and lift himself out of torpor:

> Sister & Friend of my devoutest Choice!
> Thou being innocent & full of love,
> And nested with the Darlings of thy Love,

7

And feeling in thy Soul, Heart, Lips, & Arms
Even what the conjugal & mother Dove
That borrows genial Warmth from those, she warms,
Feels in her thrill'd wings, blessedly outspread –
Thou free'd awhile from Cares & human Dread
By the Immenseness of the Good & Fair
Which thou see'st every where –
Thus, thus should'st thou rejoice!
To thee would all Things live from Pole to Pole,
Their Life the Eddying of thy living Soul –
O dear! O Innocent! O full of Love!
A very Friend! A Sister of my Choice –
O dear, as Light & Impulse from above,
Thus may'st thou ever, evermore rejoice!

(letter of 4 April 1802, CL II, 798, lines 324–40)

As a gift, this final scenario renews the giver because it demonstrates his renewed capacity to care for another's happiness. For the receiver, though, it is a double-edged sword, for while it kindly testifies to Coleridge's care for Sara's independent happiness, it nevertheless binds her back to him, as the grateful recipient of a portrait that not only evinces his best wishes but also makes her the object of his imaginings, however well intended. The terms of her absence from Coleridge are set by Coleridge; his letter, once delivered (and circulated in their family circle), presents her in his words. An act of blessing someone's independence may also be a tour de force of reclamation from the margin.

Coleridge was not unaware of the mixed motives that come from loving, yearning and craving, or of the blurred lines that come from writing to the beloved. As his own unsatisfied longings came to contrast more and more starkly with the contentment of a Wordsworth who was supported not only by the doting Dorothy but also by the devoted Mary, he turned again to confessional and self-analytic verse. 'The Pains of Sleep' (1803) engages us today for its vivid portrayal of psychological torment and for the acuity of its understanding of dreams as products of a divided self that tries to repress its shameful desires and guilty fears. Coleridge wrote it in the fallout from a walking tour of Scotland he had begun with the Wordsworths. 'I soon found that I was a burthen on them', he wrote, '& Wordsworth, himself a brooder over his painful hypochondriacal Sensations, was not my fittest companion / so I left him' (CL II, 1009–10). Self-exiled from his companions of choice, Coleridge 'walked by myself far away into the Highlands', consuming large amounts of opium and walking prodigious distances. Reaching Edinburgh, he sent 'The Pains of

Sleep' in letters to friends as a report on his mental state. It described terrifying dreams in which the dreamer felt utterly helpless:

> Desire with Loathing strangely mixt,
> On wild or hateful Objects fixt:
> Pangs of Revenge, the powerless Will,
> Still baffled, & consuming still,
> Sense of intolerable Wrong,
> And men whom I despis'd made strong
> Vain-glorious Threats, unmanly Vaunting,
> Bad men my boasts & fury taunting
> Rage, sensual Passion, mad'ning Brawl,
> And Shame, and Terror over all!
> Deeds to be hid that were not hid,
> Which, all confus'd I might not know,
> Whether I suffer'd or I did.   (*CL* II, 982–83; lines 18–30)

It is the discovery in these dreams of the inextricability of desire and loathing that causes a paralysing 'Horror, Guilt, & woe ... / Life-stifling fear, Soul-stifling Shame!' (lines 31, 33). But, compared with the 'Dejection' verse of the previous year, there is now less release from anguish in the articulation of the experience in poetry: the ordering process of writing is unable to prevent the recurrence of trauma. Release from night terrors seems possible only by another route:

> Thus two nights pass'd: the Night's Dismay
> Sadden'd and stunn'd the boding Day.
> I fear'd to sleep. Sleep seem'd to be
> Disease's worst malignity.
> The third night when my own loud Scream
> Had freed me from the fiendish Dream,
> O'ercome by Sufferings dark & wild,
> I wept as I had been a Child.   (lines 34–40)

Weeping like a child, an action of innocence and tenderness in which the responsibilities and authority of manhood are lost, proves Coleridge's best escape route, allowing him to subdue 'my anguish to a milder mood'. Neither reason nor will but an admission of vulnerability and a request for love offer the only hope for a free and stable self: 'To be beloved is all I need' (line 54). Presumably, the regular gentle stimulation of loving intimacy – lost on the walking tour when Coleridge and the Wordsworths separated in irritation and resentment – would replace the depression that was deepened by excessive doses of laudanum, restoring the balance between inner and outer worlds. Such stimulation, however, remained a forlorn hope, not a plan of action, a hope likely to be subverted by nightly imprisonment in the mental theatre of desire and loathing.

'The Pains of Sleep' leaves the reader with an image of the poet as an isolated, terrified being, in a deeper crisis than he is able to repair. A comment of 1814 shows that Coleridge had come to see 'The Pains' as 'an exact and most faithful portraiture of the state of my mind under influences of incipient bodily derangement from the use of Opium', 'a Slavery more dreadful, than any man, who has not felt it's iron fetters eating into his very soul, can possibly imagine' (*CL* III, 495). That derangement – psychological as well as physical – occurs through the breakdown of the boundaries between sleeping and waking: the pains of nightmare extend into the fully woken daytime self, rendering it doubtful whether self-control and self-knowledge can be achieved. And yet the poem, if not cathartic and curative, does stave off chaos: it achieves at least a provisional aesthetic order: controlled rhythm, rhyme and figuration allow Coleridge at least to know, and hold in check, the power of the forces that possess him. Poetic form brings some relief and also brings his troubles home to others. Readers vicariously share his grappling with trauma, a process that engenders sympathy for him: they will provide the loving support that he needs so as to keep the demons at bay. The poem exists to invoke an intimate, consolatory hermeneutic circle that might compensate for the loss of a real circle of friends; as such it offers an example that is applicable beyond Coleridge himself of how writing and reading may suspend mental anguish. A practical lesson in therapy.

Coleridge on Slavery and Race

Coleridge's imaginative insight into vulnerability and suffering – his capacity to dramatize, in figures such as the Ancient Mariner and Christabel, states of fear, loathing, guilt – states, too, of thralldom to other more powerful people – echoes in the insistence throughout his political writings of the value of personhood. This insistence is accompanied by vehement opposition to ideologies that ignore personhood so as to enable exploitation. While still a student he had written a Greek ode against the slave trade. As a radical lecturer and journalist in Bristol (a city enriched by the trade) in 1796 he asked Britons to put their own vulnerable and precious lives imaginatively in the place of Africans' – to bring the injustice of slavery home:

> Would you choose, that a slave merchant should incite an intoxicated Chieftain to make war on your Country, and murder your Wife and Children before your face, or drag them with yourself to the Market? Would you choose to be sold? to have the hot iron hiss upon your breasts, after having been crammed into the hold of a Ship with so many fellow-victims, that the heat and stench, arising from your diseased bodies, should rot the very planks? Would you, that others should do this unto you? (*Watchman*, 138)

In the same article, Coleridge argued that the poor in England were subjected to endless toil making the products that serviced the slave trade – guns, hatchets, ironwork. He thus not only opposed slavery in a city where it was inadvisable, not to say dangerous, to do so but understood that the enslavement and brutalization of Africans were parts of a nascent global capitalism that was based on the exploitation of poor, vulnerable people abroad and at home. Their minds and bodies paid the cost of investors' newfound wealth.

Coleridge spoke out against slavery. He dramatized the consequences of slavery in his poems; he insisted that human life, of whatever race, was an irreducible value not to be degraded. Persons were not things, and must not be treated so. He deserves honour for these actions and statements. But, as was typical for intellectuals of the time, he did not accept that black people were as civilized as whites, and accepted a racial hierarchy, historically produced if not inherent or biological. His ideas about race were shaped by two influences – his education in natural history at the hands of the pre-eminent authority on racial variety J. F. Blumenbach, and his Christian organicism, which led him to treat the Biblical text as a symbolic and partial account of the will of God working itself out in and as history. Blumenbach's widely accepted classification of humanity into races had aimed to include humankind and its origins in a general account of nature. Before Darwinism, it stressed not evolution by natural selection but a process of human degeneration from a perfect, Adamic, original man. Natural history was, that is to say, reconcilable with scripture even while it claimed empirical accuracy. Racial variety had been produced as the original people had gradually separated – and descended – into the different races on earth in the present day. These races were all human, and all degenerate by comparison with the Adamic original. Some, however, were more degenerate than others: degeneracy occurred unevenly as a result of historical exposure to different geographical and climatic conditions.

Coleridge was not a public commentator on or theorist of race. His views on the subject were occasional speculations left in manuscript – the tentative thoughts of a particular occasion rather than a formulated argument or published system. This fact should be remembered when considering them today. They occur as parts of drafts made in 1828 towards a theory of life. Coleridge combined Blumenbach's scheme with Biblical hermeneutics as he tried to explain how 'the Hebrew Tradition, whether it be interpreted historically or mythical [ly] ... the Idea of Shem, Ham and Japhet ... will be a guide in the attempt to connect the scheme with Historical Events & Facts' (SWF II, 1457). Where Blumenbach classified the effects on humankind of the historical past, Coleridge looked forward:

he offered a teleological understanding of racial difference as an aspect of God's providential scheme working itself out through nature and history. He substituted the term 'historic race' for Blumenbach's usual 'central race' and suggested that, of the various races classified by Blumenbach, the Caucasian was, alone at present, aspiring to the condition of the race that would fulfil the providential scheme of uniting the various races with each other and with God: 'in the idea of the Historic Race we have presented a Vision of Glory – the very … fact that its realization is the final cause of our existence in this world cannot but wonderfully raise and ennoble our nature & the Race to which we belong in our own eyes – and the eye of Reason' (SWF II, 1405–6).

While the Caucasian race could conceive for itself a vision of its divine mission, 'inferior Races' were heading, blindly, towards a 'catastrophe of Destruction' or a 'judgement', after which only 'the crowning Products that formed the final cause of the preceding Epoch [would be] carried over to the new Ledger or Page' (SWF II, 1405). The 'crowning Products', Coleridge implied, included the historic race but not the inferior ones, with the exception of those who were lifted by the historic race out of a degeneracy that they were not capable of throwing off by themselves. Thus, in his account, black people's degeneracy was a state ordained by God to allow the historic race to fulfil its civilizing and Christianizing mission. The 'children of Ham', Coleridge declared, interpreting Genesis 12:1–2,

> seem by Providence to have been impelled to the south, and there as the inhabitants of Africa, to bear witness to us of that awful prophecy which Christianity, the universal redeemer, has been lately, to the undying glory of this nation, at once fulfilling, and healing the unhappy slaves that were to be servants to their elder brethren till that time when the servant should be as the master and the master as the servant before the eye of the common Lord.

Britons, Coleridge implied, could congratulate themselves in that, by abolishing the slave trade, they had begun the holy work of raising Africans out of the gradually intensifying degeneracy to which God had condemned them when, after the fall, He sent them into a hostile climate. '[I]t is possible', Coleridge argued, 'that certain climates are inhabitable without physical degeneracy only by the animalizing changes brought about by moral degeneracy' (SWF II, 1404). Black people's animal-like bodies, he implied, suggested their moral inferiority; he speculated that white Caucasians, if they rose to the status of the historic race, would, possessing superior moral strength and scientific knowledge, deservedly supersede other races: 'a far higher state of moral and intellectual energy in the central Race, with the scientific powers & resources of that far higher state, might enable the Masters of the world to reside unharmed on any part of their Estate' (*SWF*, II, 1405). Caucasians, however, were as yet nowhere near that point.

Here Coleridge's manuscript verges on the sinister ideology (and anticipates the very language) used by those who did conquer black and indigenous peoples' land to justify their white supremacist policies (he is not far removed from the self-fulfilling concept of 'manifest destiny' that accompanied the US extirpation of Native Americans or from the notion of the 'white man's burden' that was used to portray British colonialism as a matter of a dutiful civilizing mission). And his phrases are uncomfortably close to those used in Germany by Nazi race theorists.[3] Yet, unlike these apologists for empire, he neither advocated a land-grab nor sanctioned the ill-treatment, still less genocide, of non-white races. His thinking is, in our terms, racist and unacceptable, yet it was neither unorthodox for the time nor incompatible with his argument that all people must be free and their full humanity recognized. However, in making the supposed inferiority and degeneracy of black people part of God's plan, Coleridge's manuscript speculations both historicized and spiritualized racist 'science' that placed Caucasians above others, giving that 'science' an aura of temporal inevitability and divine necessity: in this way the shaky empirical data on which natural history's categorizations depended gained an aura of ordained truth.

Notes

1 On the poem and slavery, see J. R. Ebbatson, 'Coleridge's Mariner and the Rights of Man', *Studies in Romanticism* 11 (1972), 171–206; Debbie Lee, 'Yellow Fever and the Slave Trade: Coleridge's "The Rime of the Ancient Mariner"', *ELH* 65 (1998), 675–700.

2 For Southey's poem, see *Robert Southey: Poetical Works 1793–1810*, gen. ed. Lynda Pratt, 5 vols (London: Pickering and Chatto, 2004), V, 288–92.

3 On Coleridge and race, see J. H. Haeger, 'Coleridge's Speculations on Race', *Studies in Romanticism* 13 (1974), 333–57. Peter J. Kitson, 'Coleridge and "the Oran Utan Hypothesis": Romantic Theories of Race', in *Samuel Taylor Coleridge and the Sciences of Life*, ed. Nicholas Roe (Oxford University Press, 2001), 91–116. My own chapter in *Coleridge and the Sciences of Life*, 'Theorizing Golgotha: Coleridge, Race Theory, and the Skull beneath the Skin' (117–33), has informed my discussion here.

2

JACOB LLOYD

Political Coleridge

'[L]ocal and temporary Politics are my aversion' (*CL* 1, 222) declared Coleridge in 1796, when contemplating writing for *The Morning Post*. Despite this disavowal, Coleridge was consistently a political writer. He advocated social reform and attacked the slave trade in his lectures in Bristol in 1795 and, as a Unitarian preacher, his sermons were '*preciously pep-pered with Politics*' (*CL* 1, 176). His journalism included parliamentary reports and leading articles, and he edited his own periodicals, *The Watch-man* (1796) and, later, *The Friend* (1809–10, 1818). His prose works, *The Statesman's Manual* (1816), *A Lay Sermon* (1817) and *On the Constitution of the Church and State* (1829), offered political theory and social com-mentary, while his private correspondence often discussed current affairs and political philosophy. Coleridge was also a political poet. Some poems, such as 'Ode on the Departing Year' (*CPW* 1, i, 302–11) and 'Fire, Famine, and Slaughter: A War Eclogue' (*CPW* 1, i, 428–44), are explicitly politi-cal; others are less obviously so, but are infused with the ideas and values of the Romantic Revolutionary age. Furthermore, Coleridge's ambitions as a thinker were always about synthesizing: in 1801 he promised that his proposed work '"Concerning Poetry & the nature of the Pleasures derived from it" [...] would supersede all the Books of Metaphysics hitherto written / and all the Books of Morals too' (*CL* 11, 671). Coleridge did not neatly separate literary interests from moral, philosophical or political concerns, but perceived them as deeply connected.[1]

In the 1790s, Coleridge acquired such political notoriety that a stranger (not knowing to whom she was speaking) referred to him as a 'vile jacobin villain' (*CL* 1, 321), and the satirical periodical *The Anti-Jacobin* depicted him, in the poem 'The New Morality' in July 1798, as praising the deist French Revolutionary Louis La Révellière-Lépeaux.[2] 'Jacobin' was rather a vague label, derived from the influential club of French Republicans that dominated post-Revolutionary French politics. In Britain, the term could indicate someone sympathetic to the French Revolution, opposed to war with France and advocating democratic reform in Britain.[3] For conservatives, 'Jacobinism' suggested treason and regicide.

Coleridge's radicalism in the 1790s is demonstrated by the plan he and fellow poet Robert Southey devised to found, with like-minded couples, a rural commune in America named 'Pantisocracy'. Labour would be shared and property abolished, or 'aspheterized', as Coleridge termed it (*CL* i, 84). This utopian notion informed Coleridge's religious lectures of 1795. Furthermore, his first volume of poetry contained verses which 'allude to an intended emigration to America on the scheme of an abandonment of individual property' (*CPW* i, ii, 1196).

Alongside his Bristol lectures and editorship of *The Watchman*, Coleridge's associations contributed to his Jacobin reputation. At Jesus College, Cambridge, Coleridge became friendly with the tutor William Frend. In 1793 Frend published *Peace and Union*, a pamphlet which criticized the war with France, attacked the Established Church and its clergy and denied the doctrine of the Trinity, while defending the execution of the French King Louis XVI. Frend was expelled from Cambridge as a result. Coleridge later became friends with the radical speaker John Thelwall, who had been one of the reformers arrested, tried for and eventually acquitted of high treason in 1794, owing to their attempts to organize in favour of votes for all men. In April 1796, Coleridge wrote to Thelwall that 'Pursuing the same end by the same means we ought not to be strangers to each other' (*CL* i, 204). Their ensuing correspondence covered poetry, politics, religion and science. In 1797 they planned for Thelwall to move nearby to Coleridge and William Wordsworth in the West Country, before Coleridge changed his mind due to the animosity Thelwall's politics aroused from his neighbours (*CL* i, 341–44). By 1801, Coleridge was distancing himself, intellectually, from Thelwall, claiming that they had 'irreconcileably different opinions in Politics, Religion, & Metaphysics' (*CL* ii, 723).

Coleridge's own accounts of his political journey are inconsistent. In early 1798 he wrote to his brother George (a respectable vicar), insisting that he was not an admirer of the French Revolution, nor an opponent of the British Government, but had 'snapped my squeaking baby-trumpet of Sedition' (*CL* i, 397). The adjective 'baby' associates his former politics with immaturity, and 'snapped' indicates an irreversible break, even as 'Sedition' acknowledges his previously subversive activity. The strength of his new commitment is based on admitting to having changed his behaviour.

When he discussed these years in his *Biographia Literaria* (1817), though, Coleridge denied such a change, asserting that his friends from 1796 would 'bear witness for me, how opposite even then my principles were to those of jacobinism or even of democracy' (*BL* i, 184). Southey and Thelwall contradicted this claim. Southey wondered that if Coleridge 'was not a Jacobine, in the common acceptation of the name, I wonder who the Devil was'.[4] Thelwall recalled that Coleridge 'was indeed far from Democracy, because he was far beyond it', having been 'a down right zealous leveller'.[5]

Amidst continued attacks on radicals by the conservative press, Coleridge had a tendency to revise his work and obscure his youthful radicalism. When he reprinted part of *Conciones ad Populam* (1795), a published version of two of his Bristol lectures, in 1818, Coleridge's alterations included removing attacks on tyranny and the former prime minister, William Pitt the Younger (*Lects 1795*, 9–11, 37–39; *Friend* I, 326–38). Coleridge treated his poetry similarly. In his collection *Sybilline Leaves* (1817), Coleridge altered lines in 'Ode on the Departing Year', from 'O doom'd to fall, enslav'd and vile, / O Albion! O my mother Isle!' to 'Not yet enslav'd, not wholly vile' (*CPW* II, i, 421, lines 129–30). He replaced a condemnation of Britain's corruption with an assertion of persistent national virtue. 'Fire, Famine, and Slaughter', the most incendiary of his poems, was defused with an apologetic preface, which, at twenty pages, was longer than any of the poems in the collection's political section (*CPW* I, i, 429–40).

Coleridge's changing politics were epitomized by his response to the seminal event of his lifetime: the French Revolution. Coleridge initially supported the Revolution, but his later publications frequently criticized Jacobinism. In his 1795 'Moral and Political Lecture', Coleridge had claimed that 'French Freedom is the Beacon, that while it guides us to Equality, should shew us the Dangers, that throng the road' (*Lects 1795*, 6). He indicated admiration, even as he caveated it with a warning. He publicly acknowledged changing his mind with a poem, which he published in *The Morning Post* in April 1798, following France's invasion of the Swiss Confederacy in January. This invasion was troubling for British radicals because France was indisputably the aggressor. Originally titled 'The Recantation, An Ode', 'France: An Ode' implores 'Forgive me, Freedom!' because Coleridge 'sang defeat' to Britain in her military efforts against France (*CPW* I, i, 465, line 36; 466, line 64), in his 'Ode on the Departing Year' (*CPW* I, i, 302–11). Notably, even this admission of error is undercut by a larger claim to consistency: the poem begins and ends with the natural world validating his assertion that throughout the period he 'still ador'd / The spirit of divinest Liberty!' (*CPW* I, i, 464, lines 20–21).

Coleridge changed his position on the monarchy, the Established Church and political reform. He seems to have been a republican in 1794, writing to Southey that 'The Cockatrice is emblematic of Monarchy – a *monster* generated by *Ingratitude* on *Absurdity*' (*CL* I, 84). Coleridge liked this symbol so much that he reused it in 1795 in the second of his 'Lectures on Revealed

Religion', which attacks monarchy as encouraging avarice and profusion (lavish expenditure), leading to poverty and vice, as well as taxation and idolatry (*Lects 1795*, 134).

In January 1800, though, Coleridge wrote in *The Morning Post,* 'thank Heaven [...] we have a KING and no *Monarch!*' (*EOT* I, 136), making the distinction, conventional in eighteenth-century political theory, between a constitutional ruler, bound by the law, and a tyrant. Coleridge's later royalism may have derived from his fear that republicanism and democracy could easily degenerate into military dictatorship, as he saw happening under Napoleon in France (*EOT* I, 50–53). In *On the Constitution of the Church and State*, Coleridge lauds 'the king [...] by whom alone the unity of the nation in will and in deed is symbolically expressed and impersonated' (*Church and State*, 77). No longer a monstrous creature or false idol, the king is glorified as symbol: the part of the constitution which embodies the unity of the nation as a whole.

Coleridge's attitude to the Established Church was connected to his changing religious beliefs. As a Unitarian, Coleridge was hostile, claiming that 'the Church of Rome and the Church of England' both bore 'the mark of antichrist' (*Lects 1795*, 210). By 1802, Coleridge was writing that the Church of England and its 'property are an elementary part of our constitution, not created by any Legislature, but really & truly antecedent to any form of Government in England upon which any existing Laws can be built' (*CL* II, 806). If the Church is 'antecedent' to government, it is not subject to political debate, but provides its own authority. *On the Constitution of the Church and State* insists upon the necessary interdependence of the Established Church and the government of the state.

Coleridge initially advocated radical political reform. In the lecture *The Plot Discovered* (1795), he identified three types of government: 'Government by the people, Government over the people, and Government with the people'. 'Government *over* the people' is despotic, whereas 'Government *by* the people' is democratic: power is exercised by the whole people 'actually present' or through their representatives. 'Government *with* the people' is a movement from government *over* to government *by* the people, and is as good as it is close to 'Government *by* the people' (*Lects 1795*, 306–7). Contemporary discourse often extolled the British Constitution as mixed and balanced, as combining the advantages of monarchy, aristocracy and democracy through the power held by the Crown, the House of Lords and the House of Commons, respectively (though few men got to vote for their MP). Coleridge saw this arrangement as insufficiently democratic, arguing 'that a Government, under which the people at large neither directly or indirectly exercise any sovereignty, is a Despotism' (*Lects 1795*, 308).

Coleridge's advocacy for democratic government was well outside the mainstream.

In December 1799, though, Coleridge outlined the different advantages of hereditary monarchy, democracy and government based on property, commenting that Britain contained 'all these three principles' (*EOT* I, 47–48). While not identical to the usual defence of Britain's mixed system (since Coleridge does not validate aristocracy, as represented by the House of Lords), this claim uses a similar logic and indicates Coleridge moving to a more conservative position. In *On the Constitution of the Church and State*, Coleridge suggested that the people of Britain enjoyed 'fewer restraints on their free agency' than the occupants of any country in history, in part because Britain's political system avoided the 'extremes' of either a 'democratic Republic' or 'an Absolute Monarchy', both of which delegated all power to their particular governments (*Church and State*, 95–96).

During his later years, Coleridge's scorn could be directed towards those advocating the kind of reform he had supported in his Bristol lectures. In an 1811 article he attacked the radical MP Sir Francis Burdett, denouncing as seditious Burdett's plan for a popular assembly that would make demands for constitutional reform and franchise extension: Coleridge called it tantamount to inciting 'foul rebellion' (*EOT* II, 165). In his second *Lay Sermon*, Coleridge used a passage from Isaiah to launch a sustained attack on radical speakers and politicians, characterizing them as the kind of villainous hypocrites Isaiah describes (*SM*, 142–50). Coleridge calls them 'pretended heralds of freedom' who are 'inflaming the populace to acts of madness that necessitate fetters' (*SM*, 149–50). Coleridge's adjective 'pretended' implies that the radicals are bad faith actors deliberately perpetrating a deception. Such censorious rhetoric seemed designed to prove Coleridge's credentials as a loyal patriot, and appeared hypocritical to those who still supported more radical politics. His former friend William Hazlitt was relentless in attacking Coleridge for this political apostasy.

The role of property was central to Coleridge's thinking about politics, but Coleridge changed from opposing to supporting its power.[6] He once considered property 'the Origin of all Evil' (*CL* I, 214). Pantisocracy was therefore designed on the principle of 'aspheterism', whereby 'we should remove the *selfish* Principle from ourselves, and prevent it in our children, by an *Abolition* of Property: or [...] by such similarity of Property, as would amount to a *moral Sameness*, and answer all the purposes of *Abolition*' (*CL* I, 88, 163). In his Bristol lectures, Coleridge argued that 'Property is Power and equal Property equal Power' (*Lects 1795*, 126). He offered a religious authority for radical redistribution, arguing that Jesus 'commanded his disciples to observe a strict equality' (*Lects 1795*, 218). His poetry was similarly idealistic: 'Religious Musings' offered a vision in which 'each heart / Self-govern'd, the vast family of Love / Rais'd from the common earth by common toil / Enjoy the equal produce' (*CPW* I, i, 188, lines 340–43).

Coleridge was hostile towards commercial forces in these lectures. Instead of providing necessities, Coleridge insisted, commerce was 'debauching the field Labourer with improportionable toil by exciting in him artificial Wants' and 'Its Evils are vast and various – and first, Cities Drunkenness, Prostitution, Rapine, Beggary and Diseases' (*Lects 1795*, 223–24). Coleridge saw the government as aggravating the situation, increasing the people's wants through 'Taxes rendered necessary by those national assassinations called Wars' (*Lects 1795*, 222). Coleridge's vision of agrarian equality was founded on the conviction not only that it would remove vice but also that, without material temptations, such a society could easily provide for its members.

Yet, when evaluating the new French Constitution in December 1799, Coleridge declared that 'For the present race of men Governments must be founded on property; that *Government is good in which property is secure and circulates*; that *Government the best, which, in the exactest ratio, makes each man's power proportionate to his property*' (*EOT* I, 32). By making property foundational to government, Coleridge gives it priority over other political rights. Although the insistence that property 'circulates' is a move to redress the problems of a society dominated by inherited wealth, the notion that it must be 'secure' stresses that the interests of property holders should be protected from the masses. Instead of being the means to ensure strict equality, property becomes the justification for a necessary inequality.

In *The Friend*, Coleridge offered a new analysis. Rather than seeing taxation as draining national resources, Coleridge appreciated that it enabled government to redistribute wealth more efficiently for greater productivity (*Friend* I, 228–30). He argued that 'Taxation itself is a part of Commerce, and the Government may be fairly considered as a great manufacturing house carrying on in different places, by means of its partners and overseers, the trades of the ship-builder, the clothier, the iron-founder, &c. &c.' (*Friend* I, 230). Coleridge explained how the money spent maintaining the armed forces in the war against France provided employment and incomes to British subjects (*Friend* I, 242–44). Due to this increased economic activity, Coleridge claimed that the people of Britain were materially better off than they were previously, despite being taxed more (*Friend* I, 236–39).

He had not come to see commerce solely as a positive force, though. Coleridge's second *Lay Sermon* was written to address the 'EXISTING DISTRESSES' (*SM*, 119): the economic depression and high food prices that followed the conclusion of the war. Coleridge explained the situation as caused by 'the OVERBALANCE OF THE COMMERCIAL SPIRIT IN CONSE-QUENCE OF THE ABSENCE OR WEAKNESS OF THE COUNTER-WEIGHTS' and the extension of commercial thinking 'into our agricultural system'. The depression was aggravated by the peace: an end to the taxes which had financed the war led to a reduction in government revenue and the collapse of public spending (*SM*, 159–60, 169, 214).

While recognizing the contribution of the commercial system of credit in increasing 'the power and circumstantial prosperity of the Nation' during the previous sixty years, Coleridge noted that periodic economic crashes were a feature of the system (*SM*, 202–4). However, he believed that direct state involvement to rectify the situation would be ineffective (*SM*, 169, 217–18). He also opposed state intervention because it interfered with the voluntary action of individuals. Coleridge claimed that property rights 'are the spheres and necessary conditions of free agency' (*SM*, 24–25), and free agency was the foundation of moral action (*Friend* 1, 189–90). Reform required persuading the landowners and gaining their consent. Coleridge believed that to do otherwise would be to dismantle the entire system that sustained the nation (*SM*, 217–18). He instead emphasized three predominant counter-weights to the commercial spirit the feeling of rank and ancestry, 'genuine philosophy' (as opposed to empiricism) and religion (*SM*, 170–76, 194–95). These three had all declined.

Coleridge developed a sophisticated theoretical foundation for his later positions. In *The Friend*, he distinguished three kinds of theory of the origin of government, each relating to a different claim about how the mind works: through passive sensation, Reason or Understanding. Coleridge rejected the ideas of Thomas Hobbes, that the human mind is the product of 'manifold modifications of passive sensation', and that government is based on fear. Coleridge noted that even in situations of conquest leaders will be chosen, and that fear 'is utterly incapable of producing any regular, continuous and calculable effect, even on an individual' (*Friend* 1, 166–67). Coleridge also criticized the theories, advanced by Jean-Jacques Rousseau and later the French Revolutionaries, holding that the only just political arrangements are those 'capable of being demonstrated out of the original laws of the pure Reason' (*Friend* 1, 178).

The distinction between the Reason and the Understanding was influenced by Immanuel Kant. Reason, for Coleridge, is the 'organ of inward sense' that has 'the power of acquainting itself with invisible realities or spiritual objects', such as 'God, the Soul, eternal Truth, &c'. The Understanding, by contrast, is 'the conception of the Sensuous [...] that faculty, the functions of which contain the rules and constitute the possibility of outward Experience' (*Friend* I, 156). Coleridge believed that 'the whole moral nature of man originated and subsists in his Reason' (*Friend* I, 199). Whereas morality considers 'not the outward act, but the internal maxims of our actions', matters of government concern how to 'regulate the outward actions of particular bodies of men, according to their particular circumstances' (*Friend* I, 194–95). Coleridge criticized Jacobinism as treating ideal forms as identical with their political manifestations, without seeking to mediate between the two.

Coleridge observed that Rousseau ascribes sovereignty not to people individually or collectively but to 'abstract Reason' itself. A government based on Reason was therefore not necessarily democratic or even representative, and in practice, the Constituent Assembly of France excluded both children and women, believing them incapable of exercising Reason properly. Instead, Coleridge argued, such theories led to the violent excess of the French Revolution and prepared the way for the dictatorship of Napoleon, as the man able to present himself as the incarnation of Reason's sovereignty (*Friend* I, 195–97).[7] As Coleridge would summarize in *The Statesman's Manual*, 'Jacobinism is [...] made up in part of despotism, and in part of abstract reason misapplied to objects that belong entirely to experience and the understanding' (*SM*, 63–64).

Coleridge thereby developed a distinction he first outlined in his 1802 *Morning Post* article, 'Once a Jacobin Always a Jacobin', that 'Whoever builds a Government on personal and natural rights, is so far a Jacobin. Whoever builds on social rights, that is hereditary rank, property, and long prescription, is an Anti-Jacobin' (*EOT* I, 370). Coleridge considered natural rights to be abstractions which could not meaningfully be accommodated in the real world. Coleridge's 'social rights', by contrast, are products of the Understanding, since they exist in the world we experience. Coleridge's preference for the Understanding as the basis of politics is partly because he conceived it not as operating autonomously but as offering mediation. The Understanding applies the principles derived from Reason to the world we experience (*Friend* I, 199–201).

Coleridge's analysis recalls the thinking of the MP Edmund Burke. Burke argued that:

> Government is not made in virtue of natural rights, which can and do exist [...] in a much greater degree of abstract perfection: but their abstract perfection is their practical defect. By having a right to every thing men want every thing. Government is a contrivance of human wisdom to provide for human *wants*.[8]

Having supported the American Revolution, Burke surprised many by condemning the French Revolution. His *Reflections on the Revolution in France*

(1790) presented the Revolutionaries as political metaphysicians. He pitted their abstract application of the rights of man against his cherished virtues of experience, tradition, social and familial ties, and a knowledge of human nature.[9] Although Coleridge always admired Burke's writing, he was initially incensed by Burke's supposed betrayal. In Coleridge's 1794 sonnet 'To Burke', the personification of 'Freedom' laments how Burke 'with alter'd voice [...] bad'st Oppression's hireling crew rejoice' (*CPW* I, i, 157, lines 6–7). In the *Biographia*, though, Coleridge praised Burke, writing that 'In Mr. Burke's writings indeed the germs of almost all political truths may be found' (*BL* I, 217).

Like Burke, Coleridge came to prefer the theory 'deriving the origin of all government from human *prudence*, and of deeming that to be just which experience has proved to be expedient' (*Friend* I, 176–77). Coleridge justified the protection of property on this basis, arguing that 'it is impossible to deduce the Right of Property from pure Reason' (*Friend* I, 200). Property is not the object of Reason, but is comprehended by the application of the Understanding. Since the Understanding is, unlike Reason, unevenly distributed (*Friend* I, 190), the amount of property acquired will also be uneven. Consequently, 'where individual landed property exists, there must be inequality of property: the nature of the earth and the nature of the mind unite to make the contrary impossible' (*Friend* I, 200).[10] Coleridge theorized that the original motive of people creating the state 'was not the protection of their lives but of their property' (*Friend* I, 199). By advancing this explanation, Coleridge presupposes that an unequal distribution of property 'has proved to be expedient', that it is beneficial in some way. He also suggests that the state can have only limited authority to redistribute that which it was formed to preserve.

That Coleridge should begin by denouncing Burke and end by developing some of Burke's arguments encapsulates Coleridge's altered political allegiances. In very Coleridgean fashion, however, it is also true that his political writings contained some important consistencies. Coleridge's politics were always informed by his religious beliefs. As a Unitarian, radical lecturer he claimed that a reader of the Gospels 'would learn the rights of Man and the Imposture of Priests, the sovereignty of God, and the usurpation of unauthorized Vice-gerents' (*Lects 1795*, 209). Although the phrase 'rights of Man' was widely used, it strongly evokes Thomas Paine's *The Rights of Man* (1791), which responded to Burke's criticisms of the French Revolution. Paine's book caused a sensation and Paine was convicted, in absentia, of seditious libel. Coleridge's claim audaciously associates the spirit of Christianity with the most notorious attack on the political establishment. In his lectures, Coleridge pronounced that 'Universal Equality is the object of the Mess[iah's] mission' (*Lects 1795*, 218), equating Christianity with his own Pantisocratic vision.

In his more conservative years, Coleridge continued to conceptualize political understanding as dependent upon the religious, as demonstrated by the subtitle to *The Statesman's Manual*: 'THE BIBLE THE BEST GUIDE TO POLITICAL SKILL AND FORESIGHT' (*SM*, 3). *The Statesman's Manual* argues that political leaders should consult Scripture because it is symbolic, being both 'Sacred History' and sacred prophecy. In the Bible, 'both Facts and Persons must of necessity have a two-fold significance, a past and a future, a temporary and a perpetual, a particular and a universal application' (*SM*, 29–30). In its consideration of the particular and the universal, Religion unites the Understanding and the Reason (*SM*, 62). To demonstrate Biblical wisdom, Coleridge quoted a passage from Isaiah, claiming that it prophetically 'revealed the true philosophy of the French revolution' (*SM*, 34). Coleridge directed political leaders towards the Bible as a way to correct the error of Jacobins, who conflate moral and political judgements, the abstract with the mundane. The Bible, by contrast, demonstrates the true relation of these faculties one to the other: how the Understanding should be guided by Reason rather than applying it directly. In his second *Lay Sermon*, Coleridge identified 'Religion' (meaning Christianity) as one of the essential counterweights to the 'overbalance' of the commercial spirit (*SM*, 174–75).

Coleridge's approach to politics was also consistently elitist, even in his radical years. In *Conciones ad Populam*, he declares that 'We certainly should never attempt to make Proselytes by appeals to the *selfish* feelings – and consequently, should plead *for* the Oppressed, not *to* them' (*Lects 1795*, 43). Although he subsequently referred to 'the poor and ignorant' rather than 'the Oppressed' (a notable shift of framing), Coleridge repeatedly invoked this mantra of pleading for, not to (*Friend* I, 210; *EOT* II, 376; *BL* I, 185; *SM*, 148). He saw political progress as something bestowed from above, prompted by feelings of benevolence, not something to be achieved by agitating the masses to direct political action.

In 1795, Coleridge quoted, as an epigraph for 'A Moral and Political Lecture', lines by the poet Mark Akenside, beginning 'To calm and guide / The swelling democratic tide' (*Lects 1795*, 3). The epigraph presumes that some elite group must oversee social and political transformation. In the lecture, Coleridge identifies 'thinking and disinterested Patriots', who may be distinguished from those political reformers whose motives and methods are suspect (*Lects* 1795, 7–13). These 'Patriots' appear in 'Religious Musings' as the 'Elect, regenerate thro' faith' (*CPW* I, i, 178, line 88). The Elect aid the spiritual and political transformation of humanity:

These, hush'd awhile with patient eye serene
Shall watch the mad careering of the storm;
Then o'er the wild and wavy chaos rush
And tame th' outrageous mass, with plastic might
Moulding Confusion to such perfect forms,
As erst were wont, bright visions of the day!

(*CPW* I, i, 184, lines 243–48)

Watching over the 'chaos', from which they are able to produce 'perfect forms', the 'Elect' resemble God creating the world in Genesis. Even within the context of a visionary religious poem, the elevation of the 'Elect' to quasi-divinity establishes a huge distance between them and the mass of humanity they are supposed to be helping.

Coleridge's elitism endured through his later writings. In *The Friend*, Coleridge states that it is 'To the successive Few' and their 'wisdom' that 'we owe our ameliorated condition' (*Friend* I, 61–62). Similarly, in *The Statesman's Manual*, he claims that the most important 'discoveries and improvements' have their origin 'in the closets of uninterested theorists, in the visions of recluse genius' (*SM*, 14). In 1831, when reform to Parliamentary elections was being proposed, Coleridge is recorded as criticizing the government for 'playing upon the necessary ignorance of the numerical majority of the nation' (*TT* I, 254).

Coleridge was, though, an outspoken opponent of slavery. In 1795, he delivered a lecture 'On the Slave Trade', which he subsequently revised for *The Watchman* (*Watchman*, 130–40). Coleridge denounced the evils slavery creates and urged his audience to undermine the viability of the Atlantic slave trade by boycotting sugar and rum (*Lects 1795*, 248–50). Coleridge's horror at slavery appears in his poetry. 'The Rime of the Ancyent Marinere' has been interpreted as addressing slavery, with the shooting of the albatross as symbolic of the slave trade's crimes.[11] More directly, the first two published versions of the 'Ode on the Departing Year' included a footnote which quoted from his lectures detailing Britain's global crimes, including how 'from Africa the unnumbered victims of a detestable Slave-trade [...] groan beneath the intolerable iniquity of this nation!' (*CPW* I, i, 309).

In *The Friend*, Coleridge emphasizes 'the sacred principle [...] which is the *ground-work* of all law and justice, that a person can never become a thing, nor be treated as such without wrong'. Influenced by Kant, Coleridge explained that whereas a thing 'may rightfully be used, altogether and merely, as a *means*', a person 'must always be included in the *end*, and form a part of the final cause' (*Friend* I, 190). Coleridge later explained (in an unpublished fragment) that 'A slave is a *Person* perverted into a *Thing*: Slavery therefore is not so properly a deviation from Justice, as an absolute subversion of all Morality' (*EOT* III, 235). Although the slave trade was abolished in the British Empire in 1807, slavery itself was not, and there were concerns that British capital was still being used to finance the trade. In 1817, therefore, Coleridge could still express his outrage at 'the abomination of the African commerce nominally abolished' (*SM*, 219). However, in later years Coleridge's priority shifted towards Christianizing Africans, both those in Africa and those that had been transported to plantations (*SWF* I, 241–42; *CM* III, 1082; *TT* I, 386). This imperialist religious attitude was consistent with Coleridge's approach to political amelioration through moral and religious instruction. When emancipation was finally effected by Parliament, Coleridge expressed scepticism, suggesting the legislation lacked any other principle than 'fear of the Abolition faction struggling with a fear of causing some monstrous calamity to the Empire at large' (*TT* I, 389). Nevertheless, Coleridge believed that a government which permits slavery 'is not worthy to be called a STATE' (*Church and State*, 15–16).

Coleridge consistently rejected claims that political objectives could be achieved through the application of rational thinking or by calculation. Instead, he emphasized moral obligations and personal benevolence. Coleridge's approach contrasted with those of other radicals, such as William Godwin.[12] In *An Enquiry Concerning Political Justice* (1793), Godwin argued that Reason should be the sole determinant of action, and that Truth was objective and unchanging. He contended that if people learned to be guided solely by Reason, they would perceive that their happiness would be served by acting virtuously to achieve Justice. For Godwin, the demands of Justice must take precedence over emotional consideration, even if that meant saving a great philosopher from a burning building at the expense of a loved one. He considered gratitude a vice and marriage an imprisonment.

Coleridge objected to Godwin's atheism, and dismissed *Political Justice* as teaching that 'filial Love is a Folly, Gratitude criminal, Marriage Injustice, and a promiscuous Intercourse of the Sexes our wisdom and our duty' (*Lects 1795*, 164).[13] He criticized the 'proud Philosophy, which affects to inculcate Philanthropy while it denounces every home-born feeling by which it is produced and nurtured'. Coleridge thought such an approach failed to appreciate human values and motivations. Coleridge claimed instead that 'general Benevolence is begotten and rendered permanent by social and domestic affections' (*Lects 1795*, 46). Political virtue could not be promoted by the application of Reason, but must be nurtured by existing human relationships.

Coleridge was similarly sceptical towards political claims made solely on the basis of rights. Coleridge placed equal emphasis on duties (*SM*, 64; *TT* I, 255), the promotion of which he saw as fundamental to political society.

In *Conciones ad Populam*, he argues that the best method for the reformer to diffuse truth is to 'be *personally* among the Poor, and teach them their *Duties* in order that he may render them susceptible of their *Rights*' (*Lects 1795*, 43). This is not a justification of servility but a conception of politics as based around reciprocity: that political and economic claims arise out of the performance of obligations to one another, rather than abstractly from the state of nature. The adverb *'personally'* emphasizes individual responsibility and moral agency, rather than social or legal forces. In *The Friend*, he rejects Hobbes's attribution of the origin of government to fear because such a philosophy 'denies all truth and distinct meaning to the words, RIGHT and DUTY' and 'considers men as the highest sort of animals' (*Friend* I, 166). The ability to recognize both 'right and duty' is the result of human reason, the source of morality that distinguishes humans from animals. The social contract is not an historical fact, but is 'synonimous with the sense of duty acting in a specific direction, i.e. determining our moral relations, as member of a body politic' (*Friend* I, 173–74). Civilization is thereby a product of moral thinking. Jacobinism, by contrast, is flawed because it elevates the claims of rights at the expense of duties (*EOT* II, 385, 387, 393–94). Coleridge's political prose can be understood as attempting to make all people aware of their obligations. In 1817, Coleridge would offer an exhortation similar to the one from 1795: 'let every man [...] contribute money where he cannot act personally; *but let him act personally and in detail* wherever it is practicable' (*SM*, 230).

The second *Lay Sermon* focused on the duty of landowners, partly because so much of the misery related to the scarcity and high price of food, but also because, according to Coleridge, agriculture shares the same *'ultimate* ends' as the state itself (*SM*, 216–17). Consequently, the landowner 'ought not to regard his estate as a merchant his cargo, or a shopkeeper his stock' (*SM*, 215): estates should be managed for the benefit of the many, with 'the living and moral growth that is to remain on the land' given priority over profit (*SM*, 218). Furthermore:

> Our manufacturers must consent to regulations; our gentry must concern themselves in the *education* as well as in the *instruction* of their natural clients and dependents, must regard their estates as [...] offices of trust, with duties to be performed, in the sight of God and their Country. (*SM*, 229)

This vision of social duty is articulated in opposition to the 'commercial spirit', and its related philosophy that treats *'immediate utility* [...] as the test of all intellectual powers and pursuits' (*SM*, 74). One manifestation of utilitarian philosophy that Coleridge attacked was 'Political economy', a perspective emphasizing the maximization of benefits derived from commercial activity.

According to Coleridge, political economy, 'in its zeal for the increase of food [...] habitually overlooked the qualities and even the sensations of those that were to feed on it' (*SM*, 76). It did not make moral considerations, only material ones. Political economists justified the disruption caused by credit cycles because 'in a free and trading country *all things find their level*' (*SM*, 205). Coleridge's objection was that 'Man does not find his level', that these economic forces cause miseries and hardships during times of unemployment through no fault of the labourer (*SM*, 206–7). Utility is calculated as an aggregate, but the effects of commerce are felt by individuals. Coleridge's opposition to 'ultimate utility' as a measurement of worth was similar to his earlier criticisms of Godwin's appeal to Reason's judgement.

Coleridge believed that political economy, like Jacobinism, resulted from empiricism (*EOT* I, 315; *SM*, 33–34, 108–110; *Friend* I, 446–47). He argued that empiricism, which deduced all knowledge from sense experience, led to the 'general conceit that states and governments might be and ought to be constructed as machines, every movement of which might be foreseen and taken into previous calculation' (*SM*, 33–34). This conceit was fundamental to Jacobinism. The focus on sense experience implied materialism: a philosophy that Coleridge had briefly embraced in the 1790s, but subsequently rejected. Furthermore, empiricism 'teaches that pleasure is the sole good, and a prudent calculation of enjoyment the only virtue' (*EOT* I, 315). Coleridge objected to this consequentialist approach to morality (*EOT* II, 79–81; *Friend* I, 313–17).

Coleridge began his final work of political prose, *On the Constitution of the Church and State*, as part of the debate over Catholic Emancipation: the removal of legal bars on Catholics holding public offices, most notably on being MPs. Coleridge produced a wider-ranging philosophical tract, however. He argued that the constitution is not bound by tradition and precedent (as Burke, amongst others, maintained), but evolves through a process guided by the 'idea' of the constitution, which is 'given by knowledge of *its ultimate aim*' (*Church and State*, 12–13, 19, 30). Coleridge uses this framework to explain how the constitution provided unity through the equipoise and interdependence of different forces. Coleridge identifies two 'antagonist powers' of permanence and progression, represented by the landed interest and the forces of commerce (*Church and State*, 23–25). These were already held in equipoise in the *actual* state by the bicameral system of Lords and Commons (*Church and State*, 27–29). Additionally, the *idea* of the state includes the 'National Church' as a third estate (*Church and State*, 42, 61–62). The National Church required its own wealth (which Coleridge refers to as 'Nationality'), held in trust, to act as a counterweight to propriety (*Church and State*, 35–36, 77–78). The Nationalty would provide for the maintenance of a proposed learned class, which Coleridge names the 'Clerisy'. The membership of this National Church is not limited to religious officials, but comprises all men of learning, including practitioners of law and medicine (*Church and State*, 46, 71).

The Clerisy was the latest formulation of the Coleridgean elite and reflected his enduring preoccupations. Although not themselves rulers, they would influence those who ruled. The Clerisy have an educative and cultivating function (focused on the nation's cultural rather material progress), providing every part of the country 'a resident guide, guardian, and instructor', diffusing knowledge so that all would understand their rights and duties (*Church and State*, 42–44). By educating the poor about their rights and duties, they would perform the task Coleridge had emphasized in 1795. The Clerisy would be an anti-utilitarian organization: guided by 'true philosophy', they would correct the errors of empiricism, strengthening the counterweights to the commercial spirit identified in the second *Lay Sermon* (*Church and State*, 48–49, 69–70).

Coleridge's model of the Clerisy and his conception of the moral purpose of the state helped shape the ideas of many later thinkers, including the philosopher and historian Thomas Carlyle, Cardinal John Henry Newman, the critic Matthew Arnold, the philosopher T. H. Green and Prime Minister W. E. Gladstone (*Church and State*, lxii–lxviii).[14] Perhaps most significant was Coleridge's impact on J. S. Mill, the foremost British political philosopher of the nineteenth century, and the intellectual father of liberalism.[15] Mill described Coleridge as one of 'two great seminal minds of England in their age', the other being the utilitarian philosopher Jeremy Bentham.[16] Under Coleridge's influence, Mill, the notable utilitarian, modified Bentham's philosophy with humanist values.[17] Coleridge's opposition to utilitarian thinking and *laissez-faire* economics informed later ethical critiques of capitalism, including the social thought of the Broad Church Movement, the Oxford Movement and Christian Socialism: three diverse Christian groups.[18] To the Victorians, Coleridge's politics were as vital as his poetry.

Notes

1 For some accounts of the politics of Coleridge's literary theory, see Daniel Fried, 'The Politics of the Coleridgean Symbol', *Studies in English Literature, 1500–1900*, 46.4 (October 2006), 763–69; Kir Kuiken, *Imagined Sovereignties: Toward a New Political Romanticism* (New York: Fordham University Press, 2014), 69–120; and Seamus Perry, 'Coleridgean Politics', *The Wordsworth Circle*, 49.3 (Summer 2018), 123–29.

2 'Poetry', *The Anti-Jacobin* (9 July 1798), 286, lines 327–37.

3 This was Coleridge's summary when discussing the politics of the young Robert Southey (*EOT* II, 475).

4 *New Letters of Robert Southey*, ed. Kenneth Curry, 2 vols (New York: Columbia University Press, 1965), I, 511.

5 B. R. Pollin, 'John Thelwall's Marginalia in a Copy of Coleridge's *Biographia Literaria*', *Bulletin of the New York Public Library*, 74 (1970), 73–94, at 81.

6 See John Morrow, *Coleridge's Political Thought: Property, Morality and the Limits of Traditional Discourse* (Basingstoke: Macmillan, 1990), 156–64.

7 For an analysis of this process, see Kuiken, *Imagined Sovereignties*, 97–109.

8 Edmund Burke, *Reflections on the Revolution in France* (Oxford University Press, 1993), 60.

9 While Coleridge came to share Burke's criticism of the *political* claims made for Reason, he was not sceptical of rationalism or metaphysics more generally. In fact, he objected to empiricism. See Andy Hamilton, 'Coleridge and Conservatism: Contemplation of an Idea', in *Coleridge and Contemplation*, ed. Peter Cheyne (Oxford University Press, 2017), 143–68, at 143–51.

10 See Timothy Michael, *British Romanticism and the Critique of Political Reason* (Baltimore, MD: Johns Hopkins University Press, 2016), 146–48.

11 For example, Malcolm Ware, 'Coleridge's "Spectre-Bark": A Slave Ship?', *Philological Quarterly*, 40 (1961), 589–93; J. R. Ebbatson, 'Coleridge's Mariner and the Rights of Man', *Studies in Romanticism*, 11 (1972), 171–206; Patrick J. Keane, *Coleridge's Submerged Politics: The Rime of the Ancient Mariner and Robinson Crusoe* (London: University of Missouri Press, 1994), 47–160.

12 Coleridge did have a brief Godwinian phase, writing a sonnet in praise of him (*CPW* I, i, 165–66), but was attacking Godwin only months later. It is possible that Coleridge did not read *Political Justice* until after he had written the sonnet, as his letter of 1811 to Godwin seems to indicate (CL, III, 315).

13 For Coleridge's religious-based radicalism in opposition to Godwin, see Nicholas Roe, *Wordsworth and Coleridge: The Radical Years*, 2nd edn. (Oxford University Press, 1988; rev. repr., 2018), 24–30, 88–117.

14 See Philip Aherne, *The Coleridge Legacy: Samuel Taylor Coleridge's Intellectual Legacy in Britain and America 1834–1934* (Basingstoke: Palgrave Macmillan, 2018), 202–9.

15 See Hamilton, 'Coleridge and Conservatism', 156–62.

16 *The Collected Works of John Stuart Mill*, ed. J. M. Robson, 33 vols (University of Toronto Press, 1963–1991), X: *Essays on Ethics, Religion, and Society* (1969), 77.

17 Aherne, *Coleridge Legacy*, 261–62; Hamilton, 'Coleridge and Conservatism', 156.

18 Aherne, *Coleridge Legacy*, 217–24.

3

FELICITY JAMES

Coleridge and Collaboration

July 1797. Coleridge sits alone, in conversation. He is in the arbour of Tom Poole's garden in Nether Stowey, confined there, as he tells Robert Southey, because his wife Sara 'accidently emptied a skillet of boiling milk on my foot' (*CL* I, 334). Unable to walk with his friends the Wordsworths, newly moved to Alfoxden, and Charles Lamb, visiting from London, he accompanies them in blank verse instead. The letter to Southey shifts from prose into poetry, retaining its conversational tone, but transmuting his burn into myth:

> Well – they are gone: and here must I remain,
> Lam'd by the scathe of fire, lonely & faint,
> This lime-tree bower my prison.

The solitary self-dramatizing moment opens into a vicarious vision of the pleasure the friends will enjoy, out on the 'springy* heath, along the hill-top edge'. The 'springy' is marked with a scribbled asterisk, and a note is squeezed into the right-hand margin: *'elastic,* I mean.' There are further marginal notes, almost running into the lines themselves, glossing details both literal and philosophical, bringing Southey, as reader, into the scene. This mirrors the movement of the whole poem, towards imaginative involvement with the experience of another: a sympathetic impulse which rebounds on the poet himself, as the impulse to share allows him a renewed appreciation of his own surroundings. Those surroundings, too, speak of reciprocity and relationship: the play of sunshine and shadow, the intertwined foliage of ivy 'which usurps / Those fronting elms', all facilitated by the friendly ministrations of Tom Poole himself, putting book-room and bower at Coleridge's disposal. Further in the background, the domestic labour of Sara, caring for baby Hartley, hosting, cooking, is registered only by accident.

This single-authored poem of solitude, with its many layers of allusion, personal and literary, is a good starting point for an understanding of Coleridge's complicated collaborative process, which this chapter traces across his writing life, from *Poems* (1796) to *Biographia Literaria* (1817).

30

Collaboration, strictly defined, means the act of working together. For Coleridge, however, this working together could take many different forms: co-writing (and rewriting); conversation; allusion or quotation; mentoring younger writers; or even conversing with himself. It was emotional, certainly, but also literary, philosophical and political, shaped both by Coleridge's own restless yearning for affectionate response and by his negotiations with religion and revolution in the 1790s. His poems frequently seem to dramatize and interrogate his own urge towards collaboration, as in the looping reciprocity of this conversation poem. It confers a blessing both on the discontented poet and on his friend Charles Lamb – the real 'lam'd' figure in the poem, struggling with his own physical and mental difficulties, winning his way 'thro' evil & pain / And strange calamity', in the aftermath of his sister's mental crisis and matricide. It also looks, perhaps tactlessly, to involve Southey, former collaborator, in a new version of community: Pantisocracy re-imagined in the West Country. And more broadly, it recapitulates questions Coleridge had been worrying at through the 1790s – questions around the nature of freedom, the relationship between poetry and public duty and between individual affection and wider social responsibilities. Poetic conversation, bringing together private affection and public statement, might be a way through the 'lonely & faint' feelings of self-doubt, personal sorrow and post-Revolutionary disappointment.

The poem also allows us a deeper insight into the way in which, as Alison Hickey has suggestively explored, 'Romantic texts thematize and stage collaboration in metaphors of organic relation'.[1] It figures Coleridge's favourite images of interdependence: foliage, trees, leaves which belong both to trees and to books. Those lime-tree leaves are both symbolic and real. They borrow something, as we will see, from the 'rose-leaf beds' of 'Reflections on Having Left a Place of Retirement', and their roots run deep, through eighteenth-century poetry into Milton. But Coleridge's precise depiction also owes a great deal to Dorothy Wordsworth. The friends were sharing not only walks but also ways of observing the natural world, and the blank verse of Coleridge's conversation poems borrows from the delicate, detailed prose of Dorothy's journals. She notes the weather, the woods, the 'glossy green leaves' of the trees:

> The adder's-tongue and the ferns green in the low damp dell. These plants now in perpetual motion from the current of the air; in summer only moved by the drippings of the rocks. A cloudy day. (DWJ, 7, 6)

Coleridge, too, tries hard to capture the look and the motion of these 'plumy ferns', as he describes them in the letter to Southey. Later, in the version published in the *Annual Anthology*, they become a 'dark-green file of long *lank weeds'.[2] A footnote references the 'Asplenium scolopendrium ... the

Adder's tongue' and directs the reader to William Withering's *An Arrangement of British Plants*, a book that Wordsworth had acquired in August 1800. The ferns and leaves of the poem thus reflect several years of shared walking, reading and writing about the natural world. They speak both to Dorothy's 'minute inspection' of the Stowey landscape in prose and to the creative power of the Wordsworths' friendship (*DWJ*, 8). Indeed, Coleridge's imagery of relationship is often informed by the natural world. 'The beings who know how to sympathize with me are my foliage' (CL I, 381), he writes to Tom Poole, for instance, looking at a leafless winter tree as a symbol of his solitary self. Or, more darkly, he imagines himself among the Wordsworths as a 'wither'd branch upon a blossoming Tree' (*CPW* I, ii, 685). The changing imagery evokes Coleridge's ambiguously layered feelings, and the tensions of friendship itself.

For this conversational monologue also, of course, raises key questions around collaboration, none more biting than the criticism made by its dedicatee, 'Charles Lamb, of the India House, London': 'For God's sake (I never was more serious), don't make me ridiculous any more by terming me gentle-hearted in print, or do it in better verses' (LL I, 217–18); 'please to blot out *gentle hearted*, and substitute drunken dog, ragged-head, seld-shaven, odd-ey'd, stuttering, or any other epithet which truly and properly belongs to the Gentleman in question' (LL I, 224). Lamb's criticism is, as always, acute. To have personal 'calamity' linked to his professional identity at the East India House could have had embarrassing or even harmful consequences, but his complaint is more far-reaching. What he is resisting is Coleridge's larger tendency to disrespect the creative identities of others – with which he had direct experience. Coleridge's collaborative conversations could often shade into speaking for, or drowning out, others; co-writing, as we shall see, could easily turn into over-writing.

Those bowers, leaves and branches of 'This Lime-Tree Bower' speak, then, to the organic, complicated, interwoven nature of Coleridge's collaborations. Critics have become more attuned to this entangled Coleridgean language of collaboration in recent decades, reflecting a broader shift in our critical understanding of Romanticism. Alongside the Romantic poet composing in rural solitude, our frame of reference now includes the friends and family working and walking alongside that poet, the wider networks, local and global, literary and political, which might shape their work. Our vision of the place of Romantic creativity has expanded: not only the mountainside but also the crowded Strand, Fleet Street, the periodical, coffee house and tavern. The lime-tree bower is set against its urban equivalent, the 'Salutation and Cat', where Coleridge and Lamb gathered for poetry, tobacco and egg-hot; poems of private relationship are read in their public contexts

of periodicals and contemporary news.³ This forms part of a larger critical interrogation of the concept of the Romantic author as singular genius;
recent criticism is increasingly aware of Romantic sociability itself as a 'kind
of text in its own right, a form of cultural work'.⁴ Coleridge's self-conscious
collaborations, on and off the page, might be read differently in this context, as we recognize the creative importance of different forms of literary,
religious or institutional network or coterie – the 'continuities and connect-
edness' of Romantic-era writers, attached both to a longer literary history
and to each other.⁵ The debate has broadened and deepened over the last
decades, as Coleridge's friendships have been theorized in more detail and
the importance of other writers in his circle has been recognized: Lloyd,
Southey, Thelwall, Robinson, Barbauld. We are learning to read 'the poetry
of relationship' in new ways.⁶

This impulse towards collaboration might be seen in psychological terms.
Coleridge's own portraits of his unhappy childhood lend a poignancy to
his repeated idealization of domestic affection, and his hunt for acceptance
within a family, or quasi-familial circle, stretching from the Evans sisters to
the Frickers, to the Wordsworths, to the Morgans. But this is not simply a
story of Coleridge's psyche: it is also about Romantic influence and how it
might be perceived. Recent criticism is sympathetic to Coleridge as reader
and author: myriad-minded, allusive, capacious, anxious. Moreover, his
intimate appeals for friendship and readerly sympathy can be seen as linked
to his emotional, and spiritual, urge towards community. As I will trace in
the studies which follow, he moves from the political, (im)practical project
of Pantisocracy – a scheme of shared property – to a vision of intellectual
collaboration, most notably with the Wordsworths but also through shared
reading and shared writing. From a close circle of writer–reader friends,
Coleridge moves outward, attempting – through imagery, echo, quotation –
to create a bond with a reading public akin to friendship, although it might,
like Coleridge's relationships in life, have its darker aspects.

Poems on Various Subjects, 1796

Coleridge's first major publication, *Poems on Various Subjects* (1796), reis-
sued, with some important revisions and additions, in 1797, shows this
collaborative creativity in practice. The volume gives an insight into mid-
1790s Coleridge: newly wedded, still boasting on his title page that he is
'late of Jesus College, Cambridge'. His Pantisocratic allegiances are proudly
on view, and in the closing poem, 'Religious Musings', he takes a turn in the
Dissenting pulpit, a nod to his desire in the late 1790s to become a preacher.
The collection begins with a pre-emptive interrogation, and defence, of the

'querulous egotism' of the self-absorbed poet of sensibility (*PVS* (1796), v). In a technique to which Coleridge would return throughout his life he enters into dialogue with himself. 'But how are the Public interested in your sorrows or your description?', he asks, comforting himself that there may be 'scattered individuals' who will find solace in the description of his own feelings:

> There is one species of egotism which is truly disgusting; not that which leads us to communicate our feelings to others, but that which would reduce the feelings of others to an identity with our own. (*PVS* (1796), viii)

Already, Coleridge is formulating the idea of the audience as friend, the partial answer to the perpetual anxiety to avoid 'the word *I*' which would always haunt him' (*PVS* (1796), ix). In this early work, we see collaboration emerging as a guiding principle for his writing life – and can understand, too, how closely it is linked to his early political and philosophical experiments with the 'abandonment of individual property' (*PVS* (1796), x).

The 'Preface' to *Poems* closes with allusions to that early project, immediately followed by details of others' contributions: Charles Lamb, and the would-be Pantisocrats Favell and Southey. We move from the shared ideals of the Susquehanna settlers to a shared space for poetry, and the two remain closely interlinked throughout. The opening poem, 'Monody to Chatterton', not only pays affectionate homage to the poet but actually invites Chatterton to join in the Pantisocratic scheme, settling down in 'Freedom's undivided dell', ploughing by day and rhapsodizing by night. This is an extreme version of the ways in which Coleridge seeks to bring his literary and political heroes into sympathetic community: poetic homage to Bowles runs alongside tributes to Kościuszko, Priestley and Fayette, and reproaches addressed to Burke.[7] In a series of poems to 'eminent individuals', Coleridge strives to evoke a larger ideal of freedom, inflected by the millennial rhetoric of religious Dissent and by the conflicted discourses of late eighteenth-century revolution, and deeply connected to collaboration. Writing to and with friends, or co-opting others into the language of friendship, might help the poet to navigate between individual self-interest and the larger public good.

Immediately following this run of effusions to public figures come three far more homely poems, signed 'C. L.': Charles Lamb's contributions. Their placement shows the way in which Coleridge's collaborative mode moves between public and private, so that his affectionate individual relationship with Lamb becomes part of a larger public dialogue. Seen in this light, Lamb's rather awkward poems seem to dramatize this movement, each negotiating its way through a moment of emotional crisis or excess and moving to a larger perspective. In 'Methinks, how dainty sweet it were, reclin'd', for example, the poet evokes a embowered moment of passion, lying with his lover, Anna, 'Beneath the vast o'er shadowing branches high / Of some old wood'. In the hands of Coleridge, this vision is then rejected as self-indulgent:

> On rose-leaf beds amid your faery bowers
> I all too long have lost the dreamy hours!
>
> (*PVS* (1796), 56)

The 'faery bowers' strategically anticipate the embowerment of the poet and Sara in 'Effusion XXXV' with its visions of 'Faery Land', so that Charles Lamb's work is seen as a part of a larger Coleridgean dialogue about the purpose and affections of the poet.

Yet those 'rose-leaf beds', and accompanying self-reproach, are entirely Coleridge's – revisions of Lamb's poem. As it stood originally, the poem exhibited no such anxiety, depicting instead a scene of shared storytelling and sensibility. When *Poems* was published, Lamb was dismayed to find it changed: 'I had rather have seen what I wrote myself,' he told Coleridge, defending his sonnets in terms which reproachfully recall the language of the 'Preface': 'I love my sonnets because they are the reflected images of my own feelings at different times [...] I charge you, Col. **spare my ewe lambs**' (*LL* I, 20). The poem was restored to its original, more ambiguous, version in the second edition of the volume in 1797; the rose-leaf beds, however, found a new home in Coleridge's 'Reflections on having left a Place of Retirement'. There they illustrate anxiety over the poet's self-absorbed private relationships, which entice him to dream away 'the trusted Hours / On rose leaf Beds, pamp'ring the coward Heart / With feelings all too delicate for use' (*PVS* (1797), 103). It is this same self-doubt that is voiced, and then soothed, in 'This Lime-Tree Bower'. The embowered poet can thus be seen as a special motif, a private allusion, in the Coleridge circle, used to voice anxieties about affection, friendship and public duty. But the image also offers a telling example of Coleridge's collaborative poetics in action, at first productively, as Lamb's poem is ushered into print as part of an overtly idealistic community, and then more darkly, as it is co-opted into playing an unwilling part in a Coleridgean narrative.

Lyrical Ballads (1798)

Looking again at a volume such as *Poems* helps us see the longer and more complex history of Coleridgean collaboration, before and around his relationship with Wordsworth. Yet *Lyrical Ballads* remains a powerful myth of

35

Romantic shared work and ideals, which also carries within itself the traces of future conflict and difference. Any account of the volume is shaped by the men's own self-fashioning of their 'symbiotic' relationship: writing and rewriting the story of working together in the years 1797 and 1798, coming and going between Alfoxden and Nether Stowey in a glow of mutual discovery and optimism.[8] Theirs is a 'lyrical dialogue', in the words of Paul Magnuson; for Lucy Newlyn, the two men create a 'language of allusion', which did not preclude, however, radical differences; Gene Ruoff attempts to trace and define an 'intertextual genetics' of complexly knotted and connected strands.[9] In recent years, however, critical attention has shifted, opening up those oft-repeated origin myths to help us understand a larger community around the poems. *Lyrical Ballads* should be seen as an act of 'domestic co-partnery' with Dorothy Wordsworth, containing the traces of other lost voices: John Thelwall, 'the silenced partner' of the 1790s; Charles Lloyd; the editorial work of Humphry Davy.[10] Critics have also begun to interrogate *Lyrical Ballads* in different contexts, moving out from the conversation between two men to understand interdisciplinary debates in their larger circle: Romantic disability aesthetics, for example, or ongoing discussions around eco-criticism.[11]

But, in spite of that weight of critical debate, opening that 1798 volume can still evoke feelings of 'strangeness and awkwardness' for the reader, as the first few poems bring disparate genres and tones into dialogue. After Wordsworth's brief 'Advertisement', with 'The Rime of the Ancyent Marinere', originally conceived as a joint project before being taken over by Coleridge alone; we then move to a section of Coleridge's *Osorio*, 'The Foster Mother's Tale, a Dramatic Fragment'. Only then do we come to Wordsworth's 'Lines Left upon a Seat in a Yew-Tree', followed by Coleridge's 'The Nightingale, a Conversational Poem'. Each work tells us a slightly different story of collaboration, and conflict – much like Wordsworth's own account, in later years, of the beginning of the volume, which grew out of the writing of 'The Ancient Mariner' on a walking tour. 'We began the composition together', Wordsworth told Isabella Fenwick, but very soon differences emerged: 'As we endeavoured to proceed conjointly (I speak of the same evening) our respective manners proved so widely different that it would have been quite presumptuous in me to do anything but separate from an undertaking upon which I could only have been a clog' (*LB*, 4). That language of 'clog' is significant: the writing had begun, physically and emotionally, as a shared journey, moving forward together. Now, recollecting even the development of the poem across the evening, Wordsworth uses a language of impediment.

Indeed, the poem itself is a frightening vision of stasis, by turns icy and dry as dust:

> Day after day, day after day,
> We stuck, ne breath ne motion. (LB, 773)

This tale of collaboration gone awry, of difficult storytelling and collective failure, is an ominous opening to the shared volume. In both form and content, it also dramatizes some of the issues which would cause trouble for the whole project. The two writers made various attempts, from the 'Preface' onwards, to describe and divide the subjects of the volume. In *Biographia Literaria*, Coleridge outlines 'the plan of the "Lyrical Ballads"', in which the two men divided their efforts apparently equally, so that Coleridge's 'endeavours should be directed to persons and characters supernatural, or at least romantic': 'Mr. Wordsworth on the other hand was to propose to himself as his object, to give the charm of novelty to things of every day, and to excite a feeling analogous to the supernatural' (*BL* II,7). But in practice, as the editors of *Lyrical Ballads* point out, 'Aesthetic planning for the joint volume seems [...] far more haphazard' (*LB*, 5). It proved difficult to define the boundaries of the 'every day' and the 'supernatural'; it was even harder to bring the approaches and styles of the two men into a coherent whole. Again, those first few poems bear this out: generically, as we move from the ballad form to play, to blank verse; thematically, in their portrayal of lated figures, from the mariner to the wild boy of 'The Foster-Mother's Tale', and the solitary of the yew tree. Within the lyrical space of the 1798 volume, the back-and-forth dialogue of the disparate poems is held together – as plans advanced for the second volume, however, the strains and discordances of the collaboration became more pronounced.

'Christabel' and 'Dejection: An Ode'

Wordsworth's 'Preface' to the 1800 edition of *Lyrical Ballads* sets out uneasily to explain the inclusion of Coleridge's poems in 1798; there may be 'a difference', he admits, between the two writers, but 'there would be found no discordance in the colours of our style; as our opinions on the subject of poetry do almost entirely coincide' (*LB*, 742). *Almost* entirely: his doubts are evident in his re-ordering of the 1798 volume, where 'The Rime of the Ancyent Marinere' loses its place at the head of the volume, and is accompanied by a note excusing 'the defects of the poem', in subject matter, narrative, imagery and metre. The rupture is evident, too, in the poem which is silently absent from the volume: Coleridge's 'Christabel'. Begun in early

1798, this was initially intended for the second edition of *Lyrical Ballads*. But the poem was not completed: perhaps because of Wordsworth's doubts about its suitability; perhaps because, in the words of J. C. C. Mays, 'to complete the poem in terms established by Part II requires the resolution of tensions and oppositions that Part I was content simply to present, embody, and suggest' (*CPW* I, i, 479). Neither the poets, nor the poem itself, could work together easily.

'Christabel' is a cross-generational tale of friendship and hospitality betrayed, and, when finally published, the 'charges of plagiarism or servile imitation' mentioned in its preface reinforce this narrative of anxiety (*CPW* I, i, 481). The poem obsessively returns and recasts images Coleridge had previously used to express creative power and nurture. In the place of embowering foliage, the oak tree which Christabel prays beneath has just 'One red Leaf, the last of its clan', dancing alone. Images of intertwining and responsive movement are transformed into a Gothic narrative of possession and threat: Geraldine's arms are 'the lovely lady's prison'; the snake swells around the dove's neck. It is part of a pattern of skewed echo and response, in which even the bells across the landscape of the Lake District give back a 'death-note', a mocking devilish refrain. This is the conversation poem made sinister. Again, we close the poem, in its published version of 1817, with an image of Hartley, but this time the father's tale spills over into 'words of unmeant bitterness', as the poet watches the red-cheeked child dancing alone, like the last leaf we encountered earlier. It is a portrait of self-sufficiency which should be joyful but which gives voice to discordance and doubt:

> Perhaps 'tis pretty to force together
> Thoughts so all unlike each other.   (*CPW* I, i, 503)

For all its doubts around hospitality and sympathetic response, Coleridge was eager to recite the poem in public and it was widely circulated in manuscript, exerting influence on others – most notably, Walter Scott – before publication. It was published thanks to the support of others, chiefly Byron, so that it becomes a poem which at once expresses doubt over collaboration and relies upon it.

The dynamic is not dissimilar to 'A Letter to [Asra]', intended for Sara Hutchinson, which would be revised as 'Dejection: An Ode'. It is dated in manuscript '4 April 1802. Sunday Evening', the day before Wordsworth set out to propose marriage to Mary Hutchinson. Coleridge, unable to propose to her sister Sara, registers his isolation, creative and familial, in the poem. Just as in 'This Lime-Tree Bower', we begin with an image of the lonely poet. But for all his attentive looking at each detail of the natural world – the larch tree, the 'peculiar tint' of the yellow green sky, the clouds, the stars, and the crescent moon – he remains isolated. Here it is the throstle, not the poet, who sings joyfully from within the larch tree, and although that tree – 'which pushes out in tassels green / It's bundled leafits' – is scrutinized as carefully as the lime, its leaves remain something separate, bundled away from poetic insight:

> – I see them all, so excellently fair!
> I see, not feel, how beautiful they are.   (*CPW* I, ii, 681)

This is a failure not only of creative vision but of collaboration: an answer, in a minor key, to the confidence both of Wordsworth's new direction in life and his new writing, specifically his 'Ode', 'Intimations of Immortality from Recollections of Early Childhood', which he had begun a few days earlier in 1802. Wordsworth's own lines are echoed, but sadly, faintly, without the sense of answering inspiration which had allowed the poets to develop the possibilities of blank verse in 1797 and 1798. Although Coleridge cut out the image of himself as 'wither'd branch' from 'Dejection' when published, he retains another ambiguous description of himself as tree:

> Fancy made me Dreams of Happiness:
> For Hope grew round me, like the climbing Vine,
> And Leaves & Fruitage, not my own, seem'd mine!
> (*CPW* I, ii, 687)

Looking back to the Alfoxden days, Coleridge presents a deliberately ambiguous image: are those 'Leaves & Fruitage' his own poems of that era, infused with borrowed inspiration? Or Wordsworth's poems? When does allusion become appropriation? Buried within the lines are the memory of the way the ivy 'usurps' the elms in 'This Lime-Tree Bower' and echoes, too, of *Paradise Lost* – the wedding of elm and vine in Book Five.[12] Both hint at larger literary debts, suggesting that collaboration might shade into usurpation or betrayal.

And yet behind the isolation, failure and loss narrated in the poem is a shadow story of domestic collaboration. Coleridge wrote 'Letter [to Asra]' in Greta Hall, having moved there hoping to recreate the creative intercourse of the Somerset years, with the Wordsworths thirteen miles away in Grasmere. Although there was plenty of coming and going, Grasmere proved 'too great a distance for us to enjoy each other's Society without inconvenience' (*CL* II, 671): Wordsworth's marriage, and the fraught relationship with Sara Hutchinson, must also have been complicating factors. Coleridge was soon enumerating the advantages of the Lakes to Southey, and by autumn 1803 the Southeys had joined the Coleridges at Greta Hall. This temporary arrangement was to prove permanent: Southey took over the lease in 1804 and, in Coleridge's absence, became head of an extended household, which included Coleridge's wife and children and another Fricker sister, Mary, widow of the Pantisocrat poet Robert Lovell, and their child. This was a household which had its foundations in those transatlantic visions of the 1790s, and while Keswick was not quite Susquehanna, this was a creative, caring, if fractious, community. At first a refuge for the Southeys, without a permanent home and grieving the loss of a child, the extended household then became vital for the Coleridges: an ongoing collaboration which was both self-serving and supportive.

Biographia Literaria (1817)

A pattern of collaboration emerges, with Coleridge's writing solitude facilitated by the silent domestic support of others, his creativity at once fiercely individual and interdependent with others. Similarly, *Biographia Literaria* is simultaneously a statement of independent thought and a homage to collaboration – in genre, style and composition history. An extended answer to Wordsworth's lengthy 'Preface' to *Lyrical Ballads* (1800), and subsequent revisions of his statements about their poetic differences in later years, it may be seen as a Coleridgean reappropriation of the long-discussed philosophical project of *The Recluse*. It is also the product of another, different collaborative relationship. Although we do not know the exact composition details, Coleridge seems to have dictated the majority of the material, hurriedly, in the summer of 1815, to his friend John Morgan. Coleridge had settled with the Morgan family earlier that year – one of his long series of quasi-familial domestic nests so vital for his sense of self, and a key factor in his creation of the *Biographia*. Indeed, Kathleen Coburn suggests that Morgan, 'acting as amanuensis, extracted the *Biographia* from Coleridge, almost by force'.[13] Even so, progress was slow: the printing delayed, sheets spoiled, Coleridge rewriting material in the two volumes until eventual publication in July 1817, alongside *Sibylline Leaves*. *Biographia Literaria* reflects very many years of Coleridge's collaborations and negotiations with others and with his own past writing.

From its inception the *Biographia* was a hybrid work. A notebook entry of 1803 sees Coleridge making up his mind 'to write my metaphysical works, as *my Life & in* my Life – intermixed with all the other events /or history of the mind & fortunes of S. T. Coleridge' (*CN* I, 1515). This 'intermixed' aspect has been seen both as a strength and a weakness, but recent criticism has tended to see a Coleridgean 'unity in multeity' at work in its muddle of metaphor, memoir, theory and quotation, both acknowledged and unacknowledged. For Kathleen M. Wheeler, for example, the work should be seen as a complicated but fundamentally unified whole, 'engaging the reader in a project of self-criticism and knowledge'.[14]

This active form of collaboration is prompted through the work the reader has to do: interpreting the metaphors, tracing allusion and quotation. Coleridge begins by fondly, if critically, remembering his first book, *Poems on Various Subjects* (1796), and by paying tribute to early influences, from his schoolmaster James Bowyer to the beloved poet of his youth, William Bowles – whose writings, he notes, inspired feelings of 'friendship as of a man for a man' (*BL* I, 12) – and real friends such as Southey and Lamb. The *Biographia* bristles with references – from Locke, Berkeley, Leibnitz, Hartley, to George Fox, Boehme, William Law, to name only a few – but there are still more silent borrowings and slippages. How should we read these unacknowledged forms of collaboration? Accusations of Coleridge's literary theft have a long history; Coleridge was himself, as Norman Fruman notes, often hasty in accusing others of stealing from him.[15] Recent criticism has tended towards a nuanced reading of Coleridge's appropriations, from Jerome Christensen's analysis of a larger creative pattern of 'marginal discourse' to Andrew Keanie's appreciation of Coleridge's 'inspissation', an 'organically evolved quality' of layering and thickening and overgrowth which pays little heed to literary property.[16] These different ideas are present in the work itself. While it pays homage to collaboration and friendship, it also (guiltily?) hints at the different ways this might be interpreted, in a quotation borrowed from his own earlier work, 'Dejection: An Ode':

> I would fain present myself to the Reader as I was in the first dawn of my literary life:
>
> > When Hope grew round me, like the climbing vine,
> > And fruits, and foliage not my own seem'd mine.   (*BL* II, 159)

The image registers anxiety over literary originality and usurpation, as we have seen; we might also note the way in which the reader is approached in this section, the slightly arch, self-conscious tone of 'fain present myself', challenging the reader to recognize this echo from his own work – and perhaps to contradict it.

The response of one reader shows that this appeal could meet with sympathy: Charles Lamb, dedicating his own *Works* (1818) to Coleridge. Lamb reminisces about his own early literary life, and his lack of poetry since the days of Coleridge's mentorship: 'wanting the support of your friendly elm, (I speak for myself,) my vine has, since that time, put forth few or no fruits; the sap (if ever it had any) has become, in a manner, dried up and extinct.'[17] Lamb takes on Coleridgean metaphor of elm and vine to emphasize the sustaining power of his friend's collaboration, and to register support for *Biographia*, published the previous year. As he becomes a successful periodical essayist, he returns to the idea of Coleridge's collaboration as central to his creativity; the essays of Elia not only allude to Coleridge's work but actually take on his identity in the *London Magazine* essay 'Christ's Hospital Five and Thirty Years Ago'. In excusing this, he returns to language of the 1790s, picking up Coleridge's anxious use of the term 'egotism' in the 'Preface' to *Poems* 1796 and asking the reader to consider 'If it be egotism to imply and twine with his own identity the griefs and affections of another – making himself many, or reducing many unto himself'.[18] The gift of 'This Lime-Tree Bower', ungraciously received at first, is finally reciprocated; the over-writings of Lamb's work through the 1790s not only forgiven but slyly returned with interest. These long-running, changing conversations might be glimpsed in Wordsworth's later work, even after Coleridge's death: 'Evening Voluntaries', for example, pick up the rhythms of much earlier work, willing the language of a lost community into life again.[19] Southey's friendship, too, speaks to the enduring power of those early collaborations: the writing relationship which had begun in 1794 with the *Fall of Robespierre* was renewed in 1812 with *Omniana: or Horae Otiosiores*. This collection of jointly authored notes, edited by Southey, is a wild miscellany which evokes wide-ranging, shared conversations; it also looks forward to the editing projects of H. N. and Sara Coleridge. The collaboration had started with fiery political early writing and idealistic plans: it weathered the Wordsworthian intensity of the 1790s, and Coleridge's erratic habits, 'murderous of all domestic comfort'.[20] Moreover, the familial literary community of Greta Hall, overseen by Southey, nurtured the second generation: in the lyrics of Hartley Coleridge, and the editing of Sara, we see how the collaborations of the 1790s continued in new ways.[21]

It is with Sara as her father's great 'unacknowledged collaborator' that I want to close.[22] Born in December 1802, she bears the name of her mother, but also, of course, of Sara Hutchinson: she, too, is the product of the 'Dejection' year. She was the child of Romantic collaboration, brought up by her mother, aunt and uncle Southey at Greta Hall, she knew Wordsworth 'more intimately than I knew my Father' (Swaab, 96). Yet despite not having lived with her father for more than a few weeks at a time, she would go on to become one of his first, and most important, editors.[23] While her own poetic, philosophical and theological writing deserves to be fully remembered, so too does her editing. Her 1847 *Biographia* is not only sympathetic and thorough but also creative: digressive, allusive, personal, offering astute critical and biographical readings, half the page often taken up with notes, translations and commentary. Sara commented to Isabella Fenwick, as she worked on the proofs of *Biographia*, that 'the trouble I have taken with this book is *ridiculous* to think of – it is a filial *phenomenon*: nobody will thank me for it – except a few the *wrong way* – and no one will know or see a twentieth part of it' (Swaab, xix). She frequently speaks of the 'trouble' and 'labour' of bringing his 'body' of work into coherent form, and the reminder of childbirth is significant. Sara as collaborator occupies an ambiguous part-child, part-parent role, at once heir to and protector of her father's legacy. As editor, she finds her way through questions of literary propriety and paternity skilfully and painstakingly.[24] She laboured to trace Coleridge's multiple allusions and borrowings, commenting on his 'unusual disregard' for property of thought, but maintaining a deep sympathy with his struggle towards an ideal of unity. Tackling the issue of plagiarism head-on in her edition of *Biographia,* she entitles the first section of her introduction, 'Mr Coleridge's obligations to Schelling, and the unfair view of the subject presented in Blackwood's Magazine'. Peter Swaab, noting the assiduity of her engagement with Coleridge's philosophical reading, suggests that she gives an 'extraordinarily acute psychological analysis of her father's carelessness in composition, both judicious and forgiving' (Swaab, xx).

Perhaps the most telling, and most poignant, act of retrospective collaboration is Sara's dedication of the 1847 *Biographia* to Wordsworth, evoking the time he and Coleridge met, 'in the lovely Vale of Stowey'. She signs the dedicatory letter, 'Your Child in heart and faithful Friend'. The phrase 'Child in heart' acts both as a nod to 'Ode: Intimations of Immortality' and as a personal acknowledgement of the father role the poet had played for her; she also takes on her own father's identity as 'faithful Friend'. Wordsworth did not, however, welcome this collaborative tribute, telling Isabella Fenwick that he 'could not refuse', though 'the Book contains many things not at all to my taste' (*WL* (*LY*), 833). Like 'This Lime-Tree Bower', or the wedding present of 'Dejection', the Coleridgean literary gift could be an ambiguous one.

We began with Coleridge, alone, metaphorically imprisoned, imagining the freedom that might come through friendly sympathy. We have seen how adept he was at finding that sympathy, and in prompting answers – positive and negative – to his lonely conversation. Twenty-first-century criticism will continue to show how many different voices participated in those conversations: not only exploring the family and friends and texts immediately outside the lime-tree bower but also looking across the 'western ridge' and 'blue Ocean' to global Romanticisms. Helen Thomas has suggested the ways in which we might productively read Coleridge's abolitionist writings alongside the rhythms of slave narratives; we should also take seriously the transatlantic yearning visible in *Poems*.[25] Frederick Douglass invokes the words of Coleridge, slightly changing his emphases, at the start of *My*

Bondage and My Freedom (1855) as a starting point for his definition of freedom: 'a PERSON is eternally differenced from a THING.'[26] The quotation is from *A Dissertation on the Science of Method; or, the Laws and Regulative Principles of Education* (1818), the introduction to the hotch-potch project *Encyclopedia Metropolitana*. But the principles are those which had illuminated Coleridge's sermons in the 1790s, so that his post-Revolutionary calls for freedom go forward into a new battle on the other side of the Atlantic in the 1850s. Douglass's reworking of Coleridge seems to respond to the collaborative urge of the poet himself, his urgent desire to find answering sympathy. Even posthumously, Coleridge's collaborative conversations continue to evolve.

Notes

1 Alison Hickey, 'Double Bonds: Charles Lamb's Romantic Collaborations', *ELH*, 63 (1996), 735–71, at 735.
2 *The Annual Anthology* (Bristol, 1800), 141.
3 The work begun by critics such as Kelvin Everest, *Coleridge's Secret Ministry: The Context of the Conversation Poems, 1795–1798* (Hassocks, Sussex: Harvester, 1979), and Paul Magnuson, *Reading Public Romanticism* (Princeton University Press, 1998), has been continued by, for example, Heidi Thomson, *Coleridge and the Romantic Newspaper: The 'Morning Post' and the Road to 'Dejection'* (Basingstoke and New York: Palgrave, 2016).
4 *Romantic Sociability: Social Networks and Literary Culture in Britain, 1770–1840*, eds. Gillian Russell and Clara Tuite (Cambridge University Press, 2002), 4.
5 David Fairer, *Organising Poetry: The Coleridge Circle, 1790–1798* (Oxford University Press, 2009), 1.
6 See Gurion Taussig, *Coleridge and the Idea of Friendship, 1789–1804* (Newark: Delaware University Presses, 2002), Richard Matlak, *The Poetry of Relationship: The Wordsworths and Coleridge, 1797–1800* (New York: St. Martin's Press, 1997), and Nicola Healey, *Dorothy Wordsworth and Hartley Coleridge: The Poetics of Relationship* (Basingstoke and New York: Palgrave Macmillan, 2012), for a discussion of this term.
7 For a discussion of the ways in which Coleridge uses literary predecessors as collaborators and conversation partners, see David Fairer, 'Coleridge's Sonnets from Various Authors (1796): A Lost Conversation Poem?', *Studies in Romanticism*, 41 (2002), 585–604.
8 Paul Magnuson, *Coleridge and Wordsworth: A Lyrical Dialogue* (Princeton University Press, 1987); Lucy Newlyn, *Coleridge, Wordsworth and the Language of Allusion* (Oxford University Press, 1986; repr. 2000); Gene Ruoff, *Wordsworth and Coleridge: The Making of the Major Lyrics, 1802–1804* (New Brunswick, NJ: Harvester Wheatsheaf, 1989).
9 Thomas McFarland, *Romanticism and the Forms of Ruin: Wordsworth, Coleridge, and Modalities of Fragmentation* (Princeton University Press, 1981), see particularly Chapter 1.

10 Polly Atkin, 'Collaboration, Domestic Co-Partnery and Lyrical Ballads', in *The Cambridge Companion to 'Lyrical Ballads'*, ed. Sally Bushell (Cambridge University Press, 2020), 32–48; Judith Thompson, *John Thelwall in the Wordsworth Circle: The Silenced Partner* (New York: Palgrave Macmillan, 2012).

11 Emily B. Stanback, *The Wordsworth–Coleridge Circle and the Aesthetics of Disability* (London: Palgrave Macmillan, 2016); Jeremy Davies, 'Romantic Ecocriticism: History and Prospects', *Literature Compass*, 15 (2018) gives a good guide to recent discussion.

12 Newlyn, *Language of Allusion*, 77.

13 Daniel Mark Fogel, 'A Compositional History of the "Biographia Literaria"', *Studies in Bibliography* 30 (1977), 219–34 (233). See also *Biographia Literaria*, ed. Adam Roberts (Edinburgh University Press, 2014).

14 Kathleen M. Wheeler, *Sources, Processes and Methods in Coleridge's Biographia Literaria* (Cambridge University Press, 1980), 106.

15 Norman Fruman, *Coleridge, The Damaged Archangel* (London: Allen & Unwin, 1972), 76; xix.

16 Jerome C. Christensen, 'Coleridge's Marginal Method in the Biographia Literaria', *Publication of the Modern Language Association* 92 (1977), 928–40; Andrew Keanie, 'Coleridge and Plagiarism', *The Oxford Handbook of Samuel Taylor Coleridge*, ed. Frederick Burwick (Oxford University Press, 2012) 435–54 (450).

17 Charles Lamb, *Works* (London: Ollier, 1818), vi.

18 'A Character of the Late Elia', *London Magazine*, January 1823, 19.

19 Tim Fulford, 'Wordsworth Elegizing the Lyrical Ballad in the 1830s and 1840s', *Studies in English Literature 1500–1900*, 59 (2019), 787–812.

20 *CLRS*, 1311. Robert Southey to John Rickman [*c*.24 April 1807].

21 See Healey, *Dorothy Wordsworth and Hartley Coleridge* and Andrew Keanie, *Hartley Coleridge: A Reassessment of His Life and Work* (Basingstoke and New York: Palgrave Macmillan, 2008).

22 Jeffrey W. Barbeau, *Sara Coleridge: Her Life and Thought* (New York: Palgrave Macmillan, 2014), x; Bradford Keyes Mudge, *Sara Coleridge, a Victorian Daughter: Her Life and Essays* (New Haven, CT, and London: Yale University Press, 1989), 14.

23 Alan D. Vardy, *Constructing Coleridge: The Posthumous Life of the Author* (New York: Palgrave Macmillan, 2010), 3.

24 See Alison Hickey, '"The Body of My Father's Writings": Sara Coleridge's Genial Labor', in *Literary Couplings: Couples, Collaborators, and the Construction of Authorship*, eds. Marjorie Stone and Judith Thompson (Madison: University of Wisconsin Press, 2006), 124–47.

25 Helen Thomas, *Romanticism and Slave Narratives: Transatlantic Testimonies* (Cambridge University Press, 2000).

26 Neil Roberts, *Freedom as Marronage* (University of Chicago Press, 2015), 62.

4

GREGORY LEADBETTER

Nature Lyrics

In 'The Nightingale' of April 1798 (*CPW* I, i, 516–20), Coleridge invokes a new relationship between poetry and nature, by way of wry contrast to another: an earlier verse-persona of his own, in 'To the Nightingale', written three years before (*CPW* I, i, 227–28). There, Coleridge had played along with the clichéd poeticism of a literary convention – 'Sister of love-lorn Poets, Philomel!' (line 1) – citing Milton's description of the nightingale as a 'Most musical, most melancholy' bird (line 17). Revisiting this allusion in 'The Nightingale', Coleridge counters it directly: '"Most musical, most melancholy" Bird! / A melancholy Bird? Oh! idle thought! / In nature there is nothing melancholy' (lines 13–15). The altered mood goes further, and a 'different lore' (line 41) finds its voice:

> Poet who hath been building up the rhyme
> When he had better far have stretch'd his limbs
> Beside a brook in mossy forest-dell,
> By Sun or Moon-light, to the influxes
> Of shapes and sounds and shifting elements
> Surrendering his whole spirit, of his song
> And of his fame forgetful! so his fame
> Should share in Nature's immortality,
> A venerable thing! and so his song
> Should make all Nature lovelier, and itself
> Be lov'd like Nature! (lines 24–34)

In these lines, Coleridge inscribes a radical, mutually altering dynamic between the poet and the natural world, the human and the more-than-human. His intimate pairing of poetry and nature presents both as forms of life that create more life, in and through each other. The fact that Coleridge articulates this dynamic in the performative agility of poetry itself suggests the kind of imaginative and affective possibilities woven into the workings of a poem: pre-conceptual 'influxes' of being and their mysterious correspondence to human language, thought, feeling and action.

The potency and fluency of the poem's affirmation of this 'lore' belies the intricacy of its ramifications. It connects the process of poetic composition to the poet's attitude to nature: rejecting a laboured inauthenticity in which 'building up the rhyme' becomes a literary barrier between humans and their habitat, the poem intensifies the permeability, valency and participatory character of that relationship. As so often in Coleridge's poetry, the 'forest-dell' is a subtly eroticized site of transformative commune and secret pleasure. The productive idling of the poet lying beside the brook, at once relaxed and peculiarly attentive, figures a principle at the heart of Coleridge's poetics, ethics and metaphysics: a willing exposure of the self to living 'influxes' beyond its deliberate control, a union of the active and the passive, the elective and the receptive – a voluntary state from which the poet draws both insight and power. In a stimulating paradox, 'The Nightingale' is intensely self-conscious in depicting the 'different lore' of an elect group in a certain place at a certain time – Coleridge, William and Dorothy Wordsworth, 'My Friend, and thou, our Sister!' (line 40) – while that very 'lore' speaks of transcending self-consciousness in a greater apprehension of reality, embodied not in finality, but a way of being. Similarly, the poem does not abandon poetry ('song'), despite the acknowledged artifice of the form, but rather draws poetry in a new direction, modulating the relation between the natural and the artful. Notice, too, that refracted through their forest-dell 'forgetting', the poet's 'song' and 'fame' emerge all the more strongly for being imbued by the energies to which the poet and the poetry have been exposed. The poet's 'fame' should share in the iterative life of nature itself, while his poetry casts its vivifying spell on nature in and through its human participants – a sightline to beauty, wonder and love – and as such, is loved as if it were a living natural presence. It's an exhilarating synthesis: a key to many of Coleridge's most animating concerns, and a clue to his ongoing significance for any fresh consideration of poetry and the form of human activity in relation to its ecology.

In this essay I examine the questions, patterns and impulses that stir, haunt and ultimately characterize the making of that synthesis – principally with regard to that loose grouping of poems to which the subtitle of 'The Nightingale' would give its name: the 'conversation poems', for each of which the relationship between poetry, the natural world and human life is central. These poems reveal Coleridge's acutely productive sensitivity to the tension between the 'enchanted ground of POETRY' (*SWF* I, 649) and veneration of the natural world for its own sake. 'Nature has her proper interest', he writes in 1802, '& he will know what it is, who believes & feels, that every Thing has a Life of it's own, & that we are all *one Life*' (*CL* II, 864). One productive tension exposes another – here, between individual distinctiveness and fundamental unity, the ancient dilemma of 'how the *one can be many!*' (*CN* I, 1561) – but each dilemma is in fact intimately related: the art of poetry alters nature with a self-distinguishing life of its own, even as it is rooted in the givenness of the living world and the human condition. Describing the origin of *Lyrical Ballads* in his collaboration with Wordsworth, Coleridge again brings two contending principles together, as 'the two cardinal points of poetry':

> the power of exciting the sympathy of the reader by a faithful adherence to the truth of nature, and the power of giving the interest of novelty by the modifying colours of imagination. The sudden charm, which accidents of light and shade, which moon-light or sun-set diffused over a known and familiar landscape, appeared to represent the practicability of combining both. These are the poetry of nature. (*BL* II, 5)

The givenness of 'nature' itself is not fixed, but a living dynamic: both its 'truth' and its 'poetry' involve self-altering states, analogous to the self-altering action of the imagination. Coleridge knew that he was pursuing a daring and ambitious poetics of radical simultaneity – the character of which, I argue, has extraordinary interest and value for today's readers and poets, and more broadly for the reconciliation of literary humanism and philosophical ecocentrism.

Ironically, the very subtlety that Coleridge would achieve in the conversation poems began with a quest for a new simplicity: the attempt to combine 'natural thoughts with natural diction' (*BL* I, 25), and so amend a 'garishness' in his own poetry (*CL* I, 277). He keenly admired poets from whom he felt he could learn in this respect, including William Cowper, Robert Burns and William Lisle Bowles; in the flush of his early enthusiasm, Coleridge described Bowles as 'the most tender, and, with the exception of Burns, the only *always-natural* poet in our Language' (*CL* I, 278). This principle was already well established in his thinking (if not his poetry) by 1794 (*CL* I, 147), and it was in this ongoing context that Coleridge met and became close friends with Wordsworth, in whose work he found 'no mark of strained thought, or forced diction, no crowd or turbulence of imagery', and whose poetry he would tirelessly champion for its 'freedom from false taste' and 'union of deep feeling with profound thought' (*BL* I, 79, 80). Coleridge was still wrestling with the matter in January 1798, when he complained to Wordsworth, good-humouredly, that he could not attain 'simplicity & naturalness' except by '*assumption*' (*CL* I, 379). That tension between artfulness and naturalness feeds directly into their provisional resolution, articulated three months later in 'The Nightingale' – and, as I will show, dilates into a darker undertow that invests the conversation poems with a peculiar energy.

Coleridge was well advanced with this project, though, before his intimacy with Wordsworth. He recognized a breakthrough towards his 'present ideal' (*BL* 1, 26) in certain blank verse poems composed before and after the publication of his first collection in April 1796: writing to Southey in July 1797, he identifies 'Reflections on Having Left a Place of Retirement' (November 1795) as 'the best of my poems', with 'To the Rev. George Coleridge' (May 1797) next to it 'in point of *taste*' (*CL* 1, 334). In *Sibylline Leaves*, the collection of his poetry that accompanied the publication of *Biographia Literaria* in July 1817, both poems are included in the section entitled 'Meditative Poems in Blank Verse'. In one copy of the collection, on the page where 'The Eolian Harp' begins, Coleridge inscribed a note quietly laying claim to 'having first introduced this species of short blank verse poems – of which Southey, Lamb, Wordsworth, and others have since produced so many exquisite specimens' (*CPW* 1, i, 232 n). These 'Meditative Poems in Blank Verse' include nearly all of the work that George Maclean Harper first grouped together as the 'conversation poems': Harper includes 'The Eolian Harp' (August 1795), 'Reflections on Having Left a Place of Retirement' (November 1795), 'This Lime-Tree Bower My Prison' (July 1797), 'Frost at Midnight' (February 1798), 'Fears in Solitude' and 'The Nightingale' (both April 1798), 'Dejection: An Ode' (April 1802) and 'To William Wordsworth' (January 1807).[1] It is a porous category, with which several other poems by Coleridge can be aligned. While he anticipated later critics in discerning in these poems a three-part structure of description, imaginative flight and return, Harper's grouping emerged in the context of an essay on friendship, and the theme of friendship has been prominent in readings ever since. Important a theme as it is, however, there is – as I have already shown – much more in play, and at stake, in these poems and their cousins in Coleridge's *oeuvre*: grappling with the relationship between feeling, diction and technique, between the natural, the imaginal and the artful, Coleridge saw grounds for the renovation of English poetry.

It is telling that in 1797, when he identifies it as the best of his early poems, Coleridge adds the Latin epigraph 'Sermoni propriora' to 'Reflections on Having Left a Place of Retirement': a slight misquotation of Horace, meaning 'more fitted for conversation or prose' (*CPW* 1, i, 260–61). It signals Coleridge's self-consciousness about the experimental style he was developing in these poems, and – reaching for precedent – quietly summons the shade of Horace's own personal and meditative odes in support of the formal contentions embodied in the poem. The implication (or concern) that the poem might somehow slip towards prose is balanced by an appeal to the inherently varied and lively qualities of conversation.

In 1820, Coleridge still contends for 'the possibility of improving & enriching our English Versification by digging in the original *mines* – viz. the tunes of nature in impassioned conversation' (*CL* v, 93). In this new poetry of the mid-1790s, however, confidence and diffidence still went hand in hand.

'Reflections on Having Left a Place of Retirement' (*CPW* I, i, 260–63) establishes many of the patterns and qualities that Coleridge pursues in the other conversation poems. Composed in blank verse sensitive to the rhythms of speech and transitions of affect that intensify or relax according to its mood, the poem largely achieves the 'natural language, neither bookish, nor vulgar' (*BL* I, 22) for which Coleridge was aiming. The poem opens in the lush seclusion of a 'low Dell' (line 27), and makes performative, 'conversational' use of two addressees: the poet's wife, Sara ('we'/'our'), and the 'pretty Cot' (line 1) from which the poem sets out. It follows an odic, three-part structure: a scene of dwelling, a euphoric excursion to the peak of a 'Mount sublime' – scene of an initial ecstatic climax, in which 'It was a Luxury, – to be!' (lines 43, 42) – and an altered, proleptic return. It defines itself against the worldly 'thirst of idle gold' (line 13) and presents an alternative, more communal, compassionate, levelling vision of society. More subtle patterns emerge, too, which prefigure the active psychic receptivity that Coleridge envisions for the poet in 'The Nightingale': the skylark's song is an 'Unearthly minstrelsy! then only heard / When the Soul seeks to hear; when all is hush'd / And the Heart listens!' (lines 24–26). Coleridge calls upon the human will to listen and attend to the calls of the more-than-human life that surrounds it. The poem extends its 'conversation' to incorporate the affective reality of non-human and preverbal communication: 'We could hear / At silent noon, and eve, and early morn, / The Sea's faint murmur' (lines 2–4). It is no coincidence that here, as in the other conversation poems, Coleridge blends such invocation and evocation with the technical innovations he wishes to master: a pulsing rhythm running across enjambed lines that spill from pause to pause of varying length, at once moving and lingering, gathering force and shapeliness through change and continuity. The technique is essential to the character of the invocation, in 'exciting a more continuous and equal attention, than the language of prose aims at' (*BL* II, 15).

In bringing the self into a closer communicative relationship with life beyond the self, Coleridge wanted his new poems to bear the mark of lived experience. Like 'Frost at Midnight', 'Fears in Solitude' and 'The Nightingale', 'This Lime-Tree Bower My Prison' (*CPW* I, i, 349–54) is rooted in Coleridge's energetic absorption in the Quantock landscape, refracted through meditation and imagination. Coleridge accentuates this blend of experience in the latter poem, composed after 'dear Sara accidently emptied

50

a skillet of boiling milk on my foot' (*CL* I, 334), preventing him from walking with Lamb and the Wordsworths during Lamb's stay at Nether Stowey in July 1797. As in the other conversation poems, its contemplative vicariousness is creative and dynamic: its performance of displacement intensifies the act of imagining, and provokes its utterance. Like 'To the Nightingale' before it, and 'Frost at Midnight' after, the poem contrasts the stimulus and freedom of the natural world with urban confinement, 'In the great City pent' (line 30). Turning stasis into motion, it assumes an excursive form in which the physical intimacy of walking through landscape – alert, observant, exhilarated – corresponds to the inward, wandering, exploratory life of feeling. Its verbs are motile, vivid and prominent – as in the 'roaring dell', the ash that 'flings' its trunk 'from rock to rock' and the invocation of the sunset ('Shine', 'burn', 'Live', 'kindle' (lines 9, 12–13, 34–37)) – conjuring a sense of non-human agency, an active habitat to which the life of the language responds. The imagined walk culminates in an immersive ecstasy:

> So my Friend
> Struck with deep joy may stand, as I have stood,
> Silent with swimming sense; yea, gazing round
> On the wide landscape, gaze till all doth seem
> Less gross than bodily. (lines 37–41)

In its earliest, epistolary version, the landscape here becomes 'a living Thing / That acts upon the mind' (*CL* I, 335) – an apt description of the action of the poem itself: the language of the poem, like the 'wide landscape', is charged with far more than just the dictionary sense of its words. A leaf is 'watch'd'; the play of dappling shadow 'lov'd' (lines 48, 49), so that when the poem articulates a principle – 'No Plot so narrow, be but Nature there, / No waste so vacant, but may well employ / Each faculty of sense, and keep the heart / Awake to Love and Beauty!' (lines 62–65) – it speaks from a quality of attention that the poem both summons and performs. The poet in his bower participates, in microcosm, with the macrocosm that acts upon his friends. The poem's resonant final line – 'No Sound is dissonant which tells of Life' (line 76) – creates an analogy between the sounds of the poem and the sounds of the surrounding more-than-human world: both 'tell' of life.

From Coleridge's earliest writings, the contemplation of the natural world is conceived as a healing and improving influence. In March 1795, he writes that 'In the country, all around us smile Good and Beauty – and the Images of this divine καλοκαγαθον ["beautiful good"] are miniatured on the mind of the beholder, as a Landscape on a Convex Mirror' (*CL* I, 154), and he reuses this image when lecturing in Bristol the following year: 'In the

country, the Love and Power of the great Invisible are everywhere perspicuous, and by degrees we become partakers of that which we are accustomed
to contemplate' (*Lects 1795*, 224). In March 1798, Coleridge describes his
aim 'in poetry, to elevate the imagination & set the affections in right tune
by the beauty of the inanimate impregnated, as with a living soul, by the
presence of Life', and presents the love of 'fields & woods & mounta[ins]'
as an ethical education in itself: quoting a variation of lines recently written by Wordsworth, Coleridge affirms the existential authority of 'shadowy
Sympathies with things that hold / An inarticulate Language' (*CL* I, 397).
In 'The Dungeon', extracted for *Lyrical Ballads* from *Osorio*, the play he
wrote in 1797, Coleridge's faith in the healing 'ministrations' of the natural
world finds its zenith: under the influence of the 'melodies of woods, and
winds, and waters', the 'distempered' being could 'no more endure / To be
a jarring and a dissonant thing, / Amid this general dance and minstrelsy'
(*CPW* I, i, 334).

The conversation poems evolve a greater complexity from this pattern, in
ways that reveal Coleridge's poetry and philosophy growing (inextricably)
together. In these poems – as articulated in 'The Nightingale' – the affective power of the more-than-human world exists in mutually inductive relationship to the active, inward, correlative life of the human. Observing this
relationship in the making of his own poetry, a distinct idea of the will as a
'vis motrix, and the Mind a *directive* power' (*CM* IV, 450) assumes fundamental importance in Coleridge's work.[2] He conceives the will, that is, as
an enabling act or disposition that directs, shapes and orders – without controlling or determining – our relationship to the life both within and beyond
ourselves. The active, originating power of consciousness amplifies its own
passive, receptive power, and vice versa – anticipating and informing his
idea of the imagination as 'at once both active and passive' (*BL* I, 124). The
fascinated engagement with natural and imaginary forms so characteristic of
Coleridge's writing is, as he recognized, both active and passive in this way.
The willing exposure to living forms and energies beyond the control of the
calculating ego moves, transforms and grows the self, and in this sense the
natural world becomes a gnostic medium in Coleridge's poetry – that is, a
catalyst of our epistemic, empathetic and creative powers – and poetry itself
takes on an identical role and significance, analogous to that of the natural
world. Nature's 'lovely shapes and sounds intelligible' ('Frost at Midnight';
CPW I, i, 452–56, line 59), like 'the influxes / Of shapes and sounds and
shifting elements' in 'The Nightingale' (lines 27–28), have a corresponding
life in the operative 'shapes and sounds' of the poems themselves.

For all the 'self-watching' of his 'subtilizing mind' (*CPW* I, i, 454 n) and
the 'Strange Self-power in the Imagination' (*CN* III, 3547) to which he was

so sensitive, Coleridge's extraordinary capacity for observation characteristically focuses on the *other*, and his poetry both feeds and is fed by the intensity of his attention to natural forms and processes. The opening of 'Frost at Midnight' – 'The Frost performs its secret ministry, / Unhelped by any wind' (lines 1–2) – is at once awake to the silent action of the frost itself and embodies kindred qualities of attention in its language: 'performs' slows and lengthens 'frost', bridging its whispering sibilance with 'its secret ministry', while the lighter stresses in the metrical pattern in the second half of the line condense and intensify the connection between 'secret' and 'ministry'. Attention to habitat and attention to language amplify each other. In Coleridge, noticing is intimately connected with noting, as his incomparable notebooks everywhere testify: there we find him absorbed by nature for its own sake and interest, delighting in the givenness of the living world – often in self-forgetting wonder, and often roused into verbal and speculative energy by what he has seen or heard. Exploring a 'wild, *Pan* like' river on a boat in Malta in 1804, his field-notes record what looks like 'the green bulb or tumour of a rush / Yet why did I look again? – The understanding of the obscure feelings. It was a green frog sticking to the Stalk like an old Bigot at his prayers' (*CN* II, 2212). In November 1799, he observes a murmuration of starlings, moving 'in vast Flights, borne along like smoke, mist', 'still expanding, or contracting, thinning or condensing, now glimmering and shivering, now thickening, deepening, blackening!' (*CN* I, 1589). In such moments, Coleridge intuits 'the copresence of Feeling & Life, limitless by their very essence, with Form, by its very essence limited' (*CN* I, 1561) – a 'copresence' at the heart of his poetics, in which 'Form' bears a metonymic relationship to 'Feeling & Life'.

The participatory character of Coleridge's relationship to the living world is embodied in the *involving* character of his poetic language: it summons and seeks to implicate the attention *in* the sense of the poem, which accentuates the affective power of sound, breath – and hence the body – within its verbal texture. The conversation poems establish an analogy between the poem as a dynamic experiential form and the dynamic experience of topographical encounter. In 'The Nightingale', the birds

> answer and provoke each other's songs –
> With skirmish and capricious passagings,
> And murmurs musical and swift jug jug,
> And one low piping Sound more sweet than all.   (lines 58–61)

The poem has followed its own ethos of openness to the 'influxes / Of shapes and sounds', in finding this voice: the poem answers the provocation of the nightingales' song with its own, in language modulated in response to the nightingales' non-human pattern.

53

Examples like this illuminate Coleridge's contention that 'A Poet's *Heart* & *Intellect* should be *combined, intimately* combined & *unified,* with the great appearances in Nature – & not merely held in solution & loose mixture with them, in the shape of formal Similies [*sic*]' (*CL* II, 864). When the physical eye looks upon 'some chance thing' the way the 'inward eye' contemplates its own 'ideal shapings', then, he writes in 1821, 'Nature, like an individual spirit or fellow soul, seems to think and hold commune with us' (*SWF* II, 947). The poet transmutes what he has learned by meditating upon living forms into the living stem of the poem – the principle of its ordering. In this radical sense, *forming* and *wilding* fuse in the making of a poem – like the 'wild Ducks *shaping* their rapid flight in forms always regular', which Coleridge uses as an 'image of Verse' (*CL* II, 814). Again, the will comes into play in opening an enabling, receptive, seminative relation to unwilled forms and conditions of existence – linking human creativity to the vital powers of more-than-human nature – to produce an elective organicism.[3]

Coleridge recognized a related interfusion in himself and his writing as early as 1796: 'I feel strongly, and I think strongly; but I seldom feel without thinking, or think without feeling ... My philosophical opinions are blended with, or deduced from, my feelings: & this, I think, peculiarizes my style of Writing' (*CL* I, 279). In 'Frost at Midnight', the 'idling Spirit ... makes a toy of Thought' (lines 20, 23), and we see the interplay that Coleridge describes in the way thought and feeling proceed together in the motion of the poem: the 'sole unquiet thing' (line 16) is not so much the fluttering film on the fire-grate as the feeling mind manifest in the poem's voice, disturbed by the 'strange / And extreme silentness' (lines 9–10) in which – and from which – it grows. Colloquially, thinking and feeling are often treated as different in kind, or even opposites, but Coleridge assigns a germinal role to thought in the process of feeling: in 1802 he says that Bowles, his early favourite, 'has no native Passion, because he is not a Thinker' (*CL* II, 864), and on his voyage to Malta in 1804 he puts the sailors' inhumane treatment of a hawk down to 'non-feeling from non-thinking' (*CN* II, 2090). The implications are significant, not least in acknowledging that 'natural' feeling – including our spontaneous responsiveness to the natural world – is mediated by our culture, and our education in its broadest sense: our ideas, values, attitudes. In this, poetry has a potent role, for Coleridge:

> it is by a negation and voluntary Act of *no*-thinking that we think of earth, air, water &c as dead – It is necessary for our limited powers of Consciousness that we should be brought to this negative state, & that [it] should pass into Custom – but likewise necessary that at times we should awake & step forward – & this is effected by Poetry & Religion / –. The Extenders of Consciousness.   (*CN* III, 3632)

The educative role of poetry – here akin to 'Religion', in its effects – is nothing less than the *re-animation* of our reality: the dilation of our being, our consciousness and our apprehension of life. This is the animating aspiration that courses through Coleridge's poetry, poetics and metaphysics.

Coleridge conceives a special role for poetic form in the forming of attention, and the re-animating of reality. 'The reader should be carried forward', he writes of poetry, not by 'a restless desire to arrive at the final solution; but by the pleasureable activity of mind excited by the attractions of the journey itself … Precipitandus est *liber* spiritus ['The *free* spirit must be hurried onward'], says Petronius Arbiter most happily' (*BL* II, 14). Here he echoes his earlier note on poetry as the extender of consciousness: 'The truth is, we stop in the sense of Life just when we are not *forced* to go on' (*CN* III, 3632). The heightened attention that poetry summons in the dynamics of language serves precisely this quickening of the 'sense of Life': it invokes the 'initiative thought, the intellectual seed', the vitalizing, organizing condition of experience that 'must have its birth-place within, whatever excitement from without may be necessary for its germination' (*Friend* I, 513).

Coleridge's experimental techniques in the conversation poems are geared to this purpose. They combine precision in diction and poetic syntax – 'a reason assignable, not only for every word, but for the position of every word' (*BL* I, 9) – with the diffusion and plasticity of the 'conversational' style that, as I have described, teases its relationship to prose and the rhythms of energetic speech. The description of the nightingale, 'That crowds, and hurries, and precipitates / With fast thick warble his delicious notes' (lines 44–45), shows some of the valency of diction, sound-pattern, rhythm and lineation that Coleridge achieves: the vowel-wave across the first line (a-ow, a-u-ie, a-e-i-i-a-e), varying the momentum produced by those propulsive verbs, built up by the pause of each comma at -dz, -iez, then (at -ates) spilling over the run-on line to add its force to the lingering stress of 'fast thick warble', which – in the phoneme of its last syllable – slips into the second line's lush consummation. Coleridge aimed for an integrated fluency of thought and feeling in deliberate contrast to the '*conjunction disjunctive*' (*BL* I, 19) of the epigrammatic rhyming couplet, which he associated with Pope, Johnson and their imitators: Hazlitt recalls him saying that 'the ears of these couplet-writers might be charged with having short memories, that could not retain the harmony of whole passages'.[4] 'Frost at Midnight' draws instead on the 'divine Chit chat of Cowper' (*CL* I, 279) with which it is in dialogue, both technically and intertextually.[5] The interwoven integrity and concinnity of the poem become fundamental to its effect: in 1807 Coleridge removed the six lines with which 'Frost at Midnight' originally concluded 'because they destroy the rondo, and return upon itself of the Poem. Poems of this kind & length ought to be coiled with its tail round its head' (*CPW* I, i, 456 n). The poem should conduct, recirculate and diffuse its energies without dissipation.

For Coleridge, poetic form and effect are intimately connected to metre. The underlying pattern for the conversation poems may be that of blank verse, but Coleridge took the view that 'under that form there are 5 or 6 perfectly distinct metres' (*CL* III, 434). On the face of it, that complicates matters enormously – especially given that he thought in quantity or duration, as well as accent and syllable – but in Coleridge variation is intrinsic to metre. Indeed, the depth and breadth of poetic variety to which Coleridge is sensitive – and which he achieved – suggest 'forms of metre which we have not been familiarized to' (*Lects 1808–1819* I, 222): epi-metrical forms for which we still lack a truly adequate vocabulary in prosody. The grounds of this variety, however, lie in the principle that metre does not work in isolation from sound, sense, idea or feeling. If it is to operate effectively and meaningfully, 'to increase the vivacity and susceptibility both of the general feelings and of the attention' (*BL* II, 66), metre works in concert with the aural, emotional, figurative and verbal grammar of the poem: it is a 'yeast, worthless or disagreeable by itself, but giving vivacity and spirit to the liquor with which it is proportionally combined' (*BL* II, 67). The conversation poems use metre as a pattern with which to develop their own patterning – to move with the buoyancy of dance and, crucially, the fascination of a living form that leads the eye, ear and imagination. This is quintessential to the lyric quality of the poems – their 'orphic song', as Coleridge wrote of Wordsworth's own blank verse masterpiece: 'passionate thoughts, / To their own Music chaunted' ('To William Wordsworth': *CPW* I, ii, 815–19; lines 45–47). The ends of poetry are in its means. Coleridge's purpose, in bringing these technical and thematic concerns together, is to fuse spontaneity and concinnity – 'nature' and 'art' – at once educating the character of our spontaneous response to other living forms, cultivating our intelligence and stimulating the pre-conceptual sources of life in ourselves.

These aims, like the poems to which they correspond, have deeply political dimensions. In 'Fears in Solitude' (*CPW* I, i, 468–77) – first published together with 'France: An Ode' and 'Frost at Midnight' as a pamphlet in 1798 – 'A green and silent spot, amid the hills' (line 1) becomes the scene for a meditation on the evils of war, slavery and oppression, and a call for renewed compassion between human beings founded in a loving relation to our habitat: the land from which, Coleridge writes, he has 'drunk in all my intellectual life', whose 'Sweet influences trembled o'er his frame', and whose living diversity 'seems like society – / Conversing with the mind, and giving it / A livelier impulse and a dance of thought!' (lines 187, 21, 219–21). Coleridge blends his own story with his storying of landscape, in which care for other living forms, care for ourselves as human beings and care for language go together. The vivifying action of language, embodied in the fabric of the poems, becomes political in a fundamental sense, stimulating powers at the root of both a wiser, more empathetic sociality and a greater ecological sensitivity.

Another pattern – with its own unsettling energy – is also at work in the conversation poems, which gives their more widely recognized treatment of love, friendship and revitalized community a darker canvas and a keener edge. From their very origins, the ecstatic relation to the natural world at the nucleus of the poems is entangled with figures of alienation and existential differentiation at once alluring and hazardous, filled with the promise and risk of becoming: an exaltation coeval with transgression. This drama is central to 'The Eolian Harp' (*CPW* I, i, 231–35), which invests this simultaneity with an erotic charge: the instrument in the 'clasping casement', 'by the desultory breeze caressed' (lines 13–14), is an eroticized body, yielding 'long sequacious notes / Over delicious surges' (lines 18–19) in response to the touch of the breeze, which the poem identifies with the touch of a lover. Seduced by the 'soft floating witchery of sound' (line 20) released at that touch, the poem becomes the seductive music of its own event. The poem presents a double climax, the first of which is accentuated by the lines Coleridge added in 1817 (in the errata of *Sibylline Leaves*):

> O the one life within us and abroad,
> Which meets all motion and becomes its soul,
> A light in sound, a sound-like power in light,
> Rhythm in all thought, and joyance every where. (lines 26–29)

The second climax parallels the first, where 'wild and various' thoughts traverse and rouse the idling poet's mind as he basks on a hillside:

> And what if all of animated nature
> Be but organic harps diversely framed,
> That tremble into thought, as o'er them sweeps
> Plastic and vast, one intellectual breeze,
> At once the Soul of each, and God of All? (lines 44–48)

Through its extraordinarily condensed pattern of analogies, the poem renders its speaker at once harp and breeze, seducer and seduced, 'animated nature' and animating 'Soul' – his doubled exaltation cast as an 'unhallowed' (lines 51) transgression of the religious orthodoxy ventriloquized through his fiancée, Sara: his metaphysical excursus shamed, at the very moment of its realization, as 'shapings of the unregenerate mind' (line 55).

In this, 'The Eolian Harp' prefigures the story of the foundling in 'The Foster-Mother's Tale' (*CPW* I, i, 329–33), discovered under a tree as a baby 'wrapt in mosses', who 'never learnt a prayer nor told a bead; / But knew the names of birds, and mocked their notes, / And whistled, as he were a bird himself!' – whose affinity for the more-than-human world went hand in hand with 'unlawful thoughts', 'heretical' learning and spellbinding speech (lines 24, 30–32, 44, 55), and who, in the process of evolving what in practice constituted an alternative spirituality, became an object of superstitious fear, outcast from Christianity. Coleridge was acutely aware that his 'more different mind' made him 'still most a Stranger' in society, even (and perhaps especially) among his own family ('To the Rev. George Coleridge'; *CPW* I, i, 326–28, lines 16, 41) – for which he paid a lifelong price of internalized, neurotic guilt. The voice of 'Frost at Midnight' is that of an anomalous self – alone, the 'sole unquiet thing' in a world 'Inaudible as dreams', whose very wish for his child to know nature's 'lovely shapes and sounds intelligible', and the questionings they stir (lines 16, 13, 59), is founded in contrast to his own privation as a lonely schoolchild in the city. The poem combines fulfilment with denial, integration with alienation, in a state of uncertain promise suffused with the 'secret ministry' of the living world. It is well to remember that Coleridge also composed his lyric myths of transnatural mystery and daemonic becoming in 1797–98: 'The Rime of the Ancyent Marinere', 'Kubla Khan' and 'Christabel'.

While its more classically odic form makes it something of an anomaly in Harper's grouping of the conversation poems, 'Dejection: An Ode' (*CPW* I, ii, 695–702) nevertheless plays out many of the patterns established in the earlier poems, and takes them in new directions. It begins in stillness charged with a coming storm, from which it voices its drama of alienation and vicarious benediction. Its 'Æolian lute' recalls 'The Eolian Harp', but now with a 'dull sobbing draft, that moans and rakes' upon its strings as the storm rises, now with 'a scream / Of agony' as it blows (lines 6–7, 97–98): 'nature' itself reveals a different face. The poem converses not only with Coleridge's own poetry – including its original, private version ('A Letter to – '; *CPW* I, ii, 677–91) – but also that of Wordsworth, whose 'calmer habits and more steady voice' (*Prelude* (1805), vi, 323) were increasingly pointed for Coleridge, both personally and poetically, even to the point of '*radical* Difference' (*CL* II, 812). Despite voicing fears for his own 'shaping spirit of Imagination' (line 86), however, 'Dejection' is a compelling affirmation of its regenerative power. Even the poem's lament that 'I may not hope from outward forms to win / The passion and the life, whose fountains are within' (lines 45–46) is not as distant as it first appears from the earlier conversation poems, which, as I have shown, call upon and cultivate those inner fountains, to renew the human bond with 'outward forms': this is fundamental to the 'different lore' that they embody. Critics often also fasten upon Coleridge's turn to 'abstruse research to steal / From my own nature all the natural Man' (lines 89–90) as evidence that his poetic and psychological affinity to the natural world is now somehow dead – but this misses the structural role that the poem gives to its stormy weather. The sounds of the storm itself, Coleridge writes, 'Might now perhaps their wonted impulse give, / Might startle this dull pain, and make it move and live!' (lines 19–20) – and indeed the poet is released from 'viper thoughts', re-energized, and *recovers* his capacity for the joyful exhilaration of the final stanza, by turning to 'listen to the wind, / Which long has rav'd unnotic'd' (lines 94, 96–97). 'Dejection' embodies a willing convergence with autonomous natural forces beyond the self – an elective organicism – as figured in 'The Nightingale'.

Alongside its virtuosic poetic achievement, 'Dejection' also signals the more difficult personal circumstances in which Coleridge was now writing. Wordsworth's arrogation of the second, expanded edition of *Lyrical Ballads* in 1800 – rejecting 'Christabel', and moving the 'Ancient Mariner' to near the back of the first volume with a disparaging note (*LB*, 791) – had baffled and blighted Coleridge's confidence. He was in love with Sara Hutchinson, soon to be Wordsworth's sister-in-law, while remaining unhappily married – and he was now irrevocably addicted to opium. In time, the wound in his relationship with Wordsworth – and even his emotional, mental and physical suffering – would sharpen Coleridge's sense of himself and his work, but this was a long and painful process, which increasingly involved teasing out the critical implications of his earlier poetry, rather than composing more poems of the same kind.

Coleridge's subsequent arguments regarding poetic diction, for example, and his controversy with Wordsworth in this respect (*BL* II, 42–45, 81–84) drew on the dynamics of will – and its (self-)education – developed in the conversation poems. As Coleridge puts it, 'It is not every man that is likely to be improved by a country life' (*BL* II, 44): the relation between the human and the non-human world figured in Wordsworth's poetry, as in his own, involves a certain state of mind and feeling – an enabling disposition within ourselves – that it was (in part) the purpose of their poetry to stir and develop. True poetry, for Coleridge, speaks to the creative principle by which we become active, constitutive participants in the conception and ordering of ourselves and our habitat: 'That which we find in ourselves, is (gradu mutato) the substance and the life of *all* our knowledge' (*SM*, 78). Such poetry acts upon the same principle as the sensuous force of a natural form that stirs wonder and awe: 'blending with my Thought, / Yea, with my Life and Life's own secret Joy' ('Hymn before Sun-Rise, in the Vale of Chamouny'; *CPW* I, ii, 720). 'To William Wordsworth' describes how, on hearing his friend recite the *Prelude*, Coleridge felt 'The pulses of my Being beat anew': language speaks to 'vital Breathings secret as the soul / Of vernal growth' (lines 62, 9–10). Words are nothing less than 'LIVING POWERS' (*AR*, 10), and poetry might truly be 'A power like one of Nature's' (*Prelude* (1805), xii, 312).

'To William Wordsworth' deepens Coleridge's self-characterization as a thwarted, even somehow posthumous being, but again, this does not preclude poetic affirmation – and indeed, can become its condition: 'Hopes which in lamenting I renew'd' ('The Garden of Boccaccio'; *CPW* i, ii, 1093). In his later years, however, his poor health inevitably constrained the immersive, ecstatic relationship to the natural world that had made him a poet of 'Wood-walks wild' ('To William Wordsworth', line 71), 'open glade, dark glen, and secret dell' ('A Tombless Epitaph'; *CPW* i, ii, 865). From the 1810s, the man who 'Worships the spirit of unconscious life / In tree or wild-flower' ('The Picture, or The Lover's Resolution'; *CPW* i, ii, 712–13) is usually in his study, or garden – even if Coleridge could still describe himself as 'a *Terrae Filius*', a child of the earth.⁶ In his later philosophy Coleridge was careful 'to admit the divine influence as not to exclude the agency of nature, and on the other hand so to appropriate an agency in nature as not to convert it into self-sufficeingness [*sic*] and divinity' (*OM*, 360), but it is misleading to infer in this a fundamental breach with his earlier writings on the natural world. Deeply engaged with the German *Pantheismusstreit* – particularly its fear that identifying God with nature ('pantheism') collapses all life into automatism – Coleridge strove to affirm the reality of creative and moral agency: an endeavour to which the elective organicism that grew from his poetry was vital. Poetry remained, for Coleridge, 'the highest effort of the mind' (*TT* i, 562).

The 'different lore' that Coleridge developed in the conversation poems embodied a new ecology – still radical today – in which the renewal of language and a renewed relation to the living world are inextricably entwined. In the action of the poem, communion with our more-than-human habitat is combined and reconciled with human self-cultivation. A fresh sensitivity to the life beyond ourselves – with which our own life is fundamentally involved – presents an alternative to a world in which (as Wordsworth wrote), 'Getting and spending, we lay waste our powers'.⁷ In this, the poems assume an initiatory character, as animating, quickening acts of poetic fascination analogous to the preverbal stimulus of non-human life. The participatory fabric of poetic invocation is essential to Coleridge's psychotropic purpose. This is not a complacent, self-indulgent pastoral but an exhilarating, unsettling poetry, charged with the secret life of its own formative drama: mysteries woken in 'greenery' (*CPW* i, i, 513).

Notes

1 George Maclean Harper, 'Coleridge's Conversation Poems' (1928), in *English Romantic Poets: Modern Essays in Criticism*, ed. M. H. Abrams, 2nd edn. (Oxford University Press, 1975), 188–201.
2 'Vis motrix': 'a force that moves, arouses, affects or influences'.
3 Gregory Leadbetter, *Coleridge and the Daemonic Imagination* (Houndmills: Palgrave Macmillan, 2011), 47 *et passim*.
4 *S. T. Coleridge: Interviews and Recollections*, ed. Seamus Perry (Basingstoke: Palgrave, 2000), 66.
5 In an oblique tribute to his exemplar, Coleridge incorporates the image of the fluttering 'stranger' on the fire-grate, and its associated superstition, from Cowper's then widely known poem *The Task*, IV, 286–95. *The Poems of William Cowper*, eds. John D. Baird and Charles Ryskamp, vol. II (Oxford: Clarendon Press, 1995), 194.
6 James Gillman, *The Life of Samuel Taylor Coleridge* (London, 1838), 12.
7 'The world is too much with us': *Wordsworth's Poetry and Prose*, ed. Nicholas Halmi (New York: W. W. Norton, 2014), 403.

5

JOANNA E. TAYLOR

Coleridge's Ecopoetics

> We all look up to the blue Sky for comfort, but nothing appears
> there – nothing comforts nothing answers us – & so we die.
> (*CN* III, 4294)

As the starting point for a Coleridgean ecopoetics, this translation from Jean
Paul in Coleridge's notebook (dating somewhere between 1814 and 1818) is
not comforting. Henry Crabb Robinson's assessment that Coleridge's readings of the German Romantic were little more than 'an illustration of his
absurd accumulation of images' is indicative of contemporary assessments
that criticized the poet for increasingly irrelevant abstractions and a growing distance between philosophy and reality.[1] In fact, this translation gets to
the very heart of the doubt central to Coleridge's ecopoetics: what if there
really was no connection, no communication, between human and non-
human beings? Exploring this question requires a view of Coleridge's career
that shifts away from the one more usually found in Romantic ecocriticism.
This tradition has tended to focus on the poems that were the results of
Coleridge's close collaboration with William Wordsworth, and to identify
the 'Dejection' ode as the moment when Coleridge articulates the collapse
of his ecopoetics – just as his creative relationship with Wordsworth was
also breaking down. Yet, if we read the 'Dejection' ode as a catalyst for a
Coleridgean ecopoetics that the poet was to spend the rest of his career –
some thirty-two years – developing, we find an under-explored avenue in
Coleridge's thinking. In this approach, we might situate Coleridge's dejection not as a failure in a dominant Wordsworthian ecology, but as the starting point for an alternative model of Romantic ecopoetics.

As early as 1803, Coleridge was describing '*a World*' as 'an harmonious
System where an infinity of Kinds subsist each in a multitude of individuals apportionate to its kind in conformity to Laws existing in the divine
Nature – & therefore in the Nature of Things' (*CN* I, 1619). It was twenty
to four in the morning, after a sweat-soaked night of bad dreams induced
by opium withdrawal, and Coleridge had identified a central tenet of what
would grow into the science of ecology: the recognition of 'Nature' – human
and non-human – as an infinite series of connections between individual

examples of all types of matter. This thought marked one of the 'logical development[s]' from Coleridge's 'early views on the integrity and inter-relatedness of the natural world' that James C. McKusick thinks inspired Coleridge's mature views on 'aesthetic organicism'.[2] Rather than seeing all life as 'one', as he had in 1795–96 (*CPW* I, ii, 233, line 26), now Coleridge was beginning to consider a question that would come to underpin his eco-poetics and eco-philosophies for the rest of his career: how can a world made up of disconnected 'Things' also function as an integrated whole?

This recalibration of Coleridge's ecological thought coincides with another significant moment in Coleridge's poetic life: his recognition that there was 'somewhere or other, a *radical* Difference' (*CL* II, 444) between his thoughts on poetry and Wordsworth's. One such 'Difference' was the increasingly clear disjunction between the two poets' understandings of nature. At the same time as Coleridge was developing his nascent under-standing of the world as a system of intra-material relations, Wordsworth – so it seemed to Coleridge – was elevating nature itself into a deity. In Octo-ber 1803, after a difficult afternoon of confrontations between William Hazlitt and Wordsworth, Coleridge addressed Wordsworth in his notebook: 'Would Ray, or Durham, have spoken of God as you spoke of Nature?' (*CN* I, 1616). Wordsworth's apparent deification of an abstraction worried Coleridge, but in Wordsworth's view Nature was godly: it was the 'spirit' that 'rolls through all things' (*LB*, 119, lines 101–3). In Wordsworth's per-sonal histories 'the beauteous forms / Of Nature were collaterally attach'd' (*Prelude* (1805), ii, 51–52) to his memories; 'Nature' was his most impor-tant collaborator, and no solitary in Wordsworth's corpus need be lonely if he or she was in tune with the non-human world.

Coleridge's poetic records of witnessing 'one life within us and abroad' (*CPW* I, ii, 233, line 26) expressed a similar sense of cohesion, and his early ecopoetics share with Wordsworth's what McKusick calls a 'holistic concept of the Earth as a household, a dwelling-place' that 'clearly foreshadows the modern science of ecology'.[3] But there was a consistent difference between the two poets' ecologies. As Edward Kessler recognized, even in Coleridge's youthful 'conversation' poems 'the delights of nature conceal a vacancy',[4] a perpetual sense of disconnection between himself and the world. Coleridge thought the reasons for this difference could be located in the poets' biogra-phies: whilst Wordsworth grew up among his native Lakeland mountains, Coleridge had been sent – 'transplanted', as he put it in a poem addressed to his brother, George (*CPW* I, i, 327, line 18) – to school in London at nine years old. He was, he explained to George, sent away 'ere [his] soul had fixed / Its first domestic loves' (*CPW* I, i, 327, lines 8–19), including to the non-human features of the local landscape. From that point, finding himself 'in the great city, pent' (*CPW* I, i, 455, line 52), Coleridge felt isolated from 'lovely' nature, except for the skies and stars that enveloped the school's cloisters (*CPW* I, i, 455, line 53). In 'Frost at Midnight' this confinement leads to a burst of creative energy that is embedded in visions of the natural world: from being himself 'pent' up, he releases a vivid imagining of his son Hartley's future 'wander[ing] like a breeze' by the lakes and beneath the mountains of the rural north of England (*CPW* I, i, 455, lines 54–64). He foresaw for Hartley the kind of Wordsworthian identification with nature that he was unable to find for himself.

For Tom Mole, the difference between the poets amounts to a distinction between 'a Wordsworthian desire to "share the fruitful stir / Down in our mother earth's miraculous womb"' and 'a Coleridgean dejection that "I alone / Am dead to life and joy, therefore I read / In all things my own"'.⁵ While Wordsworth describes a communion between human and non-human beings that is almost a biological imperative stemming from a shared beginning in 'our mother earth', Coleridge emphasizes a lifeless loneliness. Coleridge began exploring an ecopoetics based on a sense of severance from other life forms after 1797. An anxiety about the effects of sealing oneself off from the non-human world is at the heart of Coleridge's 'vision in a dream', 'Kubla Khan', in which Kubla encloses 'twice five miles of fertile ground / With walls and towers' (*CPW* I, i, 513, lines 6–7). For a time, the gardens overflow with life: 'sinuous rills' both make natural music and water the 'incense-bearing tree[s]' and the ancient forests (*CPW* I, i, 513, lines 8–11). But earth fights back against this unnatural containment: from a 'deep romantic chasm' bursts a 'mighty fountain' that destroys Kubla Khan's 'pleasure-dome', which becomes no more than a 'shadow' floating away on the waves (*CPW* I, i, 513, lines 12–32). The poem unwittingly documents more than an imagined catastrophe; recent investigations in the region controlled by the historic Kubla Khan have revealed that this empire was a serious early polluter through its intensive mining activities.⁶ In Coleridge's ecopoetics, though, the concern is more imaginative: what might happen, the poem worries, if we act as though we are isolated, and build over natural forces in ways that disregard the agency and power of non-human things?

A more quotidian instance of disconnection's consequences occurs in 'The Rime of the Ancyent Marinere', where the eponymous Mariner shoots a non-human bystander, an albatross, in an 'inhospitabl[e]' act of environmental violence; as Jonathan Bate explains, it 'breaks the contract of mutual dependency which binds species in a network of reciprocal relations'.⁷ Afterwards, the Mariner's disconnection from that network seems complete:

> Alone, alone, all all alone
> Alone on the wide wide Sea;
> And Christ would take no pity on
> My soul in agony.   (*CPW* I, i, 390, lines 232–35)

The stupefying stasis – both the ship's being becalmed, and the Mariner's isolation – is enacted through the repetition of that one syllable, 'all', that both gestures to ecological unity and emphasizes the Mariner's utter disconnection from it. Even Christian certainties (Christ in 1797, and 'never a saint' in revised versions after 1817) have deserted the Mariner, leaving him – it seems – utterly dissevered from living (or even metaphysical) connections. In the 1834 version, following decades of revisions to the poem, the Mariner is alone 'on a wide wide sea' (*CPW* II, i, 519). The change from the definite to indefinite article is significant: the indefinite 'a' further emphasizes the Mariner's disconnection from non-human things by extending that isolation to a geographical uncertainty, too. Yet, as Seamus Perry astutely observes, 'through what looks like a weakness, a being astray, a wandering, Coleridge arrives at something that a greater sense of purpose or intent would not have pulled off'.[8] It is in this state of complete disconnection from other life that the Mariner notices that 'a million million slimy things / Liv'd on – and so did I' (*CPW* I, i, 390, lines 238–39). At this stage, all the Mariner shares with creatures that he can only see as 'things' is life itself. Yet, this recognition of a shared life force holds open the possibility for redemption, because it acknowledges – even at a basic level – a shared experience. He is saved, and reinstated into the global ecosystem, when he names these 'things' as 'water-snakes', thereby acknowledging their status as living beings. This act of naming, and his 'bless[ing]' of them, demonstrates a new awareness that all life forms, great and small, are crucial to healthy ecological functions. The Mariner's inexorable task becomes to tell his tale, repeating his trauma with the aim of leading other human beings disconnected from the non-human world towards (re-)integration with the global ecosystem.

Like the Ancient Mariner, Coleridge was to find that he had to reach utter aloneness – and do so repeatedly – before he could recover a sense of connection with other living beings. By 1802, his inability to find oneness with the natural world seemed to encapsulate what Coleridge saw as his failure in what had been his and Wordsworth's joint poetic project: what A. S. Byatt summarizes as a performance of 'unification' between 'thought and feeling and the sense of life in the world beyond the self'.[9] In this year, his mind became even more than usually abstracting: he looked at mountains and saw only 'Curves', and stars were reduced to 'Triangles' (*CL* II, 714).

In the terms Coleridge would use in the 'Dejection' ode, he could 'see' these elements of the non-human world but not 'feel' them. Josie Dixon identifies experiences like this as a result of 'imbalance[s]' between 'the eye and the mind', a characteristic feature of the debilitating episodes of 'dejection' Coleridge experienced in the early 1800s.[10] Coleridge's daughter, Sara, explained that this tendency towards extreme abstraction – or what she thought of as everything becoming 'too real' – was a result of being 'too alive to outward impressions, & too full of speculations suspecting them'.[11] For Coleridge himself, this profound awareness of a disjuncture between eye and mind, and mind and Things, fuelled his belief that he was, now, 'no Poet' in the face of Wordsworth's 'true Poetry' (*CL* II, 714).

A version of this myth has continued to find traction in Romantic ecocriticism: Jonathan Bate's path-breaking studies *Romantic Ecology: Wordsworth and the Environmental Tradition* (1991) and *The Song of the Earth* (2000) established Wordsworthian ecopoetics as the baseline for the period's responses to the non-human world. Although Coleridge featured prominently in an early study of the Romantic environment – Arden Reed's *Romantic Weather: The Climates of Coleridge and Baudelaire* (1983), perhaps one of the last books that could claim that writing about the weather 'may seem like a rather strange undertaking'[12] – in the intervening decades the most influential Romantic ecocriticism has positioned Wordsworth at its centre: Mary Jacobus, Karl Kroeber and Onno Oerlemans each foregrounded Wordsworth in their various approaches to Romantic ecocriticism.[13] So pronounced is Wordsworth's hold on this field that J. Andrew Hubbell notices that 'Wordsworth's nature has […] been used as a synecdoche for Romantic nature.'[14] Wordsworth's centrality has been taken by Jeremy Davies as evidence of a desire to 'read Romanticism with rather than against the grain', and as a successful strategy in putting Romantic-era Britain 'at the heart of ecocritical concerns'.[15]

Wordsworth's centrality to the field is not without merit: 'it is true that Wordsworth's ecopoetics have had a more evident impact on environmentalisms than any of his contemporaries'. No other Romantic poet can be said to have inspired the same tradition of environmental concern as did Wordsworth, whose work was reinterpreted through campaigners including John Ruskin, William Morris, Hardwicke Rawnsley and Edward Thomas, and continues to be invoked as a forerunner to modern environmental activism.[16] Scott Hess has shown, though, that there has been a tendency to assume that Wordsworth's social position, and the 'ecological consciousness' it develops, can be 'taken as universal in ways that other subjectivities – women or laboring class perspectives, for instance – cannot'.[17] One result has been a serious narrowing of our understandings about the 'spectrum' of Romantic environmental thought that risks disenfranchising anyone who is not, like Wordsworth, white, male and imbricated into their local, native place.[18] Another has been a conflation of 'nature' with 'ecology', a compression that persistently locates humanity as a witness to, rather than a part of, the interactions that make up the planet. Oerlemans, for instance, found that Romantic lyrics recorded a disjuncture between mind and world. Bate's evidence was even broader: in *The Song of the Earth*, he contended that language – and, thus, literature – are in themselves symbolic of an ontological distance between the human and non-human. This distance is at the heart of an old ecocritical problem: as Vince Carducci summarizes, it evinces the tendency to put 'nature on a pedestal, casting it as the pristine other of modern civilization and of the autonomous individual self'.[19]

Elsewhere, ecocriticism has persistently demonstrated that, in Cheryl Glotfelty's words, 'literature does not float above the material world in some aesthetic ether, but, rather, plays a part in an immensely complex global system in which energy, matter, *and ideas* interact.'[20] Whilst there can be a tendency to overstate literature's importance in addressing ecological catastrophes – what Timothy Clark views as a misplaced 'faith that environmental destruction can be remedied by cultural means'[21] – ecocriticism has found in Romantic-era writings evidence of alternative modes of being that emphasize living with the world, not merely on it. Timothy Morton's work on ecomimesis, which reads into Romantic poetry attempts to mimic environmental phenomena, takes an important step towards bridging the gap that Bate identified: in Morton's readings, language offers a way of translating non-human phenomena into human-legible forms.[22] Alan Bewell, meanwhile, showed in *Natures in Translation* (2017) that understanding 'nature' as a being active, mobile and plural – rather than a static and homogenous backdrop for humanity – reveals Romantic writing about nature to contain 'complex materialities deeply linked to language'.[23]

Material ecocriticism adds to these perspectives a recognition that textual criticism is not only a literary endeavour. Material ecocriticism engages – belatedly, in Davies's view – with concerns raised by Raymond Williams and John Barrell's pioneering research in the 1970s and 1980s.[24] It examines the ways that physical space and place affect and are affected by social, cultural and material conditions. Anne-Lise François has been instrumental in effecting the materialization of twenty-first-century Romantic ecocriticism; as Anahid Nersessian finds, François's book *Open Secrets: The Literature of Uncounted Experience* 'turn[ed] Romantic ecocriticism decisively away from its earlier mimetic mode'.[25] François, like other new materialists, understands all matter as being inherently textual; in Marjorie Levinson's evocative terms, criticism in this vein aims 'to awaken the frozen forms' of our world (past and present).²⁶ Serenella Iovino and Serpil Opperman explain that material ecocriticism 'examines matter both *in* texts and *as* a text' and, moreover, recognizes an 'agentic dimension' to all things. In this understanding, there is no dichotomy between humanity and nature; rather, 'human agency meets the narrative agency of matter halfway.'²⁷ Recognizing the agential capacities of other forms of matter might have significant consequences for human responses to climate crisis; as Jane Bennett argues, viewing all matter as agential may 'catalyze a sensibility that finds a world filled not with ontologically distinct categories of beings (subjects and objects) but with variously composed materiality that form confederations'.²⁸

Coleridge's writing, in its various forms, records a lifelong fascination with what happens – or what might fail to happen – in that interstitial space between human and non-human beings, but rarely in his works are the meeting places between human and non-human agencies either so neat or so peaceful as 'halfway' and 'confederations' imply. In Coleridge's understanding, human and non-human agencies were more like a spectrum than an opposition; he came to believe that 'think[ing] of ourselves as separated beings, and plac[ing] nature in antithesis to the mind, as object to subject, thing to thought, life to death', resulted in 'mere understanding' that was disconnected from the lived experience of being in the world (*Friend* I, 520–21). Instead, Coleridge surmised that 'the organic and inorganic are necessary *relative* distinctions' (*CN* III, 4319, original emphasis), and that the places where they came together – the moments at which *relations* can be determined – were more the point than artificial assessments of what kinds of life mattered. On 13 November 1809, he explained his evolving understanding of the relationship between human perception and non-human entities:

> [I]t is by a negation and voluntary Act of *no*-thinking that we think of earth, air, water, &c. as dead – It is necessary for our limited powers of Consciousness, that we should be brought to this negative state, & that should pass into Custom – but likewise necessary that at times we should awake & step forward – & this is effected by Poetry & Religion/– The Extenders of Consciousness – Sorrow, Sickness, Poetry, Religion –. –<The truth is, we stop in the sense of Life just when we are *forced* not to go on – and then adopt a permission of our feelings for a precept of our Reason.   (*CN* III, 3632)

In material ecocritical terms, the non-human elements Coleridge lists ('earth, air, water, &c.') are part of a community engaging in what Iovino and Opperman see as conversations between human and non-human beings. Coleridge's innovation here is to recognize that a human inability to partake in that conversation has transformed from a natural into a cultural phenomenon – and, more than this, that the cure might be to register *disconnection* as a means of reintegrating into those ecosystemic communications. Yet, he goes further: what Iovino and Opperman fail to register, and what is central for understanding Coleridge's ecopoetics, is what happens when that conversation becomes a screaming match across unshared languages. Coleridge's understanding is that it takes states ('Sorrow' or 'Sickness') or interlocutors ('Poetry, Religion') of disconnection to extend the human consciousness out towards the intra-actions that make up the planet's eco-systems. As he also knew, though, this strategy was not without danger. Cautions repeat across Coleridge's verse about what might happen if the self becomes too intertwined with another being; the Mariner's experience of being very nearly overwhelmed by the intra-actions of human and non-human agencies is only the most explicit warning of what might happen to one being in a world governed by unpredictable matter. In the Mariner's case, what is most frightening – and what continued to haunt Coleridge – is the fact that he cannot converse with the non-human world, but it can respond to him; when he blesses the water snakes 'unaware', he is not speaking their language – but they are clearly comprehending his.

Coleridge's approach is distinctive in in a tradition where a 'conspicuous aspect' has been what Hubert Zapf recognizes as a tendency to emphasize 'relationality and interconnectedness on all levels'.[29] Yet these qualities do not reflect quotidian experiences of being in the world – either now or in the Romantic era. Disconnection from the non-human world was as much a characteristic of the Romantic period as connection with it: in a period of mass enclosures – that, as John Clare records, drove people off their land and away from an intra-active relationship with nature – and widespread urbanization, we might just as easily see the Romantic period as the start-ing point for the widespread apathy towards the non-human world that defined quotidian responses to it in the twentieth and twenty-first centu-ries.[30] Alongside Coleridge's Mariner, Keats's (another poet from the 'great city') Belle Dame Sans Merci might be the era's archetype for that new dis-connection: when the knight kisses her 'wild wild eyes' shut, and he lands in her 'thrall', plants wither and birds fall silent.[31] Both poems hypothesize about when a union between human and non-human turns nightmarish, and act as warnings for connecting too much with natural things. A chal-lenge for modern ecology is to work out how to connect people who are culturally severed from nature with the non-human world; in Coleridge's proto-Heideggerian terms, it is a question of what tools to use to 'extend' human consciousnesses towards conversation with non-human things. If we see Coleridge's disconnection from the non-human world as an early, indi-vidual symptom of a modern, social problem, then we can also find in his writing guidance for how to utilize – if not overcome – it. Coleridge's most important interventions in Romantic ecopoetics ask one simple, devastating question: what happens to the person (or thing) that is shut out – ontologically or semantically – from that communication chain?

Coleridge's Ecopoetical Meshes

In Coleridge's experience, the interconnectedness of all things was never clearer than at the exact moments when he felt most isolated. December 1804 was a case in point: in the middle of his self-imposed exile to Malta, Coleridge was cogently summarizing his understanding of ecosystems as being representative of 'the great game-laws of Nature', a careful balance between natural phenomena and human management: '[F]ish with nets of such meshes, as permit many to escape, & preclude the taking of many' seemed to him to encapsulate the principles of habitat sustainability: 'two races are saved', he explained, 'the one by taking part, and the other by part not being taken' (*CN* II, 2329). Central to this example are the 'meshes' that facilitate and control interactions and connections between individuals or, even, species. Like what Morton describes of Charles Darwin's 'entangled bank', Coleridge's example asks us to 'visualize interconnected life-forms as a whole', an 'entangled mess of ambiguous entities' that decentralizes any one life's importance. The 'mesh' Coleridge describes anticipates the ecocritical 'mesh' that, Morton explains, 'does away with boundaries between living and non-living forms', indicating instead 'both the holes in a network and the threading between them'.[32] In ecocritical terms, a mesh supports meeting points between 'Things'.

While it is true that Coleridge continued throughout his career to describe a 'rival conflict' between the human mind and external nature, nevertheless his ecological thinking became a prime example of the group of philosophies under the heading 'extremes meet', an axiom that Coleridge thought defined his work (*CN* I, 1725). The point, for him, was not in the extremes themselves but in their meeting points. The relationship between the self and the non-human world was Coleridge's most persistent example. Like Morton, Coleridge found that 'Nature' conceptually dies in the moment when we view the planet as an ecological mesh, because focusing in on individual elements – such as the fish in Coleridge's example – abstracts them. This shift worried Coleridge, as it would concern later poets: Tennyson, for instance, finds in Nature benevolence at the level of the species, but cruelty towards the abstracted individual: 'So careful of the type she seems, / So careless of the single life.'[33] Like Coleridge, Tennyson finds no comfort in abstraction, either ecologically or personally. Both poets worry about the risk that everything might slip through the holes in that mesh: what is to stop the self from also being abstracted, one more individual entity in a disconnected universe?

While Julie Ellison is right to say that abstraction had 'almost exclusively negative associations' for Coleridge[34] – and certainly did him no favours with the reading public, who, in his later years, 'often regarded [him] as a burnt-out case wandering in a wilderness of abstraction'[35] – the process of abstracting was nevertheless central to his experiences. His repeated explanation of his perceptions, starting with a notebook entry from October 1803, makes clear how enmeshment underpinned Coleridge's thinking:

> Nothing affects me much at the moment it happens – it either stupefies me, and I perhaps look at a merry-make & dance the hay of Flies, or listen entirely to the loud Click of the great Clock/or I am simply indifferent, not without some sense of philosophic Self-complacency. – For a Thing at the moment is but a Thing of the moment/it must be taken up in the mind, diffuse itself thro' the whole multitude of Shapes & Thoughts, not one of which it leaves untinged – between ~~each~~ w^ch & it some new Thought is not engendered/this is a work of Time/but the Body feels it quicken with me –   (CN I, 1597)

The problem for Coleridge was not simply abstraction, but rather the disorientating experience of being caught between 'Things' and 'Thoughts'. This process is not the same as Wordsworth's ability to coalesce humans with nature; rather, the enmeshment Coleridge describes creates a third space that sits between thought and thing, and combines elements of both. In the *Biographia Literaria*, this meeting point (filtered through Coleridge's reading of Schelling) becomes the esemplasticity that Coleridge sees as being a defining trait of the imagination (*BL* II, 254–55). By 1818, he could explain this process in more detail via a marginal gloss to *The Friend* (repeated in a letter from November 1819): 'from my very childhood I have been accustomed to *abstract* and as it were unrealize whatever of more than common interest my eyes dwelt on; and then by a sort of transfusion and transmission of my consciousness to identify myself with the Object' (*Friend* I, 520–21n; *CL* IV, 974–75). In the November 1819 letter, this explanation acts as a gloss to the poem 'Hymn before Sunrise in the Vale of Chamouni', which Coleridge had adapted from a German original by Friederike Brun. Coleridge recalls Wordsworth's condemnation of the poem on the grounds that it was a specimen of 'a sort of dreaminess which would not let [Coleridge] see things as they were'. Instead, Wordsworth thought, Coleridge used his 'extraordinary powers [to summon] up an image or series of images in his own mind'.[36] Wordsworth was not wrong – but nor was he entirely right. What Coleridge actually did was more interesting: he 'unrealize[d]' objects, and dehumanized himself, so that human and non-human perspectives intertwined somewhere in the middle. What Coleridge described is what Karen Barad has called 'meeting the universe halfway', in a space where matter and meaning become 'inextricably fused together' so that '[m]attering is simultaneously a matter of substance and significance'.[37] To put it another way, when extremes meet in Coleridge's intellectual habitat, they find a space for the human and non-human to hybridize. This was not a benign process, in Coleridge's view. The principal risks were twofold: that this hybridization might be fragile or, what was perhaps worse, that it might be so robust that it destroyed individual identity.

In Coleridge's thinking, this hybridization was particularly important when dealing with non-human lives; as he explained in *The Friend*, abstractions are unhelpful if they mean that 'we think of ourselves as separated beings, and place nature in antithesis to the mind, as object to subject, thing to thought, death to life'. Positioning the human in antithesis to the natural was, he thought, to explore no more than 'the science of the mere understanding' (*Friend* I, 521). A poem or a notebook entry recorded an enmeshment that went beyond that limited 'science' to document the by-product of encounters between thoughts and things. In fact, writing it down might be the most secure part of those fragile meshes. In Coleridge's works, these meeting points are felt and acknowledged most explicitly when the extremes are at their most distant, and the meetings most delicate: that is, when Coleridge felt himself to be the most disconnected from other living things – human and non-human – were also the moments at which those meetings became most perilous, and most urgent. They could be dangerous because the poet was at his most vulnerable, and in these times of dejection and disconnection Coleridge worried that the abstracting process might both be a defence against merging with other living things (a merger which, in Coleridge's fraternal and romantic experiences, inevitably bought pain), and the means by which his very identity was displaced. In November 1799, during his walking tour of the Lake District with Wordsworth, Coleridge had imagined being possessed by the 'Ghost of a mountain/the forms seizing my body as I passed & became realities – I, a Ghost, till I had reconquered my Substance' (*CN* I, 523). In early 1804, he was still wondering about 'work[ing] up' something on the 'wanderings of this Ghost thro' the world' (*CN* II, 1913). This fear, of being so profoundly enmeshed with an antagonistic ecosystem that his sense of self could be ejected from his body by a non-human life-force, was preoccupying Coleridge in the weeks leading up to the first publication of the poem which, more than any other, explored what might happen when the poet felt himself as a 'separated being': the 'Dejection' ode.

'I see, not feel': Dejection in Coleridge's Ecopoetics

In Barad's vision of an enmeshed universe constructed around the meeting points between living things, human beings are neither observers of the world nor located precisely within it; instead, she sees each individual as part of the world's intra-activity. That does not feel like the case, though, for someone experiencing profound dejection, as Coleridge was in 1802. At this moment – feeling alone in his failing marriage and increasingly isolated from his friends, as his opium addiction became painfully clear – Coleridge felt himself to be outside the rest of the world's intra-activity. It was in this state that he drafted perhaps his most profound, and certainly most moving, exploration of an ecopoetics founded not, like Wordsworth's, on interconnection with the world but on disconnection from it. The morning after hearing Wordsworth recite his draft of the 'Immortality' ode, where Wordsworth asks 'Whither is fled the visionary gleam / Where is it gone the glory and the dream?', Coleridge had started to provide an explanation for this loss in himself.[38] Ernest de Sélincourt thought that the 'root idea' of 'A Letter to — ' and the great poem that emerged from it, 'Dejection: An Ode', was Coleridge's developing realization of a 'contrast' between himself and Wordsworth as lovers and writers – but we can, I think, add to that as ecologists, too.[39] Coleridge wrote the Ode by combining separate fragments and drafts into one poem, making the poem itself a product of enmeshment: a meeting point for Coleridge's ongoing reflections on how his dejection and sense of disconnection affected his ecopoetics.

Started from his Keswick study as a storm blew across the mountains, the ode registered a profound mental anguish arising from Coleridge's feeling of total estrangement from both social and natural ecosystems. In *Sibylline Leaves*, the poem reads:

> All this long eve, so balmy and serene,
> Have I been gazing on the western sky,
> And its peculiar tint of yellow green:
> And still I gaze – and with how blank an eye!
> And those thin clouds above, in flakes and bars,
> That give away their motion to the stars;
> Those stars, that glide behind them or between,
> Now sparkling, now bedimm'd, but always seen;
> Yon crescent moon, as fixed as if it grew,
> In its own cloudless, starless lake of blue,
> I see them all so excellently fair,
> I see, not feel how beautiful they are.
>
> (Parrish, 51–53, lines 27–38)

Here, Coleridge is mourning not only the loss of his own hopes for happiness, or just his sense of not being able to reach, with Wordsworth, into the 'life of things', but a dissevering from his contemporaries' intellectual and aesthetic communities. His isolation is self-imposed, protecting him from the disorientating, sometimes even traumatizing, experiences that being close to an unfulfilled (or unrequited) connection can bring – but it is no less painful for that. The inventory of the night sky's contents, structured by the repetition of the distancing 'those', reveals the poet's disconnectedness from the 'one life' he can now *only* perceive abroad; he cannot position himself as part of the living things he lists. The half-rhyme in the final, jarring couplet emphasizes this distinction; it seems that, in the process of describing his own relationship to the nocturnal ecosystem, Coleridge cannot maintain the couplets that bind together his descriptions of the night sky.

This apparent dissonance between thought and things is even more pronounced in the earlier version of the poem. 'A Letter to — ' was explicitly addressed first to Sara Hutchinson, then to Wordsworth; the later version was redacted to protect the families' privacy, but the change also reduces the sense that part of Coleridge's sense of disconnection was specifically associated with his close friend and the woman he had already spent three years obsessing over. Naming them offers the speaker specific contrasts with his own isolated state. The earlier version reads:

> All this long Eve so balmy & serene
> Have I been gazing on the Western Sky
> And its peculiar Tint of yellow Green:
> And still I gaze – & with how blank an eye!
> And those thin Clouds above, in flakes & bars,
> That give away their motion to the Stars;
> Those stars, that glide behind them and between,
> Now sparkling, now bedimm'd, but always seen;
> Yon crescent Moon, as fix'd as if it grew
> In it's own cloudless, starless Lake of Blue,
> A boat becalm'd! Dear William's Sky Canoe!
> I see them all, so excellently fair,
> I *see*, not *feel*, how beautiful they are! (Parrish 24, lines 31–43)

The verse is a self-conscious contrast with the fast-moving 'sky canoe' from the 1798 prologue to Wordsworth's 'Peter Bell'. There, the 'living boat' gives the poet access to terrestrial and extraterrestrial communities (even if it does scold him for wanting it to make it no better than 'A Boat twin-sister of the crescent-moon!').[40] The canoe in Coleridge's hands, though, is a symbol of disconnection; unable to intra-act with the 'starless Lake of Blue', it can only hang isolated from the other elements of the night sky in a Mariner-like 'becalm'd' state. Like the Mariner, too, Coleridge is 'alone, alone, all all alone', cut out from what he perceives as an otherwise universal mesh. In the Mariner's case, that exclusion is the result of an unwitting misjudgement about the agentic powers of non-human lives; in Coleridge's, it is a knowing acknowledgment of the same agencies. Yet Coleridge does imply a glimmer of hope in his observations on the stars. At first glance, Coleridge imparts his own sense of isolation onto them: they 'glide behind' the clouds, giving nothing in return for the 'Motion' given to them. But another possibility occurs here: perhaps they don't remain 'behind', but come 'between'. In 'Peter Bell', Wordsworth goes with his boat 'between the stars' to 'pry' among the constellations, and Coleridge holds open the chance that the stars might still be meeting points for the poet who can feel them.

The tension between seeing and feeling in that final couplet is a keystone example of the chiasma which Hubbell thinks defines Romantic 'Nature' poems from 'Tintern Abbey' to Keats's odes: moments where the self confronts its opposite, Nature.[41] In the 'Dejection' ode, he finds that Nature is dead matter until the poet imbues it with life; in the poem's own terms, 'we receive but what we give, / And in our life alone does Nature live' (Parrish, 55, lines 47–48). Yet, as we have seen already, Coleridge did not experience his interactions as a straightforward dialectic between thought and thing; instead, for him each of these moments were defined by an intermediary process where thought and thing combined in a fluid, inchoate relationship that it was his aim to articulate and so comprehend. The chiastic tropes in the ode might emphasize the distance between the poet and the world he witnesses, but at the place where the chiasmus crosses we might also locate a point at which these extremes can meet.

The poem concludes by seeming to find options for these meeting points. One passage in particular, removed from the published versions of 'Dejection' until 1817 but circulated in the meantime in letters to friends, anticipates the possibility of finding new connections. The poem (ironically, as Paley notes) blames Coleridge's 'abstruse Research' (Parrish, 59, line 89) for his failure to write poetry. Yet that 'Research' explicated the abstracting process which allowed him virtually to communicate with both human and non-human beings, even in his isolation. The next stanza shows this kind of vicarious connection in progress:

> Hence, viper thoughts, that coil around my mind,
> Reality's dark dream!
> I turn from you, and listen to the wind,
> Which long has rav'd unnotic'd. What a scream
> Of agony by torture lengthen'd out
> That lute sent forth! Thou Wind, that rav'st without,

Bare crag, or mountain tairn, or blasted tree,
Or pine grove whither woodman never clomb,
Or lonely house, long held the witches' home,
Methinks were fitter instruments for thee,
Mad lutanist! who in this month of show'rs,
Of dark-brown gardens, and of peeping flow'rs,
Mak'st Devils' yule, with worse than wint'ry song,
The blossoms, buds, and tim'rous leaves among.
Thou actor, perfect in all tragic sounds!
Thou mighty Poet, e'en to Frenzy bold!
What tell'st thou now about?
'Tis of the Rushing of an Host in rout,
With groans, of trampled men, with smarting wounds –
At once they groan with pain, and shudder with the cold!
But hush! there is a pause of deepest silence!
And all that noise, as of a rushing crowd,
With groans, and tremulous shudderings – all is over –
It tells another tale, with sounds less deep and loud!
A tale of less affright,
And tempered with delight,
As Otway's self had fram'd the tender lay –
'Tis of a little child
Upon a lonesome wild,
Not far from home, but she hath lost her way:
And now moans low in bitter grief and fear,
And now screams loud, and hopes to make her mother hear.

(Parrish, 59–61, lines 94–125)

The wind, here, links disconnected things: the bare crag, the remote tarn, the blasted tree, the unvisited grove, the lonely house, the lost child and the dejected poet. Together, they form a collective of isolated – yet interconnected – things. What unites them, as well as the wind's 'tragic sounds', is their shared disconnection. Although the last stanza hopes for the 'Lady' to find herself enmeshed in the intra-actions of all things ('To her may all things live, from pole to pole, / Their life the eddying of her living soul' [Parrish, 63, lines 135–36]), in fact the poem demonstrates the poet's own ability to use disconnection to recover a sense of involvement in the ecosystem. It is, after all, the Coleridgean speaker who is able to interpret the wind's stories. By the poem's end, even if he can't see or feel, the speaker is able to at least hear the enmeshment of human with non-human life.

This is the sum of Coleridge's ecopoetics: that what starts in dejection, in disconnection, can – must – transform into self-reflexive connection with and between human and non-human ecosystems. Yet, that connection in itself brings dangers: it runs the risk that the self might be remade in other moulds, an aggressive takeover of individual agency by an ecosystemic collective. Poetry, which enmeshes the world experienced with one imagined, provides the site at which such evaluations can take place. Wordsworth's might – as Coleridge certainly believed – be the 'ideal' ecopoetics, where the poet's 'genius and originality' are in 'sympathy and [...] inter-communion with Nature' ('Comprehensive Theory of Life'; *SWF*, 551) – yet Coleridge's ecopoetics offers an alternative vision that, while darker, is no less valuable. Coleridge's sense of disconnection – his 'dejection' – has an important role to play in modern ecology, at a moment when humans (at least in the Western world) are increasingly disconnected from our non-human counterparts. Coleridge's disconnection offers some hope: in Coleridge's ecopoetics, dejection becomes the impetus needed to inspire ecological care. At a moment of environmental catastrophe and climate crisis driven to a substantial degree by widespread apathy towards – we might even say disconnection from – the non-human world, understanding the role that dejection might play in ecological thinking has perhaps never been more important.

Notes

1 Quoted in Philipp Hunnekuhl, *Henry Crabb Robinson: Romantic Comparatist, 1790–1811* (Liverpool University Press, 2020), 207.
2 James C. McKusick, 'Coleridge and the Economy of Nature', *Studies in Romanticism* 35 (1996), 383.
3 James C. McKusick, *Green Writing: Romanticism and Ecology* (Basingstoke: Palgrave, 2000), 29.
4 Edward Kessler, *Coleridge's Metaphors of Being* (Princeton University Press, 1979), 174.
5 Tom Mole, *What the Victorians Made of Romanticism: Material Artifacts, Cultural Practices, and Reception History* (Princeton University Press, 2017), 32–33.
6 Aubrey L. Hillman, Mark B. Abbott, JunQing Yu, Daniel J. Bain and TzeHuey Chiou-Peng, 'Environmental Legacy of Copper Metallurgy and Mongol Silver Smelting Recorded in Yunnan Lake Sediments', *Environmental Science and Technology* 49 (2015), 3349–57.
7 Jonathan Bate, *The Song of the Earth* (London: Picador, 2000), 49.
8 Seamus Perry, 'Coleridge's Desultoriness', *Studies in Romanticism* 59 (2020), 15–34, at 30.
9 A. S. Byatt, *Unruly Times: Wordsworth and Coleridge in Their Time* (1989) (London: Vintage, 1997), 43.
10 Josie Dixon, 'The Notebooks', in *The Cambridge Companion to Coleridge*, ed. Lucy Newlyn (Cambridge University Press, 2002), 75–88, at 83–84.

11 Sara Coleridge, 'On Nervousness', in Bradford Keyes Mudge, *Sara Coleridge, A Victorian Daughter: Her Life and Essays* (New Haven, CT, and London: Yale University Press, 1989), 201–16, at 202.

12 Arden Reed, *Romantic Weather: The Climates of Coleridge and Baudelaire* (Providence, RI: Brown University Press, 1983), 3.

13 Mary Jacobus, *Romantic Things: A Rock, A Tree, A Cloud* (Chicago University Press, 2012); Karl Kroeber, *Ecological Literary Criticism: Romantic Imagining and the Biology of Mind* (New York: Columbia University Press, 1994); Onno Oerlemans, *Romanticism and the Materiality of Nature* (University of Toronto Press, 2004).

14 J. Andrew Hubbell, *Byron's Nature: A Romantic Vision of Cultural Ecology* (New York: Palgrave Macmillan, 2018), 2.

15 Jeremy Davies, 'Romantic Ecocriticism: History and Prospects', *Literature Compass* 15 (2018), 3.

16 Dewey W. Hall, *Romantic Naturalists, Early Environmentalists: An Ecocritical Study, 1789–1912* (Abingdon: Routledge, 2016). See also 'The Times View on William Wordsworth's Activism: Poetic Justice', *The Times,* 29 April 2020. www.thetimes.co.uk/article/the-times-view-on-william-wordsworths-activism-poetic-justice-oqpd65m3r.

17 Scott Hess, *William Wordsworth and the Ecology of Authorship: The Roots of Environmentalism in Nineteenth-Century Culture* (Richmond, VA: University of Virginia Press, 2012), 10–11.

18 J. Andrew Hubbell, 'Figuring Nature: Tropics of Romantic Environmentality', *Studies in Romanticism* 57 (2018), 353–81, at 375.

19 Vince Carducci, 'Ecocriticism, Ecomimesis, and the Romantic Roots of Modern Ethical Consumption', *Literature Compass* 6 (2009), 632–46, at 633.

20 Cheryl Glotfelty, 'Introduction: Literary Studies in an Age of Environmental Crisis', in *The Ecocriticism Reader: Landmarks in Literary Ecology*, eds. Cheryl Glotfelty and Harold Fromm (Athens, GA, and London: University of Georgia Press, 1996), xv–xxxvii, at xix.

21 Timothy Clark, *Ecocriticism on the Edge: The Anthropocene as a Threshold Concept* (London: Bloomsbury, 2015), 19.

22 Timothy Morton, *Ecology without Nature: Rethinking Environmental Aesthetics* (Cambridge, MA, and London: Harvard University Press, 2007).

23 Alan Bewell, *Natures in Translation: Romanticism and Colonial Natural History* (Baltimore: The Johns Hopkins University Press, 2017), xiv.

24 Raymond Williams, *The Country and the City* (London: Vintage, 1973); John Barrell, *The Idea of Landscape and the Sense of Place, 1730–1840: An Approach to the Poetry of John Clare* (Cambridge University Press, 1974), and *The Dark Side of the Landscape: The Rural Poor in English Painting, 1730–1840* (Cambridge University Press, 1983).

25 Anahid Nersessian, 'Romantic Ecocriticism Lately', *Literature Compass* 15 (2018), 4.

26 Marjorie Levinson, 'Of Being Numerous', *Studies in Romanticism* 49 (2010), 633–57, at 657.

27 Serenella Iovino and Serpil Opperman, 'Introduction: Stories Come to Matter', in *Material Ecocriticism*, eds. Serenella Iovino and Serpil Opperman (Bloomington and Indianapolis: Indiana University Press, 2014), 1–18, at 2, 6–7, 9.

28 Jane Bennett, *Vibrant Matter: A Political Ecology of Things* (Durham, NC: Duke University Press, 2010), 99.

29 Hubert Zapf, 'Creative Matter and Creative Mind: Cultural Ecology and Literary Creativity', in *Material Ecocriticism*, eds. Serenella Iovino and Serpil Opperman, 51–66, at 55.

30 Richard Louv, *The Nature Principle: Reconnecting with Life in a Virtual Age* (Chapel Hill, NC: Algonquin Books, 2014); Selin Kesebir and Pelin Kesebir, 'A Growing Disconnect from Nature Is Evident in Cultural Products', *Perspectives on Psychological Science* 12 (2017), 258–69; Jack Gelsthorpe, 'Disconnect from Nature and Its Effect on Health and Well-Being: A Public Engagement Literature Review' (London: Natural History Museum, 2017).

31 John Keats, 'La Belle Dame sans Merci', in *The Complete Poems*, ed. Miriam Allott (New York: Longman, 1970), 500–06, lines 31–48.

32 Timothy Morton, 'The Mesh', in *Environmental Criticism for the Twenty-First Century*, eds. Stephanie LeMenager, Teresa Shewry and Ken Hiltner (Abingdon: Routledge, 2012), 19–29, at 22–24.

33 Alfred, Lord Tennyson, *In Memoriam*, ed. Erik Grey (London: W. W. Norton & Co., 2004), 40, Part LV, stanzas 7–8.

34 Julie Ellison, *Delicate Subjects: Romanticism, Gender, and the Ethics of Understanding* (New York: Cornell University Press), 208.

35 Morton D. Paley, *Coleridge's Later Poetry* (Oxford: Clarendon Press, 1996), 3.

36 Quoted in Seamus Perry, *Coleridge and the Uses of Division* (Oxford: Clarendon Press, 1999), 48.

37 Karen Barad, *Meeting the Universe Halfway: Quantum Physics and the Entanglement of Matter and Meaning* (Durham, NC: Duke University Press, 2007), 3.

38 William Wordsworth, *Poems, in Two Volumes, and Other Poems, 1800–1807*, ed. Jared Curtis (Ithaca, NY, and London: Cornell University Press, 1983), 272, lines 56–57; Stephen Parrish, *Coleridge's "Dejection:" The Earliest Manuscripts and the Earliest Printings* (New York: Cornell University Press, 1988), 2; 5–6.

39 Quoted in Parrish, *Coleridge's 'Dejection'*, 18.

40 William Wordsworth, *Peter Bell*, eds. John E. Jordan, Mark L. Reed and Stephen Parrish (Ithaca, NY, and London: Cornell University Press, 1985), 51, line 80.

41 Hubbell, 'Figuring Nature', 363–66.

6

MARGARET RUSSETT

Gothic Coleridge, Ballad Coleridge

Coleridge divided the *Lyrical Ballads* into poems of 'two sorts'. One sort, contributed by his friend William Wordsworth, addressed 'subjects … chosen from ordinary life'. In the others – Coleridge's own poems – 'the incidents and agents were to be, in part at least, supernatural', and the goal was to capture the 'dramatic truth of such emotions, as would naturally accompany such situations, supposing them real. And real in this sense they have been to every human being who, from whatever source of delusion, has at any time believed himself under supernatural agency' (*BL* II, 6). This description linked Coleridge's poems with the romances and supernatural fictions, such as Ann Radcliffe's *The Mysteries of Udolpho* and Matthew Lewis's *The Monk*, which had so captivated readers in the decade preceding the publication of *Lyrical Ballads*. Gothic novels like these certainly delivered on the 'incidents', including heroines immured in ruinous castles, murderous monks and cross-dressing novices, actual and threatened rapes, ghosts both real and imagined, and even the occasional gigantic helmet dropping from the sky. In its emphasis on supernatural agency, Coleridge's description echoes the 1765 preface to Horace Walpole's 'gothic tale', *The Castle of Otranto*, whose author – so he alleged – was 'desirous of leaving the powers of fancy at liberty to expatiate through the boundless realms of invention, and thence of creating more interesting situations' than were to be found in everyday life. But he also 'wished to conduct the mortal agents in his drama according to the rules of probability; in short, to make them think, speak, and act, as it might be supposed mere men and women would do in extraordinary positions'.[1]

Coleridge's goal, like Walpole's, was psychological verisimilitude rather than the documentary realism of Wordsworth's poetry. But where Walpole claimed to depict realistic responses to impossible circumstances, Coleridge focused on *belief* in the supernatural: in other words, the phenomenon of 'delusion', or what we would now call psychosis. He might indeed have classed his poems as exercises in 'psychoanalysis' – a word he himself coined, along with its cousin 'psychosomatic'. His interest lay not in consciousness-as-usual, but in the dysfunctions and distortions that reveal the mind's own supernaturalism: its capacity to deceive us about the nature of reality; to conceal from us our most intimate truths; even to interrupt or impair our speech and bodily functions. His gothic poetry analyses distressed psyches, and the spells cast by traumatic experience upon the actions and consciousness of the wounded subject.

It was the 'human interest' drawn from our 'inner nature' that would, Coleridge hoped, be 'sufficient to procure for these shadows of imagination that willing suspension of disbelief for the moment, which constitutes poetic faith' (*BL* II, 6). That phrase, 'suspension of disbelief' – as ubiquitous as the Shakespearean 'catch a cold' – is often used without any recognition that it too is one of Coleridge's coinages, devised to account for another psychological puzzle: how is it that we come to love or hate unreal people, or to care about the outcomes of mere stories – even to the point that, as the fictional Henry Tilney remarks of the real *Mysteries of Udolpho*, 'when I had once begun it, I could not lay down again; – I remember finishing it in two days – my hair standing on end the whole time'?[2] Or, as the fictional Hamlet asks about an actor's real tears, 'What's Hecuba to him, or he to Hecuba, / That he should weep for her?'[3]

Questions like this had been raised in eighteenth-century drama criticism – hence, perhaps, Coleridge's reference to 'dramatic' truth – in a debate which concluded with Samuel Johnson declaring that 'spectators are always in their senses, and know, from the first act to the last, that the stage is only a stage, and that the players are only players'.[4] Coleridge was not so sure about this, comparing the effect of 'stage illusion' with the 'state of the mind in Dreams. It is not strictly accurate to say, that we believe our dreams to be actual while we are dreaming. We neither believe it or disbelieve it – with the will the comparing power is suspended, and without the comparing power any act of Judgement, whether affirmation or denial, is impossible' (*BL* II, 6n [letter to Daniel Stuart, 13 May 1816]). Like dreamers, dramatic spectators and absorbed readers temporarily – wilfully – abrogate the will-power that, for Coleridge, is synonymous with sanity. Only a 'voluntary Lending of the Will to this suspension of one of it's own operations' (*BL* II, 7n) distinguishes 'illusion' from 'delusion', or insanity per se.

Coleridge knew very well how slight this distinction was, nervously castigating those 'devotees of the circulating libraries' – bad readers – whose 'delirium' consists in a 'trance or suspension of all common sense and all common purpose' (*BL* I, 48n). For, as Johnson had warned, 'delusion, if delusion be admitted, has no certain limitation.'[5] It was the credulous readers of popular fictions who, Coleridge averred, most readily strayed from illusion into delusion. He associated their 'suspense' (a lesser form of 'suspension') with romances like Radcliffe's, in which, as he remarked in an anonymous early review, 'curiosity is kept upon the stretch from page to page, and from volume to volume', so that 'the secret, which the reader thinks himself every instant on the point of penetrating, flies like a phantom before him' (CU, 361). The secret is, of course, that there is no secret – it is a kind of temporary insanity to suppose that some hidden truth will ever be revealed by a story we consume as fiction. But if this is the case, then all devoted readers are as delusional as those who believe themselves under supernatural agency. After all, who can say that readers and spectators are not literally enchanted? Only when we come to the end of a story do we awaken from the 'spell which had bound [us] so strongly to it' (CU, 362).

The slide from illusion into delusion, and from absorption into enthral-ment, is the constant theme of both Coleridge's literary criticism and his supernatural poetry. Sometimes tales of the supernatural are cast as a branch of white magic, as in the short ballad 'Love', which tells how a minstrel wins his 'bright and beauteous bride' by singing 'Songs, that make her grieve' (CPW I, ii, 606–10, lines 96 and 20). But sometimes, as in 'The Rime of the Ancyent Marinere', they leave their hearers traumatized, 'like one that hath been stunn'd, / And is of sense forlorn' (CPW I, i, 418, lines 622–23). The Wedding Guest, a transparent surrogate for the reader, is held in thrall: first by the Mariner's hand (line 13), then by his 'glittering eye' (line 17) and then by the tale itself, which he 'cannot chuse but hear' (line 22), and to which he listens with the helplessness of 'a three year's child' (line 19). Whatever Coleridge may say about 'poetic faith', there is noth-ing 'willing' about the Wedding Guest's suspension of disbelief – a point Coleridge underlines by adding that 'the Marinere hath his will' (CPW, I, i, 372, line 16).[6] The story to which the Mariner subjects his listener is indeed replete with gothic 'incidents and agents', including zombified sailors, a 'spectre ship', an animated skeleton and the most fatale of all femmes, 'The Nightmare Life-in-Death' – any of which could have been ripped from the pages of a particularly lurid romance such as The Monk, or from Lewis's ballad 'Alonzo the Brave and Fair Imogine'. But unlike Lewis, Coleridge naturalizes his supernaturalism in a way that recalls Radcliffe's 'artificial contrivance[s]' (CU, 362) for observing the conventions of realism amid a series of highly implausible events.[7] Although the Mariner 'believe[s] him-self under supernatural agency', the reader is invited to see the spectre-bark and its crew as hallucinations, brought on by a combination of guilt, ostra-cism and dehydration so severe that the Mariner is forced to 'suck [his own] blood' (line 52) just to hail the approaching ship. But in contrast with a Radcliffe novel, the listener is not released from horror when the Mariner finishes his tale. In this respect, the Mariner (or Coleridge) weaves a more powerful spell even than Radcliffe, that 'great enchantress', the 'interest' of whose stories is nonetheless 'completely dissolved when once the adventure is finished' (*CU*, 362).[8] Thus, while the Mariner's tale features supernatural events, its reception by the Wedding Guest figures the supernaturalism of literary effect – the way a tale may 'harrow up th[e] soul[s]' of readers or audiences,[9] 'stunning' them into awareness of the world's fearfulness, as well as its beauty.

It may be doubted whether all early readers of 'The Rime' were as captivated as the Wedding Guest, or as was the young Coleridge by *The Mysteries of Udolpho*. But listeners and readers alike testified to Coleridge's Mariner-like 'strange power of speech' (*CPW* I, i, 416, line 587). William Hazlitt remarked that 'there was a chaunt' in Coleridge's recitation 'which acts as a spell upon the reader, and disarms the judgment' (Howe XVII, 118–19). Thomas De Quincey told how, as a very young man, he read 'The Rime' aloud at an aristocratic gathering in 1801. His hostess mortified him by laughing at its extravagances, but De Quincey scored an unexpected 'triumph' when, several days later, 'she suddenly repeated by heart' the six-line stanza describing the ship's enchanted motion (lines 366–72). Upon being asked 'what he thought of *that*?' an elderly guest 'seemed petrified', but 'at last, and as if recovering from the spasms of a new birth, said "I never heard anything so beautiful in my whole life."'[10] We may wonder which response is the more remarkable: the old man's enchantment or the young woman's trance-like recitation of a poem in which she had taken so little apparent interest.

Even its author was in thrall to 'The Rime', to judge by his incessant tinkering and revisions to the poem: it exists in at least eighteen authorized versions, with substantive changes made in 1800, 1817 and 1834. The best-known of these changes appeared in the 1817 volume *Sibylline Leaves*, where Coleridge introduced the marginal glosses which imply that an ancient oral tale has been transcribed and interpreted by a later commentator. But the comments do nothing to explain the Mariner's delusions. For every clarifying note, at least as many are redundant, tendentious or even zany. The Mariner's remark that 'The moving Moon went up the sky' yields this effusion:

In his loneliness and fixedness he yearneth towards the journeying Moon, and the stars that still sojourn, yet still move onward; and every where the blue sky belongs to them, and is their appointed rest, and their native country and their own natural homes, which they enter unannounced, as lords that are certainly expected and yet there is a silent joy at their arrival.

(*CPW* I, i, 393 [1834, lines 263–66]).

Oh, right. If the gloss at first seems intended to methodize the Mariner's madness, its excesses imply that analysis produces only a delusion of clarity. The immediate effect is to break the spell of recitation: no one has ever figured out how to read verses and notes simultaneously. But by recasting the contest between teller and listener as one between a tale and its reception, the gloss also suggests how efforts to master the text replay its drama of wills. The attempt to be 'wiser' (line 624) may leave us more fixated than ever; thus, interpretation does not demystify so much as it rehearses the superstitions that Walpole playfully ascribed to earlier, more credulous audiences.

Perhaps it was inevitable that the notorious monologist should come to be seen as the incarnation of his preternaturally loquacious character. De Quincey recalled Coleridge's disastrous 1808 lectures as performances by the Mariner himself, complete with 'lips ... black in colour' from being 'baked with a feverish heat', despite all the water he was drinking ('with throats unslack'd, with black lips bak'd', as the Mariner recalls the 'utter drouth' of his crewmates [lines 154, 131]).[11] The Coleridge of De Quincey's portrait is less master of than mastered by his own speech, again like the Mariner, who is 'forced ... to begin [his] tale' over and over, and who suffers 'woful agony' until that 'ghastly tale is told' (*CPW* i, i, 417 [1834, lines 579–84]). If the Wedding Guest's thraldom suggests the dark counterpart of 'willing suspension', then Coleridge-as-Mariner dramatizes the suspension of will in the compulsive repetition of a story.

These days, the diagnosis of possession or enchantment doesn't hold much water (potable or otherwise) as an explanation of strange behaviour, and Sigmund Freud's hypotheses about hysterical conversions and the 'compulsion to repeat' may not seem like a great improvement – perhaps, indeed, psychoanalysis may strike us simply as latter-day magic. How, then, do we account for the supernatural effects of this gothic poem? Short of falling back on the mimetic fallacy – that a depiction of enchantment has the capacity to enchant – we may notice that Coleridge's observations on poetic power emphasize repetition and the material properties of words, just as occult ceremonies do. In the *Biographia Literaria*, Coleridge names 'two critical aphorisms' which 'comprise the conditions and criteria of poetic style.' First, 'that not the poem we have read, but that to which we return ... possesses the genuine power, and claims the name of essential poetry'. Both the Mariner's compulsion to tell and Coleridge's compulsion to retell dramatize the uncanny iterability that is synonymous with aesthetic effect for Coleridge. 'Second, that whatever lines can be translated into other words of the same language, without diminution of their significance ... are so far vicious in their diction' (*BL* i, 23). One of the Rime's most striking quirks is its literally untranslatable diction, rife with eccentric spellings and rare or obsolete words ('eftsoones', 'swound'). While the conspicuous archaism of its language is in part an attempt to 'antiquate' the poem – to give it the patina of the ancient – it also elevates sound over semantics in a way that recalls the rhythmic syllables of magical incantations ('abracadabra'). The effect is amplified by the flamboyant use of internal rhyme and alliteration, which Coleridge employs more sparingly in his odes and verse meditations. Hazlitt's throwaway comment on 'Kubla Khan' – that 'it is not a poem, but a musical composition' proving only that its author 'can write better nonsense verses than any man in England' – testifies, albeit dismissively, to the incantatory effect of Coleridge's prosody (Jackson I, 208). Algernon Charles Swinburne made the point more appreciatively when he remarked that 'Kubla Khan' possesses a 'charm … which can only be felt in silent sub-mission of wonder' (Jackson II, 147). Swinburne's 'holy dread' (*CPW* I, i, 514, line 52) conjures the ecstatic register of enchantment: the delights – as well as the terrors – of surrender to 'forms and thoughts [which] act … by their own inherent power' (*BL* I, 6n).

Suspended disbelief, and the formal qualities of iterability and untranslat-ableness, are also hallmarks of trauma as that phenomenon has been under-stood since Freud. A traumatic experience 'challenges the limits of language and even ruptures meaning altogether'.[12] And as Peter Trachtenberg writes in *The Book of Calamities*, trauma is marked by compulsive return:

> A common feature of many theories of trauma is the idea that the causative – the wounding – event is not remembered but relived, as it is in the flashbacks of combat veterans, experienced anew with a visceral immediacy that affords no critical distance. To remember something, you have to consign it to the past – put it behind you – but trauma remains in the present; it fills that present entirely. You are inside it … Some researchers believe that trauma bypasses the normal mechanisms of memory and engraves itself directly on some portion of the brain, like a brand. Cattle are branded to signify that they are someone's property, and so, too, were slaves. The brand of trauma signifies that henceforth you yourself are property, the property of that which has injured you … and elsewhere in the literature one often comes across the word 'possession'.[13]

That the Mariner has suffered a trauma is among the few indubitable points to be made about 'The Rime'. Forever possessed by extreme suffering, he passes his trauma along to the stunned Wedding Guest, who in turn assumes the woeful burden of the tale he has heard. To put these remarks in con-versation with Coleridge's poetics is to see how he depicts the wonder pro-voked by great poetry as a kind of wounding, or even possession. Consider Coleridge's choice of a single line to exemplify the power of imagination:

'What! have his daughters brought him to this pass?', spoken by King Lear when, crazed with grief, he meets Edgar in the guise of Poor Tom the beggar (quoted in *BL* I, 85). Great poetry, Coleridge suggests, casts a spell that, unlike Radcliffe's artificial contrivances, does not dissolve with the conclusion of the story. If we approach the 'Rime' as such a poem – and, further, as a 'psychoanalysis' of such poetry – we might first take note of the ways in which, despite its gothic atmosphere, the story differs fundamentally from a tale by Radcliffe or Lewis. The Mariner has no secrets – no skeletons in closets, no spectacles behind black veils. There are mysteries, to be sure, but they will never be solved: why must the crewmates suffer so grotesquely for the Mariner's sin? Why, for that matter, did he shoot the albatross in the first place? He himself evidently has no idea. Questions like these, unanswerable by any social or symbolic code, persist as the traumatic kernel of all attempts to 'translate' the poem, or lay its demons to rest. Thus it is that 'The Rime' is on the one hand a 'standard text ... for introducing students to poetic interpretation' and on the other a poem whose many published interpretations are all conspicuously unsatisfactory.[14]

Traumatic experience defies closure. It persists even past the lifetime of the sufferer, recurring, though perhaps in disguised forms, from teller to listener – or text to reader – as from parent to child. Indeed, as Walpole summarized the senseless moral of his own gothic tale, 'the sins of fathers are visited on their children to the third and fourth generation'.[15] Gothic novels hint at this sobering insight through such devices as the 'found manuscript' – the fragmentary journal or unsent letter discovered, as by accident, when the offspring of a long-lost parent unearths it in the decaying abbey where she is held captive.[16] But the literary form which, for Coleridge, best exemplified the longevity of trauma was the folk ballad – a form particularly associated with long-ago tragedies which, though perhaps unrecorded, live on in popular memory. It is the familiar stanza of folk balladry – typically, though not prescriptively, a quatrain in common metre with alternating rhymes – that Coleridge borrows for 'The Rime of the Ancyent Marinere'. He adapted the same form for the 'other poems', specifically 'The Dark Ladie' and 'Christabel', in which he 'should have more nearly realized [his] ideal' for supernatural poetry than he had been able to do in 'The Rime' (*BL* II, 7). 'Should have', rather than 'did', because neither poem was ever completed: all that remains of 'The Dark Ladie' is a fifteen-stanza fragment, barely establishing the premise of a love affair gone wrong (*CPW* I, ii, 522–25). 'Christabel' is much longer, but still breaks off before either its protagonist's fate or its antagonist's identity is revealed. (Three different and mutually exclusive resolutions, recorded by Coleridge's interlocutors much later in his life, all possess about equal authority and plausibility.)[17]

In these two poems as in 'Kubla Khan' – which also employs a variant of the ballad stanza in its first and last sections – Coleridge virtually elevated the fragment into a genre of its own. In a different way from the 'Rime', which goes on and on while its protagonist remains a cipher, 'The Dark Ladie' and 'Christabel' embody what Cathy Caruth calls the 'unclaimed experience' of trauma in their blatant failure to resolve.[18] In this respect they also allude to the allegedly incomplete or textually corrupted poems collected in Bishop Thomas Percy's *Reliques of Ancient English Poetry* (1765), an anthology which really did originate in a found manuscript. Percy was visiting the home of his friend Humphry Pitt when he noticed a sheaf of folio pages being used as kindling for the parlour fire; snatching these pages from the maid, he found them to be a seventeenth-century compilation of anonymous poems, some of which apparently dated back to the twelfth century. He took the already half-ruined sheaf to a binder, who promptly lopped off the top and bottom lines of each page. The remaining fragments, amended and expanded by their editor, formed the basis of a remarkably influential collection to which Coleridge and Wordsworth paid homage in the title of their own collaborative volume, *Lyrical Ballads*. Among Coleridge's personal favourites were 'Sir Patrick Spence', the terse, enigmatic tale of a doomed seafaring expedition, and 'Sir Cauline', a love story whose atypically happy ending moved Percy to provide a tragic conclusion which he thought more appropriate. Sir Cauline, a knight of low degree, woos the king's daughter (named 'Christabelle' by Percy); they can be united only when Sir Cauline has slain all the king's enemies. Percy excused his meddling on the grounds that he found the poem in 'so very defective and mutilated a condition (not from any chasm in the MS. but from great omission in the transcript, probably copied from the faulty recitation of some illiterate minstrell)' that he 'was tempted to add several stanzas in the first part, and still more in the second, to connect and compleat the story in the manner which appeared to him most interesting and affecting'.[19] We have not far to seek for the overzealous fictive editor of 'The Rime', though there were certainly other precedents, such as the teenage forger-poet Thomas Chatterton's elaborate annotations for the putatively medieval 'Excelente Balade of Charitie', which he had actually written himself, stuffing it with as many real or coined archaisms as he could fit.

Percy's *Reliques* went a long way towards establishing a typology of the ballad as an anonymous composition, originally recited rather than written, and relating either a domestic tragedy or a historic rout such as the fourteenth-century Battle of Otterburn (an episode in the long-standing border wars between England and Scotland). The folk ballad was, in other words, the genre of trauma, whether private or collective. Its formal devices, including catch-phrases and refrains as well as mysterious elisions, attested to the iterability of suffering and its inexplicable causes. Death comes by way of battles and family feuds, but also from mystical charms and superstitious guilt. Percy's title, *Reliques*, amplifies these connotations by evoking irrecoverable loss as well as numinous remainders – even, perhaps, the dismembered body parts revered as synecdoches of sainthood in Catholicism. The 'barbarous' poems he presented to his readers thus also served as traces of an illiterate but charismatic folk, figured by Coleridge's 'ancyent' Mariner with his glittering eye and mesmerically inarticulate speech. The popularity of Percy's collection owed something, no doubt, to the collective mourning for a lost primitive origin that characterizes societies which understand themselves to be both modern and modernizing – that is, disenchanted.

Coleridge's choice to cast his supernatural poems in ballad form suggests a synthesis of gothic suspension and folk spells. A spell is the subject of his most uncanny poem, 'Christabel', whose effect when read aloud – it circulated in manuscript and recitation for almost twenty years before being published in 1816 – can only be described as bewitching. The most susceptible respondent was undoubtedly Percy Shelley, who heard 'Christabel' recited some time after midnight on 18 June 1816, after an evening spent telling ghost stories with his host, Lord Byron, Shelley's young lover Mary Godwin and Byron's personal physician, John Polidori, later to achieve minor fame as author of the first vampire novel in English. Byron had reached the stanza describing the beautiful stranger Geraldine's striptease for her hostess, Christabel:

> Like one that shudder'd, she unbound
> The Cincture from beneath her Breast:
> Her silken Robe and inner Vest
> Dropt to her feet, and fell in View,
> Behold! Her Bosom and half her Side –
> A Sight to dream of, not to tell!
>
> (*CPW* I, i, 490–91, lines 242–47)

At this point, Polidori relates in his diary, 'silence ensued, and Shelley, suddenly shrieking and putting his hands to his head, ran out of the room with a candle'. Polidori 'threw water in his face, and after gave him ether. He was looking at Mrs. S[helley], and suddenly thought of a woman he had heard of who had eyes instead of nipples, which, taking hold of his mind, horrified him.'[20] Evidently Shelley had no trouble visualizing the 'Sight to dream of'. But if his response was unusually histrionic, other readers were just as spellbound. Byron himself, who had heard the poem recited by Walter Scott, called it 'the wildest & finest I ever heard in that kind of composition', and credited it with inspiring his own poem *The Siege of Corinth* (1816).

In short, as he told Coleridge, 'All took a hold on my imagination which I shall never wish to shake off.'[21] Scott, Byron's source, first heard 'Christabel' recited in 1802, and suddenly found himself able to complete the long verse romance *The Lay of the Last Minstrel* (1805), on which he had been stalled for several years. When the inspiration for Byron's and Scott's poems finally appeared in print, it had even been anticipated by a parodic sequel, 'Christobell, a Gothic Tale' (1815), which purported to supply the story's missing conclusion.[22] In the ghostly, barely there form of recitation or rumour, 'Christabel' exercised something more powerful than 'influence': it took hold of other poets' speech, and reproduced its rhythms in their words, like the first murmur in an elaborate game of telephone or Chinese whispers.

This effect was just what the poem itself seemed to dictate. When Geraldine has 'had [her] Will' with the heroine, she takes the precaution of locking her tongue: 'In the Touch of this Bosom there worketh a Spell / Which is Lord of thy Utterance, Christabel!' (*CPW* I, i, 490–92, lines 306, 267–68). Unable to explain what has passed between them, Christabel is condemned 'passively [to] imitate' (*CPW* I, i, 501, line 605) Geraldine's words and actions. But if Coleridge, like Geraldine, lorded it over other utterances, the price – as he tells it – was his own silencing. In his preface to the 1816 volume *Christabel, Kubla Khan, and the Pains of Sleep*, Coleridge averred that his 'poetic powers' had been 'in a state of suspended animation' since 1797, when he wrote 'Christabel' with the intention of including it in *Lyrical Ballads*.[23] By the time sleeping beauty awakened, 'Christabel' had spawned so many imitations that its author feared being accused of 'plagiarism or servile imitation from myself' (*CPW* I, i, 481).

The flip side of enchanted recitation is traumatic repetition. Coleridge performed the traumatic register in his preface, and other readers followed suit with less apparent irony. Hazlitt was, once again, both Coleridge's most perceptive and most punitive critic, accusing the poet of 'shocking [his readers'] feelings at the outset', and darkly hinting of 'something disgusting at the bottom of his subject' (Jackson I, 207). Homophobia should not be discounted as a cause of disgust; as Camille Paglia pointed out more than thirty years ago, 'Christabel' is among other things a work of 'blatant lesbian pornography'.[24] But Hazlitt's way of gothicizing his shock also makes a subtler point about the relationship between the poem's themes and its formal devices. There is 'something disgusting', but Hazlitt, like the poem's heroine, either 'cannot' or simply will not 'tell' what it is. (Variants of the phrase 'cannot tell' occur at least five times in 'Christabel': lines 40, 99, 253, 473, 619.) Readers of gothic fictions could tell well enough how to read a coy allusion like this, versed as they were in the motif of the veiled 'spectacle' that causes heroines to faint and readers to delight themselves by guessing what lies behind it.[25] Thus Hazlitt resolved his unease by recasting the uncanny power of 'Christabel' in the familiar terms of popular romance. But his admission that the poem 'is more like a dream than a reality' and that 'the mind, in reading it, is spell-bound' suggests a more disturbing half-awareness that 'Christabel', like the 'Rime', both depicts and dictates a lapse of will that reduces the supposed voluntarism of suspended disbelief to little more than a polite fiction. The reader's suspension mimes the crippled will of the poem's central figures, who 'act without power' and 'yield without resistance' (Jackson 1, 207).

Hazlitt's traumatized response to this depiction of trauma is to fixate on the same passage that possessed Shelley. He does so with a difference, however: where the published version of the poem turns on an aposiopesis ('Behold! her Bosom and half her Side –'), Hazlitt supplies a missing line which he conned from the unpublished manuscript: 'Hideous, deformed, and pale of hue' (Jackson 1, 207). This, he says, 'is the keystone that makes up the arch'. By doing so, he stabilizes the story's meaning and domesticates its power to disturb – a power that Coleridge figures as an unrevealed spectacle. While Radcliffe does, finally, reveal what lies behind her black veil, Coleridge re-imagines the veil as a screen onto which both Christabel and her readers project what Jacques Lacan might call 'the real of their desire'. Is this sight horrific? Is it perhaps unbearably alluring? The narrator will not, and we cannot, tell. It is the consequent state of 'metaphysical suspense and theoretical imbecility' that so disgusts Hazlitt, and so enchants Scott and Byron (Jackson 1, 207).

I have been arguing that the trope of enchantment is Coleridge's figure for the constellation of affects and symptoms which we now usually identify with profound psychic disturbance. That the power to disturb so closely resembles the power to delight is the mystery that Coleridge's ballads of supernatural possession both exemplify and allegorize. Thraldom, captivation, bewitchment – these states dramatize 'poetic power' as the magical ability to 'decree' delusion (*CPW*, 1, i, 512, line 2) or to suspend disbelief. Before turning, by way of a conclusion, to some remarks about why Coleridge thought it important for disbelief to be suspended now and then, let us pause to wonder how he cast such mighty spells. It may be difficult for twenty-first-century readers to hear or feel the prosodic innovations that his contemporaries found so uniquely bewitching – and which, for those readers, set Coleridge's supernatural poems apart from either prose romances or traditional ballads. Both Scott and Byron identified the originality of 'Christabel' with its 'mescolanza of measures', by which Scott meant its singular rhythm and verse form.[26] While loosely adhering to the tetrameter line of popular balladry, Coleridge greatly exaggerated the metrical irregularities that Percy had noted in older ballads like 'Sir Cauline', to the point that he could claim in his preface to have 'founded ... a new principle' of versification (*CPW* I, i, 482). For Coleridge, and for those who heard him, metrical patterns were anything but mechanical. Their effects could indeed be spellbinding: 'as far as metre acts in itself', Coleridge argued, 'it tends to increase the vivacity and susceptibility both of the general feelings and of the attention ... As a medicated atmosphere, or as wine during animated conversation; they act powerfully, though themselves unnoticed' (*BL* II, 66). Skilfully varied metre, Coleridge suggests, allures readers and listeners by calling attention to the poetic medium – and, thus, to the phenomenon of mediation as such.[27] So, for example, 'Kubla Khan' begins in tetrameter, loses a foot in line 5, and then segues into more or less standard iambic pentameter. The intricately irregular rhyme scheme, vaguely reminiscent of a Petrarchan sonnet, 'excite[s] surprise' precisely through repetition. The 'Rime' employs the 'common' ballad quatrain with an uncommon number of five- and six-line stanzas mixed in. 'Th[e] effect' this variation 'produces by ... the quick reciprocations of curiosity still excited and still re-excited' (*BL* II, 66) evokes the enchantments of the gothic novel on a more intimate scale, and at a less conscious level.

If we no longer associate poetry with compulsion, witchery or delusion, it may be salutary to remind ourselves that similar language regularly crops up to describe the hold exercised by 'new media'. Coleridge inaugurates this trope when, in his bizarre attack on 'the devotees of the circulating libraries', he imagines that their 'beggarly daydreaming' is 'supplied ab extra by a sort of mental camera obscura manufactured at the printing office, which pro tempore fixes, reflects and transmits the moving phantasms of one man's delirium, so as to people the barrenness of an hundred other brains afflicted with the same trance or suspension of all common sense and all definite purpose' (*BL* I, 48n). Whoever these 'devotees' may be, Coleridge's sally against mass culture strikingly anticipates Theodor Adorno and Max Horkheimer's 1947 critique of 'the culture industry' (their name for the dominant media of the mid-twentieth century) that manipulates citizens into passive consumers. The 'camera obscura' has, uncannily, become synonymous with the concept of ideology (roughly, collective 'belief') in the Marxist tradition.[28] Even in 1817, Coleridge suspected – as many cultural critics have since affirmed – that popular forms such as 'frantic novels, sickly and stupid German tragedies, and deluges of idle and extravagant stories in verse' (Wordsworth, 'Preface', *LB*, 747) may lay asleep or distract the passions energies and critical powers of the consuming populace. This, Coleridge feared, was the mechanism by which 'a film of familiarity' intervenes between us and a more authentic engagement with 'the loveliness and the wonders of the world before us' (*BL* II, 7). 'In consequence of [this] film', he believed, 'we have eyes, yet see not, ears that hear not, and hearts that neither feel nor understand' (*BL* II, 7). In short, we are enchanted by a black magic all the more pernicious because we cannot recognize it for what it is. This is one moral to be drawn from the plot of 'Christabel', whose most disenchanted character, Sir Leoline, is also its most deluded, while the true state of affairs is intimated only in dreams (*CPW* I, i, 499–501).

Literary art was Coleridge's technique for combating the mechanisms of indoctrination in which he also inevitably participated. The awakening was to be achieved by subjecting readers to the 'imaginative medium' of poetry itself[29]– in full ironic awareness of the paradox at stake in treating passive 'trance or suspension' with the 'suspension of disbelief'. The difference, if there is one, lies in the single word – 'willing' – which suggests the capacity to resist those lords of utterance who impose 'th[eir] Will' (*CPW* I, i, 492, line 306) on us so much more insidiously than do Geraldine or the Mariner. The attempt to fight magic with magic partly accounts for Coleridge's insistence on 'untranslatable' diction and compulsory 'return', those hallmarks of necromancy and neurosis. Supernatural incidents and agents offered him a vocabulary for both depicting and reverse-engineering the spells of ideological immersion. In this, as in much else, he took a page from Walpole, grandfather of the gothic novel, who excused the prodigies related in his gothic tale (a work 'printed at Naples, in the black letter, in the year 1529') by positing that an 'artful priest' might combat the progress of enlightenment by 'avail[ing] himself of his abilities as an author to confirm the populace in their ancient errors and superstitions'.[30]

Coleridge saw that this strategy could be turned on its head. If superstitions can be cynically manipulated, then the vicarious experience of 'supernatural agency' might just awaken readers and listeners from the medicated atmospheres in which they habitually dwell. Recall De Quincey's anecdote of the old man who first seemed 'petrified' by his hostess's recitation of 'The Rime', but who 'at last, as if recovering from the spasms of a new birth, said "I never heard anything so beautiful in my whole life."' The old man's conversion echoes Coleridge's definition of genius as the capacity 'to awaken in the minds of others ... that freshness of sensation which is the constant accompaniment of mental, no less than of bodily, convalescence' (*BL* I, 81). There is no cure to lassitude without some traumatic intervention: the wounding which gives rise to wonder, and which 'constitute[s] an epoch in the mind of the reader, [such] that no one, after he has read it, shall ever be exactly the same man that he was before'.[31] This was the avowed aim of Coleridge's friend, the philosopher

William Godwin, in his gothic novel/exposé of 'Things as They Are'. The temporary suspension of disbelief could, Coleridge hoped, interrupt the habitual 'belief' in a mediated, ideologically saturated reality which keeps people from seeing the wonders and horrors that confront them every day. Or, as Coleridge's friend Charles Lamb protested, when Coleridge added the subtitle 'A Poet's Reverie' to the 1800 version of 'The Rime': 'it is as bad as Bottom the Weaver's declaration that he is not a lion, but only the scenical representation of a lion. What new idea is gained by this title but one subversive of all credit – which the tale should force upon us – of its truth' (*LL* I, 266). If everyday reality keeps us in a state of 'suspended animation', perhaps unwilled enchantment is needed to remind us that we do, after all, have wills to exert, or to suspend.

Notes

1 [Horace Walpole], *The Castle of Otranto: A Gothic Tale* (London: John Murray, 1769), xiv–xv.

2 Jane Austen, *Northanger Abbey*, ed. Claire Grogan (Peterborough, Ontario: Broadview Press, 2002), 120.

3 *Hamlet*, Act I, scene ii, lines 568–69.

4 Samuel Johnson, Preface 1765, in *Johnson on Shakespeare*, ed. Arthur Sherbo. vols VII–VIII of the *Yale Johnson* (New Haven, CT, and London: Yale University Press, 1968), VII, 77.

5 Johnson, *Preface*, 77.

6 References to 'The Rime' cite the 1798 text unless otherwise specified.

7 Radcliffe's association with the 'supernatural explained' was established by Walter Scott, in *The Lives of Novelists* (London: Dent, 1910), 245: 'All circumstances of her narrative, however mysterious and apparently superhuman, were to be accounted for on natural principles at the winding up of the story.'

8 Thomas De Quincey, *Confessions of an English Opium-Eater, 1821–1856*, ed. Grevel Lindop, vol. II of *The Works of Thomas De Quincey*, gen. ed. Grevel Lindop, 21 vols (London: Pickering & Chatto, 2000), 147. My understanding of how Coleridge adapted gothic conventions is indebted to Michael Gamer, *Romanticism and the Gothic: Genre, Reception, and Canon-Formation* (Cambridge: Cambridge University Press, 2000), and especially to two articles by Karen Swann: '"Christabel": The Wandering Mother and the Enigma of Form', *Studies in Romanticism* 23 (1984), 533–53; and 'Literary Gentlemen and Lovely Ladies: The Debate on the Character of "Christabel"', *English Literary History*, 52 (1985), 397–418.

9 *Hamlet*, Act I, scene v, line 16.

10 Thomas De Quincey, *Autobiographic Sketches*, ed. Daniel Sanjiv Roberts, *The Works of Thomas De Quincey*, gen. ed. Grevel Lindop, XIX, 266.

11 Thomas De Quincey, 'Samuel Taylor Coleridge [II]', ed. Alina Clej, *The Works of Thomas De Quincey*, gen. ed. Grevel Lindop, X, 320.

12 Nasrullah Mambrol, 'Trauma Studies', *Literary Theory and Criticism*. https://literariness.org/2018/12/19/trauma-studies/, accessed 27 June 2021.

13 Peter Trachtenberg, *The Book of Calamities: Five Questions About Suffering and Its Meaning* (New York: Little, Brown and Company, 2008).

14 Jerome J. McGann, 'The Meaning of the Ancient Mariner', *Critical Inquiry*, 8 (1981), 35–67 (35). See, for instance, Frances Ferguson's pithy observation that 'criticism of "The Rime of the Ancient Mariner" reflects a craving for causes' ('Coleridge and the Deluded Reader: "The Rime of the Ancient Mariner,"' *The Georgia Review*, 31 [1977], 617–35 (617)).

15 Walpole, *The Castle of Otranto*, viii; original emphasis.

16 I summarize a subplot of Radcliffe's *The Romance of the Forest*, which preceded *The Mysteries of Udolpho*.

17 Two endings were proposed by Coleridge's biographer James Gillman; a third was suggested by his son Derwent. Sophie Thomas discusses all three in 'The Return of the Fragment: "Christabel" and the Uncanny', *Bucknell Review*, 45 (2002), 51–73.

18 See Cathy Caruth, *Unclaimed Experience: Trauma, Narrative, and History* (Baltimore: Johns Hopkins University Press, 1996).

19 [Bishop Thomas Percy], *Percy's Reliques of Ancient English Poetry, in Two Vols.* (London: Dent, 1906): 'Sir Cauline', I, 90–100; 'Sir Patrick Spence', I, 113–14; Percy's apology, I, 90.

20 *The Diary of John William Polidori 1816*, ed. William Michael Rossetti (Cambridge University Press, 2014), 128. Rossetti supplies a concluding line, 'Hideous, deformed, and pale of hue', apparently repeating Hazlitt's misquotation of the 'keystone that makes up the arch.'

21 [George Gordon, Lord Byron], *Byron's Letters and Journals: A New Selection*, ed. Richard Lansdown (Oxford University Press, 2015), 193.

22 *The Poetical Works of Sir Walter Scott*, ed. J. Logie Robertson (Oxford University Press, 1909), 52–53. [Anna Jane Vardill], 'Christobell, A Gothic Tale.' *European Magazine*, 67 (April 1815), 315–16. http://spenserians.cath.vt.edu/TextRecord.php?action=GET&textsid=39091, accessed 29 June 2021.

23 This sentence, omitted from *CPW*, is included in *Coleridge's Poetry and Prose*, eds. Nicholas Halmi, Paul Magnuson and Raimonda Modiano (New York: Norton, 2004), 161.

24 Camille Paglia, *Sexual Personae: Art and Decadence from Nefertiti to Emily Dickinson* (New Haven, CT: Yale University Press, 1990), 331.

25 Radcliffe does not reveal the secret until the penultimate chapter of *Udolpho*, when we learn that a realistic 'wax figure' had so frightened her heroine, Emily, that she 'let the veil drop' before her 'delusion' could be dispelled (Ann Radcliffe, *The Mysteries of Udolpho*, ed. Terry Castle [Oxford University Press, 2008], 662). The veil motif was explicitly invoked as a figure of suspensive reading by Jane Austen, in *Northanger Abbey* (ed. Grogan, 61).

26 Scott, *Poetical Works*, 52.

27 For a longer version of this argument, see Margaret Russett, 'Unconscious Plagiarism: From "Christabel" to The Lay of the Last Minstrel', in Margaret Russett, *Fictions and Fakes: Forging Romantic Authenticity, 1760–1845* (Cambridge University Press, 2006), 70–90. My understanding of Romantic mediations is indebted to Celeste Langan and Maureen L. McLane, 'The Medium of Romantic Poetry', in *The Cambridge Companion to British Romantic Poetry*, eds. James L. Chandler and Maureen L. McLane (Cambridge University Press, 2008), 239–62.

28 Beginning, of course, with Marx himself in *The German Ideology* (London: Electric Book Company, 2000), 68. For a brief redaction of the Adornian argument, see Theodor W. Adorno, 'The Culture Industry Reconsidered', in *The Culture Industry: Selected Essays on Mass Culture*, ed. J. M. Bernstein (London: Taylor & Francis, 2000), 98–106.

29 Wordsworth, Fenwick note to 'We Are Seven', quoted in *BL* II, 7.

30 Walpole, *Castle of Otranto*, vi.

31 William Godwin, 'Preface' to *Things as They Are; or, the Adventures of Caleb Williams*, ed. Gary Handwerk and A. A. Markley (Peterborough, Ontario: Broadview Press, 2000), 447.

7

EWAN JAMES JONES

Coleridge's Metres

When occasion dictated, Sara Coleridge liked to get straight to the point. 'Have you been poeticizing of late?' she asked Miss Morris, without further preamble, in a letter written on 10 June 1844: 'I do not tie you down to these longs and shorts; but, depend upon it, there is much use in them.'[1] The remainder of her short letter repeats a single emphatic claim: metre ('longs and shorts') represents the most essential yet most easily overlooked aspect of poetry. Other fine arts offer her a point of comparison: we decompose paintings into colours and tones; we break down music into its constituent harmonies and melodies. And yet, she continues, we exhibit a puzzling reluctance to consider the stuff of which verse is made. We 'imagine', that is to say, 'that Poetry must flow forth spontaneously, like the breath which we breathe, without volition or consciousness'.[2]

Sara Coleridge's continuing insistence upon the centrality of metre quickly summons the spectre of a father who had died but a decade earlier:

> All our finest metrists knew these rules: how far they went I by them I cannot say; but I know that my father, whose versification has been greatly admired by critics, was fond of talking about anapaests and iambuses; and if people admired 'Christabel,' as it were, by nature, he was never easy till he had put them in the way of admiring it more scientifically.[3]

In this survey of Samuel Taylor's Coleridge's writings on and in metre, I want to attempt to return us to something like the culture in which his daughter wrote, in which versification mattered – mattered so much that it might be the first thing that you wanted to write to a dear correspondent. To do so requires us to forget critical habits that have since taken root and become tenacious. Notwithstanding recent salutary recovery work in the field of historical poetics,[4] prosody remains generally marginal to the broader field of literary aesthetics: a forbiddingly technical subfield that often serves as a site for the narcissism of small critical differences. This generalized neglect applies specifically to Coleridge, and yet versification mattered deeply to him, and he mattered deeply to versification. Indeed, there is a strong case to be made for his being *the* single most significant theorist and practitioner of metre in the history of English verse, especially where the gradual liberation of vernacular poetry from the established but ill-fitting rules of classical prosody is concerned. T. S. Omond certainly thought as much, giving pride of place to 'Christabel' for having discovered 'a principle' through which 'our verse, and later our theories of prosody, have been revolutionized'.[5] George Saintsbury cast reasonable doubt upon the absolute novelty of Coleridge's versification; he was nevertheless wrong to conclude that his 'references to formal prosody are few and unimportant'.[6] Coleridge never did stop thinking and living the embodied patterns of poetry. His scattered reflections lie buried in the drafts of uncompleted prosodic manifestos, in the marginal annotations to numerous poets across several centuries and language traditions, in the near-illegible scribblings of semi-private diary entries, in digressive footnotes that flee from the subject at hand, within *ad hominem* attacks whose harshness threatens to obscure the insight of the ideas themselves. And this is part of the problem: Coleridge's many prosodic insights lie buried.

I

From December 1796 to March 1797, Coleridge worked as a 'hireling' for the *Critical Review*.[7] Towards the end of this stint, he offered an anonymous review of Samuel Horsley's *On the Prosodies of the Latin and Greek Languages* (1796), a text that received little attention at the time and has merited still less since. Coleridge's review pits Horsley against John Foster's *Essay on the Different Nature of Accent and Quantity with Their Use and Application in the English, Latin and Greek Languages* (1763), which Coleridge had borrowed from Bristol Library, so as to cram up on the topic at hand. A brief precis of this thorny problem of Greek prosody, which raged throughout eighteenth-century polite discourse, elucidates his changing views on the topic. Unlike English prosody, which is governed by stress, ancient Greek and early Latin versification operates according to quantity: the length of time that it takes to articulate a syllable (Sara Coleridge's 'long and shorts'). Classical poetry was generally sung or recited: syllabic quantity induced modulations of pitch. Yet the piecemeal survival of Greek poetry leaves several questions open: in particular, we cannot be sure what relation (if any) obtained between pitch and linguistic accent.

On the Prosodies of the Latin and Greek Languages ventured into this contested field. Unlike Foster, who held that syllabic quantity was the sole relevant regulator of ancient Greek verse, Horsley identified a number of antique texts, dating back to the seventh century BC, which he took to clinch the importance of accent. Coleridge's review treats these claims with understated scepticism. While offering qualified early praise for the '*probability*' of Horsley's 'system', he ultimately comes down in favour of Forster's more traditional view (*SWF* I, 53). Successively, he calls into question the nature of the archival evidence on display, regrets the 'corruption' of modern Greek and points to the distorting influence of modern vernacular languages, which similarly operate according to very different structural principles. 'We indeed of this country read the Greek and Latin as we read the English, which differs in the powers of the vowels from every other language upon earth' (*SWF* I, 52). The exceptionality of English is not, in this context, a good thing: among other crimes, it confuses long and short, mistakes dactyls for anapaests, hallucinates cretics and amphibrachs where none exist.

All of this may seem somewhat arcane, even if we bear in mind Meredith Martin's welcome reminder, in *The Rise and Fall of Meter*, that prosody remained a vital social (and ideological) factor throughout the long nineteenth century.[8] But I am interested in Coleridge's essay in large part because of the remarkable sea-change that takes place in his subsequent thinking. Reflections upon Greek prosody bookend his career: at one end, we find the anonymous review of Horsley's text; in 1833, the year before his death, *Table Talk* recorded very different views on the same topic. 'The distinction between accent and quantity is clear', Coleridge said, in August that year, 'and was, no doubt, observed by the ancients in the recitation of verse.' So far, his views remain orthodox. 'But', Coleridge then continues, 'I believe such recitation to have been always an artificial thing, and that the common conversation was entirely regulated by accent.'[9]

Coleridge's newfound focus upon accent over quantity produces two further related shifts in perspective: first, he stresses the importance of language as it is actually spoken over an 'artificial' or unknowable recitation; second, and by logical extension, the relation between classical Greek and the modern vernaculars changes drastically. 'I do not think it possible to *talk* any language without confounding the quantity of syllables with their high and low tones', Coleridge continues, going even so far as to wonder whether 'we can altogether disregard the practice of the modern Greeks'. As Henry Nelson Coleridge notes in the editorial notes to his 1836 edition of the *Table Talk*, such views stand 'in direct opposition' to Foster, to whom Coleridge had previously proven so indebted, 'and [are] scarcely reconcilable with the apparent meanings of the authorities from the old critics and grammarians'.[10]

We should here embed Coleridge within a broader cultural context that he did more than anyone to bring about, which challenged for the first time the suitability of classical metres for the modern vernacular. In the eighteenth century, as before, poets and critics unthinkingly banded around the familiar Greek feet (iambs, trochees, anapaests etc.), simply replacing stress for syllable length. Around the turn of the century, however, several figures challenged this presiding attitude: what mattered to English verse was not the number of syllables or their subdivision into feet; rather, it was a consistent number of beats, which persisted even through variations in line length.[11] Perhaps the most significant single work in this respect was Joshua Steele's *Prosodia rationalis*, whose revised second edition of 1779 represented the first systematic attempt to uncouple English prosody from foot-based metrics: '[a]s the ancient Greeks', Steele archly remarked, 'as well as their language, are all dead, I do not want to be drawn into a comparative contest about them.'[12] Like the Coleridge of 1833, Steele stressed the importance of intonational patterns in quotidian conversation, in addition to song and recitation. (Coleridge may well have known indirectly of Steele's reformist endeavour through the mediation of John Thelwall, who applied *Prosodia rationalis* in various elocutionary contexts; the pair exchanged several letters that touched repeatedly upon prosody (see *CL* I, 215–16, 258–62, 278–87).)

Viewed this way, Coleridge's volte-face might well seem to stand for a prosodic liberation. His prefatory note to 'Christabel' proves broadly consistent with the late *Table Talk* comment, in its notorious claim to be 'founded on a new principle: namely, that of counting in each lines the accents, not the syllables ... Though the latter may vary from seven to twelve, yet in each line the accents will be found to be only four' (*CPW* I, i, 482–83). Derek Attridge, who stands as the pre-eminent contemporary representative of the accentual school of prosody (as opposed to a foot-substitution model), certainly argues as much, claiming that 'Coleridge's "Christabel" constitutes a conscious revival of dolnik style'.[13] The dolnik, whose provenance and prevalence Attridge has brilliantly traced, represents a four-beat prosody common to English and Russian verse. Coleridge may not be new, on this account, but he most certainly delivers a rupture from conventional foot-based forms of versification. Yet we should pause for breath before concluding that Coleridge was a prosodic radical or thoroughgoing accentualist. The one obvious barrier that stands in the way of such a conclusion is his stubborn retention of precisely the metrical terms that for Attridge so poorly express the rhythms of poetry: in the Elizabethan dramatist Philip Massinger, for instance, he finds 'Iambic Pentameter Hyperacatalectic, their Proceleusmatics, and Dispondaeuses-proceleusmatics' (*CM* I, 376).

In an insightful article on Coleridge's early essay on Horsley, Charles I. Patterson claims that 'Christabel' recovers for English verse precisely the classical foot-based prosody that Omond, Attridge and many others deemed it to have consigned to the dustbin of history.[14] This metrical experiment, on his view, achieves temporal 'quantity' for the English vernacular: while this isochrony is underpinned by accent rather than syllable length, we can nevertheless carve up individual lines into metrical feet. Patterson does just that, reading amphibrachs into Coleridge just as Coleridge read amphibrachs into other authors. So, which is it? Does 'Christabel' mark liberation from classical precedent or the continuation of a prosodic system that, over and above being of dubious use to the modern vernacular, was the exclusive preserve of the classically educated elite? The remainder of this essay will attempt to prove that this is a false way of posing the question. In so doing, I seek to get to the heart of Coleridge's prosodic intelligence, and to suggest why it mattered to his broader thinking.

Coleridge retained traditional feet for more than elitist ends. To perceive these more fully, I wish to redirect attention from the thorny and contentious question of the 'correct' scansion of English, so as to consider more practical and enactive ways in which it figures in lived experience. The first of these contexts is pedagogical. It is no coincidence that Sara and Hartley Coleridge both gave pride of place to metrical virtuosity, in their common recollections, for their father taught many young persons the rudiments of versification with generosity of spirit and fecundity of imagination. Several instances of this pedagogy endure: the Wordsworth Library in Grasmere holds the notes for a 'Lesson in English Prosody', written for Hartley when he was then ten; between 1819 and 1824, Coleridge wrote a series of rules for scanning (and making) Latin verse, intended for both of the young sons of James Gillman, at whose Highgate residence Coleridge spent the final years of his life (*SWF* I, 201–5, 808–18; *SWF* II, 1214–50). These teaching aids are rigorous but also demonstrate a pragmatic flexibility, along with a preparedness to acknowledge the great difference between English and classical languages. 'We adopt', he sets out in the 'Lesson' for Hartley, 'the words, long and short syllables, by an abuse, or transfer of words; and should in strictness say/ (*for our own metres*) accented & unaccented, strong or light, syllables.' Accordingly, classical prosody provides several '[d]oubtful feet, relatively to the English Language – or rather transformable according to the sense & passion'. The two-word phrase 'any money' can offer a 'Proceleusmaticus', which, we recall, Coleridge observed in Massinger's verse: four lightly and rapidly stressed syllables. Or, spoken another way, it can offer a 'dispondaeus': four heavy stresses. Think of different 'passions' in which the phrase might be uttered: the relative value of stress might well make the difference between begging and demanding.

Versification, we can therefore conclude, is for Coleridge descriptive rather than normative: scansion does not offer an objective and context-independent truth; rather, it describes a given performance, in a given setting, with a given feeling. Think of it as the prosody of a situation. Each of his several examples of metrical feet communicates a miniature history: the different articulations of 'any money'; the rising aspiration of the iambic 'delight'; the dactylic trip of 'merrily'; the emphatic belief of the hyperspondaic 'God's right hand'; the similarly heavily stressed mollosus 'John James Jones'.[15] Coleridge is continually alert to the stress variations of individual words, to the extent that we nearly engage in a superstitious form of prosodic determinism.

It is significant that these prosodic sketches all take the form of individual *words*: as Coleridge is the first to admit, it is difficult to keep up such metres for any length of time. The English vernacular tends to blur any difference between dactyls and anapaests: we should nonetheless carry on trying to hear them not because they are 'out there' in any metaphysical sense but because to do so is to honour the world, as represented in language, by attempting to hear such minute discriminations (*SWF* I, 201). The most famous of Coleridge's prosodic lessons, 'Metrical Feet', both abridges his pedagogy and delights in the world-as-worded:

> Trŏchēĕ trīps frŏm lōng tŏ shōrt;
> From long to long in solemn sort
> Slōw Spōndēe stālks; strŏng fōot! yet ill able
> Ēvĕr tŏ cōme ŭp wĭth Dāctŷl trĭsŷllăblĕ.
> Ĭāmbĭcs mārch frŏm shōrt tŏ lōng; –
> Wĭth ă leāp ănd ă bōund thĕ swĭft Ānăpæ̆sts thrōng;
> One syllable long, with one short at each side,
> Ămphĭbrăchŷs hāstes wĭth ă stātelÿ stride; –
> Fīrst ănd lāst bēĭng lōng, mĭddlĕ shōrt, Amphĭmācer
> Strīkes hĭs thūndĕrĭng hōofs līke ă prōud hīgh-brĕd Rācer.
>
> (*CPW* I, i, 808)

Here, it is not just that we can imagine the amphimacer as a 'proud high-bred racer', but also that we can imagine the 'proud high-bred racer' as an amphimacer. The world around us, that is to say, falls into rhythm: once we have the words to express those rhythms, we begin to hear them everywhere.

But this is not all that Coleridge's metrical experiment achieves. This act of tender pedagogy is often published in the form in which I have cited it above: as a quick trawl through the duple and triple metres. The Canadian poet Bliss Carman, for example, extracted 'Metrical Feet' in just this way for his *The World's Best Poetry* anthology (1904), in the section marked 'Ingenuities and Oddities'. Not many read on to consider the poem's conclusion:

> If Derwent be innocent, steady, and wise,
> And delight in the things of earth, water, and skies;
> Tender warmth at his heart, with these metres to show it,
> With sound sense in his brains, may make Derwent a poet –
> May crown him with fame, and must win him the love
> Of his father on earth and his father above.
>   My dear, dear child!
> Could you stand upon Skiddaw, you would not from its whole ridge
> See a man who so loves you as your fond S. T. Coleridge.

$$(SWF \text{ I}, 441–42)$$

I find this second stanza just as interesting as its more illustrious precursor, even though – or precisely because – the showy reflexive prosody now drops out. Shorn of our metrical stabilizers (the diacritical marks with which Coleridge previously indicated stress), we must now scan on our own initiative. What results are a series of lines that lack the previously clear-cut distinctions: 'if Derwent be innocent' proves rather a prosodic mouthful, with the internal rhyme encouraging us to stress both words, unusually, on the last syllable. From then the verse stabilizes into a broadly triple metre: the second appearance of the proper name now clearly accentuates the first syllable, enforcing the anapaestic metre that runs throughout the line ('With sound sense in his brains, may make Derwent a poet – '). Yet the difference between anapaests, dactyls and amphibrachs matters less than the fast pace common to each. This pace in turn matters most, however, when it is brutally curtailed, with the abruptly catalectic apostrophe, 'My dear, dear child!' The artlessness of this expostulation depends upon art: what would otherwise count as a blurted cry accrues deeper force from the rhythmical pattern that it disrupts.

Is this suddenly irregular poem still metrical? No and yes. There is certainly no way to apply to this catalectic line any of the varied feet for which Coleridge's prior stanza primes us. We could hear in it Attridge's dolnik: for we can conceivably stress every one of its four syllables, which would raise the number of beats to that of its syllabically more populous precursors. But such a treatment of the prosodic character of the individual line, or of the poem as a self-consistent whole, leaves out what is surely the most vital component of this poem: its aliveness to metrical surprise and variation. We should not pay attention to the stress profile of a word or phrase or line so as to perform prosodic taxidermy – to attach the stuffed specimen to its proper taxonomic category. Rather, we should hear such repeated rhythms so as to expose ourselves to moments of rhythmical non-repetition. Coleridge teaches prosody with love, so as to stage that for which no amount of teaching can prepare: the disruption of expectation, which takes the form of the declaration of affection. When the final two lines of this short and touching and comic poem settle back down into a triple metre, their recovered prosodic character takes on a new force: it a shelter recovered, a fragile bond that sustains community, and which community sustains. 'See a man who so loves you as your fond S. T. Coleridge.' The father becomes so much more than a dactyl.

II

It is upon metrical surprise and variation that the remainder of my discussion focuses. Coleridge recognized this principle astutely, notwithstanding his more hyperbolic declarations of prosodic innovation. At some point in the spring of 1816, he composed a short essay, 'On the Metre of *Christabel*', which, partly on account of its unfinished nature, has received far less attention than the brief prefatory statement accompanying the poem's final publication in the same year that claimed to be based on a new accentual metre (*SWF* I, 441–42). Yet Coleridge's lesser-known fragment offers what in many respects is a humbler, more accurate and more suggestive estimation both of the poem itself, and of versification in general:

> The ~~Verse~~ meter in which I have written it is the common 8 syllable verse, in technical phrase, the tetrameter Iambic acatalectic – the liberties besides of that of using a double rhyme, ... are that of substituting ~~an~~ anapest or dactyl ~~accompany~~ followed by a trochee instead of two Iambics, either in the ~~beginning or the~~ first or latter half of the verse & sometimes of giving four anapests, sometimes four trochees, instead of the four Iambics – in brief, having no other *law* of metre, except that of ~~retaining~~ confining myself to four *strokes*, ~~of the verse~~ or accentuated syllables.   (*SWF* I, 442)

The four-beat system does not preclude adherence to a general (octosyllabic) norm, which Coleridge underlines with the use of the technical term 'acatelectic', which indicates a line that has its replete number of syllables. In place of self-perceived revolutionary novelty, we thereby observe a series of subtler and more supple breaks from a presiding pattern. Accentualism does not displace the syllabic system, but rather attunes us to its modulations.

What matters, in short, is not the manner in which we scan an individual line or foot, so much as the liberty that Coleridge buys himself for variation between them. Referring back to 'Metrical Feet', Patterson convincingly argues that we can notate individual lines of 'Christabel' as amphibrachs:

Which hung in a murky old niche in the wall

This scansion seems to be perfectly plausible: yet as Patterson confesses, we can just as easily render the same line as an initial iamb, followed by a run of anapaests.[16] The question is how such notational variations relate to *experience*. To my mind (to my experience) they do not: I neither feel nor hear a significant distinction in marking the end of a foot after 'in' or 'hung'. What I do feel or hear, by contrast, are the variations that take place between lines, which are not simply 'free', but which depend upon general conformity to have their effect. Take the famous opening stretch from 'Christabel':

> 'Tis the middle of night by the castle clock,
> And the owls have awakened the crowing cock;
> Tu–whit! Tu–whoo!   (lines 1–3)

The owlet's call pierces the poem with brilliant force. If this passage seems familiar, it is not only because the poem is a famous one. It stems, also, from the fact that Coleridge has elsewhere similarly curtailed a skipping triple rhythm, albeit to very different effect. 'Tu–whit! Tu–whoo!' 'My dear, dear child!'

The uncontrolled expression of emotion thereby continues to require the law that it breaks from. The force of the variation is all the greater for being slight: it traces a dialectic between freedom and constraint that is subtler than a hidebound allegiance to convention, on the one hand, and putative liberation, on the other. As Coleridge put it, in an 1802 letter to William Sotheby, *'metre* itself implies a *passion'* (*CL* II, 812).He later remarked in the *Biographia Literaria*, attributing the insight to his schoolteacher, the Revd James Boyer, 'poetry, even that of the loftiest and, seemingly, that of the wildest odes, had a logic of its own, as severe as that of science' (*BL* I, 9).

Coleridge's scattered reflections on prosody, along with his own verse practice, enable us to grasp anew what is by some distance his most famous and sustained treatment of metre: Chapter XVII of the *Biographia*. There, via a series of interlocked metaphors, Coleridge expresses what metre is, how it works upon its reader and the manner in which it influences the experience of temporality. These points, taken together, seek to refute Wordsworth's famous claim that 'There neither is nor can be any essential difference between the language of prose and metrical composition' (*BL* II, 392). On the contrary, Coleridge argues, versification 'resembles ... yeast, worthless or disagreeable by itself, but giving vivacity and spirit to the liquor with which it is combined' (*BL* I, 267). Metre, then, helps the brewing process; elsewhere Coleridge suggests that it works '[a]s a medicated atmosphere, or as wine during animated conversation; they act powerfully, though themselves unnoticed' (*BL* I, 266).[17] It 'tends to increase the vivacity and susceptibility of the general feelings and of the attention' (*BL* I, 266). Vivacity *and* susceptibility: what matters, here, is the manner in which it attunes us to the world. In his brilliant coupling of prosody with attention, Coleridge found a potential means of resolving what remained a problem in his more exclusively philosophical writings. His developing aversion to Lockean associationism led him to disdain any 'passive' materialist conception of mind (see *CL* II, 709). Yet Coleridge was, more than anyone, brilliantly able to capture the nature and feel of sub-intentional states, whether the mind in question be dreaming, or hallucinating, or otherwise induced into a given cognitive circumstance. His many scattered writings on what we would now call philosophy of mind often labour to draw pertinent distinctions in this regard: 'In ATTENTION, we keep the mind passive: In THOUGHT, we rouse it into activity' (*AR*, 14). Prosody shows why the former modality deserves so much more than a negative contrast with ideation proper.

Finally, Coleridge imagines the manner in which this heightened attentional capacity produces a particular capacity for temporal experience, in a remarkable evocation of rhythmical retention and protention. Metre sets up an expectation: '[w]here, therefore, correspondent food and appropriate matter are not provided for the attention and feelings just roused, there must needs be a disappointment felt; like that of leaping in the dark from the last step of a staircase, when we had prepared our muscles for a leap of three or four' (*BL* I, 266). Coleridge's miniature sketch of this poetical gymnast (drunk on prosodic wine?) is again quite brilliant. I would seek to modify the trope in only two slight ways. First, Coleridge's metaphorical pratfall, however vivid, still risks implying a binary between metre and language: we detect prosody, and expect a certain register. In addition to asserting a restrictively exclusive understanding of what properly 'poetic language' might be, this dualism overlooks the manner in which metre generates a rhythmical expectation not for language but for itself, which is to say the continuation of its own rhythmical patterns. Coleridge sometimes acknowledged this self-propelling prosodic capacity, as when he observed that 'Dryden's genius was of that sort which catches fire by its own motion; his chariot wheels get hot by driving fast' (*TT* II, 269). Second, I would stress the extent to which the disappointment of such rhythmical expectation can itself be a positive good: jumping from one step, when one expects a gap or four or five, describes nothing so well as those early lines from 'Christabel'.

III

Hitherto, my discussion has focused on Coleridge's writings on and in conventional prosodic repertoires. I have attempted to show how his variations upon established syllabic models prove ultimately more profound than any more thoroughgoing 'break' with precedent, and how his verse actuates such principles. Yet the verse that I have hitherto considered takes, in every case, a markedly metrical form. What of the other works for which Coleridge is principally known: the sequence of meditative blank verse poems that do not follow anything like so distinct a prosodic organization? The concluding section of this essay will attempt to refute this very distinction.

If by 'blank verse' we mean unrhymed iambic pentameter, then many of Coleridge's most famous conversation poems do not qualify as such. For they contain trace elements of the very substance that they might seem, in comparison to the various aforementioned works, to lack: rhyme. Rhyme can of course be considered independently from metre: yet it can also reinforce the sense that we are in the presence of language ordered according to some prosodic principle. This effect can be particularly pronounced in forms such as blank verse, where we might well forget that we are reading poetry at all, rather than passages of more or less rarefied prose that simply happen to be hammered into decasyllabic slivers.

To prove my point, I want to focus on two instances from Coleridge's magisterial sequence of conversation poems. 'Frost at Midnight' and 'The Nightingale', both composed in the *annus mirabilis* of 1798, share a common metrical structure and thematic concern. Indeed, these two features (structure and theme) prove finally inseparable, generated as they are by the ghost of rhyme. Coleridge, I am convinced, thought long and hard about such matters, as with his suggestive comment that Thomson's blank verse feels 'rhyme-less or rather rhyme-craving' (*CL* IV, 782). With conscious artifice, he sought to generate effects that would evade conscious awareness.

What kind of blank verse might 'crave' rhyme? A poem both troubled by and desirous of self-identity, for a start. 'Frost at Midnight' answers pretty well to this description (*CPW* I, i, 443–45). The work tells of a subject disconcerted by a quiet night in which he is the only living thing, who seeks to escape the blank self-evidence of the world through recollecting childhood. But this drama, such as it is, turns on a series of sonorous shifts whose subtlety Coleridge would never again attain; these devices are quieter than the metrical pyrotechnics of 'Christabel' and 'The Rime of the Ancyent Marinere', yet no less significant as a result. Smothered rhyme counts among them. The poem begins with an eye-rhyme that does not quite chime ('The Frost performs its secret ministry, / Unhelped by any wind. The owlet's cry', with the /ī/ phoneme then soon emerging at another terminal rhyme ('side' (line 6)). We might well pass these phonemic coincidences over, where it not for the quickly ensuing monorhyme that wonderfully captures the perceived redundancy of the world:

> Sea, hill, and wood,
> This populous village! Sea, and hill, and wood,

Metre here helps us perceive what would otherwise pass merely for rhetorical repetition; terminal rhyme in turn reminds us of a metre whose looseness might otherwise pass for prose. 'Frost at Midnight' continues to employ terminal rhymes (or pseudo-rhymes) in this way, with the subsequent echoing of 'oft' (lines 24, 27), and the successive near-rhyme 'dreamt'/'dreams!' (lines 34–35).

These monorhymes express a mind tying itself in knots ('Echo or mirror seeking of itself'). But they also attune us to a series of further echoes that win more difference from coincidence. Having recalled his childhood self, the speaker turns back in the fourth verse paragraph to the 'Dear Babe, that sleepest cradled by my side' (line 44). We may or may not hear the dangling monorhyme of 'side' from the very beginning of the poem. But we cannot deny the subsequent aural coincidence of 'And think that thou shalt learn far other lore' (line 50) and 'Which image in their bulk both lakes and shores' (line 57), the answering terminal rhyme being underscored by its supplementary repetition of 'lakes and sandy shores' from two lines ago. Rhyme, then, migrates from terminus to within the line itself: the phoneme is picked up and transformed in its passage from 'sole unquiet thing' to 'articulate sounds of things' to come, to 'soothing things', to 'gentle breathings', to God, 'all things in himself'; or from 'calm indeed! so calm, that it disturbs' to 'heard in this deep calm'. The poem gives us ears to hear the appropriate terminal repetitions of 'ear', 'reared' and 'hear'. All rhyme (even monorhyme) insinuates difference into repetition: in this dense aural patterning, the 'strange' silentness of the present world (line 9) gives rise to the recollected wish for a future 'stranger' (lines 26, 41). The unforeseeable figure that the child was nervously expecting turns out to be a later version of himself. The later subject escapes himself through the recollection of what had been foreclosed. Intolerable difference and intolerable sameness heal one another. Buried rhyme is what puts them on speaking terms. With it, 'Frost at Midnight' stages a drama that is both local and universal: how to escape from the narrow cottage that is also your mind.

Some ambiguity attaches to these rhymes, with regard to both the reader (do we cognize them?) and the author (did Coleridge intend them?). Certainly, were we to take yesterday's copy of the *Daily Mail* and chop its articles into decasyllables (making in the process the worst avant-garde blank verse poem of all time), there is a statistical likelihood that inadvertent terminal rhymes would arise. But 'The Nightingale: A Conversation Poem' (*CPW* I, i, 264–67), written only two months later, renders such sceptical concerns moot (or mute): its rhymes are too pervasive and patterned to be incidental, even though, as with 'Frost at Midnight', they remain underground.

Where buried rhyme previously served as means of linking the subject to a world beyond him, this later and more joyful poem worries only that such links will one day have to be broken. From the start, terminal rhymes prove more conspicuous: 'grove' repeats itself at three separate line-ends (lines 49, 57, 73); 'notes' occurs twice (lines 45, 74); 'love', phonemic kin to 'grove', occurs twice (lines 18, 42). Where in 'Frost at Midnight' 'minstrelsy' near-rhymed with 'cry', this later poem pairs the same word with 'sky' (lines 78, 80): strong proof that the device was intentional. 'Silently' occurs at the very beginning and the very end of the poem (lines 6, 103), training our ears to hear the endurance of simple circumambience. Just as with 'Frost at Midnight', rhyme migrates from periphery to centre: 'love' and 'grove' multiply within the line. But the biggest giveaway, in this respect, is the nightingale itself, whose appearance on line 83 ('Many a nightingale') rhymes with line 81 ('As if some sudden gale'). (In both cases, 'gale' falls on the stressed sixth position.)

By the time that we get to the valedictory final verse paragraph, rhyme has sprouted within what we now have to call unblank verse:[18]

> Farewell! O Warbler! till tomorrow eve,
> And you, my friends! farewell, a short farewell!
> We have been loitering long and pleasantly,
> And now for our dear homes. That strain again!
> Full fain it would delay me! (lines 87–91)

'Strain' rhymes not only in quick succession with 'again' and 'fain', but also with earlier iterations of itself ('melancholy strain' (line 22), 'pity-pleading strains (line 39)'). Monorhyme, a source of such anxiety within 'Frost at Midnight', here seeks to forestall leave-taking, with the word 'farewell' repeating itself twice in the following line, and at the end of the final two lines, and distilling itself into the single-syllable 'well', which communicates first benignity ('knows well' (line 97)), and then a simple expostulation ('Well! – ' (line 105)), which does no more – and no less – than waylay us in this pleasant place. But the one key rhyme throughout the poem is, appositely, 'song', which recurs at the end of no fewer than five separate lines. When we hear it, smuggled within the third-from-last line, it triggers a host of associations: like Coleridge's son, who here recurs, we have become 'Familiar with these songs'. No less than the formal lessons on prosody with which this chapter began, Coleridge's verse lovingly teaches the children that we keep on becoming. Associationism is no longer an arbitrary set of associations imposed from without, but a series of patterns that our bodies induce and that then induce our bodies. Metre is not an abstract grid but a shelter that we found ourselves building without knowing. By rhyming 'farewell' with itself, we sublimate its meaning.

It is important to acknowledge that in a real sense I am disfiguring these poems by excavating their buried rhymes. For this aural coincidence exists on the threshold of our perceptual capacities; they are factors to which we do not pay conscious attention, but which condition the manner in which we pay attention. They are, that is to say, the 'medicated atmosphere, or ... wine' that induces susceptibility. In this manner, Coleridge's verse actuated truths to which his philosophical writings only groped. This truth traverses comparatively 'free' works such as the conversation poem sequence, and more obviously metrical productions, such as 'Kubla Khan', which shuttles between tetrameter, tetrameter catalectic, pentameters, hendecasyllables and alexandrines.[19] This prosodic virtuosity might seem to give the lie to Coleridge's claim to have composed the work in a visionary trance. Yet, just as was the case in 'Frost at Midnight' and 'The Nightingale', such prosodic structure can exist on the very threshold of conscious awareness. Freud held that we dreamed in language; we can certainly dream in prosody.

The kind of prosody in which we dream depends, of course, on the rhythms and cultural influences that have constituted our upbringings. For Coleridge, the rhythms that came naturally were those in which he had been initiated as a young man, after which the scansion of ancient Greek lay on the tips of his fingers. Many of us will have had different forms of upbringing, which may make Coleridge's prosodic descriptions seem forbidding by contrast. Yet the specific terms and references that he reflexively employed (the iambs and dactyls that the earliest sections of this essay considered at length) matter less than the broader truth that they uncover: that our experience of poetry (and the world) is conditioned by rhythmical expectation and surprise.

Notes

1 *Memoir and Letters of Sara Coleridge*, ed. Edith Coleridge (London: H. S. King, 1875), 157.
2 Ibid., 157.
3 Ibid.
4 For a survey of this development, see Yopie Prins, 'What is Historical Poetics?', *Modern Language Quarterly*, 77.1 (2016), 13–40.
5 T. S. Omond, *English Metrists* (Oxford: Clarendon Press, 1921), 115.
6 George Saintsbury, *History of English Prosody: From the Twelfth Century to the Present Day*, 3 vols (London: Macmillan, 1906), III, 58.
7 For more on Coleridge's journalism for this venture (and the disputed nature of his contributions), see Derek Roper, 'Coleridge and the Critical Review', *Modern Language Review*, 55 (1960), 11–16.
8 Meredith Martin, *The Rise and Fall of Meter* (Princeton University Press, 2012).

9 *Specimens of the Table Talk of Samuel Taylor Coleridge* (London: John Murray, 1836), 264.

10 Ibid., 265n.

11 Edwin Guest, *A History of English Rhythms* (London: William Pickering, 1838).

12 Joshua Steele, *Prosodia Rationalis: or, an Essay towards Establishing the Melody and Measure of Speech, to Be Expressed and Perpetuated by Peculiar Symbols* (London, 1779), 89.

13 Derek Attridge, 'The Case for the English Dolnik; or, How Not to Introduce Prosody', *Poetics Today*, 33 (2012), 1–26 (at 11).

14 Charles I. Patterson, 'An Unidentified Criticism by Coleridge Related to "Christabel"', *PMLA*, 67 (1952), 973–88.

15 The first three of these examples come from *SWF* I, 205; the final one comes from marginal notes entered into a fly leaf of the Theobald edition of Shakespeare, which can be found in *Coleridge's Shakespearean Criticism*, ed. T. M. Raysor, 2 vols (Cambridge University Press, 1930), II, 121.

16 Patterson, 'An Unidentified Criticism by Coleridge', 983.

17 *BL* I, 266. On metre as an intoxicant see Anya Taylor, 'Coleridge and the Pleasures of Verse', *Studies in Romanticism*, 40 (2001), 547–69 (at 566).

18 I borrow the phrase from Oliver Goldstein, in his brilliant reading of blank-verse rhymes within Charles Doughty's *The Dawn in Britain*, in 'Radical Conservatism and Victorian Poetry: 1830–1906' (unpublished dissertation, University of Cambridge, 2020).

19 I have explored this metrical hybridity in more depth, in 'The Sonic Organization of "Kubla Khan"', *Studies in Romanticism*, 57 (2018), 243–64.

8

MICHAEL GAMER AND JEFFREY N. COX

Coleridge and the Theatre

Coleridge's career as a playwright has been obscured by a long-standing, now outdated, view about the nature of 'Romantic drama'. Writers from Joanna Baillie to William Wordsworth, scholars contended, were either ignorant of the stage or else rejected it.[1] Their reasons lay in the supposed corrupt taste of the times: theatres dominated by the gothic sensationalism of Matthew Lewis, the morally questionable plays of August von Kotzebue and the rising domestic melodrama. The only option, they maintained, was writing for the closet: what Byron called 'mental theatre'.[2]

Coleridge's literary career firmly contradicts such views. We often forget that the first half of the famous 'golden year' that produced *Lyrical Ballads* (1798) yielded not poetry but rather two plays: Coleridge's *Osorio* and Wordsworth's *The Borderers*. So hopeful were the authors that their tragedies would be produced that the Wordsworths travelled to London to lobby for their acceptance (*WL* I, 195). It was only after receiving rejections that the two began to hatch various plans that would culminate in *Lyrical Ballads*. Had Richard Brinsley Sheridan at Drury Lane or Covent Garden's manager, Thomas Harris, accepted these early works, the history of Romanticism would look very different. Writing to a friend after the triumphant opening night of Coleridge's *Remorse* (1813), Robert Southey surmised that, had *Osorio* been accepted, 'the author might have produced a play as good every season: with my knowledge of Coleridge's habits, I verily believe that he would'.[3]

Even with this early rejection, Coleridge remained committed to the stage throughout his career. From *The Fall of Robespierre* (1794) to *Zapolya* (1818), he reworked not only traditional tragedy but also popular gothic drama and melodrama. His *Remorse* (1813) was the most successful new tragedy of the period. *Zapolya*, written at Byron's request for Drury Lane Theatre, though eventually rejected there, found a home at the Surrey Theatre, revised with Coleridge's blessing by Thomas John Dibdin as a melodrama. And while his reasons for writing plays were many, certainly much of the drama's attraction lay in the theatre's elevated cultural status and significant financial rewards. A novel or collection of poems might fetch an established author between £50 and £200 at the turn of the nineteenth century, but a successful play could earn many times that sum. Reflecting on *Remorse*'s success, Coleridge noted with satisfaction, 'It has been a good thing for the Theatre. They will get £8,000 or £10,000 by it, and I shall get more than all my literary labours put together, nay, thrice as much' (*CL* III, 437).

Like other Romantic playwrights, Coleridge had to overcome a series of cultural divisions arising from ingrained notions of 'high' and 'low'. Some of his best dramatic writing, in fact, traverses oppositions between 'high' dramatic tradition and 'low' theatrical tactics, uniting tragedy (fit for treating history and its men of high estate) and other popular genres (seen as suitable only for comedy and common domestic life). It also shows an acute awareness of the divided theatrical terrain of the age. Coleridge wrote at a time when the so-called 'patent' theatres – called such because the government granted them a monopoly on the performance of spoken drama – had to compete with the many 'illegitimate' or 'minor' houses, which had to traffic in new stage techniques and forms. In all of his plays he draws both on tragedy, from the Greeks to Shakespeare, and on the newest developments in the contemporary theatre. His hybrid dramas also reflect the struggles his characters face in working out the relations between private emotions and public actions.

This balancing act had Friedrich Schiller as its pivot. While by the late 1790s the German drama was largely identified with the works of Kotzebue and seen as salacious and possibly seditious, early British interest had centred on Schiller and other young German playwrights inspired by Shakespeare. Henry Mackenzie's groundbreaking 'Account of the German Theatre' (1788) had started the cultural trend, singling out Schiller's *The Robbers* as proof that German writers were emerging, thanks to English models, from the thrall of false French standards of taste. Given first as a public address and later published as an essay, Mackenzie's account found enthusiastic reception throughout Britain, and *The Robbers* was translated into English in 1792. Borrowing a copy in November 1794, Coleridge could not contain his excitement: 'My God, Southey, who is this Schiller, this convulser of the heart? Did he write his tragedy amid the yelling of fiends? [...] Why have we ever called Milton sublime?' (*CL* I, 122). Publishing his first volume of *Poems* (1796) two years later, he included a sonnet lavishly praising Schiller as a 'Bard tremendous in sublimity'. His note to the poem goes even further:

A Winter midnight – the wind high – and 'The Robbers' for the first time! – The readers of SCHILLER will conceive what I felt. SCHILLER introduces no supernatural beings; yet his human beings agitate and astonish more than all the *goblin* rout – even of Shakespeare. (*CPW* II, i, 72–73)

Coleridge's sonnet and note show him positioning himself in relation to the most popular English literary mode of the 1790s, the gothic, whose fondness for depicting supernatural scenes of horror and terror was especially reviled by late eighteenth-century reviewers.[4] What renders Schiller superior to other writers, even Shakespeare and Milton, is his ability to 'agitate and astonish' readers without introducing the supernatural. Instead, his 'human beings' produce this feeling of sublime encounter by containing the infinite and impossible within themselves. The best dramatic writing, Coleridge suggests, is that which moves audiences without recourse to spirits or stage tricks, producing the effect of the supernatural by tapping the seemingly unknowable depths of the soul.

Writing two decades later, in Chapter 14 of *Biographia Literaria* (1817), Coleridge revisited these issues in his account of the writing of *Lyrical Ballads*. In planning that volume, he recounts, he and Wordsworth chose to divide their labour via this same question of the supernatural:

> [M]y endeavours should be directed to persons and characters supernatural, or at least romantic [...] Mr. Wordsworth on the other hand was to propose to himself as his object, to give the charm of novelty to things of every day, and to excite a feeling analogous to the supernatural. (*BL* II, 6–7),

In this clean designation of roles, Wordsworth was to awaken readers to 'the wonders of the world before us', while he himself would infuse his supernatural poems with 'a human interest' to procure 'that willing suspension of disbelief [...] which constitutes poetic faith' (*BL* II, 7). Readers examining Coleridge's two most significant contributions to the *Lyrical Ballads* project, 'The Rime of the Ancyent Marinere' (1798) and 'Christabel' (intended for but not published in 1800), however, will find muddier waters. Each presents scenes exuberantly supernatural, such as the Spectre Ship of the 'Rime' or the visitation of Christabel's ghostly Mother as she and Geraldine prepare for bed. Yet both also cultivate haunting effects from nature and the everyday, whether a sight of sea-snakes swimming in ocean waters (which triggers the Mariner's redemption) or a guard dog howling at an April moon half-hidden by clouds (the scene of Christabel's night adventures). In his own poems, then, Coleridge consistently plays both sides of this supernatural–natural divide, and another passage from the *Biographia* potentially captures why. '[T]he excellence aimed at' in the supernatural poetry, he explains, 'was to consist in the interesting of the affections by the dramatic truth of the emotions, as would naturally accompany such situations' (*BL* II, 6). Here, the phrase 'dramatic truth' is especially telling. It shows Coleridge not only insisting on psychological realism regardless of supernatural subject matter, but also locating that sense of 'truth' – even in poetry – in a 'dramatic' medium.

Coleridge's admiration for Schiller as a dramatist of truth in emotion was lifelong rather than a passing fancy. His esteem led him, after the publication of *Lyrical Ballads*, to undertake a monumental translation of the second two parts of Schiller's seminal *Wallenstein* trilogy, which he published in 1800. Throughout his career, Coleridge would return not just to Schiller's sublimity but also to his depictions of inner emotion and external action in conflict. Among his many excellences, Schiller embodied for Coleridge above all things a way of imagining how a *modern* tragic drama – one retaining Shakespeare's virtues while eschewing his '*goblin* rout' – could be imagined for the Romantic stage.

We can already see this balancing of old and new, public and private, in *The Fall of Robespierre, an Historic Drama* (1794). Written with Robert Southey in Bristol while the two were hatching plans to form a communal 'Pantisocracy' in Pennsylvania, the play offers a compressed account of the events of 8 and 9 Thermidor (26 and 27 July), when Bertrand Barère (Barrere in the play) joined allies of the already executed Danton to condemn Robespierre for seeking a dictatorship. After a brief escape, Robespierre was seized on 27 July 1794 and summarily guillotined. News of the events reached London on 16 August, and Southey later indicated to Henry Nelson Coleridge that his part was 'written with newspapers before me, as fast as newspaper could be put into blank verse'.[5] Coleridge and Southey were not alone in finding Robespierre's death suitable for tragedy. As Matthew Buckley notes, newspapers including *The Times* drew on Shakespearean prototypes to describe the rapidly changing situation.[6] Such reports even shaped Coleridge's Shakespeare-influenced first act, which opens not by putting public events into blank verse, but rather by imagining the private motives behind them, the kind of internal emotional struggles he admired in Schiller.

The play begins with Barrere in private contemplation of Robespierre's motivations:

> I fear the Tyrant's *soul* –
> Sudden in action, fertile in resource,
> And rising awful 'mid impending ruins;
> In splendor gloomy, as the midnight meteor,
> That fearless thwarts the elemental war.
> When last in secret conference we met,
> He scowl'd upon me with suspicious rage,
> Making his eye the inmate of my bosom.
> I know he scorns me – and I feel, I hate him –
> Yet there is in him that which makes me tremble! *[Exit.]*
>
> (I, 3–12)[7]

Barrere may refer in passing to the stormy external world of revolutionary and counter-revolutionary violence, but ultimately he seeks insight into the 'Tyrant's *soul*', that elusive entity discernible only in unguarded moments of 'secret conference'. Differences of political principle may provide public justification for Barrere's opposition, but it is personal animosity ('I feel, I hate him') that motivates him. The scene even re-inscribes this internalization as the Thermidorians Tallien and Legendre in turn examine Barrere to find 'Th'imprison'd secret struggling in the face' (I, 21).

This embrace of the private is most pronounced in the second scene, centred on the one character Coleridge invented: Tallien's mistress Adelaide. Adelaide laments the losses she sees attending political change – 'this new freedom! at how dear a price / We've bought the seeming good! The peaceful virtues / [...] / All sacrificed to liberty's wild riot' (I, 198–99, 202) – and then sings to Tallien of domestic pleasures:

> Tell me, on what holy ground
> May domestic peace be found?
> Halcyon daughter of the skies,
> Far on fearful wing she flies,
> From the pomp of scepter'd state,
> From the rebel's noisy hate.
>
> In a cottag'd vale she dwells
> List'ning to the Sabbath bells!   (I, 210–25)

Adelaide's song invites us to leave behind both the monarchy's 'scepter'd state' and the 'rebel's noisy hate' to find solace in a rural spot. There, one might find an untainted point of view from which political criticism can still be made. As a literary device in British poetry, the figure of the rural retreat from worldly strife goes back through William Cowper's *The Task* (1785) to, at least, Anne Finch's 'Nocturnal Reverie' (1713). Coleridge would return to it repeatedly in the poems of the 1790s: sometimes as a literal spot (his rural cottage in 'Reflections on Having Left a Place of Retirement'), sometimes as a purely imaginative refuge (as with the frost and the fire-grate in 'Frost at Midnight') and sometimes a combination of both (as with 'This Lime-Tree Bower My Prison'). That such a retreat from the world of politics might also enable political critique of a cooler sort is most apparent in his 'Fears in Solitude', where Coleridge first places himself in a quiet nook and from that place of seclusion calls on his countrymen to reflect on their own warlike nature.

No such retreat is available in *The Fall of Robespierre* as Tallien effectively dismisses Adelaide's plea, dragging her back into the world of political strife by reminding her that her brother has been executed by the Revolution.

All thought of a separate peace, he argues, must give way to 'vengeance on these patriot murderers' (I, 237). Other conspirators (including Barrere) then enter, and any hope of private respite is swept aside by calls to public duty. Accompanied by cries from the street of '*No Tyrant! Down with the Tyrant!*' (I, 271), they rush off to the Convention, Tallien swearing by 'the holy poniard, that stabbed Caesar' that he will kill Robespierre.

While his opponents seek an inner self behind public masks, Robespierre, the 'Incorruptible', believes there should be no gap between words and inner thought. Where others seek secret meanings, he lives entirely in public language as a supposedly unmediated image of his inner life. This is why he can be quickly defeated once his opponents publicly label him 'tyrant'. With Robespierre's public speech silenced by the Convention, there is nothing left: no secret self to fall back on when his public voice is stilled. Significantly, he does not appear at all in the final act, as his fate is sealed. His death is not Tallien's promised private stabbing but a juridical murder. The journalistic nature of Southey's second and third acts reinforce this erasure of the private, as the private lives evoked in Coleridge's first act are overwhelmed by public events.

The Fall of Robespierre already stages the struggle between public life and private retirement that would play out in different ways not just in *Osorio/Remorse* and *Zapolya* but also in 'Ode to the Departing Year', 'Fears in Solitude' and 'France: An Ode'. The play also confirms Coleridge and Southey's awareness of the contemporary stage, since they were not the only dramatists responding to contemporary events. Since news of the storming of the Bastille first reached Britain in July 1789, London theatres had seized on events in France as fodder for new plays: Robert Merry and Charles Bonner's pantomime *The Picture of Paris* (1790) epitomizes this trend. By the summer of 1794, there already existed several dramatic representations of Robespierre as a villain, including John Bartholomew's *Fall of the French Monarchy; or, Louis XVI* (1794) and Edmund John Eyre's *Maid of Normandy; or, The Death of the Queen of France* (1794).[8] Composed in their wake, *The Fall of Robespierre* shares a number of features with these plays, chronicling events in Paris while pointedly asking whether revolutionary liberty might mask darker urges towards violence and libertinism. Coleridge and Southey's play thus stands at the end of an interesting but short tradition of revolutionary docu-dramas.

For by the time Coleridge came to draft *Osorio* in 1797, the situation at home in an England at war had deteriorated – particularly for British writers sympathetic to revolutionary principles. The autumn of 1794 saw William Pitt's government crackdown on radical activity, placing several members of the London Corresponding Society on trial for treason and suspending habeas corpus. The government's Licenser of Plays, John Larpent, began to block stage productions referring to events in Paris, silently expressing the fear that an audience hearing the radical speeches of a figure like Robespierre – even when presented as a villainous tyrant – might be spurred to radical action. With the possibility of staging a play on current events effectively barred, radical-leaning writers like Southey and Coleridge turned to historical subjects to explore their ideas. Southey responded with *Joan of Arc* (1796), an epic poem set in fifteenth-century France to which Coleridge contributed several passages. And in the following year, Coleridge began work on *Osorio*, a tragedy set in sixteenth-century Spain. Like *Joan of Arc*, *Osorio* takes place against a backdrop of war and religious oppression, the forces of the Inquisition acting as agents of repression in ways that would have resonated with audiences familiar with government tyranny at home.

In *Osorio*, Coleridge pits a Schillerian analysis of internal emotion against the popular sensationalist drama; at the same time, he self-consciously wields sensational tactics while critiquing them. With increasing competition from the so-called 'minor' houses – which, legally barred from performing 'legitimate', spoken drama, were inventing new kinds of theatre – the patent theatres at Drury Lane and Covent Garden had to turn to music and sensational action to please changing audiences. We can see these forces at work most vividly in the play that Sheridan chose to stage in the same month that he rejected *Osorio*: Matthew Lewis's *The Castle Spectre* (1797). *Osorio* shares many traits with Lewis's play, which features a riveting ghost scene, thrilling escapes and a gripping musical score composed by Michael Kelly. Both place situations of distress and daring before their audiences, and both deal in the slow accumulation of tension punctuated by involuntary displays of emotion. But while Lewis focuses on thrilling his audience through plot twists – treating them to a roller-coaster ride of sensational feeling – Coleridge instead foregrounds how memory and powerful emotion impact character action. Lewis haunts from without, Coleridge from within.

Osorio thus opens not with the event that most fundamentally shapes its story – Osorio's attempt to have his older brother Albert assassinated and his subsequent disappearance – but with its aftermath three years later. His brother presumed dead, the villainous Osorio continues to press Maria, Albert's fiancée, to accept his death and to marry him. In this he is supported by his ageing father, Velez, who urges her in the play's opening scene to 'Not make the living wretched for the dead' (I, ii, 3). Albert, meanwhile, has returned home to Granada disguised as a Moor, determined not to reveal himself until he can probe his brother's conscience and determine whether Maria has kept her vows to him.

Centred on the machinations of one brother to displace his sibling and claim his betrothed, *Osorio* strongly recalls Schiller's *The Robbers* in its backstory and characterization. Like Albert, Schiller's Karl Moor returns disguised to a home where his brother now rules; like Albert, he uses his disguise to ascertain whether his fiancée Amalia still loves him. However, Coleridge is interested less in bold actions than in pursuing Schiller's exploration of the self by dramatizing his characters' emotions when placed under stress. Thus Albert, on seeing Maria for the first time – in conference with a Moresco woman, Alhadra, who has come to plead on behalf of her imprisoned husband, Ferdinand – '*sinks down, & hides his face in his garment*' (1, i, 265). Overcome by her presence, he is unable to act in the face of his own bewildered emotions. For, while her voice convinces him that 'She is no Traitress' (1, i, 274), her not appearing in mourning for him makes him believe that she has married Osorio. Rather than propelling the action, intense emotion, if anything, stymies action by shutting people down. Act 1 closes in stalemate: with Maria sworn to remain faithful to Albert against Osorio's urgings; with Albert refusing to come forward until he has fully tested Maria's love and Osorio's capacity to atone for his previous sins; and with Osorio believing his brother dead and determined to win Maria at any cost.

Such emotionally complex situations become a staple of the play as it progresses. Act 11 begins with Osorio attempting to employ his previous co-conspirator, Ferdinand, to conduct a mock-seance to trick Maria into believing Albert to be dead. Having previously employed Ferdinand to assassinate Albert, Osorio expects him to have no scruples over 'play[ing] the Sorcerer' (11, i, 28). What he does not bank on is Ferdinand's duplicity and moral conscience: that, years earlier, he was moved to spare Albert's life on learning his identity. What emerges is a scene with little action but replete with tension, underwritten by each character's distrust of the other. Wishing not to be Osorio's unwitting tool a second time, Ferdinand voices concern that he will be recognized, persuading Osorio instead to approach a 'Stranger' (11, i, 27) new to the neighbourhood who claims to be able to 'bring the dead to life again' (11, i, 40). This 'Wizard' (11, i, 134) is, of course, the recently arrived Albert in disguise. In one of Coleridge's most highly wrought scenes, a disguised Albert finds himself not just negotiating with the brother who arranged his attempted murder but also agreeing to stage a mock-religious ritual to convince his love that he is dead:

> ALBERT.   Declare your business!
> OSORIO. I love a Lady, and she would love me,
>   But for an idle and fantastic scruple.
>
>   ...

In truth, this Lady lov'd another Man,
  But he has perish'd –
ALBERT.   What? you kill'd him? hey?
OSORIO. I'll dash thee to the Earth, if thou but think'st it.
  Thou Slave, thou Galley-slave! thou Mountebank!
  I leave thee to the Hangman!
ALBERT.   Fare you well!
  I pity you, Osorio! even to anguish!
      (*Albert retires off the stage*)
OSORIO (*recovering himself*). 'Twas ideotcy! I'll tie myelf to an Aspen
  And wear a Fool's Cap. – Ho! (*calling after Albert*)
ALBERT. (*returning*) … I listen to you.
OSORIO.   In a sudden tempest
  Did Albert perish – he, I mean, the Lover –
  The fellow –
ALBERT.   Nay, speak out, 'twill ease your heart
  To call him Villain! – why stand'st thou aghast?
  Men think it natural to hate their rivals!
OSORIO (*hesitating and half doubting whether he should proceed*).
  Now till she knows him dead, she will not wed me!
ALBERT (*with eager vehemence*).
  Are you not wedded then? merciful God!
  Not wedded to Maria? –
OSORIO.   Why, what ails thee?
  Art mad or drunk? why look'st thou upward so?
  Dost pray to Lucifer, prince of the Air?
ALBERT. Proceed. I shall be silent.
      (*Albert sits, and leaning on the Table hides his face*)   (II, ii, 83–85, 91–98, 101–12)

This passage exemplifies *Osorio*'s rapid exchanges of intense feeling: a scene almost embarrassingly bare of incident nevertheless crackles with the electricity of a duel. Where a similar scene in *The Castle Spectre* would produce swashbuckling action, as when the hero leaps from a window into the arms of rescuers, here little is resolved and much felt. Concealed by his disguise, Albert tries to probe his guilty brother's conscience without being discovered. Yet the life-and-death nature of the encounter renders him perpetually vulnerable to emotional turmoil as Osorio reveals his own treachery and Maria's fidelity.

Acts III and IV intensify this regimen of sparse action and deep play. With Velez, Osorio and Maria assembled in a '*Hall of Armory with an altar*' (III, i), the disguised Albert conducts his seance, featuring sensational lighting effects and accompanied by strange music and a chorus. He has been instructed by Osorio to have the ritual yield a token from Albert's spirit: in this case, a picture that Maria gave to Albert years earlier, but that Osorio has since procured secretly. Wishing to sting his brother into remorse and repentance, Albert covertly substitutes a picture of his own attempted assassination. Each character's response to the appearance of this new image on the altar foregrounds the complexities at play. The sceptical Maria, suspecting 'some trick' (III, i, 12) yet acknowledging the power of 'Fancy' and 'bodily creepings' to 'give substance to the shadow' (III, i, 113–14), swoons at the appearance of the conjured picture. Assuming it to be the one she gave Albert, she faints without taking in its details. In spite of having commissioned the entire scene, Osorio is thrown *'in a state of stupor'* (III, i, 118) as the picture appears, and in his absence of mind also fails to take in its actual content. Velez in many ways acts the most ambiguously: snatching up the picture and hiding it in his robes, he momentarily exits the scene with Osorio to prevent Maria examining it when she regains consciousness. Apparently, he is so bent on duping her into marriage with his son that he, too, is unable to interpret the image.

Albert's substitution of one picture for another thus produces none of the effects on his audience that he intended. In each case, their anxieties and predispositions prevent them from seeing what is before their eyes. The situation is further compounded by the disguised Albert's unwillingness to act boldly. As Velez and Osorio exit, he finds himself alone with a disorientated Maria, yet fails to disclose his identity. Instead, he merely informs her that Albert 'was not murder'd' (III, i, 136) and urges her to meet him the next day. The scene dramatizes a great deal of emotional reaction, but these responses do not lead to immediate action, as Coleridge debunks the power of spectacle to determine, or even mould, behaviour. The characters instead remain true to their predilections and experiences, so much so that their emotional states literally obstruct their vision. While in the second edition of *Lyrical Ballads* (1800) Wordsworth would criticize the Ancient Mariner as someone who 'does not act but is continually acted upon' (*LB* 791), *Osorio* demonstrates the degree to which questions of passivity, emotional stasis and incapacity are central to understanding the poetry and plays of the 1790s. We can further trace the influence of poems like the 'Rime', 'Christabel' and 'Love' most immediately in longer poetic romances such as Walter Scott's *Lay of the Last Minstrel* (1805) and *Marmion* (1808), but it extends well into the nineteenth century: from the poetry of John Keats (both 'The Eve of St Agnes' and 'La Belle Dame sans Merci') to that of Alfred Tennyson, whose 'Lady of Shalott' dramatizes a heroine in stasis spurred into acting on her desire.

Osorio's drama of emotional stasis only moves forward after its central incantation scene, and then only when Velez congratulates his son on his stratagem, especially the picture of the assassination. At this point, Osorio finally perceives that he has been duped by Ferdinand, to whom he had provided the original picture to give to the disguised Albert for the ritual. Vowing revenge, he arranges for Albert's imprisonment by the Inquisition and plans to confront Ferdinand alone in some nearby caves. Even in this climate of renewed action, however, emotional responses still predominate – as when Albert, trying to convert Osorio, is '*almost over-come by his feelings*' (v, ii, 101) – until we get to the climax to the play, which gave Coleridge considerable difficulties when he came to revise *Osorio* for the stage.

Writing on the transformation of *Osorio* into *Remorse*, J. C. C. Mays concludes that Coleridge made few revisions to his play before late spring of 1812 (*CPW* III, ii, 1028), when two developments probably turned him back to it. The first was his entering into negotiations, first with the Haymarket and then with Drury Lane, to produce his tragedy for the stage. The second was the publication of volume III of Joanna Baillie's *Plays on the Passions* (1812), a series of dramas Coleridge admired. In the introduction to that volume, Baillie had written, 'Of all our passions, Remorse and Jealousy appear to me to be the best fitted for representation'.[9] We cannot know for certain whether this comment served to spur Coleridge to revision. What we do know is that Coleridge changed the title of his play to *Remorse* at this time, as if to announce its allegiance with Baillie's works.[10]

Remorse had its premiere at Drury Lane Theatre on 25 January 1813. It played for twenty nights: the longest run of a tragedy in the still young nineteenth century. Staged during the Peninsular Wars, it appeared at a time profoundly different from that in which *Osorio* was first conceived. As John David Moore and Julie Carlson have shown, audiences interpreted Coleridge's villain not as an embodiment of 1790s Pittite repression, but rather as a commentary on Napoleon.[11] His play having acquired a different political valence, Coleridge rewrote significant portions to improve its stageability. These revisions, some made on the advice of the theatre, included renamed characters, significant cuts, an altered ending and a new opening scene to establish the background to the play. While Coleridge complained of the expositional scene as 'Prologue play[ing] Dialogue with Dumby', he did agree to the changes requested.[12]

Among its many clarifications, *Remorse* strengthens its characterization of Alvar (renamed from Albert) as a freethinker on religious matters. Retaining the lines from *Osorio* that Teresa (renamed from Maria) 'hath no faith in Holy Church [...] / Her lover school'd her in some newer nonsense (II, i, 34–35), *Remorse* adds that in the battle for the Belgic states Alvar has fought on the 'better cause' (I, i, 169) against his Catholic homeland.

This detail strengthens our sense of his religious nonconformity by attaching it to political action. Thus, while Ordonio (renamed from Orsorio) repeatedly proclaims his intellectual independence from moral checks and social bonds, Alvar is presented by Coleridge as a competing model of liberation, but one who is reassuringly Protestant, carefully principled and selflessly conscientious. It is easy to see how, presented with this contrast, British audiences aligned the hero of *Remorse* with their own cause and its villain with that of Napoleon.

Most suggestive of all of Coleridge's revisions, however, are those attending Alhadra's final speech, which had closed *Osorio*:

> I thank thee Heaven! thou hast ordain'd it wisely,
> That still extremes bring their own cure. That point
> In misery, which makes the oppressed Man
> Regardless of his own life, makes him too,
> Lord of the Oppressor's — Knew I an hundred Men
> Despairing, but not palsied by despair,
> This arm should shake the Kingdoms of the World;
> The deep foundations of iniquity
> Should sink away, Earth groaning from beneath them;
> The strong-holds of the cruel Men should fall,
> Their Temples and their mountainous Towers should fall;
> Till desolation seem'd a beautiful thing.
> And all that were and had the Spirit of Life,
> Sang a new song to him who had gone forth,
> Conquering and still to conquer! (v, i, 201–15)

In the speech from *Osorio*, the emotion of despair – if one isn't 'palsied' by the strength of the emotion – can lead to revolt. Finally locating a feeling that can spur deeds, Coleridge in *Osorio* seems to grant the last word to the proponent of revolutionary emotion. Here we encounter, rather than inward remorse, outward revenge. As with *The Fall of Robespierre*, the play moves outward from private emotion to public action.

In the revised *Remorse*, the ultimate status of Alhadra's speech is far more elusive, and depends on which version of the play one encounters. For, although approved by the government's Licenser of Plays, the speech was excised in performance. Whether this decision was made by Coleridge or Drury Lane's management is unclear, but it is part of a larger pattern of radical revision to the play's final scene. In the stage version of the play, '*The doors of the dungeon are broken open, and in rush ALHADRA, and the band of Morescoes*' (v, i, 182); Ordonio, accused of Ferdinand's murder, confesses and dies at the hands of Alhadra, who is then hurried off the stage by the Morescoes. This means that the version of *Remorse* seen by audiences ends not with Alhadra's call to 'shake the Kingdoms of the World' but rather with a closing speech by Alvar, who describes how 'Just Heaven instructs us' through our 'inward Monitress' of 'Conscience' and, where conscience fails, remorse (V, i, 215–17). In the stage version, remorse trumps revenge and morality cordons off revolt. This melodramatic resolution – where domesticity provides a check against rebellious emotions – defeats any tragic turn.

Coleridge restored Alhadra's speech when he published the text of *Remorse* in February of 1813. In its printed form, *Remorse* offers a more ambivalent political vision, where Alhadra's vision of a transformed world remains in unresolved tension with Alvar's embrace of more traditional values. His claims to be able to tame passion within marriage and violent feelings within the moral structure of atonement stand uneasily next to his brother's fate. This mixed ending extends to its handling of genre, where Alvar and Teresa kneel to receive Valdez's blessing as in a comic denouement, but must do so with Ordonio's corpse lying nearby: a joining of comedy and tragedy that would become an often criticized feature of stage melodrama.

Coleridge would turn again to issues of tradition and innovation, domesticity and revolt, in his final play, *Zapolya: A Christmas Tale, in Two Parts*. Like *Remorse*, *Zapolya* loudly proclaims its canonical ties: to Shakespeare's *Winter's Tale* (to justify the significant gap in time between the two parts) and to Aeschylus (as a source of its two-part structure of prelude and play). Such links have allowed later commentators to align *Zapolya* with dramatic tradition against newer models. In opposition to this portrait, however, are two competing factors. First, Coleridge chose to invoke Schiller, the great exemplar of contemporary historical tragedy, by borrowing the villain's name, Pestalutz, from Schiller's *Death of Wallenstein* (*CPW* III, ii, 1334). Second, he allowed *Zapolya* to be performed in revised form at a so-called minor theatre, the Surrey, as a melodrama. The combination suggests that Coleridge, always a champion of Shakespeare and canonical tragedy, also cared deeply about the stageability of his plays, believing that dramatic tradition could be placed in fruitful dialogue with new forms.

Zapolya tackles history in a layered way. While presenting itself as a dramatization of a remote episode of Hungarian history, its two parts – 'The Usurper's Fortune' and 'The Usurper's Fate' – suggest a more general exploration of politics and governance. This allegorical tendency is confirmed by its patterns of allusion. The play's setting of 'Illyria', for example, may just be another Shakespearean nod – this time to *Twelfth Night* – but it also is the name that Napoleon chose to create an imperial province in the Balkans. As with *Osorio* and *Remorse*, Coleridge's choice of a remote setting offers him the opportunity to inscribe into his play an allegory of the French Revolution and the subsequent rise of Napoleon. Rent by military usurpation and internal conflict, Coleridge's Illyria looks a lot like Robespierre's France.

The first part or prelude to *Zapolya*, not unlike the part of Schiller's trilogy Coleridge did not translate, *Wallenstein's Camp*, begins with a great deal of military bustle and hints of various plots. Emerick, a fairly stock villain, connives in the death of Andreas, the lawful king, and in a slander against the queen that her son is a bastard. With the exception of the heroic Raab Kiuprili, he has united the military behind him; even Kiuprili's son Casimir sides with him against his father. Like Claudius from *Hamlet*, Emerick hopes that Zapolya will 'Offer[s] at once the royal bed and throne!' (I, i, 401); like Coleridge's own Ordonio, he occupies the roles of murderer, usurper and would-be seducer. As an illegitimate ruler who forces out the true royal family, he would also have appeared to audiences as yet another stage Napoleon. The prelude ends with Emerick moving to seize power, but Kiuprili manages to escape the pretender's clutches and to rescue the pregnant queen. He is aided by Chef Ragozzi, who perishes in a civil war that follows, leaving an orphaned daughter, 'one of numberless / Planks from the same vast wreck' (II, i, 149–50) of Illyria taken over by a usurping villain.

While there is a dynastic struggle here and references, for example, to chieftains assembling at Temeswar, a one-time informal regional capital, *Zapolya* is not, like *The Fall of Robespierre*, so much 'An Historic Drama' as a romance of hidden identities and predestined lovers. Rather than picking up where its prelude left off, the play's second part opens twenty years later to allow various characters to grow into adulthood. Act I opens with Sarolta, the wise and virtuous wife of Casimir, discussing life at court with her attendant Glycine and echoing *The Fall of Robespierre*'s Adelaide in praising a quiet life in the country. Glycine has been betrothed to one of Casimir's lackeys, the villainous and cowardly Laska, but Sarolta already senses of Glycine that 'Something above thy rank there hangs about thee' (I, i, 65). Her premonition proves accurate: we learn that Glycine is not only the daughter of the deceased Chef Ragozzi but also beloved by a peasant boy, Bethlen, whose lowly upbringing during the civil war also conceals his noble heritage as Prince Andreas, the son of Queen Zapolya and true heir to the throne. Zapolya herself is revealed to be still alive in the second scene, but she and Kiuprili have had to remain hidden in a cave, wearing *'rude and savage garments'* (stage direction, II, i). Emerick, meanwhile, has proven himself to be a truly despicable ruler.

Publicly a tyrant and privately a libertine, he lusts after his supporter Casimir's wife, Sarolta, and plans to murder him and rape her.

Coleridge called this second part of *Zapolya* 'The Usurper's Fate', matching the prelude's 'The Usurper's Fortune'; but it is also labelled before Act I as 'Usurpation Ended; or, She Comes Again'. While the subtitles on the title page suggest the overarching orders of fate and fortune, the additional subtitle suggests more agency on the character's parts in ending the usurpation, with 'she' potentially referring to any of the three main women in the second part. Most obviously, Zapolya 'comes again', surviving to proclaim her son the rightful king, but Glycine and Sarolta also intervene at key moments. The warrior's daughter, Glycine, saves Bethlen/Andreas from the treachery of Emerick and Laska. Sarolta, meanwhile, defies Emerick, leads Casimir back to virtue and welcomes the restored royal family to her home at the play's close. With Emerick unmasked and the true identities of Glycine and Bethlen revealed, the 'assembled chieftains' of Illyria announce that they 'have deposed the tyrant' (IV, iii, 6) and unite Andreas and Glycine as king and queen. All the dangers of tyranny and the usurpation of power are resolved through the disguises and love plots of romance, managed here by the female characters.

The other feature Coleridge takes from romance or fairy tale involves the legend of the war-wolf or, to use the familiar term, werewolf: Glycine reveals that everyone believes the local forest to be the den of werewolves, vampires and other monsters (I, i, 337). In fact, Kiuprili, in his 'savage garments', has pretended to be a war-wolf to keep anyone from discovering that he and Zapolya have been hiding in a cave for twenty years. This ruse provides for much of the plot, with, for example, the lackey Laska claiming to have killed the war-wolf. Of course, the term 'war-wolf' also probably evoked the decades of war that had finally ended at Waterloo in 1815, the time when Coleridge commenced work on *Zapolya* (*CPW*, III, ii, 1329): here again Coleridge uses a play to think through the era of Napoleonic usurpation.[13]

Not offering actual Hungarian history, *Zapolya* appears more a meditation on the issues of the revolutionary Napoleonic era. In this, it joins *The Fall of Robespierre* and *Remorse* in its turn against the Terror and Napoleonic strongmen. William Hazlitt confirms this political valence when, in attacking the Lake Poets in the *Yellow Dwarf*, he links a speech by Kiuprili ('Prelude', I, 351–72) to a pro-monarchist speech given in the 'French House of Commons' (Howe xix, 202). Placing Kiuprili on the one side and Emerick and Casimir on the other, the prelude effectively restages the 1790s' pamphlet wars over the revolution led by Edmund Burke and Thomas Paine. The would-be king rehearses Paine's assault on inherited authority and tradition:

> Is it conscience,
> That a free nation should be handed down,
> Like the dull clods beneath our feet, by chance
> And the blind law of lineage?   ('Prelude', 1, 303–6)

Kiuprili offers a conservative quizzing of these arguments, asking what are the 'shallow sophisms of a *popular choice*? / What people? How convened?' ('Prelude', 1, 354–55). At times, Kiuprili sounds like all the opponents of Robespierre in Coleridge and Southey's play, trying to forestall Emerick's seizure of power by labelling him a 'remorseless tyrant' who will amuse the crowds 'with *sounds* of liberty' and warning of an Illyrian terror when 'liberty shall be proclaimed alone [...] Till Vengeance hath her fill' ('Prelude', II, 99–101, 103). Casimir looks beyond Paine and the early days of the Revolution to argue for the kind of military dictatorship created by Napoleon: 'What better claim can sov'reign wish or need, / Than the free voice of men who love their country? / Those chiefly who have fought for't?[...] Whence sprang the name of Emperor? Was it not / By Nature's fiat?' ('Prelude', 1, 315–17, 321–22). Against such claims, there is a running commentary on Emerick/Napoleon as sham king, as Emerick is described as 'this king of the Buskin! ... That from some vagrant actor's tyring room, / Hath stolen at once his speech and crown!' (III, ii, 102, 104–5). While Emerick can only play the ruler, the true nobility of Glycine and Bethlen shines through the masks they have been forced by circumstances to wear.

This Burkean sense of 'natural' nobility leads to a sense of the political order itself as a 'natural' extension of the family, as the political is dissolved in the domestic. While *The Fall of Robespierre* stages the absorption of the private and domestic into the public and political – and while *Remorse* ultimately refuses to choose between private emotion and public action – *Zapolya* readily presents the nation as an affective reflection of the family. As Andreas accepts the throne, he thanks not his supporters but his 'Heroic mother! — / But what can breath add to that sacred name?' (IV, iii, 43–44). In praising Kiuprili, he proclaims, 'loyalty is but the public form / Of the sublimest friendship'; here the political is literally the personal. Sarolta closes the play, claiming the right to serve still as their host and directly linking the national scene with hearth and home:

> None love their country, but who love their home:
> For freedom can with those alone abide,
> Who wear the golden chain, with honest pride,
> Of love and duty, at their own fire-side:
> While mad ambition ever doth caress
> Its own sure fate, in its own restlessness!   (IV, iii, 77–82)

'None love their country, but who love their home': this could easily be the motto of most of Coleridge's reflective poems of the later 1790s, from 'The Eolian Harp' and 'Frost at Midnight' to the more overtly political 'Fears in Solitude'. Here, however, it is worth noting just how different the context is. First published in 1817 and then performed at the Surrey Theatre the following year, *Zapolya*'s statement on local and national attachment appears in the years of civil unrest that followed the end of the Napoleonic Wars in 1815. His references to 'mad ambition' leading to 'Its own sure fate in its own restlessness' may invoke the fallen French emperor, but they also caution against those whose 'restlessness' might lead them to shed their 'golden chain / Of love and duty' to pursue reform at home. Such sentiments, while recalling the politics of the earlier poetry, are more closely aligned with the emerging dramatic form in which *Zapolya* would eventually appear: the melodrama, a form, as Peter Brooks argues, arising during the French Revolution to contain its radicalism on stage.[14]

Adapted by Thomas John Dibdin with Coleridge's approval, *Zapolya; or, The War Wolf: A Grand Melodrama* had its premiere at the Surrey Theatre on 9 February 1818. Given its many shifts in form during its composition, its final transformation into the popular melodrama should probably not surprise us. *Zapolya* is, in many ways, a play in search of a genre. Approached by Byron in March 1815 to write another play, Coleridge first indicated his desire to try his hand again at tragedy; by October, however, he had begun to call his play a 'dramatic Entertainment' (*CL* IV, 591) and by January had altogether abandoned 'tragedy' for other labels. When Byron left England for the Continent, Coleridge continued his negotiations with the theatre, working through Byron's friend Douglas Kinnaird and his publisher, John Murray. Writing to the latter on 6 June 1816, he states that he is completing 'two musical entertainments', working with 'the advice of a [theatre] manager'. He goes on to say that, while he wants *Zapolya*, as a *poem*, to be published as written, he understands that Kinnaird and the Drury Lane managers need to present it 'as a Melo-drama, with songs and choruses, & the Story transmuted into a domestic not a political occurrence – the Usurper to be made a Baron &c &c' (*CL* IV, 644). As J. C. C. Mays notes, Coleridge's decision to publish *Zapolya* as a 'poem in dialogue' had Drury Lane's blessing, 'on the reckoning that publication in this form would be an advantage to the melodrama' (*CPW* III, ii, 1330). *Zapolya* is thus resolutely a creation of the Regency stage, its text serving at once as the foundation of, and promotional tool for, the eventual stage drama. While the play was never performed at Drury Lane – and while Coleridge would be angered that Charles Robert Maturin's spectacular, gothic *Bertram*, considered on the recommendation of Walter Scott, would prove a success there – he nevertheless continued to search for a venue, finally hitting on the Surrey when Dibdin moved there as manager. Dibdin's adaptation played for ten nights; its success was great enough for Dibdin to choose it for his benefit night to close the season.

Like all of Coleridge's plays, *Zapolya* embodies his lifelong attempt to unite traditional drama with the contemporary stage practice, and to produce plays for a modern theatre open to the struggles of his day. Coleridge's interest in the drama extends well beyond these few plays: to various abandoned dramatic projects, to his translation of Schiller and to his famous critiques of Shakespeare. The concerns of a play such as *Zapolya* are also found in Coleridge's earlier poetic works, which explore the boundaries of public and private and how they might map onto the new political and domestic realities of the Revolutionary and then post-Waterloo years. As with his finest political poem, 'Fears in Solitude', Coleridge's dramatic works display a persistent antipathy not just to political violence and war but also to the simplistic dualisms (activity and passivity, patriotism and treason) that such unnatural states produce. It is also striking that 'conversation' as a path to 'dramatic truth' moves as a mode throughout Coleridge's most famous poems, whether the staged dialogues of 'The Rime' and 'The Foster Mother's Tale' or the imagined listeners of 'Frost at Midnight', 'This Lime-Tree Bower My Prison' and 'Dejection'. Coleridge the dramatist is also a creator of dramatic poems.

Notes

1 Such views both are on display in standard histories of the drama and theatre such as Allardyce Nicoll's *Early Nineteenth-Century Drama 1800–1850*, vol. IV of *A History of English Drama 1660–1900* (Cambridge University Press, 1960), and shape such fine critical readings of the *poetic* drama as Alan Richardson's *Mental Theater: Poetic Drama and Consciousness in the Romantic Age* (State College: Penn State University Press, 1988) and Michael Simpson's *Closet Performances: Political Exhibition and Prohibition in the Dramas of Byron and Shelley* (Stanford University Press, 1998).
2 *Byron's Letters and Journals*, ed. Leslie Marchand, 12 vols (London: John Murray, 1978), VIII, 210.
3 Letter to Grosvenor Charles Bedford, 27 January 1813, *CLRS*, 2212.
4 Cf. Michael Gamer, *Romanticism and the Gothic: Genre, Reception, and Canon Formation* (Cambridge University Press, 2000), 48–89.
5 *Literary Remains of Samuel Taylor Coleridge*, ed. Henry Nelson Coleridge, 4 vols (London, 1836–39), I, 3n.
6 Matthew Buckley, '"A Dream of Murder": The Fall of Robespierre and the Tragic Imagination', *Studies in Romanticism*, 44 (2005), 515–49. Cf. Daniel E. White, 'Introduction to *The Fall of Robespierre*', Introduction | Romantic Circles (romantic-circles.org).

7 All references to this and other plays by Coleridge are to *CPW*, III, and are cited parenthetically either by act and line number or by act, scene and line number.

8 Cf. Jeffrey N. Cox, 'Ideology and Genre in the Anti-Revolutionary Drama of the 1790s', *ELH*, 58 (1991), 579–610.

9 *Joanna Baillie, A Series of Plays ... on the Passions*, 3 vols (London: Longman, 1798, 1802, 1812), III, xiv–xv.

10 At least one reviewer noted the resemblance. Cf. *The Satirist* 12 (March 1813), 270.

11 Cf. John David Moore, 'Coleridge and the "modern Jacobinical drama": *Osorio, Remorse,* and the Development of Coleridge's Critique of the Stage, 1797–1816', *Bulletin of Research in the Humanities,* 85 (1982), 443–64; and Julie Carlson, *In the Theatre of Romanticism: Coleridge, Nationalism, Women* (Cambridge University Press, 1994).

12 Cf. note to the copy of the second edition of *Remorse* given to Sarah Hutchinson; cited in *CPW* II, 819n.

13 Cf. Frederick Burwick, *Playing to the Crowd: London Popular Theatre, 1780–1830* (New York: Palgrave, 2011), 55, which connects the war-wolf figure to Coleridge's political attacks upon the '"the hybrid monster" of Jacobinism'.

14 Peter Brooks, *The Melodramatic Imagination: Balzac, Henry James, Melodrama, and the Mode of Excess* (New Haven, CT: Yale University Press, 1995), 15.

9

ALAN VARDY

Coleridge the Walker

First, Coleridge was a prodigious walker. The recently completed Coleridge Way footpath from Nether Stowey to Linton covers fifty-one miles. Guides recommend completing the route in either four or seven days, depending on your fitness. Coleridge regularly walked it in a day, a 'jaunt down the Bristol-Channel' as William Hazlitt described it as they set off in the spring of 1798. That particular walk illustrates several things about the experience of walking with Coleridge. The first, and perhaps most commented on by his companions, was the outpouring of discourse while he walked. Kinetic energy converted into mental energy. Hazlitt described the process in comic terms via the addition to the scene of John Chester, Coleridge's neighbour in Stowey and later his companion in Germany, as a spellbound acolyte: '[he] kept on a sort of trot by the side of Coleridge, like a running footman by a state coach, that he might not lose a syllable of sound that fell from Coleridge's lips ... He scarcely opened his lips, much less offered an opinion the whole way.'[1]

Hazlitt mocks Chester, but clearly envies his closeness to Coleridge. Chester spoils Hazlitt's prospective experience by his presence. Nonetheless, part of the pleasure was in their shared physical prowess: 'We had a long day's march – (our feet kept time to the echoes of Coleridge's tongue) – through Minehead and by the Blue Anchor, and on to Linton, which we did not reach till near midnight, and where we had some difficulty in making a lodgement' (226). Coleridge's speech provided the rhythmic beat propelling them forward. Arriving around midnight, they had some difficulty finding lodging, but in the end managed to roust someone and, in Hazlitt's phrase, were 'repaid ... for their fatigue by some excellent rashers of fried bacon and eggs' (226–27). Their pleasure is complex: biochemical muscle fatigue (a pleasant ache), satisfaction at their physical prowess and relish in devouring their reward. Hazlitt's memory of this particular moment remains vivid twenty years later. The walk itself provided aesthetic pleasure, especially along the Somerset coast into Devon: 'We walked for miles and miles on the brown heaths overlooking the Channel, with the Welsh hills beyond, and at times descended into little sheltered valleys close by the seaside' (227). They strode across headlands, down to beaches and up again – visual pleasure becomes inseparable from physical pleasure, beauty and sublimity unfold as they move. Such varied aesthetic events draw them on.

The following day the plan was to walk out from Linton to see the Valley of the Rocks, the towering rock formation just outside the village. Before they could set out, 'a thunder-storm came on ... and Coleridge was running out bare-headed to enjoy the commotion of the elements in the *Valley of the Rocks*, but as if in spite, the clouds only muttered a few angry sounds, and let fall a few refreshing drops' (227). Despite Hazlitt's gentle mockery, the scene reveals another Coleridgean mode – the ecstatic, impulsive letting go that risks everything. He makes himself subject to the weather. The day proceeded as planned: a tour of the rocks, a long walk along the sands and a steady stream of conversation. Coleridge descanted on his plan with Wordsworth to write a poem set in the valley, on Virgil, on Thomson's 'greatness', on Cowper as the 'best modern poet', on the plan for *Lyrical Ballads*, on poetic diction and 'ordinary language', on Shakespeare's language, on his dislike of Gray, Pope and Dr Johnson, on Burke's superior political rhetoric compared with Fox and Pitt, on Richardson over Fielding and on and on, culminating with a discussion of 'disinterestedness' – one of Hazlitt's favourite topics (228).[2]

Hazlitt's account was written twenty years after the fact and has its own motives, primarily self-fashioning. As a result, irony enters his descriptions, post facto. The most extensive and contemporaneous accounts of walking with Coleridge are provided in Dorothy Wordsworth's journals, beginning with the 'Alfoxden Notebook' and more extensively in her journal of their 1803 tour of Scotland. In the late winter of 1798, they walked together continually, particularly in February, culminating (from a literary perspective) with their walk on the 26th:

> [W]alked with Coleridge nearly to Stowey after dinner. A very clear afternoon. We lay sidelong on the turf, and gazed on the landscape till it melted into more than natural loveliness. The sea very uniform, of a pale greyish blue, only one distant bay, bright and blue as a sky; had there been a vessel sailing up it, a perfect image of delight. Walked to the top of a high hill to see a fortification. Again sat down to feed upon the prospect; a magnificent scene, *curiously* spread out for even minute inspection, though so extensive that the mind is afraid to calculate its bounds. A winter prospect shows every cottage, every farm, and the forms of distant trees, such as in summer have no distinguishing mark. (*DWJ* 8)[3]

It's easy to imagine the reciprocity of this walk: shared curiosity, Coleridge's interest in Roman fortifications, Dorothy's precise rendering of the scene, Coleridge's discourse on the nature of the sublime – a view 'so extensive that the mind is afraid to calculate its bounds'. The similarity to Kant's mathematical sublime notwithstanding, this Burkean anxiety is probably one of Coleridge's contributions to their shared experience. Dorothy shows Coleridge the world in its transitory particularity, the sea's 'pale, greyish blue'. They drink in the scene in a state of extreme languor 'sidelong on the turf', a Coleridgean principle of seeing, feeling and composition since 'Effusion XXXV' ('The Aeolian Harp'). The revelation of so many visual objects simultaneously delights and intimidates. The walk with its rich textures and intense intellectual engagements is the product of their growing relationship, an ongoing series of negotiations as they negotiate the terrain. The result is clearly productive in literary terms, as the journal entry attests and as the echo of his similar speculation in 'This Lime-Tree Bower My Prison', 'some fair bark perhaps' (*CPW* I, i, 352, line 24) confirms. This walk reconstitutes the site where he imagined Charles Lamb and his friends experiencing the sunset, including the speculation about whether a ship sailing up the Bristol Channel would aesthetically complete the scene – 'delight', in Dorothy's phrase. This walk literally provides compensation for the missed walk from the previous summer.

Coleridge displayed intense visual acuity before he met Dorothy, the 'moment' when he glimpsed the skylark 'gleaming on sunny wing' in 'Reflection on Having Left a Place of Retirement', for example, or the 'transparent foliage' capturing the light of the sunset in Thomas Poole's garden at the end of 'This Lime-Tree Bower My Prison'. Dorothy shares this penchant for 'minute inspection'. One of her most famous isolated details, 'One only leaf upon the top of the tree – the sole remaining leaf – danced round and round like a rag blown by the wind' (*DWJ* 9) migrates to 'Christabel':

> The one red leaf, the last of its clan,
> That dances as often as dance it can,
> Hanging so light, and hanging so high,
> On the topmost twig that looks up at the sky.
>
> (*CPW* I, i, 484, lines 51–54)

This passage is often understood as an instance of Coleridge making use of Dorothy's journal, which doubtless it is, but the *use* isn't simply the borrowing of an image. The poem invokes their shared experience of the original sight, and memorializes their fleeting aesthetic pleasure. A small ephemeral event, directing their attention to the 'sole leaf', preserves the moment; neither account has any other purpose – the lines in the poem are apropos of nothing – beauty and its memorialization for its own sake.

Their fervent walking in the Quantocks confirmed Coleridge's famous first impression of Dorothy at Racedown the previous summer:

> Wordsworth & his exquisite Sister are with me ... her manners are simple, ardent, impressive –. In every motion her most innocent soul Outbeams so brightly, that who saw would say, Guilt was a thing impossible in her. Her information various – her eye watchful in minutest observation of nature – and her taste a perfect electrometer – it bends, protrudes, and draws in, at subtlest beauties & most recondite faults.
>
> (Letter to Joseph Cottle, c.8 July 1797; CL I, 329–30)

More than her ability to isolate individual objects for 'minute inspection', it was the quick kinetic play of her mind that most impressed him. She registered each thing, and her active 'taste' was subtly alive to each stimulus, measuring the merest shifts. Her 'perfect electrometer' self constantly adjusted and interacted with the unfolding scenes they shared. The evident excitement of this activity energized Coleridge and both Wordsworths as they learned 'a different lore'; their engagement with the objects of nature transformed them, made them joyous. Coleridge claimed this fundamental value of their walking in 'The Nightingale', as he performed his elation with a breathless outpouring, standing with his friends on the bridge in Stowey:

> Come, we will rest on this old mossy Bridge!
> You see the glimmer of the stream beneath,
> But hear no murmuring: it flows silently
> O'er its soft bed of verdure. All is still,
> A balmy night! and tho' the stars be dim,
> Yet let us think upon the vernal showers
> That gladden the green earth, and we shall find
> A pleasure in the dimness of the stars.
> And hark!   (CPW I, i, 516, lines 4–12)

It takes the nightingale's song to disrupt this rush of experience as Coleridge tabulates his sensations. The association of 'dim stars', 'vernal showers' and the 'green earth' creates proleptic pleasure. Pleasure occurs at the intersection of thinking and feeling – Coleridge become 'electrometer'.

This extraordinary attentiveness, the stuff of their walks, nonetheless usually occurs while they're stationary: on the bridge in Stowey, lying sidelong on the turf on the Quantock ridge, sheltering under the hollies near Alfoxden etc. During the 1803 tour of Scotland, however, Coleridge and Dorothy develop a taste for a more kinetic pleasure produced while in motion. Coleridge describes the experience in a notebook entry in late August 1803:

Reaches [of the upper Clyde], short & quite land-locked, the rocks of each from 460 to 500 feet high, as high as possible Effect could require: now one green Drapery of flowing woods from the summit to the very water; now blank, naked, and staring; now half clad, now in patches: – the Rocks retiring in Bays &c.; & now bulging out in Buttresses; – now in Giant Stairs, now in needle point, now in huge Towers with chimneys on the Top. – The single Trees on the very Edge of the Top, Birch and Ash, O how lovely!

(CN I, 1452)

The passage begins in aesthetic distance, commenting that the towering crags meet the requirements for the desired 'effect'; the scene then unfolds rapidly via a series of 'now's creating the illusion of travelling through the scene at pace. The rapidly changing views create a 'new' pleasure to consider outside the conventional aesthetic categories of the prospect. The passage ends with a quasi-mathematical account of how the experiences worked:

Larches & Firs a Repetition of units in time rather than an Assemblage in Space / units without union consequently without Greatness no character of relationship, no neighbourhood which Fir trees would gain, no motion / nor all this till tamed down by exceeding number & exclusion of all things to be compared with. (CN I, 1452)

Relational scale, repetition, movement – the physics of the unfolding scene presents a stark contrast between the affective response 'O how lovely!' and the dispassionate 'Repetition of units in time'. This seems an extreme instance of a fundamental pattern in Coleridge's walking, the practice of taking things in as an almost ecstatic reverie, followed by intellectual distancing in which he takes the measure of things experienced or his personal experience more broadly. He and Dorothy shared this back-and-forth as they travelled together. Physically shattered at the end of a long day, Dorothy set cushions on some chairs in the back room of a pub to lie down. Lying there, she discovered something she called a 'side peep':

while I lay stretched upon the carriage cushions on three chairs, I discovered a little side peep which was enough to set the mind at work. It was no more than a smoky vessel lying at anchor, with its bare masts, a clay hut and the shelving bank of the river, with a green pasture above. Perhaps you will think that there is not much in this, as I describe it: it is true; but the effect produced by these simple objects, as they happened to be combined, together with the gloom of the evening, was exceedingly wild.[4]

The static scene is brought alive by a shift in thinking about seeing. The 'little side peep' offers a partly occluded view and its incompletion fires the imagination. This seems the near-opposite of the aesthetic mastery of the prospect view, and as a walking aesthetic she had clearly been working on it with

Coleridge. He deployed the same terms to describe the various visual effects produced as they moved through the landscape the following day:

> as we moved along, there formed new pictures, sometimes shutting out, sometimes admitting a Peep, sometimes pouring in a full view of the large mass of water. / But our Road, our wild moorland Path thro' the most luxuriant Heaths, the purple, the white, the pale purple, the deep crimson, or rose-colour Purple / thro' a mountain Pass, like a Giant Gate-way.   (*CN* I, 1469)

The kinetic nature of seeing in transit meant that views were occluded, became partially visible, admitted the occasional 'Peep' and so on. Coleridge was sensually overwhelmed by each view 'pouring in'. Here, the 'peep' was produced not by a small aperture delimiting the view but by constant motion through the visual field. It was something that arose, a series of pleasing partial views.

Moving through the landscape, their ongoing discussion of ways of seeing and the pleasure inherent in them focused on a kind of furtive uncertainty, not knowing what was next; nevertheless, they often discussed the details of the tour in more conventional aesthetic terms. Early in the tour one of their ongoing conversations was put to the test. Dorothy shared the anecdote in her journal. Walking in the upper Clyde Valley, they arrived at the famous series of waterfalls at Cora Linn:

> A lady and gentleman, more expeditious tourists than ourselves, came to the spot [a viewpoint of the Cora Linn falls]; they left us at the seat, and we found them again at another station above the Falls. Coleridge, who is always good-natured enough to enter into conversation with anybody whom he meets in his way, began to talk with the gentleman, who observed that it was a *majestic* waterfall. Coleridge was delighted with the accuracy of the epithet, particularly as he had been settling in his own mind the precise meaning of the words grand, majestic, sublime, etc., and had discussed the subject with William at some length the day before. 'Yes, sir,' says Coleridge, 'it *is* a majestic waterfall.' 'Sublime and beautiful,' replied his friend. Poor Coleridge could make no answer, and, not very desirous to continue the conversation, came to us and related the story, laughing heartily.[5]

'Poor Coleridge', post-Kant, had little tolerance for mixing distinct and incompatible aesthetic categories willy-nilly, but at least he realized the episode was funny – not all tourists can be philosophers. The incident also highlighted how difficult, even futile, formalizing a distinction between the majestic and the sublime might be. Not only were various individuals bound to produce different aesthetic judgements, but such judgements were constantly amended and revised as they moved through the landscape. He and his friends were still at work on understanding the aesthetic pleasure of the 'peep'.

Walking in company for Coleridge produces distinct pleasures: an occasion for discourse, best represented in Hazlitt's account of the walk to Linton where the sights of the Somerset–Devon coast were barely mentioned; a process of shared discovery exemplified by his walking with Dorothy in the Quantocks and Scotland; and the movement back and forth between an ecstatic experiential pleasure captured in his movement between joyousness and the dispassionate consideration of visual 'units in time' as they made their way through the upper Clyde Valley. The alternation at the heart of this third mode, intense sensual experience followed by abstractions derived from the experience (aesthetic and otherwise), dominates his accounts of walking by himself. The best-known of his solo walks, the nine day walk through the Lake District in August 1802, chronicles this productive creative mode. He designated a notebook especially for the tour.[6] Having disassembled the kitchen broom at home (Greta Hall, Keswick), he set off up the Newlands Valley for Buttermere and the coast beyond, besom stick in hand. The first entry describing the walk through Newlands struggles to find a suitable form. Should he write in the present tense, in the first person? He deployed Dorothy's *Alfoxden Journal* practice of dropping the first-person pronoun: 'Quitted My house on Sunday morning, August 1. 1802 over the bridge by the Hops / Skiddaw to my right, upper halves of Borrodale mountains behind me, Newlands Arch & the 3 M.[ountains] within it, to my left' (*CN* I, 1207). Like Dorothy, he began in the past tense, but that immediately gave way to a moving panorama as he turned to his right, behind him and to his left. The illusion of present motion took over the entry as he described looking around while walking forward up the valley. He experiments with the second person, drawing in his imagined reader: 'you come into the Road Carsleddam lying flat upon Skiddaw, like a Painting / the Bridge / view at the shoemakers in Portinscale / the Birch & Oak' (*CN* I, 1207). This is reminiscent of guidebook second person, in which the reader is conducted to a series of established views;[7] here we get caught up in Coleridge's perceptual flow as he walks out of Keswick. There is no scenic destination;[8] rather, we quite literally experience one thing after another:

> mossy soft ground, every man his own path-maker – skip & jump – where rushes grow, a man may go – Red Pike peeps in on you upon your left / on the right you cross the pretty Beck that goes to Loweswater – you again ascend & reach a ruined sheep fold.　　　　　　　　　　(*CN* I, 1207)

A ruined sheepfold seems a good place to rest. The writing that conducted us here is experimental. The variety of cognitive and physiological experiences creates an illusion of being present in the scene. 'Every man his own path-maker' sounds like a transient thought as we pick our way through the 'mossy ground'; 'skip & jump' launches the body forward, a performative event; 'Where rushes grow, a man may go' is a local rhyme designed to help pick our way etc. The 'peep' in this passage is reversed as Red Pike looks down on us, not vice versa. We look left and right until we ascend to our temporary destination, the sheepfold. At this point in the entry, he ends his experiments with the second person in favour of complete immediacy. He composes in situ:

> – here I write these lines / a wild green view, bleating of Sheep & noise of waters / right opposite the upper Halves of Grasmere / & the huge mountains, his Equals, with Skiddaw far behind / Two fields peep, the highest cultivated Land on the Newlands side of Buttermere. (CN I, 1207)

Fully present, he has an immersive sensual experience, surrounded by sounds as much as expansive views. From here he projects his future route: 'I write this, the sun with a soft & watery gleam setting behind the hill which I am to ascend / I am to pass with a bulging green Hill to my left – to the left of it a frightful craggy precipice with shivers, & all wrinkled – & a chasm between the Hill & it' (CN I, 1207). Sublime terror becomes a distinct possibility; the 'shivers' are his as he faces the 'frightful' vertical terrain. Gathering himself while plotting his next immediate route, he sets off again: ' – I ascend / straight before a high round-headed Hill, (the Dodd) evidently the highest point between Buttermere and Ennerdale, bisects the ridge / I take it on my right hand / get above the bulging green hill on my left – and am now just above it' (CN I, 1207). Here he creates the illusion of being present in the moment; he can't compose while moving, but creates a composite present tense by writing and moving, writing and moving, and so on. The ascent description is composed at his next resting point at Flatern Tarn and at the summit of the pass. From there he takes in the view, a view earned by labour – risk and reward:

> I never beheld a more glorious view of its kind – I turn & look behind me / what a wonderful group of mountains – what a scene for Salvator Rosa / and before the glorious Sea with the opposite high shores & mountains.
> (CN I, 1207)

The panorama of sublime views is presented as physiological as he turns and twists his head and body. No picturesque view this: he chooses Rosa to paint it; danger and drama dominate the experience.

The temporal complexity of this first entry cannot be overstated. He began conventionally in the past tense of recollection ('Quitted my house'), makes readers his imagined companions by describing his experiences en route as our present tense experiences ('you ascend'), finally locating himself in the moment of composition at the foot of the Dodd, gathering energy for a final ascent ('here I write'). Only the speculation on Rosa as the ideal painter for the scene breaks our shared verisimilitude. Such experimentation and variety in the first entry show his ambitions for the journal. The best-known incident from his tour, the ascent and nearly disastrous descent of Scafell, is the minor masterpiece of the journal, and benefits from being recorded twice: once in his notebook and once in the letter he was writing for Sara Hutchinson (*CL* I, 833–44). He worked on both in situ. Given the circumstances, this was no mean feat. The ferocity of the wind on the summit made writing difficult. The panorama from the summit appears out of order on the back leaf of the notebook, suggesting that he couldn't risk opening the pages and improvised a single flat writing surface.[9] He begins the ascent with a subtle phenomenological portrait: 'Ascend, stooping, & looking at my shadow, stooping down to my shadow, a little shorter than myself – Dial plate Flower, & wild Thyme roam up the Fells in company – with them the Fox's Tail – Fern, Rushes, &c' (*CN* I, 1216). The sun behind him, he leans into the incline, tracking his movement by his moving shadow. The experience unfolds as he passes through the plants that roam up the slope with him. The plants 'roam' and this switching of subject position, a repetition of Red Pike 'peeping' at him, imbeds him in the scene as part of a moving series of relational actions: Coleridge, his shadow, Coleridge, Fox's Tail, Coleridge, his shadow, Coleridge, Fern and so on. He writes from the summit:

> [s]tand facing the Sea / behind me a little, & to my right, Bow fell – to the right of that Great Gavell, & close to my right Kirk Fell, T. Tyson's at the foot of it – then a noble Bason two thirds of a compleat Round, its Walls formed by Kirk Fell, Green Fell & Keppel Fell – before me & to my right, Keppel Fell & Yewbarrow Crag, with a tarn on the Top of it – behind Green Crag & Kirk Fell the Pillar, the Steeple, & the Hay Cock / all before is the dying away of all the Fells / apparently in an elevenfold ridge, running down West-ward
>
> (CN I, 1217)

He performs the panorama, turning clockwise and revealing what he sees as he turns. He begins 'facing the Sea'; no surprise: having ascended from Wasdale, this is the view he earned. He interjects the sense of real time with the use of 'then' as he swings round, finally finishing his pirouette back where he started, looking out to sea and noting the 'trident' formed by the Rivers Esk, Irt and Duddon. He draws the trident and a diagram of his position on the sheet. He shares this final view, introducing the second person: 'before you three Vales with three Rivers from their very sources falling into Sea' (*CN* I, 1217). The sweeping turn creates a sense of revelation, an unfolding series of sublime views. The motion prevents a conventional sublime view, and the diagram locates him as an insignificant speck (quite literally) in a vast perceptual field.

Coleridge's account of his descent alternates between past and present tense: 'I descended Sca Fell' (CN I, 1218). Locating him on the descent proves difficult; he writes this initial account from a sheltered spot near the summit where he feels 'lownded'.[10] From his sheltered spot he recounts the immediately past events: 'from the spot that lownds me, I see Derwentwater plainly O for a better & less *hazy* day ... had the weather been tolerably I could have seen my own House / I saw the spot where it was. – The clouds came on fast – & yet I long to ascend Bowfell' (CN I, 1218). Pitched in a moment between past ('the clouds came on fast') and future ('I long to ascend Bowfell'), Coleridge composes at a midpoint, suspended above the Mickeldore Gap. It's sheltered enough for him safely to take out his ongoing letter to Sara Hutchinson. In the letter he describes the scene in more detail:

> And here I am lounded – so fully lounded – that tho' the wind is strong, & the Clouds are hast'ning hither from the Sea – and the whole air seaward has a lurid Look – and we shall certainly have Thunder – yet here (but that I am hunger'd & provisionless) here I could lie warm, and wait methinks for tomorrow's Sun / and on a nice Stone Table am I now at this moment writing to you – between 2 and 3 o'Clock as I guess / surely the first Letter ever written from the Top of Sca' Fell! But O! what a look down just under my Feet! The frightfullest Cove that might ever be seen / huge perpendicular Precipices, and one Sheep upon it's only Ledge, that surely must be crag! (CL II, 839)

The vertigo translates into anxiety as he sees the crag-fast sheep, trapped on a ledge. To be crag-fast is to be doomed, the choice between falling to your death or dying of exposure. His longing to ascend Bowfell spells disaster as he focuses on a 'low Ridge that runs' between the two mountains. There is no safe route to that ridge. His notebook entry presents a succinct account of the terror of the descent: 'I thought I could descend ... & look down into the wild *savage, savage* Head of Eskdale / Good heavens! what a climb! dropping from Precipices and at last should have been crag fast but for the chasm – ' (CN I, 1218). This is the Coleridge who ran into the Valley of the Rocks in a storm without his hat. He recorded the full extent of his folly in a letter to Sara the following day:

> There is one sort of Gambling, to which I am much addicted; and that not of the least criminal kind for a man who has children & a Concern. – It is this. When I find it convenient to descend from a mountain, I am too confident & too indolent to look round about & wind about 'till I find a track or other symptom of safety; but I wander on, & where it is first possible to descend, there I go – relying upon fortune for how far down this possibility will continue. (CL II, 840)

The combination of confidence and indolence lead to these reckless episodes; the addiction is such that in this instance the urge overwhelms his acknowledged duty to his family. He dropped down a series of rock ledges of various heights, drawn on by the elation and excitement of his physiological pleasure until he suddenly recognized his mistake: 'I began to suspect that I ought not to go on / but then unfortunately tho' I could with ease drop down a smooth Rock 7 feet high, I could not climb it / so go on I must.' The descent, the lost wager of his gambling metaphor, culminated on a ledge too high to drop from without risking falling backwards: 'if I dropt down upon it I must of necessity have fallen backwards & of course killed myself' (*CL* II, 841). The 'of course' signals his recognition of his plight and pulls him out of the reverie that brought him there. In this state of exhaustion and trepidation, he does something sensible; he lies down to rest:

> I lay upon my Back to rest myself, & was beginning according to my Custom to laugh at myself for a Madman, when the sight of the Crags above me on each side, & the impetuous Clouds just over them, posting so luridly & so rapidly northward, overawed me / I lay in a state of almost prophetic Trance & Delight – & blessed God aloud, for the powers of Reason & the Will, which remaining no Danger can overpower us! O God, I exclaimed aloud – how calm, how blessed am I now / I know not how to proceed, how to return / but I am calm & fearless & confident / if this Reality were a Dream, if I were asleep, what agonies had I suffered! what screams! – When the Reason & the Will are away, what remain to us but Darkness & Dimness & a bewildering Shame, and Pain that is utterly Lord over us, or fantastic Pleasure, that draws the Soul along swimming through the air in many shapes, even as a Flight of Starlings in a Wind.   (*CL* II, 841)

To experience terror and delight would simply echo Burkean aesthetic categories, but Coleridge instead combines overwhelming affective experiences in a religious epiphany. If 'Reason & Will' are divinely ordained, then he can become present in the scene and negotiate that which seems impossible. Otherwise, we (he introduces the plural) suffer a complete loss of agency: 'bewildering Shame', 'Pain that is utterly Lord over us, or fantastic Pleasure'. He inserts the present tense in the midst of his account to dramatize the moment of recognition: 'how blessed I am now', 'I am calm & fearless & confident'. Physiologically recovered, the trembling in his legs dissipated, he can look around with new eyes. Dopamine had probably created tunnel vision; now past, he could look around and find the 'chasm' he mentioned in the notebook entry, a vertical shaft splitting the rock. This provided an easy 'chimney' descent to safety after skirting a rotting sheep, a victim of being crag-fast, the fate he narrowly avoided.[11]

The 1802 tour of the Lakes stands as the quintessential account of Coleridge walking and experimenting with language in an effort to find modes of description adequate to such intense experiences. A few years later, he recorded some of his walking as he travelled to Malta. Travelling abroad doubled the need for negotiation; he adapted to the physical terrain and took in the newness of unfamiliar places and cultures. For the most part his intellectual curiosity held him in good stead, but his English chauvinism occasionally undermined his ability to take in new places. Coming ashore in Gibraltar, for example, he climbed to the top of the precipice for the commanding view: 'The Mountains around me did not anywhere arrange themselves strikingly' (CN II, 2045). Nonetheless, as he looked out over the African coast, he finally did arrange the view to create maximum aesthetic pleasure:

> the Sea so blue, calm, & sunny, so majestic a Lake where it is enshored by Mountains, & where it is not, having its indefiniteness the more felt from those huge Mountain Boundaries, which yet by their greatness prepared the mind for the sublimity of unbounded Ocean.　　　　(CN II, 2045)

Despite the detailed account of his sublime experience, culminating in 'an inseparable character of Unity' (CN II, 2045), very high Coleridgean praise, he cannot help but compare the scene to his familiar English mountains: he 'had looked from far loftier mountains over a far far more manifold Landscape, the fields & habitations of Englishmen, children of one family, one religion, & that my own, the same sweet language, & manners, & every Hill & every River some sweet name familiar to my ears' (CN II, 2045). This retrenchment, and sudden sense of defamiliarization, culminates in anti-Catholic xenophobia, and bigotry: 'the Spaniards, a degraded Race that dishonour Christianity' and 'Moors ... wretches that dishonor human Nature' (CN II, 2045). These attitudes are, in a word, appalling, and point to the complex challenges of social conditioning, even in someone as brilliant as Coleridge. His homesickness pathologizes difference.

Once he arrived in Malta such challenges came to the fore as he settled into his new professional and social role. After a few days getting acclimatized he went for a walk to explore the town and harbour:

> Lizard half-erect stands still as I stop – I stop a long while / he turns his head & looks sidelong at me / Crawls two or three paces by stealth – stops again / I walk off briskly, turning my head tho' & looking at him / he is too cunning – & has not moved – at length I really move away – and off – he is gone!
> 　　　　(CN II, 2144)

His interaction here, not with a local human inhabitant, is intense, written as a present tense event. The change from his inability to see the local inhabitants of Gibraltar couldn't be more stark. The interpersonal connection with the lizard is complete, their behaviour identical – stop, gaze, dart, stop etc. The resulting dance is initiated by chance in this first instance. He discovers the lizards of Malta as part of his orientation. By the end of the walk he further complicates the relationship by becoming the initiator:

> one pretty fellow whom I had fascinated by stopping & gazing at him as he lay in a <thick> network of Sun & Shade, after having turned his head from me so as but for the greater length of its Tail to form a crescent with the outline of its body – then turned his Head to me, depressed it, & looked up half-watching; half-imploring, at length taking advantage of a brisk breeze that made all the Network dance & Toss, & darted off as if an Angel of Nature had spoken in the Breeze – Off! (*CN* II, 2144)

The opportunistic lizard uses the breeze to escape the controlling gaze. Coleridge's concentration wavered for just a moment and the lizard was 'off'. Coleridge was clearly fascinated by the lizards, and he makes the effect mutual by 'fascinat[ing]' a lizard in turn.[12] The radical sympathy produced during his walk becomes a mode of negotiation as he comes to know the terrain and the living creatures concealed by its turns and contours.

Late in life, Coleridge's walking was mostly confined to Hampstead Heath, adjacent to Gillman's house in Highgate. There, once again, Coleridge the walker and Coleridge the talker merged into one. The best-known account of this phenomenon is Keats's letter from spring 1819:

> I met Mr. Green our Demonstrator at Guy's in conversation with Coleridge – I joined them, after enquiring by a look whether it would be agreeable – I walked with him at his alderman-after-dinner pace for near two miles I suppose. In those two Miles he broached a thousand things – let me see if I can give you a list – Nightingales – Poetry – on Poetical Sensation – Metaphysics – Different genera and species of Dreams – Nightmare – a dream accompanied by a sense of touch – single and double touch – a dream related – First and second consciousness – the difference explained between will and Volition – so say metaphysicians from a want of smoking the second consciousness – Monsters – the Kraken – Mermaids – Southey believes in them – Southey's belief too much diluted – a Ghost story – Good morning – I heard his voice as he came towards me – I heard it as he moved away – I had heard it all the interval – if it may be called so. He was civil enough to ask me to call on him at Highgate. Good-night![13]

Keats's amusement is palpable; the scene returns in spirit to Hazlitt's account of the flow of information, speculation, genius that propelled them down the Bristol Channel in 1798. Hazlitt's essay and Keats's letter are roughly contemporaneous and leave us with the same sense of the man – portraits of Coleridge's peripatetic mind.

Notes

1 William Hazlitt, 'My First Acquaintance with Poets', in *William Hazlitt: Selected Writings*, ed. Jon Cook (Oxford University Press, 1991), 226. Subsequent references given intext with page number.

2 He references his work on the subject in *Remarks on the System of Hartley and Helvetius* (1805).

3 Moorman offers no note on this entry despite its obvious relationship to 'This Lime-Tree Bower My Prison', perhaps because it seems backwards, with the poem pre-dating the journal entry. Journals are often read as the raw material for poems, but the reciprocal relationship between the two writers was such that here the poem serves as source. In fact it can be read as the source of the actual walk, the aesthetic pleasure that was its goal.

4 *Recollections of a Tour Made in Scotland (1803)* in *The Journals of Dorothy Wordsworth*, vol. I, ed. William Knight (London: Macmillan, 1897), 213.

5 Ibid., 195.

6 For Coleridge's notebook practices, see Tom Owens's essay in the present volume. The tour is recorded in *CN* I, 1205–29. For fuller accounts see: Alan Vardy, 'Coleridge on Broad Stand', *Romanticism on the Net*, 61 (April 2012), www.crudit.org/fr/revues/ravon/2012-n61-ravon0834/1018600ar/ (Accessed 31 May 2022), and Alan Hankinson, *Coleridge Walks the Fells: A Lakeland Journey Retraced* (London: Harper Collins, 1993).

7 The present tense of 'you come', 'you view', 'you ascend' etc. gives guidebooks a sense of paradoxical immediacy. They are consumed as proleptic wishes; the reader 'views' future moments.

8 There's no guide to the scenic bogs of the Newlands Valley.

9 The account of climbing Scafell and descending via Broad Stand is on the twelfth leaf of the notebook, except for the view from the top, which falls in the middle, which is recorded separately on leaf 24 at the back of the notebook. In order to maintain chronology, Kathleen Coburn assigns the account three numbers (1216–18).

10 Coleridge chooses the Lakeland dialect word 'lownded' ('lounded' in the letter to Sara) to convey his experience. It means 'calm', as in 'out of the wind', 'sheltered', but carries with it the internalized sense of being calmed and feeling calm. For Coleridge it makes the act of composition possible – a temporal pause, a respite before moving on. Here it translates into a profound sense of well-being after the ecstasy of the summit.

11 This episode is often offered as the birth of rock climbing, but rock climbers are involved in intentional acts, and most focus on difficult ascents. Coleridge's understanding of his impulsiveness as a gambling addiction, however, may get at the visceral attraction of the sport.

12 For a superb account of Coleridge's interactions with lizards on Malta and Sicily, see Gregory Leadbetter, 'The Venom of Beauty, or, Geraldine under the Sun: Coleridge's Lizards in Malta and Sicily', *The Wordsworth Circle*, 43 (2012), 90–94.

13 'To George and Georgiana Keats', February to May 1819, *The Letters of John Keats*, ed. Sidney Colvin (London: Macmillan, 1925), 244.

IO

THOMAS OWENS

Notebook Coleridge

Nov. 27th, Awoke from the uneasy Doze-dream of the Coach / a rich orange sky like that of a winter Evening save that the fleecy dark Blue that rippled above showed it to be morning / – soon became a glowing Brass colour, fleeces of Brass like sand – convolves high up in to the Sky – the Sun rose o'er the plain like a Kite / rose wholly, & a column in the waters, and soon after, a Hill meeting with it, rose thro' other clouds – with a different Glory – Starlings –

(CN I, 581)

So Coleridge recorded the beginning of a new day in late November 1799, at which time he was travelling from Sockburn in the north of England to London. He scribbled his description in pencil into a small, sixty-one-leaf black leather pocketbook which he used inconsistently from both ends whilst on several trips and walking tours that year.[1] It is one of many entries that evokes what Kathleen Coburn has called 'the rough unfinished vitality of the studio', and its impressionistic energy suggests it was written hurriedly and possibly from the coach itself shortly after Coleridge woke up, which would be in keeping with other observations jotted down immediately on mountainsides or in darkness (CN I, xviii, xxxiii). The distinctive mixture of dashes and oblique strokes structures the abruptly shifting rhythms of a refractive delight in language which preserves both the momentary scene itself and the momentum of Coleridge's mind as he tracks its unfolding. This dual trajectory is further emphasized by the ordering of action ('Awoke'), perception ('a rich orange sky') and temporality ('soon became'), which reflects a desire to trace an emerging encounter with sunshine from its origins in consciousness. In this mode, it is not just dawn that is captured but the dawning of comprehension as Coleridge's proliferative imagination works through a sequence of images ('fleecy dark Blue', 'a glowing Brass', 'fleeces of Brass') and relations ('like that of a winter Evening', 'like sand', 'like a Kite') to picture time passing at daybreak. It is a style which brings into the light 'a different Glory' of its own making: the course of Coleridge's evolving and excited responsiveness.

This is a triumph of the notebooks more generally, which not only document what Coleridge was thinking about – his ordinary and imaginative commitments – but which frequently dramatize the fragile activity of the mind's endeavour to articulate experience into language:

> The Soul within the Body, can I any way compare this to the Reflection of the Fire seen thro' my window on the solid Wall, seeming of course within the solid wall, as deep within as the distance of the Fire from the Wall? – I fear, I can make nothing out of it / but why do I always turn away from any interesting Thought to do something uninteresting – as for instance, when this Thought struck me, I turned off my attention suddenly, & went to look for the Wolff which I had missed – / Is it a cowardice of all deep Feeling, even tho' pleasurable? or is it Laziness? or is it some thing less obvious than either? – Is it connected with my epistolary Embarrassments?   (CN I, 1737)

By providing space for Coleridge to practise ways of looking and discerning, the notebooks stimulated the freely speculative and analogical methods of inquiry which were fundamental to his creative engagement with the world, and which in turn fostered a stylistic idiom that excelled at evoking off-duty apprehensions (and apprehensiveness) rather than the more tightly marshalled argumentation of published prose.[2] The expansive, provisional nature of the form nurtured an intelligence dedicated to exploration ('can I any way compare this[?]') and indirection ('why do I always turn away[?]') which, in this entry's confession of honest incapacity, fused a perception about the material world with the psychological reality of distractedness ('I turned off my attention suddenly'). A lost thought prompted a rumination on the inscrutability of loss which had the unintended felicity of showing Coleridge how his mind really worked, even if its reasons for doing so remained mysterious to him ('Is it a cowardice of all deep Feeling ... is it Laziness?'). A more generous assessment than Coleridge's own would note that the shift from critique to self-critique, and from outer to inner worlds, echoes the initial imaginative gambit that the 'Reflection of the Fire' might serve as a symbol for the 'Soul within the Body', which was precisely the sort of lateral conjecture that notebook-keeping encouraged, and which in turn spurred Coleridge's deep philosophical allegiance to demonstrating the reciprocal interaction between subjective and objective states of being.

The fact that Coleridge cast many memorable entries as crepuscular visions of some kind – indistinct or incomplete – not only testifies to the unruliness of mental behaviour and the difficulties of sustaining focus but also intimates his larger suspicion about states of conviction by exhibiting a predilection for suspending judgement in favour of limitlessly tentative investigation, even if such a procedure guaranteed an *'undesigningness'* (*CN* v, 5226) of mind which often provoked anguish in its author and his critics. William Hazlitt characterized Coleridge's temperament as '*tangential*', which he meant as a shortcoming of his generalist tendencies, but this habit of askance scrutiny had the potential to keep intellectual complacency at bay through a continual process of interrogation and reflection that Coleridge considered more rigorous than the inertia of surety.[3] On a number of occasions, Coleridge explicitly condoned the inchoate and inconclusive kinds of contemplation which the notebooks promoted: 'I trust, that these Hints & first Thoughts, often too cogitabilia rather than actual cogitata a *me*, may not be understood as my fixed opinions – but merely as the suggestions of the disquisition; & acts of obedience to the apostolic command of Try~ing~ all things: hold fast that which is good' (*CN* III, 3881). Indeed, the notebooks were the archetypal Coleridgean testing-ground for budding ideas rather than final proofs, serving to protect a spirit of incipience both materially in the haphazard abundance of their proximate reflections and intellectually as an ally to the mind's life and fashioner of its diversitarian vigour.

And yet, despite his mistrust of 'fixed opinions', Coleridge was also governed by an instinctive 'desire of totalizing' that he recognized as a basic human need, and which threatened to usurp his happy omnivorousness in even the most trivial circumstances:

> Seeing a nice bed of glowing Embers with one Junk of firewood well placed, like the remains of an old Edifice, and another well nigh mouldered one, corresponding to it, I felt an impulse to put on three pieces of Wood, that exactly completed this perishable architecture, tho' it was 11 °clock, tho' I was that instant going to bed, & there could be in common ideas no possible use in it. Hence I seem (for I write, not having yet gone to bed) to suspect, that this desire of totalizing, of perfecting, may be the bottom-impulse of many, many actions, in which it never is brought forward as an avowed, or even agnized <*anerkennt*> as a conscious motive / – thence I proceed to think of restlessness in general, its *fragmentary* nature, and its connection if not identification, with the <*pains correlative* to the> pleasures derived from *Wholeness* – i.e. plurality in unity – & the yearning left behind by those pleasures ~once~ often experienced. (*CN* II, 2414)

Out of loyalty to ceaseless speculation came a contrary impulse 'of perfecting' which nicely exemplifies the competing tendencies of Coleridge's double nature, caught between the experience of the '*fragmentary*' and an over-riding aspiration for '*Wholeness*'.[4] Plentifulness cannot so easily be left alone after all, but needs to be envisaged as going somewhere purposeful: 'i.e. plurality in unity'. This was reflected in the early poetry, which explored a range of oppositional responses to abundance. In *Religious Musings* (1794), for instance, mankind is 'A sordid solitary thing' (*CPW* I, i, 181, line 149), bewildered and blind in the universe without faith in God, but for whom salvation is promised in a spiritual vision of cohesion based on the extension of 'sacred sympathy' (*CPW* I, i, 181, line 153):

> 'Tis the sublime of man,
> Our noontide Majesty, to know ourselves
> Parts and proportions of one wond'rous whole!
>
> (*CPW* I, i, 180, lines 126–28)

By this incorporative logic, intuiting only 'Parts and proportions' of reality is a sign of small-mindedness that ultimately leads to being cast adrift in the world, a motif which 'The Rime of the Ancyent Marinere' (1798) re-interrogates, quite literally, by pitching the debilitating intensity of the Mariner's unific religiosity against the nightmarish terror of an infinite plenitude at sea:

> Water, water, every where,
> Ne any drop to drink.   (*CPW* I, i, 380, lines 121–22)

The claims of unity, then, by turns redemptively reconciling or chronically self-thwarting, were envisaged elsewhere in the notebooks as a quest for '*oneness*, there being infinite Perceptions' (*CN* I, 556), and incited a compulsion to rescue insights from their momentary and stubborn independence, but which the local splendour of their individuality repeatedly frustrated: 'Exquisite Network of Film so instinct with gentle motion which, now the Shower only steadies, & now it melts it into such a mistiness as the Breath leaves on a mirror' (*CN* I, 518). The tension was clearly exacerbated by the notebooks themselves, which, in honing Coleridge's receptivity to the fleeting, encouraged the centrifugal psychodrama which enduringly preoccupied him, and which was still a source of inspiration and exasperation in his final years: 'O how pregnant & multiplicative is every truth' (*CN* V, 6405). He had explicitly conceived intelligence as a matter of deferral in the Prospectus to the 1809–10 edition of his periodical *The Friend*, where he acknowledged that 'in Order fully to comprehend and develope any one Subject, it was necessary that I should make myself Master of some other, which again as regularly involved a third, and so on, with an ever-widening Horizon' (*Friend* II, 16). The 'Memorandum or Common-place Books' that he invoked to cope with this infinitely recessive approach to thinking were really symptom and cure of the perplexity, invariably motivating the production of 'desultory Fragments' even as they supported Coleridge's intentions to document 'both Incidents and Observations; whatever had occurred to me from without, and all the Flux and Reflux of my Mind within itself' (*Friend* II, 16–17). In aspiring to juggle the actualities of what lay 'without' and what resided 'within', the notebooks depict the machinations of consciousness itself as somewhat 'desultory' or erratic, which the style and succession of the entries symbolically confirm, and which Coleridge seemed to appreciate too: 'a cracked Looking-glass – such is man's mind – Spinoza' (*CN* I, 705). In Coleridge's case, the fissure was emblematic of his antiphonal intellect: whilst the transmissibility and transience of thinking encouraged suspended judgements that pulled him in an endlessly provisional direction, this tendency was countered by a dependency upon closure, thus consolidating a central predicament which Coleridge was obliged to re-experience over the forty years (1794–1834) that he regularly wrote in notebooks (*CN* I, xix).

In all, over seventy of Coleridge's notebooks have survived, in many shapes and sizes, and with different patterns and purposes of usage. One of their basic functions was to serve as a repository for mundane, instructive, chastising and imaginative memoranda: 'Mem. Write an Ode to *Meat & Drink*' (*CN* I, 62); 'Mem – not to adulterize my time by absenting myself from my wife' (*CN* I, 73); 'Mem. I asserted that Cato was a drunkard – denied by S. – to examine it –' (*CN* I, 167); 'Mem – A Cheese Toaster' (*CN* I, 284); 'To analyse the pleasures received from Gates, in corners of Fields, at twilight / Vide Wordsworth – Evening Walk' (*CN* I, 1707); 'Mem. to collect facts for a comparison between a *wood* and a *coal*, fire, as to sights, sounds, & bodily Feeling' (*CN* II, 2414). Reminders of this kind are one instantiation of the vigilance which notebook-writing stimulated, and which show ideas moving reciprocally in and out of collaborative dialogues that were crucial to Coleridge's development. They fed a commitment to continual noticing in which nothing was irredeemable or beneath examination:

> What a beautiful Thing Urine is, in a Pot, brown yellow, transpicuous, the Image, diamond shaped of the of the [*sic*] Candle in it, especially, as it now appeared, I having emptied the Snuffers into it, & the Snuff floating about, & painting all-shaped Shadows on the Bottom. (*CN* I, 1766)

Indeed, Coleridge was magnetized to proximate brilliance of all sorts and a sense of perceptual vividness links the disparate snapshots of existence which he strikingly collected in the recursive guise of writing about the Lake District, his children and nocturnal happenings:

> I have come suddenly upon Ulswater, running straight on the opposite Bank, till the Placefell, that noble Promontory runs into it, & gives it the winding of a majestic River, a little below Placefell a large Slice of calm silver – above this a bright ruffledness, or atomic sportiveness – motes in the sun? – Vortices of flies? – how shall I express the Banks waters all fused Silver, that House too its slates rain-wet silver in the sun, & its shadows running down in the water like a column – the Woods on the right shadowy with Sunshine, and in front of me the sloping hollow of sunpatched Fields, sloping up into Hills so playful[.] (*CN* I, 549)

October, 1802. Hartley at Mr. Clarkson's sent for a Candle – the *Seems*
made him miserable – what do you mean, my Love! The Seems – the Seems –
what seems to be & is not – Men & faces & I do not [know] what, ugly, &
sometimes pretty & then turn ugly, & they seem when my eyes are open, &
worse when they are shut – & the Candle cures the SEEMS.

(*CN* I, 1253)

Wednesday Midnight, one o clock or near it ... I for the first time in my Life
felt my eyes near-sighted, & tho' I had 2 Candles near me, reading in my bed,
I was obliged to magnify the Letters by bringing the Book close to my Eye – I
then put out the Candles, & closed my eyes – & instantly there appeared a
spectrum, of a Pheasant's Tail, that altered thro' various degradations into
round wrinkly shapes, as of <Horse> Excrement, or baked Apples – indeed
exactly like the latter – round baked Apples, with exactly the same colour, the
same circular intra-circular Wrinkles – I started out of bed, lit my Candles, &
noted it down, in order to state these circular irregularly concentrical Wrinkles, something like Horse dung, still more like flat baked or <dried> Apples,
such as they are brought in after Dinner. – *Why those Concentric Wrinkles?*

(*CN* I, 1681)

As these vignettes demonstrate, Coleridge made a virtue in the notebooks
out of incomprehension and incapacity, attending closely to those aspects
of experience which tested language's competence at resolving the dispari-
ties between psychological and material realities. He wrote winningly about
trials of description, exploiting the limits of expressiveness and perception
with the immediacy of a freely associative style which dramatized the act of
thinking through something without the pressure of definitive or dogmatic
closure. It was a probing and accumulative notebook method he enthused
about to his son Hartley around 1820:

There is no way of arriving at any sciential End but by finding it at every step.
The End is in the Means: or the adequacy of each Mean is already it's end ... I
do not care twopence for the *Hare*; but I value most highly the excellencies of
scent, patience, discrimination, free Activity; and find a Hare in every Nettle,
I make myself acquainted with. (*CL* v, 98)

The value Coleridge placed on semblance, indeterminacy and process
stemmed from four decades of thinking in notebooks, an unfixed and
unfinished form which Charles Lamb playfully included in the category of
'*books which are no books – biblia a-biblia*', but whose inconclusive het-
erogeneity was a major source of attraction.[5] Their immensely wide-ranging
contents, comprising hybridized elements of diary, scrapbook, travelogue,
journal and commonplace book, defy categorization and exhaustive listing
but encompass: medicinal and food recipes; reminders; regrets; accounts of
poetic metres together with portions of original and copied poems; literary

criticism; excerpts from reading materials; drafted passages of work for publication; dreams; desires; diagrams; memories; records of illness; fears; perceptions of foreign peoples and cultures; philosophical discussions and disputes; interrogations of selfhood and self-expression; metaphysical reflections; debates on social issues; language acquisition and usage; travelling notes; aesthetic theorizing; landscape descriptions; botanical lists; childhood behaviour and psychology; religion (both personal and public) and the wider relationship between church and state; contemporary politics; self-reflection and self-castigation; the serious study of chemistry and the Bible; and bowel complaints.[6]

To match this inner array, itself a tribute to Coleridge's sustained curiosity and capaciousness, idiosyncrasies of outward appearance abound. One notebook was discovered with 'twigs of myrtle' in a small envelope in an inside pocket, ostensibly gathered from a tree Coleridge planted at Clevedon, whilst others were enterprisingly concocted for the job: 'Brown paper, handmade, stitched together' (CN III (Notes), xxxv; CN v (Notes), xxvi). The little pocketbooks, typically composed of leather or cardboard and fitting nicely into a jacket or knapsack, were often used sporadically over a period of many years, even decades, whenever they turned up, and were regularly filled from back to front as well as from front to back simultaneously. Whole pages could be left blank for Biblical passages, language learning, lecture notes and long excerpted quotations, whilst other entries were squeezed into whatever space remained and cordoned off unpredictably with lines; inside covers 'came to be used for jottings like addresses, appointments, titles of books, laundry lists' (CN I, xxiii).[7] The handsomer and larger deskbooks, by contrast, clad in 'Red leather with a leather tongue' or 'Vellum, with a metal clasp', were mostly used more systematically, in one place and largely in ink (CN I (Notes), xl; CN III (Notes), xxix). These were geared towards specific future projects rather than eclectic observations and so contained, amongst other things, working notes for lectures and passages which informed, sometimes verbatim, Coleridge's own publications. It was routine for several notebooks to be employed at any one time, and in 1809, as Paul Cheshire's helpful tabulation illustrates, up to fourteen were in use.[8] Whilst Coleridge dated some entries himself: 'Monday Night, 20 Sept^r, ~~Sept^r~~ 1830 – Mr G. extracted without pain & scarce any hæmorrhage my loose tooth, which Mr Parkinson is to try to replace' (CN v, 6460), many more remain undated and have been assigned to a time editorially through contemporary events or contexts discussed therein, though sometimes only the first and last entries in a notebook are known with much certainty (CN I, xxii, xxvi).[9]

Other writers in the notebooks are rare. The presence of Sara Hutchinson's inked hand, for example, in a hypnotizingly beautiful list of alphabetical transcriptions taken from the index to William Withering's *An Arrangement of British Plants* (1796) around December 1800 is highly unusual, and includes, under 'T':

> Tansy. Tare. Tassel Grass. Teasel. Tent Wort. Thistle. Thorn Apple. Thorough Wax. Three-faces under a hood. Thrift. Thrum Wort. Thyme. Timothy Grass. Toad Flax. Toad Grass. Tooth Wort. Tormentil. Touch me not. Tower mustard. Tower Wort. Travellers' Joy. Treacle Mustard. Tree Mallow. Trefoil. True love. Tube root. Tulip. Tun hoof. Turkey pod. Turneps. Tutsan. Tway-blade. (*CN* i, 863)

This prose-poem incantatorily conjuring forgotten riches ran to over nine leaves of the fine and spacious desk-book known as Notebook 21 and commemorates Coleridge's interest in the materiality of language and sound as well as his affection for Sara and for botany at that time.[10] Similarly, Coleridge never intended for the majority of his notebooks to be read by anyone but himself, and with the exception of a few friends it is evident that he did not envisage a larger audience for them until the mid-1820s.[11] The distinct tones of private and public address can sometimes be registered in the later notebooks through vocal shifts which indicate that an entry was either meant for a specific person around the time of writing or for a projected, posthumous collective once Coleridge sensed that the volumes 'were developing into a legacy that he would pass on to a growing circle of disciples and admirers' (*CN* v, xxi). An example of the first kind is the following note on perception, which was rather solemnly and inscrutably written to a forbearing friend and philosophic pupil, J. H. Green, in 1828:

> I need not remind you, that Perception is the Intermediate, or PARTICIPLE, of Life and Mind – the florescence of Sensibility into Sense – nor that Life is the *Indifference* of Action and Passion / while the manifestation of Life consists in the polar differencing of this, not so that Action is the one Pole, and Passion the other; but that Passion with a predominance of Action forms the Positive Pole, and Action with a predominance of Passion the Negative[.] (*CN* v, 5784)

This forthright and personalized opening contrasts with the exhortatory tone which Coleridge struck when considering his philosophical achievement as a whole, and which seems to be simultaneously self-directed and outward-looking, rather as if he were reaffirming to himself his principal ambitions whilst guiding a future readership through the morass of his notes to a single, major achievement:

> Let me by all the labors of my life have answered but one end, if I shall have only succeeded in establishing the diversity of Reason and Understanding, and the distinction between the *Light* of Reason in the Understanding, viz. the absolute Principles presumed in all Logic and the conditions under which

alone we draw universal and necessary Conclusions from contingent and particular facts, and the Reason itself, as the Source and birth-place of IDEAS.

(CN IV, 5293)

Advancing years and the prospect of an audience both heightened Coleridge's monomania, and so the core epistemological victory hoped for here – 'establishing the diversity of Reason and Understanding' – is also conceived as the crowning act of the equally central philosophical task of threading 'all the labors' of a life through 'one end': 'i.e. plurality in unity'. The omniform nature of the notes and notebooks tacitly exemplified this, too, as an enduring instance of 'the co presence of Feeling & Life, limitless by their very essence, with Form, by its very essence limited' (CN I, 1561).

Coleridge's preoccupation with the constraints of form on 'the co presence of Feeling & Life' was a province he surveyed across multiple domains, including dreams and infant experience, which lent themselves especially well to the partially delineated configuration of the notebooks. These two subjects substantiate Coleridge's 'interest in the totality of our mental life' and his abiding desire to provide children, whom he considered to be 'the secreting-organ of Hope in the great organized body of the whole Human Race' (CN II, 2549), with 'a continuing education in consciousness'.[12] There are 'about three hundred entries on dreams and sleep' alone in the notebooks, a vast *terra incognita* which underlines Coleridge's valiant efforts to understand, and draw affinities between, conscious and unconscious experience.[13] Through these topics Coleridge explored how 'Language & all *symbols* give *outness* to Thoughts' (CN I, 1387) by probing the parameters of awareness and the expressive stages of psychological development:

Friday Night, Nov. 28, 1800, or rather Saturday Morning – a most frightful Dream of a Woman whose features were blended with darkness catching holding of my right eye & attempting to pull it out – I caught hold of her arm fast – a horrid feel – Wordsworth cried out aloud to me hearing my scream – heard his cry & thought it cruel he did not come[.]   (CN I, 848)

Derwent extends the idea of Door so far that he not only calls the Lids of Boxes Doors, but even the Covers of Books / a year & 8 months[.]
(CN I, 1192).

Whilst the adults were screaming incredulously and clutching at shadows, Coleridge's young son intuitively and precociously grasped a genuine analogy which needed no further verification. In writing about his children, Coleridge found a relaxed mode untroubled by second-guessing or half-truths, partly because in doing so he aimed to 'deduce instincts from obscure recollections of a pre-existing State', which gave philosophical credence to a form of retrospective self-discovery: 'Ey! have I said, when I have seen certain tempers & actions in Hartley, that is *I* in my future State / so I think oftentimes that my children are my Soul. / that multitude & division are not (o mystery) necessarily subversive of unity' (CN II, 2332).

Coleridge's tenacity for system-building in his later years was up to the task of trying to shepherd his diffuse thoughts in a single direction, and he developed something of an ingeniously comic proclivity for making 'Extremes meet' – unsurprisingly his 'favorite adage' (CN IV, 5402) – even working the variegated textures of his dreams into sturdy exemplars of much-cherished philosophical tenets:

> Mem. the Kitchen, the good-natured Servant Maids – my necessities compelling me to beg the way to their Necessary – their regret – but Lord Podringham (I must preserve his name in case I should have any opportunity of consulting a Spiritual DEBRETT) and something I imperfectly understood about his Lordship's angry solicitude about his WALNUTS (– n.b. about a fortnight before my Conscience had twitted me for having eat some Walnuts) – then the fantastic puppet-old-man that threw himself in my way and under my feet where ever I went – my intreating some one to take him away – and a huge bloater fat fellow came & sat on him, saying, there was no other way – I went it – and a villainous little *dog* contrived to fly at me & bit me, with a sharp nip (the nearest imitation of proper pain, that I have found occur in sleep[)] ... from these dreams (and no week occurs in which I have not one or two; always originating in the Kidneys, or Bladder, or Intestinal Canal) I derive convincing confirmation of the diversity between Reason & Understanding. (CN v, 5641)

Plainly, an experience in which the 'Understanding' ran riot as 'Reason' slumbered was not unpromising epistemological fodder, and from this shining trail of his subconscious life in 1827, commencing with an urgent and refused request to use the lavatory, Coleridge ends resoundingly with success seemingly of another order, but which only confirms that the laws of nature and the laws of the mind are one and the same after all. Once again, then, 'one end' is reached through 'diversity'.

It is a distinction of the later notebooks in particular to thread together disparate kinds of observations and ideas in pursuit of governing dynamics, and for that reason, as Josie Dixon noted in describing the evolution of the entries, 'the abstraction of the "thesis" increasingly overtakes the materiality of the "illustrations"'.[14] Notably, this phrase almost exactly inverts the intellectual tendency Coleridge recognized in himself decades earlier, at which time he used 'five hundred more ideas, images, reasons &c than there is any need of to arrive at their object', and which he diagnosed with exemplary plentifulness:

Now this is my case – & a grievous fault it is / my illustrations swallow up my thesis – I feel too intensely the omnipresence of all in each, platonically speaking – or psychologically my brain-fibres, or the spiritual Light which abides in thate brain marrow as visible Light appears to do in sundry rotten mackerel & other *smashy* matters, is of too general an affinity with all things / and tho' it perceives the *difference* of things, yet is eternally pursuing the likenessnesses.

(*CN* II, 2372)

As he grew older, though, he started compensating too much the other way as 'likeness' began to predominate over '*difference*' in the search for judgement, a paucity of illustration corresponding to the increasing stasis of Coleridge's actual life. This is reflected in the shape and substance of the entries as an early predilection for the short and self-contained gave way to lengthier, holistic inquiries with a moral, theological and philosophical focus that were 'less elliptical and more argumentative than in the earlier volumes', and in which Coleridge drafted passages for treatises such as *The Friend*, the *Biographia Literaria* and the *Lay Sermons* (*CN* III, xix.).

The style of the entries also changed accordingly as youthful delight waned in natural description, literary criticism and aphorism – 'Unbiased mind – an absurdity' (*CN* I, 59); 'Doing nothing ends in being nothing' (*CN* I, 319) – and as there were fewer opportunities to travel widely, which always used to elicit alertness: 'pigs in Naples tried for their lard-fat by running a hot wire into the nape of their neck, & instantly stopping when the pig squeaks – the wire shows the fat's depth' (*CN* II, 2309). A resurgence of this writerly energy in later years is therefore immediately perceptible, and Coleridge's tour through Belgium, Germany and the Netherlands with William Wordsworth and his daughter Dora in mid-1828 attests to the ways in which being in the world produced a different kind of responsiveness in his notebook prose from living in his head: 'Thursday, 26 June – by a Caravan / O Lord! O Lord! – to Waterloo – the slipping down on the Roof to avoid having our Brains knocked out by passing under the Gateway at [? Hugo] Sainte & literally scorched our my Nadir' (*CN* V, 5884).

Such effects are observable not simply across time but also across notebooks. In an attempt 'to get launched on creative work' during a slump in October 1803, Coleridge returned to the sunrise he had sketched in a pocketbook on his way to London in November 1799, this time copying out the entry – a common practice – from Notebook 5 into Notebook 21 as part of a collage of old observations to which he reverted for inspiration (*CN* I (Notes), xli):[15]

Nov. 27th – a most interesting morning. 1799. Awoke from one [of] my painful Coach-Sleeps, in the Coach to London. It was a rich Orange Sky like that of a winter Evening save that the fleecy dark blue Clouds that rippled above it, shewed it to be Morning – these soon became of a glowing Brass Colour, brassy Fleeces, wool-packs in shape / rising high up into the Sky. The Sun at length rose upon the flat Plain, like a Hill of Fire in the distance, rose wholly, & in the water that flooded part of the Flat a deep column of Light. – But as the Coach went on, a Hill rose and intercepted the Sun – and the Sun in a few minutes *rose* over it, a compleat 2nd rising, thro' other clouds and with a different Glory.   (*CN* I, 1589)

In revisiting the original, Coleridge rewrote his impression of the dawn that day with fresh sensations ('my painful Coach-Sleeps'), images ('wool-packs in shape'), similes (like a Hill of Fire') and other details ('a compleat 2nd rising') which he transposed into a more sedate and fluent style, thereby changing the nature of his experience of the past. This is corroborated by the punctuation of the 1799 version, which holds open the possibility that the 'different Glory' might be attributable to 'Starlings', an ambiguity that is foreclosed in the 1803 account, in which the phrase refers only to the sun, thus proving that a first reaction need not be a shallow one. In essence, Coleridge sought revitalization by imaginatively re-purposing his memory in the hope of creating himself anew.

Gaining access to different versions of himself through revision was also familiar to Wordsworth, who inveterately returned to the autobiographical poem he addressed to Coleridge and which, for much of its fifty-two-year gestation, he similarly never intended to publish. When that poem did appear in 1850, as *The Prelude, or Growth of a Poet's Mind*, it gave permanent expression to a form of self-reflection which, like Coleridge's notebook entries, had always been exploratory and subject to change. Although blank verse lent Wordsworth's life a rhythmic continuity which the rhizomatic appearance of notes less obviously possessed, it did not entirely subdue the fractal and palimpsestic design of recollected experience because poetic emendation was commonplace. From this perspective, *The Prelude* and the notebooks are both epics of introspective evolution.

Re-examining a poem or notebook was therefore not only a means of returning to the preoccupations of a prior self and to some remembrance of that person at the time of composition; it also enabled reinvention. In this way, Coleridge's preservation and modification of his mental life in notebooks had productively paradoxical effects: it allowed him to chart his growth, but self-curation also made selfhood into a momentary and unstable phenomenon rather than a consistent entity.[16] The technique of re-tuning oneself by reading over previous records has a precursor in the ancient Greek ethos which Michel Foucault has described as 'taking care of oneself ... and keeping notebooks in order to reactivate for oneself the truths one needed'.[17] Through this process, it was not the secretive dimensions of a life – 'the unspeakable … the hidden … the unsaid' – which this culture of notation (*hupomnēmata*) was designed to pursue and expose, but rather the intention was, as Foucault outlined in 'Self Writing': 'to capture the already-said, to collect what one has managed to hear or read, and for a purpose that is nothing less than the shaping of the self'.[18] Coleridge documented both 'the hidden' and 'the already-said' in order to see, shape and understand himself, and at several junctures the practice of noting down his secrets led him to express concern about what would happen were he to die 'without having the power of destroying these & my other pocket books, the history of my own mind for my own improvement' (*CN* II, 2368). Indeed, entries in cipher or in multiple languages attest to that worry and to the pressure he sometimes felt to conceal his inmost thoughts (cf. *CN* III, 3325), not least as they presented a chronicle of intense love for Sara Hutchinson. In moods of dejection or despair, the notebooks offered Coleridge a way of dealing with the unshakeable feeling 'that I have been always preyed on by some Dread' (*CN* II, 2398), as he put it in 1805, and were a surrogate companion to him in especially intense bouts of loneliness: 'Ah! dear Book! Sole Confidant of a breaking Heart, whose social nature compels *some* Outlet' (*CN* III, 3325). Nonetheless, although they periodically took on a cathartic function to assuage depression, sometimes enabling Coleridge to turn pain into something productive, far more often he found solace and self-improvement in going back through his notebooks to re-engage with the 'history of [his] own mind', much like Wordsworth, rather than through expressly remedial acts of writing.

Coleridge derived his respect for speculative thinking, tentative expression and partial judgements from using notebooks, whilst acts of re-reading and revision dialogically schooled his awareness of the fragmentary and fickle nature of selfhood, liable to be momentarily certain but subsequently found to be 'in error', as he proclaimed to a prospective readership in 1830:

> If any Stranger should light on this or the preceding Numbers of the 'Fly-catcher,' let him read them not as asserted truths but as processes of a mind working toward truth – & construe the occasional *positiveness* of the language as expressing only the conviction of the moment, which however lively is yet quite compatible with an unfeigned, yea, at the very moment co-present, sense of the probability of my being in error, or at least of half-truth.
>
> (*CN* V, 6450)

'Fly-catcher' was a term with which Coleridge referred to his notebooks from the late 1820s, labelling Notebook 35 the 'Fly-Catcher / or / Daybook for impounding / Stray Nota-benes', a title more fulsomely incarnated in Notebook 56 as 'Volatilia / or / Day-book / for bird-liming / Small

Thoughts, / Impounding Stray Thoughts / and / holding for Trial doubtful Thoughts / March 1827' (*CN* v, xxvii, l). These headings link the piecemeal and serendipitous nature of thinking with the belief that the activity itself was an infraction which the notebooks were supposed to contain. They suggest that Coleridge conceived his observations to exist on a spectrum of unboundedness which ranged from unbiddable dog ('Impounding Stray Thoughts') to caught conspiracist ('holding for Trial doubtful Thoughts'), which is nicely confirmed by the way in which the senses of 'Volatilia' shuttle between the fleeting, the flying and the erratic.

The trope of the 'Fly-catcher' fitted Coleridge's 1828 note that 'From the earliest time I can remember, I discovered I lived with my Thoughts, as my fellow-creatures' (*CN* IV, 5268), and he consistently summoned a lowly kingdom of the emergent imagination to characterize his cerebralism, invoking his reflections variously as 'shapeless Jellies' (*CL* II, 962), 'a pregnant Polypus ... clung all over with young Polypi' (*CN* II, 2431) and 'Surinam Toads' (*CL* III, 95). Although this imagery emphasizes the potential for organic intellectual growth, it also typifies thinking as a proleptic practice – 'as if I were on the *brink* of a Fruition still denied' – as Coleridge put it in looking carefully 'at a beautiful Object or Landscape' (*CN* III, 3767), which he often did in the notebooks. A 'Fly-catcher' was thus an apt repository for someone who once confessed that 'Nothing affects me much at the moment it happens ... For a Thing at the moment is but a Thing of the moment / it must be taken up into the mind, diffuse itself thro' the whole multitude of Shapes & Thoughts, not one of which it leaves untinged' (*CN* I, 1597). However, this need for rigorous dissemination exacerbated Coleridge's tendency to 'lay too many Eggs <in the hot Sands of this Wilderness, the World!> With Ostrich Carelessness & Ostrich Oblivion' (*CN* I, 1248), and such failures of gestation were a direct corollary of his notebook prodigiousness: 'If one thought leads to another, so often does it blot out another ... My Thoughts crowd each other to death' (*CN* III, 3342). When dejected, Coleridge felt that his heroically attentive engagements with the world were unsustainable, resulting in 'endless fruitless Memoranda' (*CN* II, 2474) rather than sparking anything fully fledged. This left him ironically trapped in a web of his own making, as he once lamented in an 1806 note on the relation of primary and secondary consciousness: 'O Lord! What thousands of Threads in how large a Web may not a Metaphysical Spider spin out of the Dirt of his own Guts / but alas! it is a net for his own super-ingenious Spidership alone!' (*CN* II, 2784).

Moreover, there was the additional danger that such modest and far-reaching habits of collection promoted a degenerative rather than developing model of inquiry: 'Merely not to exclude any fly from this Fly-catcher, or any grain that *may* be a maggot which *may* become a Fly, I ask –' (*CN* v, 5679). Whilst amassing flies was all very well for a spider, it did not make much of a meal for a man, and the alias could inadvertently engineer a tragicomic bathos which brought the nickname into question: 'The great importance of the distinction between the Mesothesis or Indifference, & the Synthesis in the Noetic Pentad is stated at large in a former Number of the Fly-catcher' (*CN* v, 5726). In fact, the more emphasis Coleridge placed on 'Synthesis', the less value he ascribed to the provisional and the experimental, which the note-books did so much positively to condition as a constitutive part of his intel-lect. It was yet another dilemma of quantity and arrangement – 'i.e. plurality in unity' – which Coleridge's modern editors have been obliged to recapitulate in necessarily forcing coherency on the multifariousness of the notebooks for the scholarly edition: 'At the cost of some consistency, an attempt has been made where possible to reconcile two irreconcilables, that is, to preserve the run of entries in a given notebook but also to hold to the chronology, i.e. to maintain the two orders of time and place' (*CN* I, xxviii).[19]

The 'Fly-catcher' is an appropriately mutable figure that permits the note-books to be re-imagined not as spider-webs randomly and passively detaining thought-flies in a 'Brain-factory' (*CN* v, 6291) but rather as birds capable both of individual selection and soaring above particulars as the occasion demanded, much like the twinned persuasions of Coleridge's embattled psyche. Indeed, in an 1810 entry on birdsong that was drawn from his anno-tations to the 1802 edition of Gilbert White's *The Natural History and Antiq-uities of Selborne*, Coleridge recorded: 'The Fly-catcher, mutest Bird, save only when maternal anxiety extort an inward plaintive note' (*CN* III, 3959). Consequently, the spider was not the sole psychological avatar available for a man whose trained curiosity, perceptive powers and diffuse conscious-ness caused him to see something in everything, thus spurring a diligent hope to catch his quarry before it escaped. The dimensions of Coleridge's intelligence, by turns fixed and free, straddled arachnid and avian poles which made the notebooks, alongside the *Biographia Literaria*, equally exemplary of Coleridge's early insight that he seemed 'to have made up my mind to write my metaphysical works, as *my Life, & in* my Life – inter-mixed with all the other events/ or history of the mind & fortunes' (*CN* I, 1515). Although the notebooks periodically induced the neurosis they were meant to satisfy, given that Coleridge's relentless assiduity left a troubling history of ambitions or aspirations unfulfilled, system could give way – and did – to pure delight in observation and feeling, which allows them to shine with the processive freedom of a mind which early on half-saw that it was instinct with the vitality of yet another kind of 'Fly-catcher': 'I would glide down the rivulet of quiet Life, a Trout!' (*CN* I, 54).

Notes

1 For details of the physical characteristics and usage of this pocketbook, referred to in the scholarly edition as Notebook 5, consult *CN* I (Notes), xxix–xxx.

2 Cf. H. J. Jackson, 'Coleridge as Reader: Marginalia', in *The Oxford Handbook of Samuel Taylor Coleridge*, ed. Frederick Burwick (Oxford University Press, 2012), 271–87 (279).

3 William Hazlitt, 'Mr. Coleridge', in *The Spirit of the Age: or Contemporary Portraits* (London, 1825), 61–79 (62).

4 The classic study on this subject is Seamus Perry, *Coleridge and the Uses of Division* (Oxford University Press, 1999); for a more recent re-examination see Seamus Perry, 'Coleridge's Desultoriness', *Studies in Romanticism*, 59.1 (2020), 15–34. Cf. Kathleen Dugas, 'Struggling with the Contingent: Self-Conscious Imagination in Coleridge's Notebooks', in *Coleridge's Imagination: Essays in Memory of Pete Laver*, eds. Richard Gravil, Lucy Newlyn and Nicholas Roe (Cambridge University Press, 1985), 53–68 (57).

5 Charles Lamb, 'Detached Thoughts on Books and Reading', *London Magazine*, 6 (July 1822), 33–6 (33).

6 On Coleridge's use of the notebooks for science and theology in the 1820s and beyond consult *CN* IV, xiii; *CN* V, xxii–xxiii. For the argument that the notebooks should be 'reassessed as a new stage in the evolution of the commonplace book tradition', see Jillian M. Hess, 'Coleridge's Fly-Catchers: Adapting Commonplace-Book Form', *Journal of the History of Ideas*, 73.3 (2012), 463–83 (464).

7 Kathleen Coburn's 'Introduction' to the *Notebooks* in this volume is indispensable for giving a sense of their myriad life and contents; see *CN* I, xvii–xli.

8 Paul Cheshire, 'Coleridge's *Notebooks*', in *Oxford Handbook of Coleridge*, ed. Burwick, 288–306 (289–90).

9 For further difficulties of dating and presentation in the scholarly edition, consult Coburn's comments on the Gutch book, which was used 'with a wild extravagance that scandalized Coleridge later' (*CN* I, xxviii).

10 Charles Lamb also infrequently wrote in the notebooks during Coleridge's lifetime (*CN* I, xxxiv). For details of Notebook 21 see *CN* I (Notes), xl–xlii.

11 Anthony John Harding, 'Coleridge's Notebooks and the Case for a Material Hermeneutics of Literature', *Romanticism*, 6.1 (2000), 1–19 (8): 'Some of the later notebooks were clearly circulated, with Coleridge's full knowledge and consent, among close friends (Anne Gillman, Charles Lamb, John Sterling) and collaborators (Joseph Henry Green, James Gillman).'

12 Kathleen Coburn, *The Self Conscious Imagination: A Study of the Coleridge Notebooks in Celebration of the Bi-Centenary of His Birth 21 October 1772* (Oxford University Press, 1974), 21, 50.

13 Kathleen Coburn, *Experience into Thought: Perspectives in the Coleridge Notebooks* (London: University of Toronto Press, 1979), 21.

14 Josie Dixon, 'The Notebooks', in *The Cambridge Companion to Coleridge*, ed. Lucy Newlyn (Cambridge University Press, 2002), 75–88 (86). Cf. Patricia M. Ball, *The Science of Aspects: The Changing Role of Fact in the Work of Coleridge, Ruskin and Hopkins* (London: Athlone Press, 1971), 46.

15 Cf. *CN* III, 3420: 'O let me rouse myself – If I even begin mechanically, & only by aid of memory look round and call each thing by a name – describe it, as a

trial of skill in words – it may bring back fragments of former Feeling – For we can live only by feeding abroad.'

16 For the creation of 'a momentary self' in the notebooks see Anthony John Harding, 'Coleridge's Notebooks: Manuscript to Print to Database', *Coleridge Bulletin*, 24 (2004), 1–10 (7).

17 *Technologies of the Self: A Seminar with Michel Foucault*, eds. Luther H. Martin, Huck Gutman and Patrick H. Hutton (Amherst: University of Massachusetts Press, 1988), 27.

18 *The Essential Works of Michel Foucault 1954–1984*, vol. 1, *Ethics: Subjectivity and Truth*, ed. Paul Rabinow and trans. Robert Hurley (New York: The New Press, 1997), 210–11.

19 For a condensed one-volume edition with its own numbering scheme arranged chronologically and by place see Seamus Perry, *Coleridge's Notebooks: A Selection* (Oxford University Press, 2002).

II

KURTIS HESSEL

Coleridge and Science

In the margin of *Aurora*, a religious work by seventeenth-century Christian mystic Jakob Böhme, Coleridge jotted an encomium to the age's pre-eminent English chemist: 'Humphry Davy in his Laboratory is probably doing more for the Science of Mind, than all the Metaphysicians have done from Aristotle to Hartley, inclusive' (*CM* I, 566). Surprising as it is to find Coleridge praising a nineteenth-century chemist in the margins of a seventeenth-century Christian text, the association makes sense. This odd palimpsest symbolizes Coleridge's relationship to science, especially his need to integrate it with other forms of knowledge. Böhme's chapter frames an analogy around the Trinity, explaining how a trifold arrangement inheres in God, humanity and nature, uniting them all. Coleridge expected Davy's research would reveal the divine laws governing matter, reconciling human mind, nature and the divine as ably as Böhme, and fulfilling his religious vision scientifically.

Coleridge's engagement with science developed out of his position straddling two different scientific paradigms: eighteenth-century 'natural philosophy' and the burgeoning nineteenth-century disciplinary framework. He yearned for the syncretism of eighteenth-century science and recoiled from the narrow scope of individuated fields. Indeed, the above note indicates that Coleridgean consilience united science conceptually with religion across broad swathes of time. Other commitments were more transitory. Coleridge came to science through radical politics, though this association lingered even after he had disowned his former enthusiasm. As he turned increasingly to philosophy and metaphysics in his later life, his engagement with science took an inward turn that also reshaped his expectations about its social utility. This chapter will trace some of these developments, highlighting important figures who shaped Coleridge's changing relationship to science.

Breaking the Glass, or the Crisis of 'Natural Philosophy'

Picture Coleridge's first image of science lit by the flames reflecting in the shards of smashed glassware littering the cobbles outside Joseph Priestley's ransacked Birmingham home. Priestley (alongside other Birmingham Unitarians in 1791) had been punished for his reformist sentiments by a church and king mob, his home and scientific instruments made casualties to reactionary rage. Coleridge didn't see the riots himself, but their grim shadows played across the scrim of his imagination, and in 1795 he wrote in 'Religious Musings' of how 'Statesmen blood-stain'd and priests idolatrous / By dark lies mad'ning the blind multitude / Drove [Priestley] with vain hate' 'from his loved native land' (*CPW* I, i, lines 373–76). Priestley – and other dissenting intellectuals, including Erasmus Darwin – gave shape to Coleridge's political and religious radicalism and fostered his interest in natural philosophy. Priestley famously described, in the preface to his *Experiments and Observations on Different Kinds of Air* (1774), how the 'rapid progress of knowledge' would 'be the means, under God, of extirpating *all* error and prejudice, and of putting an end to all undue and usurped authority in the business of *religion*, as well as of *science*'. Indeed, science would reform the state, Priestley asserted, and 'the English hierarchy (if there be anything unsound in its constitution) has equal reason to tremble even at an air-pump, or an electrical machine'.[1]

During the eighteenth century, science took the form of what historians of science call 'natural philosophy', a largely undifferentiated pursuit, neither riven into disciplines with hard boundaries nor alienated from politics, fancy or faith. Natural philosophers, primarily supported by aristocratic patronage or royal charter, rarely confined themselves to a single course of study; the modern university's professionalized and stabilized disciplines were absent from eighteenth-century science. Priestley, for instance, began his scientific studies investigating optics, shifted to electricity and then took up the chemistry of airs, all while writing metaphysical and theological treatises. From our vantage point, these pursuits appear eclectic because we assign the studies of optics and electricity to physics and the study of the composition of matter (Priestley's work on airs) to chemistry. But as historian of science Simon Schaffer argues, our 'historical preconception of the real map of knowledge' can obscure 'the existence of a set of practices which centred on the climate, meteorology, the atmosphere, and electricity'. Experimenters could explore these areas together because natural philosophy 'extended itself through a whole cosmos of active powers in which the role of the natural philosopher was central: the task was to exploit control over these powers to draw out and make manifest the theological and moral implications for the audience' – sometimes through spectacular demonstration.[2]

Ultimately, though, natural philosophy's reliance on spectacle led to a crisis of authority by century's end. Scientific elites became increasingly concerned about charlatans who abused public credulity with extravagant demonstrations, simultaneously undermining faith that the 'powers' they revealed were actually divine.[3] Partisans like politician Edmund Burke exploited this distrust to undermine the natural philosophers' credibility. In *A Letter to a Noble Lord* (1796), Burke argues that 'the geometricians, and the chymists bring, the one from the dry bones of their diagrams, and the other from the soot of their furnaces, dispositions that make them worse than indifferent about those feelings and habitudes, which are the supports of the moral world'.[4] This conceit so roused Coleridge's indignation that he singled it out in *The Watchman*'s first issue, where he lauds the chemist, 'whose faculties are swallowed up in the great task of discovering those perfect laws by which the Supreme Wisdom governs the Universe!' (*Watchman*, 34). At the time, Coleridge venerated Priestley because his scientific studies were inextricable from his metaphysical beliefs and informed by his Unitarian faith. This appreciation for the syncretic joint investigation of science, religion and politics recurs in *The Watchman*'s third issue, in which Coleridge favourably reviews a letter by his Bristol friend, the chemist and doctor Thomas Beddoes, cataloguing how natural philosophy could help the poor. Coleridge praises Beddoes's observation that 'while the French have pressed into their service all the inventive powers of the chemist and mechanic, the sons of science in Britain (almost without exception) are known to regard the system and measures of the Minister with contempt or abhorrence' (*Watchman*, 100). This point inverts Burke's depiction of French science as immoral because abstracted from real circumstances: the French, in fact, are to be praised for pressing science into the service of social improvement. Meanwhile, the 'sons of science' in England (for Beddoes and Coleridge, a dissenting scientific tradition based in the west and the Midlands and separate from the scientific establishment and the Royal Society) cannot serve their country because their moral convictions prevent them from cooperating with Prime Minister Pitt's repressive government.

In his early poetry, Coleridge discussed science's central role, when intertwined with religion, in human moral development, a clear debt to the natural philosophy tradition. In 'Religious Musings' he begins by framing early humanity's invention of property and

> th' inventive arts, that nurs'd the soul
> To Forms of beauty, and by sensual wants
> Unsensualiz'd the mind, which in the means
> Learnt to forget the grossness of the end,
> Best pleasur'd with its own activity. (*CPW* I, i, lines 208–12)

Property and 'th' inventive arts' encourage both vice and virtue: on the one hand they gratify ease and greed, but on the other they inspire a love of beauty and encourage ingenuity. For Coleridge, the senses were productive of knowledge but could not serve as an endpoint in themselves (relying on the senses exclusively was the mistake of materialist science). Reflection, by contrast, 'unsensualized the mind', enabling the consideration of ideas and ultimately supersensual natural laws. Coleridge describes how envy, competition, violence, civic hierarchy and poverty are the immediate products of 'the inventive arts', but eventually 'From Avarice thus, from Luxury and War / Sprang heavenly Science; and from Science Freedom' (*CPW* I, i, lines 224–25). The achievement of science, by which Coleridge means systematic knowledge inclusive of natural philosophy and philosophy more generally, allows us to query our place in nature, understand our relationship with God and repudiate destructive acts arising from the passions. Coleridge drew the outlines of this developmental narrative from David Hartley's *Observations on Man* (1749), in which Hartley lays out a system of associative psychology positing a material basis for how sense impressions are received and transmitted to the mind as vibrations, combining in increasingly complex ways to form all human ideas.[5] Hartley's philosophy lays out a trajectory from 'Imagination' to 'Ambition', with higher intellectual pleasures being sympathy, piety and 'the moral sense'. In 'Religious Musings', natural philosophers such as Hartley and Priestley display and disseminate the highest forms of knowledge:

> O'er waken'd realms Philosophers and Bards
> Spread in concentric circles: they whose souls
> Conscious of their high dignities from God
> Brook not wealth's rivalry; and they who long
> Enamour'd with the charms of order hate
> Th' unseemly disproportion.   (*CPW* I, i, lines 226–31)

In these later stages of development, the philosopher's self-awareness drives his repudiation of wealth and 'unseemly disproportion'. Likewise, he turns 'from the victor's car / And the low puppetry of thrones' (*CPW* I, i, lines 232–33), suggesting that science fuels a rejection of repressive government and an embrace of the dispossessed.

Irreligious natural philosophers drew criticism from Coleridge. For instance, he disapproved of Erasmus Darwin's dismissal of religion: 'Dr. Darwin would have been ashamed to have rejected Hutton's theory of the earth without having minutely examined it ... but *all at once he makes up his mind* on such important subjects, as whether we be the outcasts of a blind idiot called nature, or the children of an all-wise and infinitely good God' (*CL* I, 177). More generally, Coleridge expressed hostility to any materialist science with no place for divinity. His contribution to Robert Southey's *Joan of Arc* (1796), reworked as 'The Destiny of Nations: A Vision', captures this antipathy:

> But some there are who deem themselves most free
> When they within this gross and visible sphere
> Chain down the winged thought, scoffing ascent
> Proud in their meanness: and themselves they cheat
> With noisy emptiness of learned phrase,
> Their subtle fluids, impacts, essences,
> Self-working tools, uncaused effects, and all
> Those blind Omniscients, those Almighty Slaves,
> Untenanting Creation of its God.   (*CPW* I, i, lines 27–35)

A note in Southey's *Joan of Arc* indicates that Coleridge was criticizing Newton's 'very subtle and elastic fluid, which he calls æther' as incapable of explaining the phenomena it sought to reconcile (æther supposedly pervaded all bodies and acted as the medium for gravitation and electricity).[6] George S. Erving explains how 'Destiny of Nations' rejected an eighteenth-century Newtonian tradition that Coleridge perceived as fanciful and mechanistic, instead embracing in Priestley's thought an alternative to Newtonianism, which offered a 'metaphysical monism that effaced the distinction between matter and spirit, mind and brain, man and nature'.[7] Nevertheless, when Coleridge later abandoned his Unitarianism for Trinitarian Anglicanism, he found godlessness in Priestley's theories where God had been before. An 1805 notebook entry criticizes the '*hollow faith*' and '*ambiguous purpose*' of Coleridge's youth, when his mind was 'wavering in its necessary passage from Unitarianism (which as I have often said is the Religion of a man, whose Reason would make him an Atheist but whose Heart and Common sense will not permit him to be so) thro' Spinosism into Plato and St John', ultimately pronouncing that 'Unitarianism in all its forms is Idolatry' (*CN* II, 2448). Priestley's rejection of Jesus' divinity ultimately rendered his whole system irreconcilable with Coleridge's growing Trinitarianism, and subsequent notebook entries enrolled Priestley (unjustly) in the godless lineage of John Locke (see *CN* II, 2598, *CN* II, 2627, and *CN* III, 3281).

Nevertheless, during this period of *'ambiguous purpose'* Coleridge cemented many expectations about science's moral and social utility, particularly through his exposure to the pneumatic research that Thomas Beddoes pioneered from 1794 and that took institutional form in the Bristol Pneumatic Institution (which opened in 1799). This research aimed to produce medical applications for the science of airs developed from Priestley's experiments, including his discovery of 'dephlogisticated air' (oxygen), which he determined was better able to support life and combustion than common air and which was therefore more 'virtuous'.[8] According to Schaffer, Priestley's experiments inspired pan-European research in which 'the atmosphere was taken to be a major site at which principles of health and disease were produced', occasioning 'a new practice of policy recommendations for the better management of the social economy and the human body'.[9] Along these lines, Beddoes hoped to develop aeriform medical treatments to administer free to the poor. He drew upon the system of Scottish physician John Brown, who posited that sickness resulted from excessive or inadequate internal stimulation. Beddoes hoped that breathing newly discovered airs would help regulate stimulation.[10] The connection to Beddoes influenced Coleridge's poetry as much as his philosophy. Tim Fulford argues that Wordsworth's and Coleridge's nature poems of the period – the so-called 'Greater Romantic Lyric' – 'were interventions in contemporary social and political debate rather than idealizing and transcendent escapes from it', as critics since the 1980s have argued. Pneumatic Institution research involved self-experimentation, with Beddoes and his assistant Humphry Davy (and volunteers including Coleridge and Southey) breathing gases and chronicling the effects. Fulford emphasizes how these accounts 'foregrounded, in their narrative voice and form as well as their content, the effects of individual subjectivity on experimental results: subjectivity both as affected by the tested nature and also as affecting that nature'.[11] In Fulford's reading, poems including 'Effusion xxxv', 'Frost at Midnight' and 'Kubla Khan' embraced this model – turns in the thought stream narrated by the poet arise from changes in the body, typically accompanied by references to breathing, air and atmospheric conditions. These poems offer minute narrations of shifting subjectivities responding intimately to their environments. Far from transcending the material world, Coleridge's early poetry, and his understanding of a person's relationship to the world, were marked by his exposure to Beddoes's science. Long after he had abandoned materialist methods as atheistic, he continued to assert that the science of nature needed to unite a study of nature's laws with a careful account of subjectivity.

Coleridge formed a close affinity with Beddoes's assistant Humphry Davy, attracted to his enthusiasm for unified scientific theories that joined disparate phenomena and displayed poetic vision. Looking back on this period from 1823, Coleridge characterized Davy as 'the Father and Founder of philosophic Alchemy' (*CL* v, 309), highlighting Davy's scientific accounts of dynamic transformations and distancing him from the field-bound designation 'chemist'. Davy's first publication, 'An Essay on Heat, Light, and the Combinations of Light' (1799), certainly made alchemical promises (which Davy later disowned as fantastical), arguing that oxygen gas was actually 'phosoxygen', a chemical combination of light and oxygen, which humans respired and which then played a role in the nervous system. Davy grounded his views on a fundamental polarity between 'repulsive' and 'attractive' forces, and he sketched a ranging theory attributing myriad phenomena to these forces' differential and opposed influences, ultimately positing that 'one law alone may govern and act upon matter: an energy of mutation, impressed by the will of the Deity, a law which might be called the law of animation, tending to produce the greatest possible sum of perception, the greatest possible sum of happiness'.[12] The argument's simplicity, universality and piety must have appealed to Coleridge. Davy also shared Coleridge's scepticism about establishment science, claiming to have disproved both Newton's theory of æther and prominent French chemist Antoine Lavoisier's theory of 'caloric', the imponderable matter of heat and a theoretical replacement for Priestley's phlogiston.[13] As he elaborated these visionary theories, Davy also wrote his own poetry. Coleridge lauded his trajectory as 'the Man who *born* a Poet first converted Poetry into Science and *realized* what few men possessed Genius enough to *fancy*' (*CL* v, 309). Davy's poetic writing fed his capacity as a philosophical alchemist, and he drew upon his Bristol friends' poetic language when composing his account of breathing nitrous oxide for his *Researches, Chemical and Philosophical, Chiefly Concerning Nitrous Oxide and its Respiration* (1800), thereby becoming an embodiment of their hopes, a scientist/poet interpreting nature's significance for body and mind. Davy's poem 'The Spinosist', written in a notebook from this period, captures in verse his commitment to Coleridgean unity:

> All, All is change, the renovated forms
> Of ancient things arise & live again.
> The light of suns the angry breath of storms
> The everlasting motions of the main
> Are but the engines of that powerful will. –
> The eternal link of thoughts where form resolves
> Have ever acted & are acting still.[14]

Spinozist monism, which Davy probably gleaned from Coleridge, frames an account of matter's recycling throughout the cosmos. The reference to the 'light of suns' recalls Davy's theory about phosoxygen, while the passage also links material changes in nature to the exercise of a divine will. Part of what must have excited Coleridge about Davy was his ability to ruminate on cosmological unity through multiple interlocking frameworks.

Davy likewise aligned the arts and sciences with reform. In the same notebook where he jotted 'The Spinosist', he noted how English elites had 'squandered away much of their thought in luxury & the vanity of pleasure' and wondered 'what might we not hope for in a state [of] society in which the character of the philosopher was united to that of the artist & in which it became the business of men & property & power eminently to patronise the sciences'. Davy doesn't seem to have held radical convictions, given that he qualifies his views: 'In this hope we do not amuse ourself with visionary theories; with thoughts concerning the infinite perfectibility of the human species, the annihilation of disease, labor & even death. – We look to a time which we may reasonably expect, to a bright day of which we already perceive the dawn.'[15] Despite his gradualist views, he nevertheless engaged the sociality of the Bristol circle post-radicals, writing to inform a friend in 1800 that Southey's *Annual Anthology*, 'your favorite poeticojacobinical Anthology', would soon be printed.[16] Regardless, Coleridge associated Davy with radical politics, as is evident from an 1802 notebook entry on Davy's lectures, which closes, 'If all aristocrats here, how easily Davy might poison them all' (*CN* I, 1098). The natural philosophy of the Bristol circle, personified in Davy, remained linked to radical politics well after Coleridge had claimed, in 1798, to have broken his 'squeaking baby-trumpet of Sedition' (*CL* I, 397). He could not separate science from the millenarian hopes it had fed, leaving him fantasizing about Davy single-handedly carrying off the French Revolution's aims, and fulfilling Priestley's prophesy about the threat science posed to an unjust state.

Re-Fusing the Shards of Science

But science was changing and would become mostly institutionalized, formalized and disciplined by the middle of the nineteenth century. Over the early decades discrete scientific disciplines gradually formed: specialist societies proliferated, field-specific journals were established and new arts and sciences institutions reorganized public knowledge.[17] According to Jan Golinski, 'this was a time in which new scientific disciplines such as geology, biology and physiology were founded and existing ones (especially physics and chemistry) dramatically reconfigured'. The stabilization of scientific disciplines was central to this process: 'Disciplinary boundaries, although they were sometimes to be breached or relocated, became a structuring feature of natural knowledge.'[18] These changes did not happen suddenly, and especially during the Romantic period significant cross-pollination occurred among intellectual pursuits. Nevertheless, scientists, poets and artists devoted rhetorical energy to evangelizing for their fields (often at the expense of other fields).[19] Jon Klancher explains how in the early nineteenth century, prominent institutions including the Royal, the British, the Surrey, the London, the Russell and the Metropolitan presented scientific and cultural knowledge to public subscribers as part of an arts and sciences matrix, from which fields emerged 'with dramatically uneven criteria of what counts as "knowledge" and which of these fields could most strongly lay claim to it'.[20] Even if these fields evinced diverse proprietary methods for authenticating information, their overall commitment to disciplinary coherence constituted the epistemological innovation of the age.

This inchoate disciplinarity inspired Coleridge's uneasy relationship with the newly systematized discipline of chemistry. Antoine Lavoisier and a group of French chemists had provided a new nomenclature and focus to chemistry during the 1770s and 1780s.[21] Their 'revolutionary' system focused on chemical elements, reconceived from the classical four (earth, air, fire, water) into a more disciplinarily situated concept: 'if we apply the term *elements* or *principles of bodies*, to express our idea of the last point which analysis is capable of reaching, we must admit, as elements, all the substances into which we are able to reduce bodies by decomposition.'[22] The modern element was tied to the chemical discipline's techniques; it no longer designated a universally stable set of fundaments, but a provisional endpoint of experimentation. This innovation shifted the discipline towards stoichiometry – chemists would break substances into their constituents to categorize them. According to Bernadette Bensaude-Vincent and Isabelle Stengers, 'the chemical reaction was no longer an object of study in itself but a means of determining the elementary composition of the products of reaction'.[23] John Dalton heightened this focus with his theory of chemical proportions and the conceptual reintroduction of atoms, rendering chemistry a counting science and offering it a legible programme, easy to frame in public lectures, that established it as 'the very image of an exemplary science, a model of positivity'.[24] Coleridge responded ambivalently. He thrilled at chemistry's potential, describing his intellectual interests in 1796 thus: 'Metaphysics, & Poetry, & "Facts of mind" … are my darling studies … Of useful knowledge, I am a so-so chemist, & I love chemistry' (*CL* I, 260). In 1801, he wrote excitedly to Davy for advice about setting up a chemistry laboratory in the Lake District (*CL* II, 670–72). But Coleridge also expressed impatience with the discipline's public form. In another letter the same year he claims,

> As far as *words* go, I have become a formidable chemist – having got by heart a prodigious quantity of terms &c to which I attach *some* ideas ... That which most discourages me in it is that I find all *power* & vital attributes to depend on modes of *arrangement* – and that Chemistry throws not even a distant rush-light glimmer upon this subject. (*CL* II, 727)

For Coleridge, chemical 'arrangement' was an inadequate endpoint because it didn't explain '*power* & vital attributes'. He expected chemists to unveil the forces behind chemical combination, putting himself at odds with an establishment that had shifted from studying 'the chemical reaction' itself to 'the elementary composition of the products of reaction'.[25]

To ground the sciences on deeper principles, Coleridge integrated them into his metaphysics. In this way, his epistemological vision for the sciences hearkened to the natural philosophy model, though with a more rigorous conceptual framework. *The Friend* conveys how the sciences' 'full evolution' would require integrating them as 'the organs of one vital and harmonious body' (*Friend* I, 493). Incomplete science relies exclusively on 'the Understanding' to form 'theories' based on aggregated observations about natural phenomena; exemplary of this faculty's limitations, the experimentalism of benighted materialists flashes from explanation to explanation (Coleridge might have considered in this light Lavoisier's replacement of Priestley's phlogiston with caloric). The Understanding, for Coleridge, is 'the conception of the Sensuous, or the faculty by which we generalize and arrange the phænomena of perception', giving it a central role in organizing an individual's sense impressions into coherent experience (*Friend* I, 156). True science, by contrast, draws upon 'the Reason', which Coleridge describes as 'an organ of inward sense' that grants the mind 'the power of acquainting itself with invisible realities or spiritual objects' (*Friend* I, 156). The Reason is Coleridge's supersensual faculty, the divine ordering impulse in humanity subjecting experience to systematic scrutiny and aiming to unveil universal 'Laws'. These are science's proper objects, relations between objects established by 'the Supreme Being, whose creative IDEA not only appoints to each thing its *position*, but in that position, and in consequence of that position, gives it its qualities, yea, gives its very existence, as *that particular* thing' (*Friend* I, 459). Framing Laws requires reconciling nature with mind: 'Yet in whatever Science the relation of the parts to each other and to the whole is predetermined by a truth originating in the *mind*, and not abstracted or generalized from observation of the parts, there we affirm the presence of a *law*' (*Friend* I, 459). For Coleridge, the quintessential system of pure Reason is geometry, and he argues that practitioners of empirical sciences should form explanations of mathematical precision for the relations between their objects of scrutiny. The Understanding aids the Reason, just as theories can be 'tentative exercises in the hope of discovering' laws (*Friend* 1, 465–66), but it offers an imperfect (because individual and particular) explanation. Much of Coleridge's criticism of popular nineteenth-century science hinged on his conviction that it was too much a product of the Understanding and not enough of the Reason.

Coleridge applied the same set of categories when he engaged public controversy around the nature of life, and once again he found disciplinary tools inadequate to philosophical ends. Between 1814 and 1819 and into the 1820s, two prominent physicians, John Abernethy and William Lawrence, argued bitterly over the nature of life.[26] Abernethy believed that life was the result of a 'superadded' substance, analogous to electricity, which infused vitality into the body's dead matter. Lawrence, by contrast, held the materialist position that life arose from the organization of the body, and he forcefully rejected Abernethy's analogy between the matter of life and electricity. In increasingly acrimonious lecture series, Abernethy and Lawrence jousted, and the controversy spilled into the periodical press as a full-blown scandal. Partisans on either side accentuated its theological and political dimensions: Abernethy's position was outmoded, reactionary and empirically unprovable; Lawrence's was atheistic French radicalism warmed over. The debate seemed tailor-made to attract Coleridge's attention, and in his 'Theory of Life' (unpublished during his lifetime, but written contemporaneously to the fracas) he took a position that both engaged and superseded the debate. In the essay, he predictably rejects Lawrence's materialism as sensualist. By contrast, Coleridge supports Abernethy's position for its 'presentiment of a great truth' (*SWF* 1, 531) but wishes the doctor had 'developed his opinions systematically, and carried them yet further back, even to their ultimate principle!' (*SWF* 1, 487). The problem with then current definitions of life, Coleridge maintains, is that they fail to frame 'the *law* of the thing, or in such an *idea* of it, as, being admitted, all the properties and functions are admitted by implication' (*SWF* 1, 492–93). Previous commentators had selected individual processes like nutrition or reproduction as the basis of life; these theories failed for their reliance on the partial Understanding. Instead, Coleridge proposes as the central law of life 'the *power* which discloses itself from within as a principle of *unity* in the *many*' (*SWF* 1, 510). Life consists in an internal drive to proliferation coalescing into unified kinds: differentiated organs working together within a body or differentiated species linked by complex relations in nature. Coleridge expands the law's scope by relating life to non-life and positing a 'ladder' (*SWF* 1, 509) linking in ascending order 'the life of metals, as the power which effects and determines their comparative cohesion' (*SWF* I, 508), growing crystals, vegetable life and animals of increasing complexity, from molluscs to men. In this totalizing hierarchy, inorganic powers of electricity, magnetism and chemical affinity are folded into higher vital powers of reproduction, irritability and sensibility (*SWF* I, 526). The law of 'unity in *multeity*' (*SWF* I, 510) offers a simpler principle than Abernethy's that nevertheless governs a wider array of phenomena, and because this system is sprawling, pursuing it requires synthesizing many types of knowledge – chemistry, comparative physiology, geology, mathematics, philosophy and religion.

In Essays on Method, sets out a programme for forming such laws as 'Method', 'the science common to all sciences' (*Friend* I, 459–60). Method internalizes a habit of purposive arrangement that links all science. Coleridge believed that Method applied to all types of thought, so the essays begin with a reading of Method in Shakespeare's *Hamlet*, before taking up Plato's philosophy, botany, chemistry, the study of electricity and Francis Bacon, finally closing with a synthesized history of human Reason's providential development. Coleridge clarifies that 'the term, Method, cannot ... be applied to a mere dead arrangement, containing in itself no principle of progression' (*Friend* I, 457). Such an arrangement would be a product of Understanding. The arrangement of objects, observation, ideas and so on must be guided by a unifying purpose and, in the sciences, oriented towards articulating laws. Such a purpose 'can never in the sciences of experiment or in those of observation be adequately supplied by a theory built on generalizations' (*Friend* I, 476); rather, it must come from the Reason, with the scientist's mind identifying a focusing eternal principle that frames the selection, relation and generalization of objects and ideas. Coleridge characterizes Botany as an immethodical discipline that never progresses beyond 'an enormous nomenclature; a huge catalogue, *bien arrangé*, yearly and monthly augmented, in various editions, each with its own scheme of technical memory and its own convenience of reference!' (*Friend* I, 469). Such basic ordering offers an initial step, but Botany would need to engage a 'principle of progression' to attain a methodical character; it would need to pursue 'the central idea of vegetation itself, by the light of which we might have seen the collateral relations of the vegetable to the inorganic and to the animal world', or the field could take up 'the constitutive nature and inner necessity of sex itself' (*Friend* I, 467). Coleridge similarly maintains that chemists satisfied to identify and collate elementary substances have only taken their first step, and that a more complete accounting (the kind promised by Davy's electrochemical experiments) must achieve 'unity of principle through all the diversity of forms' (*Friend* I, 470). By contrast,

Coleridge describes how methodical thinking rapidly advanced the study of electricity through a host of 'insecure hypotheses' (*Friend* I, 478), which nevertheless yielded

> abstract from all these suppositions, or rather imaginations, that which is common to, and involved in them all … the idea of *two – opposite – forces*, tending to rest by equilibrium. These are the sole factors of the calculus, alike in all the theories. These give the *law*, and in it the *method*, both of arranging the phænomena and of substantiating appearances into facts of science.
>
> (*Friend* I, 478)

The ideal product of science is a rational law of relation, that of polarity. *The Friend*'s best-known chiasmus displays how important Coleridge considered the law of polarity to be: 'If in SHAKSPEARE we find nature idealized into poetry, through the creative power of a profound yet observant meditation, so through the meditative observation of a DAVY, a WOOLASTON, or a HATCHETT … we find poetry, as it were, substantiated and realized in nature' (*Friend* I, 471). Poetry and science stage the meeting of opposed mental and natural powers, approached from opposite poles. Ultimately, Coleridge sought to teach Method to his readers and expected it to serve the same socially improving function that had been fulfilled by his public radicalism in the past. By teaching readers to see Reason as connecting them with God and the world, he was preparing them to achieve what he then believed the revolution never could.

Coleridge evaluated his relationships to other thinkers by where they fitted in his life's evolving intellectual system at any given point, as is clear from his shifting assessment of Davy. His estimation of Davy proceeded in three stages. First came the period of fawning correspondence and passionate intellectual exchange described in my first section. However, some time after 1812, when Davy was knighted, Coleridge appended a new note in the margins of Böhme's *Aurora,* revising his opinion of his once friend: 'Alas! Since I wrote the preceding note, H. Davy is become Sir Humphry Davy, and an *Atomist!*' (*CM* I, 572). Davy was never, strictly speaking, an atomist,[27] so why would Coleridge, a careful thinker, mischaracterize him thus? This slight reflects changes in how both Coleridge and Davy conceived of science during Davy's time in the London chemical establishment. The change in Davy's social status discomfited Coleridge: Davy had become 'Sir Humphry Davy' (*CM* I, 572), and he would serve as President of the Royal Society from 1820 to 1828, leading Coleridge to cast a suspicious eye on his popularity and establishment credentials. He had written to a friend in 1804 that Davy seemed 'more and more determined to mould himself upon the Age in order to make the Age mould itself upon him' (*CL* I, 1042). Davy took pains in his lectures to distance himself from the radicalism of the Pneumatic Institution and appear more genteel in his Royal Institution lectures. The persona of 'H. Davy', who had joked about 'poeticojacobinical Anthologies' was a professional liability for Davy's London life. Though the Royal's original plan had included demonstrations and facilities to instruct the lower classes in the arts, its mission quickly shifted to benefit London's commercial elite and the aristocracy.[28] Even having repudiated his own radicalism, Coleridge must have chafed at the Royal's vision of science as infotainment for the leisure class, denuded of improving ambitions. Far from fulfilling Coleridge's hopes about 'philosophical Alchemy', Davy devoted himself to chemistry as a discipline, offering in his *Elements of Chemical Philosophy* (1812) a history of the field that posited stark breaks from its classical and alchemical forebears. Greek matter theories had been, in Davy's view, 'rather poetical than philosophical', a formulation that emphasizes poetry and philosophy as distinct – not opposed and mutually intermingled, as in Coleridge's conception. Likewise, this framing highlights poetry's inadequacy to scientific ends. Davy argues that the Greeks failed as philosophers 'because they reasoned more upon an imaginary system of nature, than upon the visible and tangible universe'. Far from embracing Coleridge's universal method, for which classical knowledge was pivotal to cultivating human Reason, Davy criticized classical knowledge like a narrowly disciplined materialist, while seemingly participating in the discipline's vogue for analysis. Though he always focused on understanding the forces behind chemical combination, his most famous discoveries consisted in isolating new elementary substances. Even though he rejected the facticity of Dalton's atoms, his demonstrations provided rhetorical ballast to a theory of elemental substances increasingly allied to atomism. Perhaps worst of all, Davy had made peace with Lavoisier, referring to his contention that 'every body which was not yet decompounded, should be considered as simple' as a 'logical and truly philosophical principle'.[29] For Coleridge, this would have been tantamount to atomism because elementary substances were not, in fact, elementary; they were 'the symbols of elementary powers, and the exponents of a law, which, as the root of all these powers, the chemical philosopher, whatever his theory may be, is instinctively labouring to extract' (*Friend* I, 470). Coleridge's opinion softened and improved some time before 1818, leading him to characterize Davy in *The Friend* as the scientific exemplar of Method, the opposite pole to Shakespeare, but the two never resumed the warm personal connection and intense affection of their youth.

In the end, we can identify several lasting components of Coleridge's relationship to science. He expected it to be consonant and eventually metaphysically intermingled with religion and philosophy. He detested the fragmentation of knowledge and sought explanatory continuities across epochs. While he repudiated his revolutionary enthusiasm, he never abandoned the expectation that science serve the moral purpose of social improvement; he merely shifted the medium by which he expected it to do so. When young, Coleridge thought men of science would shape society to achieve reformist results, while in later years he hoped individuals could be internally guided by science to moral ends. In these ways, we find a yearning for the syncretism of natural philosophy in Coleridge, though his reverence for Davy's exceptional genius as intrinsic to scientific development is a conspicuously nineteenth-century obsession.[30] Coleridge's residual sympathy to reform must have exacerbated his disappointment at Davy's social climbing, which, combined with Coleridge's aversion to disciplines, led him for a time to fabricate an atomist–mechanist Davy. Nevertheless, both men sought to reunify the sciences. In his later years Davy wrote *Consolations in Travel* (1830), a text modelled on medieval mystic Boethius's *Consolation of Philosophy* (523), in which Davy tries to reconcile religion and science, anticipates a future beyond disciplines and crafts an intellectual history spanning ages. Both men looked to the future and found themselves curiously drawn to the past. Perhaps this was a marker of their ambivalence as they entered a new age, our own age, when knowledge itself would be divided, subjected to regimes of authentication and regularization, and sold. And maybe Coleridge offers hints about how to respond to our own fragmented and atomized moment, an alternative pathway to discovering the world's interconnected plenitude.

Notes

1 Joseph Priestley, *Experiments and Observations on Different Kinds of Air* (London: J. Johnson, 1774), xiv.
2 Simon Schaffer, 'Natural Philosophy and Public Spectacle in the Eighteenth Century,' *History of Science* 21 (1983), 16, 5.
3 Schaffer, 'Natural Philosophy', 27–34.
4 Edmund Burke, *A Letter from the Right Honourable Edmund Burke to a Noble Lord* (London: J. Owen and F. and C. Rivington, 1796), 62.
5 For a concise account of Hartley's ideas see Trevor H. Levere, *Poetry Realized in Nature: Samuel Taylor Coleridge and Early Nineteenth-Century Science* (Cambridge University Press, 2002), 9–10. On Coleridge's engagement with brain science, see Alan Richardson, *British Romanticism and the Science of the Mind* (Cambridge University Press, 2001), 39–65.
6 Robert Southey and Samuel Taylor Coleridge, *Joan of Arc*, ed. Jonathan Wordsworth (Oxford: Woodstock Books, 1993), 41.

7 George S. Erving, 'The Politics of Matter: Newtonian Science and Priestleyan Metaphysics in Coleridge's "Preternatural Agency"', *European Romantic Review*, 19 (2009), 225.

8 'Phlogiston' was key to eighteenth-century theories of combustion: it was a 'principle', an imperceptible substance whose presence in a body made it flammable. During combustion, it was presumed that an inflammable substance gave off its phlogiston until the air around was saturated. Air that was 'dephlogisticated' would therefore be free of phlogiston and better able to sustain combustion.

9 Simon Schaffer, 'Measuring Virtue: Eudiometry, Enlightenment and Pneumatic Medicine', *The Medical Enlightenment of the Eighteenth Century*, eds. Andrew Cunningham and Roger French (Cambridge University Press, 1990), 283.

10 On Beddoes's influence on Coleridge, particularly his embrace of the medical system of John Brown, see Neil Vickers, *Coleridge and the Doctors* (Oxford University Press, 2004), 37–78.

11 Tim Fulford, 'Science and Poetry in 1790s Somerset: The Self-Experiment Narrative, the Aeriform Effusion, and the Greater Romantic Lyric', *ELH*, 85 (2018), 87, 89. For an alternative reading that finds the scientific inspiration for the GRL in Coleridge's engagement with William Herschel's astronomical theories see Dometa Wiegand Brothers, *The Romantic Imagination and Astronomy* (Houndmills: Palgrave Macmillan, 2015), 50–74.

12 Humphry Davy, 'An Essay on Heat, Light, and the Combinations of Light', *Contributions to Physical and Medical Knowledge, Principally from the West of England*, ed. Thomas Beddoes (Bristol: Biggs & Cottle, 1799), 145.

13 Lavoisier had 'overthrown' the phlogiston theory, renaming Priestley's 'dephlogisticated air' 'oxygen' and declaring the gas combustion's fuel. He proposed 'Caloric' to explain the heat from combustion.

14 Quoted in Wahida Amin, 'Appendix 2b: "The Spinosist" (RI MS HD 13c 7–10)', in 'The Poetry and Science of Humphry Davy', PhD thesis, University of Salford, 2013.

15 Humphry Davy, Personal Notebook (1801–1802), Royal Institution, MS HD/13/C, 57–59.

16 Humphry Davy to [James Webbe Tobin], 21 March 1800, *The Collected Letters of Sir Humphry Davy*, eds. Tim Fulford and Sharon Ruston, 4 vols (Oxford University Press, 2020), I, 44.

17 On the eighteenth-century philosophical changes leading to specialization and disciplinarity, see Robin Valenza, *Literature, Language, and the Rise of the Intellectual Disciplines in Britain, 1680–1820* (Cambridge University Press, 2009), 1–36.

18 Jan Golinski, *Making Natural Knowledge* (University of Chicago Press, 2005), 67.

19 On the professional rivalry between Davy and Wordsworth see Catherine Ross, '"Twin Labourers and Heirs of the Same Hopes": The Professional Rivalry of Humphry Davy and William Wordsworth', *Romantic Science*, ed. Noah Heringman (Albany: SUNY Press, 2003), 23–52.

20 Jon Klancher, *Transfiguring the Arts and Sciences* (Cambridge University Press, 2013), 4.

21 For a thorough engagement with Lavoisier's innovations and his use of revolutionary rhetoric see Mi Gyung Kim, *Affinity, That Elusive Dream* (Cambridge, MA: MIT Press, 2003), 279–334.
22 Antoine Lavoisier, *Elements of Chemistry in a New Systematic Order*, trans. Robert Kerr, 3rd edn. (London: William Creech, 1796), xxiii.
23 Bernadette Bensaude-Vincent and Isabelle Stengers, *A History of Chemistry*, trans. Deborah van Dam (Cambridge, MA: Harvard University Press, 1996), 105.
24 Bensaude-Vincent and Stengers, *History of Chemistry*, 93. On the centrality of elements to public chemistry lecturing, see Kurtis Hessel, 'The Romantic-Era Lecture: Dividing and Reuniting the Arts and Sciences', *Configurations*, 24 (2016), 501–32.
25 Bensaude-Vincent and Stengers, *History of Chemistry*, 105.
26 See Sharon Ruston, *Shelley and Vitality* (New York: Palgrave Macmillan, 2005), 1–23 and 38–73, and Levere, *Poetry Realized in Nature*, 36–57.
27 See David Knight, *Atoms and Elements* (London: Hutchinson of London, 1967), 16–59.
28 On the Royal's early years see Morris Berman, *Social Change and Scientific Organization* (Ithaca, NY: Cornell University Press, 1978), 1–31.
29 All quotations from Davy in this paragraph are from his *Elements of Chemical Philosophy*, *The Collected Works of Sir Humphry Davy*, ed. John Davy, 9 vols (London: Smith, Elder, and Co., 1840), IV, 3, 5, 31.
30 See Simon Shaffer, 'Scientific Discoveries and the End of Natural Philosophy', *Social Studies of Science*, 16 (1986), 406–13.

12

JEFFREY W. BARBEAU

Religious Coleridge

Shortly after Coleridge's death, his daughter lamented his passing: 'we mourn not only the removal of one closely united to us by nature and intimacy, but the extinction of a light which made earth more spiritual, and heaven in some sort more visible to our apprehension'.[1] Sara Coleridge expressed a sentiment that many felt at the time. For the death of her father was also the loss of a religious thinker. In the same letter, Sara recalled her father's final days and, despite a complex religious biography, his attachment to the Christian faith: 'When he knew that his time was come he said, that he hoped by the manner of his death to testify the sincerity of his faith; and hoped that all who had heard of his name would know that he died in that of the English Church'.[2] These words are a reminder of Coleridge's epitaph:

> Stop, Christian Passer-by! stop, Child of God!
> And read with gentle heart. Beneath this Sod
> A Poet lies: or that which once seem'd He.
> O lift one thought in prayer for S. T. C.
> That he who many a year with toil of Breath
> Found Death in Life, may here find Life in Death.
> Mercy for Praise, to be forgiven for Fame,
> He ask'd, and hoped thro' Christ. Do Thou the Same.
>
> (CPW I, ii, 1145–46)

Lifting a prayer for the dead – for one who sought mercy and forgiveness from God – may seem contrived. Yet a closer look at Coleridge's life and writings suggests otherwise: these sombre lines capture something of the pervasive spirituality and religious character of his life. For while Coleridge was never an individual of great piety or public churchmanship, there is no period of his life in which religion fails to appear as among its most generative aspects.

In this essay, I introduce the role of religion in Coleridge's life and writings through a series of life stages that reveal his reputation as an 'inquiring spirit'.[3] The first period reveals his growth as a boy in the home of an Anglican vicar through his early political and religious life as a dissenting Unitarian. This radical period was his most productive one as a poet and popular lecturer in Bristol and the West Country. The next period reflects his embrace of Trinitarian Christianity amidst severe personal turmoil. This intellectual shift gave fresh vitality to earlier beliefs and manifest a growing political attachment to the Church of England. The last period shows Coleridge as a theologian and Biblical scholar of public influence. In his these years, he sought to reform Christianity in Britain as he built on earlier insights related to faith and life. Throughout his life, Coleridge engaged in dialogue with a range of religious beliefs, drawing him into conversation with sources from diverse Christian, Islamic, Hindu and Jewish religious traditions.

I   Unitarian Dissenter

S. T. Coleridge was the youngest son of John Coleridge, vicar of Ottery St Mary, from whom he received his earliest education in Latin and Greek.[4] In a letter to Thomas Poole, Coleridge describes how his father would 'take me on his knee, and hold long conversations with me' and how, as an eight-year-old, he walked alongside him under the stars one evening near Ottery. The boy listened as his father described the heavens and their courses through the night sky: 'I heard him with a profound delight & admiration' (CL I, 354). This attraction to the vastness of the world inculcated in the boy a sense of awe and a value for the many in the unity of the one. Coleridge was only nine years old when his father unexpectedly died during the night. The memory of his mother's scream haunted him long into the future. This singular event changed the trajectory of his life, for almost immediately the boy was sent to boarding school at Christ's Hospital. Coleridge was now effectively an orphan, struggling to find his way in the world. He would not return to Ottery for another seven years.

Nearly a decade later, Coleridge matriculated at Jesus College, Cambridge, where the Socinian theology of Joseph Priestley and the rising Unitarian movement brought Coleridge into the sphere of religious and political Dissent. He was radicalized by the tutor William Frend, who opposed subscription to the Articles of Religion of the Established Church in *Thoughts on Subscription to Religious Tests* (1788) and in 1793 published *Peace and Union*, a work that challenged the commonplace belief that religious Dissent endangered the security of the state. Publication coincided with the execution of Louis XVI and the beginning of war between Britain and France. The fellows of the College called for a trial, and Frend was formally dismissed from the University. Coleridge's participation was among the most memorable aspects of the hearings: he led other students in frequent and noisy interruptions of the proceedings.

Subsequently, Coleridge's connection to wider Dissenting circles led him to London and Bristol, where he became a lecturer, writer and Unitarian preacher. Dissent in the 1790s comprised a network of connections that included diverse Protestant sects such as Presbyterians, Baptists and Quakers, educational institutions such as Warrington Academy and publishing outlets such as Joseph Johnson's *Analytical Review*.[5] Coleridge associated with many of the leading critics of the Church and political establishment: the Old Blue George Dyer, the atheists William Godwin and John Thelwall, and the Baptists John Foster and Robert Hall. He formed a Pantisocratic scheme with Robert Southey, envisioning a utopian community on the banks of the Susquehanna in Pennsylvania.

As with many other Dissenters, Coleridge's writings from these years reflect the political turmoil of the French Revolution and war with France. In *Religious Musings*, a long poem that he hoped would establish his reputation, Coleridge opens with the image of Christ, the 'Man of Woes' and 'Despised Galilæan ... whose Life was Love!' (*CPW* I, i, 174–75, lines 9–10, 29). His messianic, millenarian vision echoes not only the Biblical book of Revelation but also the writings of Joseph Priestley ('Patriot, and Saint, and Sage'), David Hartley and George Berkeley.[6] Moreover, if 'Life is a vision shadowy of Truth' sparked concern among some readers, his pantheistic tendencies and thinly veiled attack on Bishop Samuel Horsley for nurturing atheism undoubtedly demonstrated his distance from the established Church (*CPW* I, i, 189, line 372; I, i, 190, line 397). This tendency towards pantheism and materialism also appears in other poems, including reference to the 'one life within us and abroad, / Which meets all motion and becomes its soul' in 'The Eolian Harp' (1795) and the divine unity with creation in one who 'doth teach / Himself in all, and all things in himself' in 'Frost at Midnight' (1798).[7]

Coleridge's journalism and public lectures proved equally inflammatory. In his 'Essay on Fasts' (1796), Coleridge criticized with Swiftian wit the government's declaration of a national day of fasting and prayer, blasting the establishment for the hypocrisy of its shallow appeals for spiritual repentance amidst an unjust war with France. Simultaneously, he levelled a damning assessment of the economy: the poor already fasted, even as the rich lived in abundance (*Watchman*, 51–55).[8] As with many other nonconformists, Coleridge also wrote and lectured against the slave trade. He won the Browne prize at Cambridge in 1792 for his poem on 'The Unhappy Fate of the Slaves in the West Indian Islands', and in later years lectured and published on the same topic in overtly religious language: 'They, who believe [in] a God, believe him to be the loving Parent of all men – And is it possible that they who really believe and fear the Father, should fearlessly authorize the oppression of his Children?' (*CPW* i, i, 72–78; *Watchman*, 136). In other lectures, Coleridge echoed Joseph Priestley in energetic denunciations of the 'corruptions of Christianity' during the earliest centuries of the church, railed against the Trinity as 'superstition' and claimed that popular notions of a vicarious, redemptive sacrifice amount to little more than 'irrational' confusions of metaphorical language (*Lects 1795*, 75–229).

Denunciations of the established Church and its doctrine, however, should not be mistaken as a rejection of religion. Coleridge rather sought to reform it in the spirit of nonconformity. He was already a careful reader of the Bible and, like the eighteenth-century Biblical exegete Robert Lowth, drew from Hebrew literature in paraphrase exercises based on passages from the Psalms. Indeed, despite his refusal of Anglican doctrinal teaching, it is difficult to appreciate much of his early poetry without reference to such beliefs. Although later editions capitalized on the overt religiosity of the poem, the 'Rime of the Ancyent Marinere' (1798) amounts to an Augustinian portrait of human sinfulness even in its earliest form. The Mariner commits an offence against an innocent, 'Christian soul' that can only be remedied by an act of grace: 'a spring of love gushed from my heart / And I blessed them unaware' (*CPW* i, i, 376, line 65; i, i, 393, lines 284–85). Fewer readers still recognize that Coleridge composed the 'Ancient Mariner' immediately after a failed attempt to collaborate with William Wordsworth on 'The Wanderings of Cain' (1797). In that work, Coleridge developed a mythology around the afterlife of the fratricidal Cain, drifting through the land in an agonized dream-sleep. When Cain meets the ghostly figure of his brother, he bemoans his wretched state in language comparable to the parched, tormented Mariner: 'Abel, my brother, I would lament for thee, but that the spirit within me is withered, and burnt up with extreme agony' (*CPW* i, i, 364).

In 1797, Coleridge preached in Unitarian chapels and considered an opportunity to serve full-time as a minister at Shrewsbury but, in January 1798, accepted an annuity from the Wedgwood brothers instead. This freed him for research and writing, and by the end of 1798 he was in Germany, where he gathered materials for a life of G. E. Lessing and studied the Biblical criticism of Eichhorn, Michaelis and others at the University of Göttingen.[9] This period of metaphysical inquiry proved remarkably important to Coleridge's philosophical and theological development. Yet, even before his trip to Germany, Coleridge's commitment to Unitarianism had begun to falter.

JEFFREY W. BARBEAU

Upon his return to Britain, Coleridge continued to move within Dissenting circles and imagined new works with strong religious themes. One of the most intriguing was a projected collaboration with Robert Southey on a poem about Muhammad (1799–1800). During the eighteenth century, Arabic-Islamic literature gradually came into English translation, resulting in a period of increasing visibility for 'Asiatic' ideas. These 'orientalist' texts exercised a considerable influence on the imagination of British writers (Coleridge's 'Kubla Khan' originated during these same years).[10] Southey had already read George Sale's English translation (1734) of the Qur'an, and Coleridge had made an English translation of an address by a Muslim priest to a dying man (*EOT* II, 262). Although 'Mahomet' was never completed, the fragmentary remains give some insight into Coleridge's thinking. While his contribution to the poem's depiction of the Prophet is less than glowing, the language used is consistent with the rhetoric of Dissent. He positively contrasts the figure of Muhammad ('th' enthusiast Warrior of Mecca') with those 'idolatrous Christians' who had obscured the truth about Jesus in allegedly 'orthodox' teachings. The latter had, at 'best', corrupted the message of Christ and proved 'worse than the vilest' in their dishonesty (*CPW* I, i, 571, line 6).[11] In this comparison, Coleridge echoes the belief that Unitarians and Muslims share a common commitment to monotheism that historic orthodoxy had polluted with Trinitarian doctrine.[12] In later years, Coleridge described his growing unease in matters of religion as fundamentally a dilemma over a doctrine of God: 'For a very long time indeed I could not reconcile personality with infinity; and my head was with Spinoza, though my whole heart remained with Paul and John' (*BL* I, 201).

II Philosophical Trinitarian

Coleridge's inner turmoil during the late 1790s led gradually back to the church of his childhood. Even as he affirmed his commitment to Dissent and Unitarianism in various outlets, he also wrote privately with increasing uncertainty. In the notebooks, Coleridge's search for a different path is evident: 'Socinianism Moonlight – Methodism &c A Stove! O for some Sun that shall unite Light & Warmth' (*CN* I, 467). Socinian and Unitarian belief emphasized the rational intellect in matters of religion. The appeal to logic and rationality provided a Biblical foundation allegedly uncorrupted by later church teachings and the basis for decidedly modern acts of social and political reform. Methodism, by contrast, was the faith of the enthusiast. But an overheated imagination – marked by the reviving work of the Spirit in open-air preaching by evangelical Anglicans such as John Wesley and John Fletcher – could never appeal as a lasting alternative to such a philosophically and theological inquisitive thinker.[13]

Coleridge's troubled personal life undoubtedly played some role in the formation of his philosophical theology. When Southey and Coleridge created the Pantisocratic scheme, they rapidly married two sisters. For Coleridge, the marriage was almost immediately unhappy. He spent increasingly long periods away from his wife and children, including during his studies in Germany. He was also in love with another woman, Sara Hutchinson, who served as both an object of his obsession and a symbol of poetic failure. Moreover, his personal battle with addiction to opium had left his health in a shambles. He faced daily anxiety over a host of issues and nightmares when he sought refuge in sleep.[14] In short, Coleridge believed that his personal failings and bodily weakness resulted from an enslaved will that left him utterly paralysed. Rationality or duty made little difference in such a state. He required a Redeemer who could reconcile him to God.

Simultaneously, Coleridge's study of German philosophy provided the intellectual framework that weakened the sway of rationalist Unitarianism. Kant, he says, 'took possession of me as with a giant's hand', snipping the binds that linked him to the rationalism of Hartley's necessitarianism, Priestley's Unitarianism and Spinoza's pantheism (*BL* I, 153). In its place, Coleridge took up Kant's understanding of human perception, namely, a rejection of the mind's passivity in favour of an active construction of reality through categories of human understanding. Coleridge's epistemology may be traced to precursors in Cambridge Platonists such as Henry More and Ralph Cudworth, but reading Kant (and pressing his thought to new ends) allowed him to counter the empiricism and materialism that seemed everywhere to distort Christian teaching. For Coleridge, Reason bears the same relation to spiritual knowledge as the Understanding does to material phenomena (*Friend* I, 155–56). Thus, the mind not only organizes sensory data through the Understanding but also contains its own constitutive basis for a knowledge of otherwise inaccessible, transcendent divine ideas. Reason informs the human conscience and, combined with will, leads to right moral action. At times, especially in later years, Coleridge linked Reason to the gracious work of the Holy Spirit, illuminating the mind to the things of God.[15]

These biographical and intellectual aspects of Coleridge's life set the stage for his alleged 'conversion' in 1805. At the time, Coleridge was working as acting public secretary in Malta under Sir Alexander Ball. He felt isolated from friends and family (many of whom believed he might never return home alive) and turned to studies to make use of the time. He read the debates between Samuel Horsley and Joseph Priestley, and soon discovered that the bishop's argument, which he had earlier dismissed for fostering atheism, was now utterly convincing:

> Thinking during my perusal of Horsley's Letters in Rep. to D^r P[riestley's] objections to the Trinity on the part of Jews, Mahometans, and Infidels, it burst upon me at once as an awful Truth what 7 or 8 years ago I thought of proving with a *hollow Faith* and for an *ambiguous purpose*, my mind then wavering in its necessary passage from Unitarianism ... thro' Spinosism into Plato and St John. (CN II, 2448)

The notion that this 'burst upon' Coleridge from out of thin air deserves closer scrutiny but the language here is startling nonetheless. Less than a decade since he filled Unitarian pulpits and considered an invitation to full-time ministry, Coleridge now described Unitarianism as 'the Religion of a man, whose ~~Understanding~~ Reason would make him an Atheist but whose Heart and Common sense will not permit him to be so' (CN II, 2448). Whereas earlier Coleridge rejected the divinity of Christ and doctrine of the Trinity as a corruption of faith, he now wrote confidently, 'No Christ, No God!' and 'No Trinity, no God' in a newfound conviction that the Logos is the principle of all life.[16] Of course, Coleridge's assertion of belief in the Trinity was not really a conversion (despite Coleridge's own use of the word in *Biographia Literaria*), if by the term one means a belief in something entirely new. Rather, Coleridge experienced something much closer to a 'homecoming', the return to an earlier faith nurtured first as a child and again at Christ's Hospital.[17]

Coleridge's embrace of Trinitarianism shaped a new outlook on the relationship between God and nature. At times, the sway of Schelling and the *Naturphilosophie* tradition reinforced an earlier commitment to pantheism. Some sign of this may be evident in 'Ne plus ultra' (1811), for example, where Coleridge alludes to an apparent polarity within the godhead that seems to equate God and the universe: 'Sole Positive of Night! / Antipathist of Light! / Fate's only Essence! Primal Scorpion Rod! / The one permitted Opposite of God!' (*CPW* I, ii, 884, lines 1–4). Yet, even in 'Ne plus ultra', the assertion of the 'Dragon foul and fell' is itself an affirmation of that which is not God (*CPW* I, ii, 885, line 10). By 1818 Coleridge was fully convinced of the inadequacy of pantheism as a denial of the self-sufficiency of the divine, explaining the error of Schelling's philosophy in notebooks and to correspondents (*CN* III, 4445; *CL* IV, 873–74, 883). When lecturing on the history of philosophy a year later, Coleridge identified pantheism with Hinduism specifically, commenting on a lengthy passage from the Bhagavadgita as 'a great poem of India where pantheism has displayed its banners and waved in victory over three hundred millions of men' (*Lects 1808–19* I, 130; cf. *CPW* I, ii, 997–98).[18] Coleridge's rejection of the Bhagavadgita, 'a very interesting poem', was at heart a philosophical and theological dispute about God and nature: 'in the utmost attempts of a pantheistic philosophy to reduce religion to any objects of the senses, or any object to be apprehended by men ... the infinite of a something that works like gravitation works without any consciousness' (*Lects 1808–19* I, 132).[19]

Coleridge's doomed relationship with Sara Hutchinson even played a role in this struggle to explain the connection between the subjective and objective. Early signs of this shift appear in 'Dejection: An Ode', with the poet's affirmation of a light that issues forth from the soul, 'And from the soul itself must there be sent / A sweet and potent vice, of its own birth, / Of all sweet sounds the life and element!' (*CPW* I, ii, 699, lines 56–58). Amidst his intense devotion to Hutchinson, Coleridge recognized that love requires the discovery of the self in the embodied life of another person, as Graham Davidson observes: 'Our conscience is that which requires us to seek the perfection of our nature, our true personality, in someone not ourself, but who yet re-presents our humanity to us'.[20]

Coleridge reflected on the problem in his formation of a theology of the symbol. His best-known articulation of this concept appears in *The Statesman's Manual* (1816), where he defines the symbol as 'characterized by a translucence of the Special in the Individual ... It always partakes of the Reality which it renders intelligible' (*LS*, 30). While that work addresses the language of the Bible and its representation of truths to the imagination, Coleridge previously recognized the implications of symbols for nature. As early as 1805, Coleridge remarks on symbols and love of another: 'The best, the truly lovely, in each & all is God. Therefore the truly Beloved is the symbol of God to whomever it is truly beloved by!' (*CN* II, 2540). The otherness of love for another human – this search for a 'perfection of our nature' – leads us to a recognition of the Logos in ourselves. In *The Statesman's Manual* and at still greater length in his unfinished *Opus Maximum*, Coleridge uses the image of the infant child asleep at its mother's breast to signal the formation of the self in just such an embodied fashion: 'for the infant the mother contains his own self, and the whole problem of existence as a whole' (*LS*, 71; *CPW* I, ii, 830; *OM*, 131). This sensory engagement between the self and other, he claims, is the basis of a knowledge of God: 'The reverence of the invisible, substantiated by the feeling of love ... is the essence and proper definition of religion' (*OM*, 127).[21] In this, against a tendency he saw in the German *Naturphilosophie* tradition, Coleridge avoided a confusion between objective and subjective that made the 'I am' no different from either the 'thou' or the 'it is'.

III Anglican Sage

On 25 December 1827, Coleridge opened his notebook and made a surprising entry: 'Christmas day. Received the Sacrament – for the first time since my first year at Jesus College' (CN v, 5703). For a little more than a decade, he had been living in Highgate, London, with the surgeon James Gillman and his family, hoping to manage his opium addiction more effectively. The move stabilized Coleridge's life. Yet, with this entry, Coleridge confirmed what might only have been guessed by his readers: for more than three decades, Coleridge wrote on matters of profoundly Christian concern but neglected to participate fully in the Church's liturgy.

What led to this lengthy gap? Hostility? Hypocrisy? Part of his negligence goes back to long-standing criticisms he had levelled against the Church as a Dissenter in the 1790s. Coleridge devoted himself to reflection on the *invisible* church and distrusted the tendency of *visible* institutions to fall into superstition and fanaticism. Many true Christians ranked among the Methodists, for instance, but he worried that such an enthusiast, schismatic body risked descending into the same egotism he discerned in its founder.[22] Overcoming this distrust of institutions and returning to the established Church involved an increasing need for embodied participation, a strong sense of the power of evil and an unrelenting distrust of the sinful weakness of his character. Nature – that is, human nature as well as the object world, he remarked in 1830 – was the 'devil in a strait waistcoat' (TT I, 95).[23] This aspect of his return is consistent with earlier meditations on identity and personality discovered in love for others. In the same Christmas entry, noting that the Prayer Book service is 'solemn & affecting', Coleridge distinguishes the Anglican service from the liturgies of Roman Catholics and Dissenters. The former inspire 'awe & wonder' in their miraculous claims to 'the real transmutation of the Bread & Wine', while the latter allow for only a 'cold and flat' reminder, 'a mere and very forced visual metaphor', in their memorialization of the Lord's Supper. By contrast, the Anglican liturgy – rightly understood, since Coleridge complained that too many clergy teach only the same beliefs as Dissenters – allows for a middle way: 'The Eucharist is at once symbol & instance' of the mystery fulfilled in the crucifixion of Jesus.

The combination of thought and action is particularly evident in Coleridge's writing on prayer, a topic to which he frequently returned in his late writings. In prayer, the individual submits the finite will to the Absolute Will of God. In the months before his reception of the Eucharist, Coleridge repeatedly linked sacramental life to the meaning of prayer, describing it as a duty whereby the relation of 'a Will to a Will', 'a Person to a Person' and the combination of 'the Light with a *Life*' is realized in embodied action (*CN* IV, 5383; V, 5566, 5664). 'It is the *whole* man that prays', he wrote in his personal copy of the Book of Common Prayer (*CM* I, 702), and, only days before Christmas, he explicitly linked prayer and redemption: 'The best preparation for taking the sacrament ... [is] to read over and over again, and often on your knees, at all events with a kneeling and praying heart, the Gospel of St John, till your mind is familiarized to the contemplation of Christ, the Redeemer and Mediator of Mankind' (*CM* I, 712). Prayer brought Coleridge comfort and a renewed expectation that 'Thy Kingdom come!' might bring about a surer hope than he observed among the followers of his friend, the preacher Edward Irving (*CN* V, 5486). Irving's attempts to revive enthusiastic worship in the Anglican church, at first encouraged by Coleridge, culminated in schism and the formation of yet another millenarian sect.

Even as Coleridge prayed the Scriptures, he continued to study the Biblical text with critical eyes. In fact, although he remained familiar with the latest trends in Biblical criticism, he still consulted some of the same scholarly resources he first discovered in the 1790s. By the 1820s, he devoted lengthy periods of daily study to reading the Bible, checking critical literature and composing extended notes on his findings. He also consulted regularly with his close friend Hyman Hurwitz, who was elected as first professor of Hebrew at University College London in 1828. The two collaborated on two translations of Hurwitz's poetry from Hebrew into English – 'Israel's Lament' and 'The Tears of a Grateful People' (*CPW* I, ii, 945, 975) – and the friendship deepened Coleridge's appreciation for Jewish interpretive traditions.[24] Although he had earlier theorized publicly on the Bible and politics in *The Statesman's Manual*, his most incisive and contentious work remained private, including a series of 'Letters on the Inspiration of the Scriptures' that circulated only among friends during his life (published posthumously in 1840 under the title *Confessions of an Inquiring Spirit*). Coleridge withheld from print much of his writing on the Bible for fear that such thoughts might damage his growing reputation as a churchman: he denied plenary Biblical inspiration in an effort to counteract what he deemed a damaging literality that made Biblical authors little more than mouthpieces of a divine ventriloquist. Against the tendency towards Bibliolatry, which made the Bible a rival to God, Coleridge recommended theological catechesis in the church, introducing the Christian faith as a system of belief prior to disputations over thorny historical matters in the Biblical text. He thought modern religious controversies wrongly placed the weight of Biblical authority on evidentiary proofs such as miracles and fulfilled prophecy rather than its spiritual meaning.[25] For this reason, he memorably declared that in reading the Bible he had found 'words for my inmost Thoughts, Songs for my Joy, Utterances for my hidden Griefs, pleadings for my Shame and my feebleness' (*SWF* II, 1121). This emphasis on the personal – '*whatever finds me*' – was not his only concern, of course, but his pointed accent on interiority shifted the weight of Biblical authority from the objective to the subjective.

Coleridge's attention to Christian faith and doctrine similarly informs his single most influential religious writing: *Aids to Reflection* (1825). Ostensibly an anthology of earlier divines such as Robert Leighton and Jeremy Taylor, *Aids to Reflection* contains deftly edited selections with lengthy notes and commentary by Coleridge himself. The result was a new Anglican theological primer, drawn from the heritage of British Christianity toward a uniquely English development of Kantian philosophy. As with F. D. E. Schleiermacher's *On Religion: Speeches to Its Cultured Despisers* (1799), Coleridge struck a decidedly modern apologetic tone, charging readers to embrace doubt in the search for truth: 'Never be afraid to doubt, if only you have the disposition to believe' (*AR*, 107). Moreover, he cautioned against sectarianism in a memorable aphorism that immediately follows: 'He, who begins by loving Christianity better than Truth, will proceed by loving his own Sect or Church better than Christianity, and end in loving himself better than all' (*AR*, 107). Still, Coleridge's attention to theological language distinguishes *Aids to Reflection* from evangelical works such as Hannah More's *Practical Piety, or The Influence of the Religion of the Heart on the Conduct of the Life* (1811), for he rejected popular explanations of original sin and Christ's redemptive work that confused metaphorical language with the mystery of divine action. In such an innovative work of scholarship, combining critical inquiry with religious devotion, Coleridge showed himself to be a truly pioneering thinker, setting the stage for later twentieth-century theological investigations of religious language, human personhood and Trinitarian theology by recent academics such as Colin Gunton, Daniel Hardy and Janet Soskice.

Reflection on Biblical language also prepared Coleridge to make critical contributions to political theology. At least since the French Revolution, thousands of Roman Catholics had emigrated to Britain, seeking refuge from persecution and violence. The increasing presence of Catholicism, alongside a growing Jewish population, brought questions of religious toleration, legal representation and political reform to the fore. What role, if any, should a national church play in a modern, pluralistic society? Coleridge's answer came in his last major prose publication, *On the Constitution of the Church and State* (1829), which addressed the question of Catholic emancipation but also proposed a new Anglican ecclesiology (or doctrine of the church) through a distinction between the idea of a truly *Christian* church and a properly *national* church. The former is marked by universality and the absence of any visible sovereign, since Christ alone is its invisible Lord; the latter, by contrast, supports the 'cultivation' or improvement of the nation, particularly through the work of the clerisy, or learned scholars drawn from all denominations and professions (*Church and State*, 46–49). Such a vision, marked by education and wisdom drawn from every part of the realm, had (once again) a distinctly religious character. Harkening back to classical and Christian models of the liberal arts, Coleridge placed the work of theologians 'at the head of all', since they fostered the unity of all knowledge as 'the circulating sap of life to all other sciences', without which the diversity of the many might descend into cacophonous epistemological fragmentation.

IV Religious Legacy

In his final years, Coleridge's widened fame and intellectual influence as the 'Sage of Highgate' hinted at what would become an enduring religious legacy in both Britain and North America. Sara Coleridge, with her husband, Henry Nelson Coleridge, stands foremost among those responsible for shaping his theological reception. They produced new editions of his poetry and prose, enabling his theological writings to contribute to contentious public debates over the Church and State, the inspiration of the Scriptures and the doctrine of regeneration.[26] Some in the Oxford Movement hoped to claim Wordsworth and Coleridge as their own, while other Tractarians politely distanced themselves from Coleridge's mottled reputation. (Newman priggishly wrote that Coleridge 'installed a higher philosophy into inquiring minds, than they had hitherto been accustomed to accept' but 'indulged a liberty of speculation, which no Christian can tolerate'.[27]) Yet his most devoted followers comprised a disparate group of writers including Thomas Arnold, F. D. Maurice and Julius Hare.[28] Each claimed Coleridge as a source of inspiration, even though none relied slavishly on any single idea or concept among his works.

In North America, Coleridge's religious reputation was secure. At the earliest meetings of the group that became the New England Transcendentalists, Coleridge was discussed with James Marsh's 'Preliminary Essay' to the new American edition (1829) of *Aids to Reflection* at hand (*AR*, 487–529). Ralph Waldo Emerson visited Coleridge in 1833, listening (in disappointment) to the man who had so dramatically shaped his thinking in prior years. Less prominent figures included the writers associated with Mercersburg Theology, a German Reformed tradition that embraced various aspects of Coleridge's philosophical theology, and the Presbyterian theologian W. G. T. Shedd, who produced an American edition of Coleridge's works.[29] Finally, among Coleridge's leading American disciples is the Congregationalist minister Horace Bushnell, whose controversial writings on language and Christology link Coleridge to a robust heritage within American Protestant liberalism.[30]

Notes

1 *Memoir and Letters of Sara Coleridge*, 2 vols, ed. Edith Coleridge, 2nd edn. (London: Henry S. King, 1873), I, 109.

2 *Memoir and Letters of Sara Coleridge*, I, 110.

3 Many have applied the appellation to Coleridge – from the posthumous *Confessions of an Inquiring Spirit* (1840) to Kathleen Coburn's anthology, *Inquiring Spirit* (1979). I regard this essay as a complement to the focused treatment of the Logos as the 'seminal principle in Coleridge's system' in Mary Anne Perkins, 'Religious Thinker', in *The Cambridge Companion to Coleridge*, ed. Lucy Newlyn (Cambridge University Press, 2002), 187–99.

4 John Coleridge not only wrote a Latin grammar (1772) but also a theological study of the Book of Judges, *Miscellaneous Dissertations* (1768); see J. C. C. Mays, *Coleridge's Father: Absent Man, Guardian Spirit* (Bristol: The Friends of Coleridge, 2014).

5 Felicity James, 'Christianity: Protestant Dissent' in *The Cambridge Companion to British Romanticism and Religion*, ed. Jeffrey W. Barbeau (Cambridge University Press, 2021), 31–49, and Daniel E. White, *Early Romanticism and Religious Dissent* (Cambridge University Press, 2007).

6 On Unitarian political themes, see Stuart Andrews, *Unitarian Radicalism: Political Rhetoric, 1770–1814* (Basingstoke: Palgrave Macmillan, 2003).

7 On Dissent and Coleridge's early poetry, see Kelvin Everest, *Coleridge's Secret Ministry: The Context of the Conversation Poems, 1795–1798* (Hassocks: Harvester, 1979).

8 See Andrews, *Unitarian Radicalism*, 64–72.

9 On his studies, see Maximiliaan van Woudenberg, *Coleridge and Cosmopolitan Intellectualism, 1794–1804: The Legacy of Göttingen University* (Abingdon: Routledge, 2018).

10 On the rise of 'orientalism', see Michael J. Franklin, *'Orientalist Jones': Sir William Jones, Poet, Lawyer, and Linguist, 1746–1794* (Oxford University Press, 2011), and Nigel Leask, *British Romantic Writers and the East: Anxieties of Empire* (Cambridge University Press, 1992).

11 Cf. Jeffrey Einboden, *Islam and Romanticism: Muslim Currents from Goethe to Emerson* (London: Oneworld, 2014), 81–91.

12 Coleridge later described his plan for Muhammad to serve as 'the Representative of Unipersonal Theism' in the poem (*CN* IV, 4973).

13 Cf. Christopher W. Corbin, *The Evangelical Party and Samuel Taylor Coleridge's Return to the Church of England* (New York: Routledge, 2019).

14 On his personal life, see Rosemary Ashton, *The Life of Samuel Taylor Coleridge: A Critical Biography* (Oxford: Blackwell, 1996), 213–38.

15 Nicholas Halmi, 'Coleridge's Philosophies' (this volume). On Reason and Spirit, see Jeffrey W. Barbeau, *Coleridge, the Bible, and Religion* (New York: Palgrave Macmillan, 2008), 127–42.

16 On Coleridge and the Logos, see Perkins, 'Religious Thinker', 187–99.

17 Mays, *Coleridge's Father*, 39.

18 Charles Wilkins's English translation of *The Bhagvat Geeta, or Dialogues of Kreeshna and Arjoon* first appeared in 1785.

19 On Coleridge and Hindu mythology, see Nishi Pulugurtha, 'Hinduism', in *The Cambridge Companion to British Romanticism and Religion*, 105–20; cf. Aparajita Mazumder, 'Coleridge, Vishnu, and the Infinite', *Comparative Literature Studies*, 30 (1993), 32–52.

20 Graham Davidson, *Coleridge's Career* (Basingstoke: Macmillan, 1990), 160.

21 On *Naturphilosophie* and Coleridge's Trinitarianism, see Raimonda Modiano, *Coleridge and the Concept of Nature* (London and Basingstoke: Macmillan, 1985), 186–204.

22 See, for example, Coleridge's marginalia on Robert Southey's *Life of Wesley* (*CM* v, 120–93).

23 Anthony John Harding, 'Imagination, Patriarchy, and Evil in Coleridge and Heidegger', *Studies in Romanticism*, 35 (1996), 3–26; Nicholas Reid, 'The Satanic Principle in the Later Coleridge's Theory of Imagination', *Studies in Romanticism*, 37 (1998), 259–77.

24 On Hurwitz and Coleridge as poetic collaborators, see Karen A. Weisman, *Singing in a Foreign Land: Anglo-Jewish Poetry, 1812–1847* (Philadelphia: University of Pennsylvania Press, 2018), 70–122; cf. *CPW* I, ii, 945–53; on Kabbalah and symbolism, see Tim Fulford, *Coleridge's Figurative Language* (New York: St. Martin's Press, 1991), 130–62.

25 Cf. Jeffrey W. Barbeau, 'The Mirror of Faith: Samuel Taylor Coleridge and Figural Interpretation', in *All Thy Lights Combine: Figural Reading in the Anglican Tradition*, eds. David Ney and Ephraim Radner (Bellingham: Lexham Press, 2021), 172–83.

26 Jeffrey W. Barbeau, *Sara Coleridge: Her Life and Thought* (New York: Palgrave Macmillan, 2014); Robin Schofield, *The Vocation of Sara Coleridge: Authorship and Religion* (Cham, Switzerland: Palgrave Macmillan, 2018).

27 John Henry Newman, *Apologia pro Vita Sua*, ed. Ian Ker (London: Penguin, 1994), 100.

28 Tod E. Jones, *The Broad Church: A Biography of a Movement* (Lanham: Lexington, 2003).

29 James Hastings Nichols, *Romanticism in American Theology: Nevin and Schaff at Mercersburg* (University of Chicago Press, 1961).

30 Philip Aherne, *The Coleridge Legacy: Samuel Taylor Coleridge's Intellectual Legacy in Britain and America, 1834–1934* (Cham, Switzerland: Palgrave Macmillan, 2018).

13

CHARLES W. MAHONEY

Coleridge the Lecturer and Critic

Near the end of Chapter 10 of the *Biographia Literaria* (1817), Coleridge goes to some lengths to exculpate himself from the charge of having 'dreamt away [his] life to no purpose', pointedly querying his reader, 'But are books the only channel through which the stream of intellectual usefulness can flow? Is the diffusion of truth to be estimated by publications; or publications by the truth, which they diffuse or at least contain?' (*BL* I, 221, 220). Conscious of not having published anything in book form since 1800, Coleridge is understandably sensitive on this topic. Rather than sheer volume of publication, he speculates, 'Would that the criterion of a scholar's utility were the number and moral value of the truths, which he has been the means of throwing into the general circulation; or the number and value of the minds, whom by his conversation or letters, he has excited into activity, and supplied with the germs of their after-growth!' (*BL* I, 220). Were these the criteria, Coleridge might be awarded a 'distinguished rank', in support of which he would 'appeal to the numerous and respectable audiences, which at different times and in different places honored my lecture-rooms with their attendance' (*BL* I, 220, 221). In what has come to be regarded as his most important book of criticism, Coleridge pointedly invokes his lectures as proof of the value of his reasonings, the truths which he has disseminated and the minds which he has catalysed into critical thinking. Coleridge the lecturer made Coleridge the critic possible.

For over 200 years, students of Coleridge have turned to the *Biographia* for the critical dicta for which he is most remembered and cited, such as his formulation regarding the 'willing suspension of disbelief for the moment, which constitutes poetic faith', his multifaceted definition of the imagination as the 'synthetic and magical power' that 'reveals itself in the balance or reconciliation of opposite or discordant qualities', his method of 'practical criticism' and his critique of Wordsworth concerning the 'true nature of poetic diction'. Indeed, there remains a tendency to think of Coleridge as a critic in terms of his published criticism. But these written pronouncements wouldn't have been possible without the oral, often extemporaneous, delivery of the lectures, beginning in 1808, on the 'principles of poetry', largely though not exclusively illustrated with reference to Shakespeare. Lecturing in 1818, Coleridge brought the *Biographia* with him to the lectern, where his notes indicate that he read aloud from Chapter 15, on 'poetic power' in Shakespeare (*Lects 1808–1819* II, 115). Such is the tangled, inextricable link between Coleridge the lecturer and Coleridge the critic: taken together (as they must be), the Shakespeare lectures and the *Biographia* constitute Coleridge's most consequential criticism. The lectures made the written criticism possible (not just the *Biographia* but also the 1814 *Essays on the Principles of Genial Criticism* and the essays on method in the 1818 *Friend*), while the published criticism further disseminated Coleridge's principles and grounds of reasoning, overcoming the transient nature of the lectures.

Between 1808 and 1819, Coleridge delivered over 100 literary lectures. Not coincidentally, these were the years during which he produced the criticism for which he continues to be remembered. The first series, delivered at the Royal Institution in 1808, was advertised as 'Lectures on the Principles of Poetry', an emphasis on *principles* which Coleridge retained in his 1811–12 series, 'Lectures on Shakespeare and Milton in Illustration of the Principles of Poetry', and as late as the 1818 series, 'Lectures on the Principles of Judgement, Culture, and European Literature'. Paradoxically, at the same time as the lectures seem to represent Coleridge's most sustained critical activity, the archival record is radically incomplete. Despite the admonishments of Wordsworth and Southey (who felt strongly that a shorthand account of the lectures was 'a duty which [Coleridge] owes to himself, and his friends and his family and the world' (*CLRS*, 1983)), Coleridge never prepared the lectures for publication; neither did he ever write out a lecture in its entirety. While there are detailed entries in numerous of his notebooks relating to some of the lectures, and equally detailed marginalia for others, there are in most instances no records.

One reason for the incomplete record we have of the lectures is that it was Coleridge's tendency as a lecturer to speak extemporaneously – or at least to appear to do so, as if spontaneously digressing from his prepared notes. As he explained, 'my Lectures, with exception only of the general Plan & leading Thoughts, are literally & strictly *extempore* – the words of the moment!' (*CL* III, 471). According to Henry Crabb Robinson, it could be difficult to distinguish between 'his conversation which was a sort of lecturing & soliloquizing and his lectures which were colloquial' (quoted in *Lects 1808–1819* I, xlvii). Either way, the effect could be mesmerizing. After hearing Coleridge lecture in 1811, Mary Russell Mitford wrote that she returned from London 'quite Coleridgified; much in the same way, I suppose, as Boswell was after a visit to Johnson', due in no small degree to 'the electric power of [Coleridge's] genius'.[1]

It is important to remember that one paid to be 'Coleridgified': nearly all of Coleridge's literary criticism was occasional, 'and the occasion was in each case the urgent need to make money'.[2] As central as the lectures were to the development of Coleridge's critical principles – and as much as he retrospectively valorized them – he was consistently ambivalent about undertaking them. As Sarah Zimmerman has argued, Coleridge's first course of lectures in 1808 represent him trying to banish his radical political persona in the 1795 Bristol lectures and reinvent himself as a culturally approved literary critic.[3] Even as he did so, however, he consistently criticized the practice and utility of public lectures, and registered his discomfort at presenting himself as part of an increasingly commercial literary marketplace. Undertaking the lectures to make money, Coleridge worried that he was '*merely* a man of letters', a figure he disparaged in the *Biographia* as someone who 'in any degree depends on the sale of his works for the necessaries and comforts of life' (*BL* I, 229, 228). Far more appealing to Coleridge was the figure of 'the man of lectures' (as Byron described him in December 1811), not a tradesman but a literary critic and theorist of 'the new Art of Poetry'.[4] It was important to Coleridge to develop a 'vocation' of criticism, a 'German-inspired philosophical criticism', as Jon Klancher has argued, that 'asserted autonomy against the economics of literary authorship and reviewing'.[5] Coleridge wanted to be regarded not as a 'Lecture-monger' but as a 'Poet-philosopher' (*CL* IV, 855; II, 668).

It was Humphry Davy who described Coleridge as a 'Poet-philosopher', an epithet that Coleridge relayed to Thomas Poole in a February 1801 letter. The timing is consequential for any account of Coleridge as a critic, for it was during the autumn of 1800 that Coleridge began to identify himself first and foremost in terms of his critical interests. He announced his intention to 'abandon Poetry altogether ... & reserve for myself the honorable attempt to make others feel and understand [Wordsworth's and Southey's] writings, as they deserve to be felt & understood' and reiterated his intention to write 'an Essay on the Elements of Poetry' (*CL* I, 623; I, 632).[6] Coleridge's interest in isolating the 'Elements of Poetry' – and, attendant upon this, the principles of criticism – informs all of his literary lectures. As he explained,

> In the course of these [lectures at the Royal Institution] I shall have said, all I know, the whole result of many years' continued reflection on the subjects of Taste, Imagination, Fancy, Passion, the source of our pleasures in the fine Arts .... The advantage of this plan to myself is – that I have all my materials ready, & can rapidly reduce them into form – for this is my solemn Determination – not to give a single Lecture till I have in fair writing at least one half of the whole course – for as to trusting any thing to immediate effort, I shrink from it as from guilt – & guilt in me indeed it would be. (*CL* III, 30)

This remarkable letter brings to the fore a number of points that pertain not only to the 1808 lectures but to nearly all of the literary lectures: a concern from the start with 'principles'; the importance of 'the genius & writings' of Shakespeare as Coleridge's first and most significant example; the prominent roles that 'Taste, Imagination, Fancy, [and] Passion' play in Coleridge's aesthetics; and the productive tension between 'many years' continued reflection' and 'immediate effort' in any consideration of Coleridge's style and procedure as a lecturer. The key term here is the seemingly innocuous 'principles', a term (and a priority) that preoccupied Coleridge throughout his lectures and his criticism. Coleridge was consistently concerned with the establishment of principles, whether in political, philosophical, theological, aesthetic, methodological or literary-critical terms. As early as the 1795 Bristol lectures, Coleridge emphasized 'the necessity of *bottoming* on fixed Principles' (*Lects 1795*, 5, 33), and in the *Biographia* he called for a 'fair and philosophical' investigation in which 'the critic announces and endeavors to establish the principles, which he holds for the foundation of poetry in general, with the specification of these in their application to the different *classes* of poetry' (*BL* II, 107).

Concerned as he was in the 1808 lectures with establishing the 'principles of poetry', Coleridge began by defining his terms, often a matter of 'desynonymizing' conflated terms, because the 'road' (the forward movement that Coleridge aligned with method) into Shakespeare begins with the consideration of such key terms as taste and beauty, fancy and imagination, poetry and the poet, the difference between a copy and an imitation. A critical term for Coleridge is 'taste', which is not to be understood in terms of *personal* enjoyment or the absence thereof, but as an *intellectual* 'perception of any object' or 'of any arrangement conceived as external to us' (*Lects 1808–1819* I, 30). Similarly, 'beauty' is also to be understood intellectually, 'a pleasurable sense of the Many ... reduced to unity', with 'many' understood as what Coleridge later terms 'multëity', a perception of each part in relation to a harmonious whole (*Lects 1808–1819* I, 35; see also *SWF* I, 371–73). And imagination, inflected less as individual fancy than as an intellectual principle, is initially defined in these lectures as the 'power of modifying one image or feeling by the precedent or following ones' (*Lects 1808–1819* I, 68). Coleridge was constantly searching for such 'regulative principle[s] ... independent of local and temporary circumstances' (*SWF* I, 365), and to illustrate them he invoked Shakespeare.

Whatever the announced topic, the lectures were invariably concerned with Shakespeare, a crux of Coleridge's critical thinking: in Walter Jackson Bate's memorable formulation, Coleridge 'so habitually turns to Shakespeare as the grand exposition of his entire aesthetic theory that we begin to feel, in reading Coleridge's criticism, that Shakespeare is almost the only poet, and Coleridge is his prophet'.[7] Shakespeare represented for Coleridge 'the poet, described in *ideal* perfection' (*BL* II, 15). At the same time, Shakespeare remained sublimely indescribable, breathlessly characterized by Coleridge in terms of '[a]n endless activity of Thought, in all the possible associations of Thought with Thought, Thought with Feelings, or with words, or of Feelings with Feelings, & words with words' (*Lects 1808–1819* I, 66). Coleridge repeatedly compared Shakespeare to Proteus, due to his ability 'to become by power of Imagination another Thing' 'yet for ever remaining himself' (*Lects 1808–1819* I, 69, 244) and celebrated him for his 'most profound, energetic & philosophical mind' (*Lects 1808–1819* I, 82), for it was his conviction that 'no man was ever yet a great poet, without being at the same time a profound philosopher' (*BL* II, 25–26). As early as 1808, Coleridge was arguing that Shakespeare was not a wild genius, a mere child of nature (a commonplace of eighteenth-century criticism), but that his genius and judgement were commensurate: Shakespeare's 'deep Feeling & exquisite sense of Beauty … were under the command of *his own Will*' (*Lects 1808–1819* I, 80).

Between the 1808 lectures and those of 1811–12, Coleridge's most important critical activity concerned *The Friend*, the (more or less) weekly periodical he published from June 1809 through March 1810. *The Friend* represents a sustained effort in both Coleridge's establishment of principles and the development of his thoughts regarding the best ways to transmit principles to others (in this case readers rather than auditors), not by delivering them ready-made positions but by impressing upon them 'the propriety of cultivating the thinking faculties' (*Lects 1808–1819* I, 192). Concerned that he had up to that point in his career 'layed my Eggs with Ostrich carelessness & Ostrich oblivion' (in lectures which he hadn't written out and for which no one had taken meaningful notes), Coleridge intended *The Friend* as 'the main Pipe, thro' which I shall play off the whole reservoir of my collected Knowledge', in order 'to found true PRINCIPLES, to oppose false PRINCIPLES, in Criticism, Legislation, Philosophy, Morals, and International Law' (*CL* III, 131, 143). Coleridge consistently denounced what he perceived to be the obstacles to sound judgement, which he made the explicit topic of the first lecture in his 1811–12 series on Shakespeare and Milton. In delineating the causes of 'false Criticism', Coleridge distinguished the permanent (e.g. the vague use of terms) from the accidental, including the negative effects of reviews, magazines, newspapers and novels. Reviews were pernicious because the critics 'decided without any reference to fixed principles' (as he argued again in the *Biographia*) and, consequently, 'taught people rather to judge than to read' – precisely the contrary of Coleridge's own ambitions in his lectures not to deliver a body of knowledge but to teach his auditors to think for themselves (*Lects 1808–1819* I, 189).

The 1811–12 lectures are Coleridge's best-known, due in large part to the detailed notes taken by M. Tomalin and John Payne Collier of ten of the seventeen lectures, and Coleridge's initial engagement with two topics that would resonate through much of the rest of his career as a lecturer and shape his reputation as a critic: the criticism of August Wilhelm Schlegel and the character of Hamlet. In lecturing on *The Tempest* as an 'ideal play' in which Shakespeare had 'at the beginning of the piece pitched the note of the whole' (*Lects 1808–1819* I, 357, 359), Coleridge remarked that he had just received from a friend the work of a German critic, which he conceded he would praise even 'more highly were it not that in truth it would be praising himself, as the sentiments contained in it were so coincident with those [I] had expressed at the Royal Institution' in 1808 (*Lects 1808–1819* I, 354). The work in question was Schlegel's *Ueber dramatische Kunst und Litteratur* (translated into English in 1815 as *A Course of Lectures on Dramatic Art and Literature*), to which Coleridge turned in lectures from 1811 through 1813, often taking his copy of Schlegel into the lecture room, translating extemporaneously, while debating Schlegel's ideas and formulations. In mentioning 'coincident' positions, Coleridge had in mind their shared conviction that 'Shakespear's Judgement was if possible still more wonderful than his Genius, or rather that the contra-distinction itself between Judgement and Genius rested on an utterly false theory' (*CL* IV, 839), which he consistently maintained (against later accusations that he had plagiarized from Schlegel) that he had argued as early as 1808. Of particular importance to Coleridge were Schlegel's distinctions between 'classical' and 'romantic' art ('romantic' designating the creative irregularity of post-classical art, as exemplified by Shakespeare) and between 'mechanic and organic regularity', the latter designating 'a law which all the parts obey conforming themselves to the outward symbols & manifestations of the essential principle' (*Lects 1808–1819* I, 358), essentially a more detailed and systematic method for thinking about what Coleridge had to that point been designating 'unity of interest'. As Coleridge formulated it in a later lecture (drawing on 'a Continental Critic'), 'The organic form ... is innate, it shapes as it developes [*sic*] itself from within, and the fullness of its developement [*sic*] is one & the same with the perfection of its outward Form. Such is the Life, such the form' (*Lects 1808–1819* I, 495). Explaining the inseparability of form and content, organic unity also explains the inseparability of the part from the whole (and, relevant to Coleridge's method, of the particular example from the general principle). Organic unity is a key component of Coleridge's critical method, integral to his interpretations not only of so many individual

Shakespearean plays (in which he reads 'the unity of interest in the whole and in the apparent contrast of the component parts' (*Lects 1808–1819* II, 254)) but also to his understanding of the imagination as the copula of the mind, the 'intermediate faculty ... at once both active and passive' which reconciles and unifies the opposing powers of reason and understanding (*BL* I, 124). The principle of organic unity thus provides Coleridge with a way to describe not only an imaginative work but also the imaginative mind that creates it, and it is central to what he will come to denominate 'method', where the 'initiative' may be understood as the informing principle that corresponds to the all-pervading life of an organic body.[8]

In Coleridge's consideration of Hamlet, he directs our attention to the absence of such an 'intermediate faculty' in Hamlet's character, something that might serve to balance the opposing tendencies of action and meditation. Coleridge's Hamlet suffers from 'an overbalance in the contemplative faculty' (*Lects 1808–1819* I, 543): he is 'a man living in meditation, called upon <to act> by every motive human & divine but the great purpose of life defeated by continually resolving to do, yet doing nothing but resolve' (*Lects 1808–1819* I, 390). His auditors immediately recognized the covert self-portrait he was offering (Crabb Robinson characterized it as a self-elegy (*Lects 1808–1819* I, 391)), lecturing on *Hamlet* as a way to recuperate and heroicize his own reputation for irresolution, for talking instead of doing. Coleridge returned to this play more than any other, concentrating even more explicitly on the character of Hamlet in 1813 (when he remarked on 'that subtle trick to pretend to be *acting* only when we are very near *being* what we act' (*Lects 1808–1819* I, 541), again underscoring his proximity to the character of Hamlet), then in his final courses of lectures in 1818 and 1819 offering three detailed considerations of the play – his most sustained close reading of any one play and character. In a marginal note from January 1819, Coleridge underscores the personal as well as critical significance of this play, claiming that 'Hamlet was the Play, or rather Hamlet himself was the Character, in the intuition and exposition of which I first made my turn for philosophical criticism, and especially for insight into the genius of Shakespear' (*CM* IV, 836): here, 'philosophical criticism' manifests itself as 'intuition and exposition', with intuition understood as 'a direct and immediate beholding or presentation of an object to the mind thro' the senses or the imagination' (*SWF* I, 369) and exposition naming the setting forth of a claim in detail, which became integral to Coleridge's understanding of practical criticism. This is, in short, Coleridge's critical procedure as a lecturer.

Coleridge's first *published* attempt to delineate what he meant by 'philosophical criticism', the establishment of incontrovertible principles of criticism instead of the prejudices of individual disposition or association, is the series of *Essays on the Principles of Genial Criticism* which he wrote in 1814 for *Felix Farley's Bristol Journal*. The term 'genial' designates something akin to critical affinity, an attempt on the part of the reader or spectator 'to judge in the same spirit in which the Artist produced, or ought to have produced' (*SWF* I, 360). 'The genial Judgement', he later observed in a note on Milton, 'is to distinguish accurately the character & characteristics of each poem, praising them according to their force & vivacity in their own kind' (*CM* III, 886), and is to be distinguished from negative criticism or reprehension. Drawing freely on Kant's terms in the *Critique of Judgement* (notably the agreeable and the beautiful), Coleridge sought in these essays to set forth principles of sound criticism' through 'establish[ing] and exemplify[ing] the distinct meaning of terms, often confounded in common use, and considered as mere synonymes' (*SWF* I, 364). These terms include 'agreeable', 'beautiful', 'picturesque', 'grand' and 'sublime', with the 'beautiful' of particular importance here, defined as the way 'in which *the many*, still seen as many, becomes *one*', or, 'Multëity in Unity' – an increasingly important component of the Coleridgean imagination (*SWF* I, 371, 372). The essays also mark the first publication addressing Coleridge's development of a theory of organic unity, his attempt to reconcile the 'two conflicting principles of the FREE LIFE, and of the confining FORM!' (*SWF* I, 374) in terms of that '[s]omething there must be to realize the form, something in and by which the forma informans reveals itself' (*SWF* I, 377; 'form that forms from within'). Although Coleridge sets forth in the *Essays* what he considers to be irrefutable principles of criticism, he doesn't explain how to put them into practice, as a result of which the undertaking may seem incomplete. The *Essays* nevertheless mark Coleridge's first published attempt to lay the foundation firmly and distinctly for the establishment of 'fixed principles' – and are in this regard unprecedented in English Romantic critical writing.

Coleridge's systematic, written attempt in the *Essays* to set forth the principles of his critical practice (combined with the preliminary exposition of many of his fundamental beliefs about great poetry in the lectures on Shakespeare) makes possible his next and most sustained attempt 'to reduce criticism to a system, by the deduction of the Causes from Principles involved in our faculties' (*CL* IV, 598) – the *Biographia*. It is here that he both systematically and immethodically applies 'the rules, deduced from philosophical principles, to poetry and criticism' and, more pointedly, defines 'the real *poetic* character of the poet', Wordsworth, whose writings concerning both poetic diction (the Preface to the 1800 edition of *Lyrical Ballads*) and the distinction between fancy and imagination (the Preface to the 1815 *Poems*) provided first the long-standing then the immediate catalyst for Coleridge to undertake the *Biographia* (*BL* I, 5). Coleridge had observed as early as 1802 that he 'suspect[ed] that some where or other there is a radical Difference in our theoretical opinions respecting Poetry', which he planned to address through 'lay[ing] down some plain, & perspicuous, tho' not superficial, Canons of Criticism respecting Poetry' (*CL* II, 830), but it wasn't until he read Wordsworth's distinction between fancy and the imagination in the 1815 Preface that he was provoked to set forth his own principles and definitions in writing, to establish himself in the public eye as the *philosophical* critic of the imagination.

While both poet–critics treat the imagination as a mental faculty, Wordsworth confines himself to 'the influences of fancy and imagination as they are manifested in poetry' (and how these terms influence the classification of his own poems in 1815), whereas Coleridge's object is 'to investigate the seminal principle, and then from the kind to deduce the degree' (*BL* I, 88). This is a critical distinction: if Wordsworth has sketched the '*poetic* fruitage' of the imagination, it is left to Coleridge as the 'philosophical critic' to 'add the trunk, and even the roots' (*BL* I, 88). Coleridge's 'philosophical' definition of the 'esemplastic power' (that which shapes into one (*BL* I, 168)) is often thought to culminate in the tortured labyrinth of Chapter 13, with its highly compacted distinction between the primary and the secondary imagination, and the attendant distinction of both of these from fancy (nothing more for Coleridge than a 'mode of memory'). Whereas the primary imagination is 'the living Power and prime Agent of all human Perception ..., a repetition in the finite mind of the eternal act of creation in the infinite I AM', the secondary imagination (differing not in kind but only in degree and the '*mode* of its operation') 'dissolves, diffuses, dissipates, in order to re-create; or where this process is rendered impossible, yet still at all events it struggles to idealize and to unify' (*BL* I, 304): in other words, the primary imagination is the faculty by which we perceive that which is external to us, while the secondary imagination is the faculty by which we (re-)create (what Coleridge later delineates as the poetic imagination). This much-anticipated definition of the 'principle' or faculty of imagination as the fusing power occurs at what appears to be the fulcrum of the *Biographia*, the structural as well as intellectual hinge between the philosophical chapters of volume I (notably Chapters 5–13) and the more 'practical' chapters of volume II (Chapters 17–20 and 22). In order to understand it not only as a mental faculty but also as the crucial intellectual link between Coleridge's definition of poetry and of the ideal poet, however, it is necessary to contextualize this cryptic pronouncement within Coleridge's various definitions of a poem, poetry and the (ideal) poet across the critical arc of Chapters 13, 14 and 15.

With his philosophical definition of the imagination seemingly in place, Coleridge immediately returns in Chapter 14 to his discussion of Wordsworth (which he paused in Chapter 4), in order to address the controversy occasioned by Wordsworth's use of 'the language of *real* life' (*BL* II, 8). Poised to declare 'in what points I coincide with [Wordsworth's] opinions, and in what points I altogether differ' (*BL* II, 10), Coleridge interrupts himself to announce that he cannot do so until he explains his ideas, 'first, of a POEM; and secondly, of POETRY itself, in *kind*, and in *essence*' (*BL* II, 11). He draws on the 1811–12 lectures in defining a poem as a species of composition which proposes its immediate object to be pleasure and furthermore proposes 'to itself such delight from the *whole*, as is compatible with a distinct gratification from each component *part*' (*BL* II, 13). Poetry proves to be a less tractable term, prompting Coleridge to combine it with the question 'what is a poet?', which leads in turn to a valorization of the poet, 'described in *ideal* perfection' as one who 'brings the whole soul of man into activity' (*BL* II, 15–16), who 'diffuses a tone, and spirit of unity, that blends and (as it were) *fuses*' by means of what Coleridge now and climactically terms 'that synthetic and magical power, to which we have exclusively appropriated the name of imagination':

> This power, first put in action by the will and understanding ... reveals itself in the balance or reconciliation of opposite or discordant qualities: of sameness, with difference; of the general, with the concrete; the idea, with the image; the individual, with the representative; the sense of novelty and freshness, with old and familiar objects; a more than usual state of emotion, with more than usual order ... and while it blends and harmonizes the natural and the artificial, still subordinates art to nature; the manner to the matter; and our admiration of the poet to our sympathy with the poetry.   (*BL* II, 16–17)

As a synthetic power, the Coleridgean imagination is a reconciling and 'completing power', a bridge between various faculties of the mind without which there cannot be 'poetic genius'.

With this rhapsodic definition of the imagination in place, Coleridge would appear poised to return (again) to Wordsworth and the 'real *poetic* character of the poet'. But not yet: he instead introduces a 'critical analysis' of Shakespeare (Chapter 15) in order to elucidate the 'specific symptoms of poetic power', or the imagination (*BL* II, 19). As is also the case throughout the lectures, Coleridge cannot define poetry – let alone the ideal poet or the imagination, or even Wordsworth – without Shakespeare. Integral to Coleridge's method of 'critical analysis' is what he now terms 'practical criticism'. As Coleridge explains, '[i]n the application of these principles [i.e. of the poem, poet, poetry, imagination] to purposes of practical criticism as employed in the appraisal of works more or less imperfect, I have endeavoured to discover what the qualities in a poem are, which may be deemed promises and specific symptoms of poetic power' (*BL* II, 19). The (Shakespearean) standards of 'poetic power' as isolated by Coleridge include: 'the perfect sweetness of the versification'; the ability to enter into the experiences of subjects 'remote from the private interests and circumstances' of the poet (i.e. the sympathetic imagination); the modification of images 'by a predominant passion' (which has the effect of 'reducing multitude to unity'); and 'ENERGY OF THOUGHT' (*BL* II, 20, 23, 25) – all of which, to one degree or another, inform his critical evaluation of Wordsworth.

Coleridge's analysis of the language appropriate to poetry, along with his extended consideration (not entirely genial) of Wordsworth's poetry in Chapters 17–20 and 22, offers a practical counterpart to the more philosophical concerns of volume I. It is here that Coleridge takes issue with Wordsworth's contention in the 1800 Preface that 'the proper diction for poetry in general consists altogether in a language taken ... from the mouths of men in real life' (*BL* II, 42). In 'adopt[ing] the very language of men' for the purposes of poetry, Wordsworth appeared to claim that that the language of poetry was to be regarded as a copy of ordinary language.[9] For Coleridge, however, poetry is one of the '*imitative* arts; and that imitation, as opposed to copying, consists either in the interfusion of the SAME throughout the radically DIFFERENT, or of the different throughout a base radically the same' (*BL* II, 72). The distinction is a crucial one for Coleridge: whereas a copy is merely a reproduction, an imitation requires creative mimesis in combining 'a certain degree of dissimilitude with a certain degree of similitude' (*Lects 1808–1819* I, 223–24). Coleridge furthermore disagrees with Wordsworth's seemingly reductive definition of 'language' as individual words (as if language were strictly a matter of diction). For Coleridge, 'language' is not a matter of 'such words exclusively' but implies a much richer practice, incorporating such vital concerns as the arrangement of words as well as sentences, the affinities between words and the effects of metre, a matter of 'the *order*, in which the words of such men are wont to succeed each other' (*BL* II, 58). And whereas Wordsworth maintained that the language of poetry 'does not differ from that of prose',[10] Coleridge countered that 'there must exist a [difference] between the ordonnance of poetic composition and that of prose' (*BL* II, 61): as he had written as early as 1802 (when he first articulated his disagreement with Wordsworth's Preface), 'Poetry justifies ... some new combinations of Language, & *commands* the omission of many others allowable in other composition' (*CL* II, 812).

When Coleridge turns from Wordsworth's Preface to the poetry, he outlines both its 'defects' and its 'beauties' in relation to 'the principles from which the judgement ... is deduced' (*BL* II, 119). Beginning with the defects, Coleridge identifies the 'inconstancy' of Wordsworth's style: 'the sudden and unprepared transitions from lines or sentences of peculiar felicity ... to a style, not only unimpassioned but undistinguished'; his *'matter-of-factness'*, often manifested as a 'laborious minuteness and fidelity in the representation of objects'; 'an undue predilection for the *dramatic* form' unsuited to his essentially meditative poetry; the disproportion between the 'intensity of feeling' and the 'value of the objects described'; and, closely related, 'thoughts and images too great for the subject' (*BL* II, 121, 126, 135, 136). Emphasizing that these defects are only 'occasional', Coleridge proceeds to the 'characteristic excellences' of Wordsworth's poetry: the 'purity of language ... a perfect appropriateness of the words to the meaning'; the correspondence of thoughts and sentiments, as drawn from Wordsworth's own 'meditative observation'; the originality and felicity of his language; the 'perfect truth of nature in his images and descriptions'; 'meditative pathos' or 'sympathy with man as man'; and, pre-eminently, 'IMAGINATION in the highest and strictest sense of the word' (*BL* II, 142, 144–45, 148, 150, 151). In Coleridge's final estimation, Wordsworth 'stands nearest of all modern writers to Shakespear and Milton; and yet in a kind perfectly unborrowed and his own' (*BL* II, 151).

Coleridge's critique of Wordsworth raises important questions regarding his method (in the written criticism as well as in the lectures), specifically the relation between the general and the particular, the theoretical and the practical, the critical principles and the textual examples. At the same time as Coleridge was systematically committed to the establishment of fundamental, 'philosophical', principles, he also advocated – and practised – what he denominated 'hypercriticism', convinced as he was as to 'how little instructive any criticism can be which does not enter into minutiæ' (*CN* III, 3970). The complicated interplay of principle and practice precludes any final determination as to whether the philosophical principles dictate the appraisal of individual poems or whether the close reading of specific passages of poetry makes possible the establishment of general principles. When Coleridge commenced work on the *Biographia* in 1815, he drew on material regarding the 'principles' of poetry from particular textual instances that he had been accumulating for years in his notebooks as well as his lectures. That is to say, he had been proceeding *inductively*. At the same time, however, Coleridge typically began a course of lectures with an historical survey or the exposition of the principles of poetry. He repeatedly argued that he was applying rules '*deduced* from philosophical principles' to the 'purposes of practical criticism' (*BL* I, 5 (emphasis added); II, 19; see also II, 107), all the while acknowledging that 'A strong sense of a particular FACT cannot be reasoned away by a general Logic ... a *general* Logic, and therefore of necessity plausible, but yet false because it is not universal, & yet is applied to a particular case, as if it were so' (*Lects 1808–1819* I, 63). What, then, is the relationship between philosophical principles and poetic examples, between the theoretical and the practical, in Coleridge's criticism?

Coleridge explicitly addresses this question in the 'Essays on the Principles of Method' (written for inclusion in the 1818 edition of *The Friend*), in which, as Dahlia Porter has argued, he attempts to establish the inductive method of his *practical* criticism as itself a *philosophical* principle.[11] Coleridge defines method via its Greek etymology as 'literally *a way*, or *path of Transit*' (*Friend* I, 457), with particular emphasis on the continuity of the transit, or transition. To teach what Coleridge calls the '*Science of Method*' is to teach someone 'to contemplate not *things* only, or for their own sake alone, but likewise and chiefly the *relations* of things' (*Friend* I, 450, 451). The uneducated mind that thinks about '*things* only' is immethodical due to its 'habitual submission of the understanding to mere events and images as such'; its neglect of all mental relations precludes all method (*Friend* I, 451), whereas the educated mind attempts to classify things in relation to . one another, 'proportionate to the connecting energy' (*Friend* I, 455), which leads to reflection and generalization. To illustrate his point, Coleridge juxtaposes Mistress Quickly and Hamlet, both of whom are immethodical, the former due to the absence of connective thinking (sterility of mind) and the latter due to its surplus (exuberance of mind). For there to be method, there must be 'the sense of a principle of connection given by the mind', which Coleridge variously calls '*the leading Thought*' or 'the INITIATIVE', in order to bring 'things the most remote and diverse in time, place, and outward circumstance ... into mental contiguity and succession' (*Friend* I, 471, 455). These essays are the only published statement of Coleridge's philosophical views when his reputation as a literary critic was at its height. Whether or not the method outlined in them is consistently, or ever, the method of Coleridge's criticism, they afford a unique opportunity to consider the relations between his method and his practice (he maintained that the essays on method were 'the ground-work ... the general views of my Philosophy' (*CL* IV, 776)). One needs to consider Coleridge's method if one is to understand his criticism.

The theoretical essays on method were written at the same time as Coleridge's most sustained exercises in practical criticism, in the three courses of lectures he gave in 1818 and 1819 not only on Shakespeare but also on other English writers (e.g. Spenser, Jonson, Beaumont and Fletcher,

Massinger, Milton), and European writers including Dante, Ariosto, Cervantes and Rabelais (he was in this regard an early comparatist). Conceiving of the 1818–19 lectures on Shakespeare (which alternated with his philosophical lectures) in terms of 'particular and practical Criticism' (*Lects 1808–1819* II, 34), Coleridge proposed to analyse individual plays 'scene by scene, for the purpose of illustrating the conduct of the plot, and the peculiar force, beauty, and propriety, of the language, in the particular passages', thereby illustrating 'the unity of interest in the whole and in the apparent contrast of the component parts' (*Lects 1808–1819* II, 254). In doing so, Coleridge could methodically delineate the work of the imagination in developing what he called 'the key note', or 'the *germ* of all the after events', announced in the opening scenes (*Lects 1808–1819* II, 268; I, 559), under the aegis of the play's imaginative coherence and organic 'unity of interest in the whole'. Delivered at the height of his reputation as a public speaker, these lectures were immediately celebrated for the 'mysterious spell' Coleridge cast over his auditors in pouring forth a 'torrent of fine, and of *extraordinary* ideas', which produced 'the finest poetry in his criticism, as if he had caught inspiration from his subject' (*Lects 1808–1819* II, 275, 274).

Coleridge returned in these lectures to his critical distinction between imitation and copy (whereas 'a certain quantum of Difference is essential to the former, and an indispensable condition and cause of the pleasure ..., in a Copy it is a defect, contravening its name and purpose' (*Lects 1808–1819* II, 264)). He also reanimated his preoccupation with identifying an intermediate state between full consciousness and delusion, which he repeatedly characterized as illusion, in which we '*chuse* to be deceived' – in other words, 'a suspension of the voluntary and therefore of the comparative power', or judgement (*Lects 1808–1819* II, 266), which he most memorably formulated in the *Biographia* as 'that willing suspension of disbelief for the moment, which constitutes poetic faith' (*BL* II, 6). Although at the time they were not conceived of as valedictory lectures, the Shakespeare lectures of 1818–19 offer final formulations of many of Coleridge's critical dicta apropos of both some of the plays on which he lectured most frequently (*The Tempest, Macbeth, Othello, Hamlet*) as well as others, such as *King Lear*, 'La Terribilitá of Shakspeare's tragic Might' (*CL* IV, 915).

These lectures are furthermore noteworthy for their reliance on marginalia, an important genre of critical writing for Coleridge later in his life. Coleridge's annotations in his interleaved copy of Samuel Ayscough's edition of *The Dramatic Works of William Shakespeare* demonstrate that he prepared for these lectures by writing long introductory notes on the blank leaves, as well as shorter, sometimes cryptic, notes on the passages on which he planned to comment, so that he was effectively offering close readings of his chosen passages, sometimes as discrete as individual lines or specific words. Spontaneously developing his thoughts in relation to his marginal cues (stage directions, as it were), Coleridge hoped to present a sense 'of order in the matter, and of animation in the manner', all the while lecturing 'without book' (*CL* IV, 812). It is in the marginalia that Coleridge succinctly sums up particular insights with a definitive formulation, such as when he describes Iago's first soliloquy as 'the motive-hunting of motiveless Malignity', or distinguishes Banquo's responses to the weird sisters from Macbeth's in terms of the *'unpossessedness'* of Banquo's 'unintröitive' mind, or singles out the *'credibilizing* effect' of the word 'again' when Marcellus exclaims of the ghost of Hamlet's father, 'Look where it comes again!' (*CM* IV, 862, 787, 839). Coleridge's marginalia serve both as prompts for the lecturer to elaborate extemporaneously and as the first articulations of ideas for the critic to develop in his notebooks. They are the marks of a practised lecturer, reading both for himself and his audiences.

When Coleridge delivered his final lectures in March 1819, he was exhausted: as he wearily recorded in his notebook, 'Fourteenth of the Phil. Course and the Last (O pray Heaven, that it may indeed be the Last) of All' (*CN* III, 4504). He was also very much in demand as a lecturer. Asked if he would reprise an earlier course of lectures delivered at the Surrey Institution in 1812–13, Coleridge defensively admitted that he couldn't repeat them because he hadn't written them out, before proceeding to explain that the critical purpose of a lecture was 'to leave a *sting* behind – *i.e.* a disposition to study the subject anew, under the light of a new principle'. The Coleridgean 'sting' required a great deal of effort on the lecturer's part, both deliberate preparation and the animated spontaneity of the delivery, in order to 'give the subject a new turn' – because, as he insisted, '[s]uch is *my way*, for such is *my nature*' (*CL* IV, 924). Coleridge was acutely aware of the double price exacted by the lectures: in providing 'employment for the bread and beef of the day', they simultaneously kept him from working on 'PERMANENT' projects and, paradoxically, provided him with 'the only means by which I can enable myself to go on at all with the great philosophical work' we now refer to as the *Opus Maximum* (*CL* IV, 925, 838, 893). Lecturing made the writing possible, even as it seemed to impede it.

In 1803, Southey had lamented, 'It vexes and grieves me to the heart, that when he is gone, as go he will, nobody will believe what a mind goes with him, – how infinitely and ten-thousand-thousand-fold the mightiest of his generation' (*CLRS*, 802). By 1819, however, Coleridge had created a body of work, unpublished as well as published, that would both testify to the 'mightiness' of his mind and eventually establish him as one of the greatest critics in the English tradition. One of the qualities that makes Coleridge so compelling a critic is that, with such an extraordinarily wide range of interests both intellectual and imaginative, his procedure as a critic is invariably combinatory, based on the tangled relationship between the practical parts and the theoretical whole. Coleridge knew as much, commenting in an early notebook entry that 'a grievous fault it is / my illustrations swallow up my thesis – I feel too intensely the omnipresence of all in each', and it is his dual tendency to 'perceive the *difference* of things' all the while 'pursuing the likenesses' that contributes to the difficulty of summing up his critical practice and achievement (*CN* II, 2372).

Nevertheless, one might provisionally assemble the qualities of his critical temperament under four headings.[12] First, Coleridge exceeds every other English critic in his depth of thought, which in turn made possible his 'philosophical criticism', based on a fixed, impersonal set of principles for critical evaluation.[13] Second, Coleridge remains the essential point of reference for the practice of 'practical criticism' (a coinage later popularized by I. A. Richards in *Practical Criticism* (1929) and disseminated throughout the American New Criticism), his 'hypercritical' attention to form, metre, diction and all the local details of literary language that remains an essential point of reference for 'close reading'. Third, and closely related, is Coleridge's development of a theory of 'organic criticism': his principle of organic unity allowed him to explain the organization of a literary work, all the while it provided a critical principle for his definition of the creative imagination. Fourth, Coleridge championed the practice of what he denominated 'just and genial criticism', or the celebration of the beauties of a work of art rather than its defects, a critical practice attuned to the imagination, or genius, of the artist. In undertaking all this, Coleridge fundamentally redefined the nature of critical activity.

Coleridge once defined the 'true Critic' as that critic who could locate himself 'on some central point, in which he can command the whole – i.e. some general rule, which founded on Reason, on faculties common to all men, must therefore apply to all men' (*Lects 1808–1819* I, 491) and valued what he termed '*surview*', that 'prospectiveness of mind ... which enables a man to foresee the whole of what he is to convey, appertaining to any one point' (*BL* II, 58). Throughout his lectures as well as his criticism, he repeatedly strove to 'combin[e] many circumstances into one moment of thought to produce that ultimate end of human Thought, and human Feeling, Unity' (*CN* III, 3247). If one were to try to isolate such a 'moment of thought' in Coleridge's lectures and criticism, it would have to be articulated in terms of the dynamic *interpenetration* of reason and imagination that characterized his genius, that 'sublime faculty' which he shared with Shakespeare, 'by which a great mind becomes that which it meditates on' (*Lects 1808–1819* I, 80–81).

Notes

1 *The Life of Mary Russell Mitford*, ed. Rev. A. G. L'Estrange, 3 vols (London, 1870), I, 162–63.
2 J. R. de J. Jackson, *Method and Imagination in Coleridge's Criticism* (Cambridge, MA: Harvard University Press, 1969), 1.
3 Sarah Zimmerman, *The Romantic Literary Lecture in Britain* (Oxford University Press, 2019), 32–33.
4 *Byron's Letters and Journals*, ed. Leslie A. Marchand, 12 vols (Cambridge, MA: Harvard University Press, 1973–82), II, 140–41; cited in Jon Klancher, 'The Vocation of Criticism and the Crisis of the Republic of Letters', in *The Cambridge History of Literary Criticism*, vol. V, *Romanticism*, ed. Marshall Brown (Cambridge University Press, 2000), 316.
5 Klancher, 'Vocation of Criticism', 315.
6 See also the contemporaneous 'Memoranda for a History of English Poetry' (*SWF* I, 107–8).
7 Walter Jackson Bate, *Coleridge* (New York: Macmillan, 1968), 152.
8 Richard Fogle, *The Idea of Coleridge's Criticism* (Berkeley: University of California Press, 1962), 12.
9 *The Prose Works of William Wordsworth*, eds. W. J. B. Owen and Jane Worthington Smyser, 3 vols (Oxford University Press, 1974), I, 130.
10 Ibid., I, 132.
11 Dahlia Porter, *Science, Form, and The Problem of Induction in British Romanticism* (Cambridge University Press, 2018), 231.
12 See also Bate, *Coleridge*, 143–45, and Angela Esterhammer, 'The Critic', in *The Cambridge Companion to Coleridge*, ed. Lucy Newlyn (Cambridge University Press, 2002), 153–54.
13 As Herbert Read noted, '[t]he distinction of Coleridge, which puts him head and shoulders above every other English critic, is due to his introduction of a philosophical method of criticism'. *Coleridge as Critic* (London: Faber & Faber, 1949), 18.

14

NICHOLAS HALMI

Coleridge's Philosophies

In conversations recorded by Thomas Medwin, Lord Byron, recalling his reading of the *Biographia Literaria*, expressed a widely shared view that Coleridge's philosophical interests were fundamentally antithetical to his poetic gifts: 'If he had never gone to Germany, nor spoilt his fine genius by the transcendental philosophy and German metaphysics, nor taken to write lay sermons, he would have made the greatest poet of the day.'[1] Coleridge himself accepted neither that poetry and philosophy were opposed to one another, nor that his immersion in German philosophy was superfluous or detrimental to his intellectual development. On the contrary, he insisted that '[n]o man was ever yet a great poet, without being at the same time a profound philosopher' (*BL* II, 25–26), and he explained that his increasing recognition of the inadequacy of the empiricist philosophies of John Locke, George Berkeley and David Hartley had led him to Immanuel Kant's transcendental philosophy (*BL* I, 140–41, 153–54). But despite his sustained interest in and commitment to philosophical thought from his youth to the end of his life, Coleridge's claim to be considered an original philosophical thinker remains as contested today as it was in his lifetime.[2]

Several factors complicate the assessment of Coleridge's engagement with philosophy: his syncretic use of established philosophers; his deliberate tendency, connected to his religious concerns, to associate thought with feeling; and the tensions involved in his persistent desire, also connected to his religious concerns, to overcome epistemological and metaphysical dualisms (thought/reality, mind/body, self/world) while maintaining moral dualism (good/evil). From his 'Lectures on Revealed Religion' (1795) onwards, his philosophical commitments were inseparable from, if not always conceptually compatible with, his vindication of Christian revelation, even as his understanding of that revelation changed over time. Since the limited space available here forces me to be ruthlessly selective, thus neglecting the important but complex topic of Coleridge's reception of German *Naturphilosophie*,[3] I shall focus on his troubled engagement with three thinkers of especial importance for him – Joseph Priestley, Benedict de Spinoza and Kant – and conclude with a very brief consideration of his use of F. W. J. Schelling in the *Biographia Literaria* (1817). Because Coleridge's early associationist phase – which he presented in the *Biographia* as an error – reveals preoccupations that persisted for the rest of his life, more attention is given to it than is usual in accounts of his philosophical thought.

While a notoriously monological talker, Coleridge was also a profoundly dialogical thinker, dependent on the intellectual stimuli provided by his reading, as the remarkable extent of his marginalia attests. His translated plagiarisms from such figures as Kant and Schelling are the most obvious manifestations of this dependence, although there is some truth to the claim that 'the more undigested a borrowing is, the more peripheral [...] to Coleridge's real interests' (*P Lects* I, lvii–iii). The account given in Chapter 9 of the *Biographia* of his philosophical journey from David Hartley's associationism to Schelling's transcendental idealism by way of Leibniz, Böhme, Spinoza, Kant and others lends support to Robert Southey's much-quoted verdict that Coleridge embraced and discarded philosophical systems successively without finally settling on any: 'The truth is that he plays with systems, & any nonsense will serve him for a text from which he can deduce something new & surprizing' (*CLRS*, 1479).[4] If his habit of working out his own philosophical positions in response to others' made him an acute critic, it also inhibited him from becoming a systematic philosopher in his own right. Hence the plural of my title.

To be sure, Coleridge long aspired to a kind of system, which he described in 1831 as identifying 'the insulated fragments of truth' in different intellectual disciplines and synthesizing them to 'frame a perfect mirror' (*TT* I, 248). Yet while the reference here to mirroring seems to assume a traditional conception of truth as the correspondence of a mental representation with a reality external to the mind, and hence also the separation of knowing subject from known object, Coleridge persistently denied that reflective self-consciousness and discursive reasoning – the first principles of most Western philosophy from Descartes to Kant – could by themselves arrive at an adequate comprehension of reality and truth.[5] In one of the fragments of the so-called *Opus Maximum*, for example, he argued that 'the inevitable result of all consequent reasoning, in which the Speculative intellect refuses to acknowledge a higher or deeper ground than it can itself supply [...] is [...] pantheism, under one or other of its modes [...] and in all alike [...] practically atheistic' (*OM*, 106–7; cf. *Friend* I, 522–23 n. 1). This ground, being inaccessible to ratiocination, could be disclosed to reason only if reason itself *were* it. Thus in *The Friend* and elsewhere Coleridge defined reason less as a mental faculty than as an ontological reality in which subject and object were united (as the condition of the possibility of knowledge) and the individual was united with God (as the condition of the possibility of faith): 'it is an organ identical with its appropriate objects. Thus, God, the Soul, eternal Truth, &c. are the objects of Reason; but they are themselves *reason*' (*Friend* I, 156; *CL* VI, 600; cf. *CM* I, 239, and II, 1151–52).

In his argument that self-consciousness must be grounded in something transcending itself, and his consequent insistence on the limits of discursive reason and on the necessary incompleteness of any philosophical system predicated on the primacy of reflective self-consciousness, Coleridge had affinities with German contemporaries such as Friedrich Hölderlin, Novalis (Friedrich von Hardenberg) and Friedrich Schlegel. But unlike the three German thinkers, Coleridge was not content to postulate an impersonal Absolute or state of Being (*Sein*) as the ground of self-consciousness – an Absolute that the Germans accepted was not directly accessible to cognition.[6] For Coleridge, whether in his early Unitarianism or his later Trinitarianism, the ground of self-consciousness and of reality itself was conceivable only in terms of God. Thus he insisted equally that 'the office and object of philosophy' was to demonstrate the identity of subject and object (*BL* I, 260), and that 'Religion [...] is the ultimate end of philosophy' (*Friend* I, 463; also *BL* I, 283).

Coleridge may have been exaggerating when he told Robert Southey in December 1794, 'I am a compleat Necessitarian – and understand the subject as well almost as Hartley himself – but I go farther than Hartley and believe the corporeality of *thought* – namely, that it is motion.' For he immediately made a joke of this philosophical position with a mock letter of consolation, usually overlooked by commentators (*CL* I, 137–38). Yet there is no doubt that David Hartley's associationism, especially as radicalized by Joseph Priestley, appealed to Coleridge in the 1790s. Hypothesizing a parallel between natural laws and the principles of mental operations, Hartley explained thought as consisting in the formation and recollection of correspondences between physical sensations and 'ideas' (including feelings). Free will, in the sense of an ability to act without cause or motivation, was therefore illusory. The determinism of this theory was reconcilable with theism insofar as God, by definition benevolent, was assumed to be the ultimate cause of both sensations and the principles by which they were processed in the mind. Hence Coleridge's recommendation of the theory to Southey, also in December 1794, as an antidote to scepticism: 'I would ardently, that you were a Necessitarian – and (believing in an all-loving Omnipotence) an Optimist' (*CL* I, 145).

NICHOLAS HALMI

While Hartley himself, unwilling to abandon the idea of an immortal soul, had resisted committing himself fully in his *Observations on Man* (1749) to a materialist theory of consciousness, Priestley overcame this obstacle by declaring the soul unknowable and therefore philosophically irrelevant. In the introduction to *Hartley's Theory of the Mind* (1775), his abridgement of the *Observations* and again in his *Disquisitions relating to Matter and Spirit* (1777) – both of which Coleridge almost certainly read – Priestley argued that once matter is recognized to be not inert and impenetrable but active, possessing forces of attraction and repulsion, its apparent difference in kind from the activities of sensation and thought disappears. So it was reasonable to assume that man is composed of a single, uniform substance comprising both material and mental attributes.[7] Having thus dissolved the dualism of mind and body, Priestley proceeded more daringly to dissolve that of God and world, arguing that the 'Divine Being', to which everything owes its existence, could not act on the world if it were not also in some sense material (since otherwise it would require the assistance of an intermediary between the immaterial and the material): 'matter is, by this means, resolved into nothing but the *divine agency* exerted according to certain rules' (Priestley, *Disquisitions*, 1, 39). And if 'every thing is really *done* by the divine power, what material objection can there be to every thing *being* the divine power'. The advantage of this scheme, Priestley added disarmingly, is 'that it supposes *nothing to be made in vain*' (*Disquisitions*, 1, 40) – including apparent evil, which becomes teleologically explicable as an instrument of divine benevolence. 'Reasoning strictly and with logical Accuracy', Coleridge lectured in 1795, 'I should deny the existence of any Evil, inasmuch as the end determines the nature of the means and I have been able to discover nothing of which the end is not good' (*Lects 1795*, 104). From God's perspective, 'All things are pure, his strong controlling Love / Alike from all educing perfect good' (*CPW* 1, i, 177).

In these early years Coleridge expressed his philosophical convictions in poetry as well as prose. Composed in 1794–96 and published in 1796, 'Religious Musings', from which the lines just quoted come, attests to his attraction to Hartley's associationism and Priestley's materialism; and the poem explicitly praises both thinkers (lines 369–77). A note added to the poem in 1797 specifies that lines 39–42, in which Coleridge traces a progression from hope to faith to love and finally to 'consciousness of God', versify Hartley's argument that all human pleasures lead by association to the idea of God as the source of all good (*CPW* 1, i, 176).[8] Assurance that this train of thought is ontologically justified follows in lines 126–31, where Coleridge invokes Priestley's conception of divine immanence:

212

'Tis the sublime of man,
Our noontide Majesty, to know ourselves
Parts and proportions of one wond'rous whole!
This fraternizes man, this constitutes
Our charities and bearings. But 'tis God
Diffus'd thro' all, that doth make all one whole [...]
                                               (*CPW* I, i, 180)

Reinforcement of this idea of a providentially organized world, although without a theological inflection, came from Erasmus Darwin's poem *The Economy of Vegetation* (1791), which itself praised Priestley. The juxtaposition in the fourth canto of an account of nature's regenerative tendency (vital winds succeeding pestilential ones) with reports of Enlightenment scientific and technological advancements implied a parallel between nature and human society, such as Priestley hypothesized: 'one great comprehensive law shall be found to govern both the material and the intellectual world' (Priestley, *Hartley's Theory*, xxv).[9] In lines contributed in 1795 to Southey's epic *Joan of* Arc (and subsequently republished in 1817 as part of his own poem 'The Destiny of Nations'), Coleridge elaborated that although God works in diverse ways, all his actions are directed towards the single end of perfection:

Glory to Thee, Father of Earth and Heaven!
All-conscious Presence of the Universe!
Nature's vast ever-acting Energy!
In will, in deed, Impulse of All to all;
Whether thy Law with unrefracted Ray
Beam on the Prophet's purged Eye, or if
Diseasing realms the Enthusiast, wild of thought
Scatter new frenzies on the infected Throng,
Thou both inspiring and predooming both,
Fit Instruments and best of perfect End.   (*CPW* I, i, 223)

In 1795 Coleridge found Priestley's deterministic theism consonant both with the traditional teleological argument for God's existence, or argument from design (*Lects 1795*, 93), and with the idea, which he derived variously from Mark Akenside's poem *The Pleasures of Imagination* (1744) and George Berkeley's *New Theory of Vision* (1709), that nature is a kind of divine language. The morally educative value of learning to comprehend this language – that is, recognizing in natural phenomena the operation of divine providence – was a theme that found repeated expression in Coleridge's works of the 1790s, from his 'Lectures on Revealed Religion' (*Lects 1795*, 94 and n. 3) to his contribution to *Joan of Arc* ('For all that meets the bodily sense I deem / Symbolical, one mighty alphabet for infant minds' (*CPW* I, i, 210)) to 'Frost at Midnight', in which he promised his infant son Hartley,

> so shalt thou see and hear
> The lovely shapes and sounds intelligible
> Of that eternal language, which thy God
> Utters, who from eternity doth teach
> Himself in all, and all things in himself.   (*CPW* I, ii, 572)

Coleridge's desire to interpret nature as God's symbolic self-representation was sufficiently deeply rooted, however, not to require the specific philosophical underpinning of Priestley's ontology of divine immanence – even if it did require an alternative anti-dualist ontology, one that allowed the symbol to be declared the same as, by virtue of itself being or at least participating in, its referent.[10] And although one of the arguments that Coleridge later deployed against Hartley – namely, that his dualism could not explain interaction between the material and immaterial (*BL* I, 117) – was taken from none other than Priestley, in the later 1790s Coleridge began to entertain serious doubts about necessitarianism, particularly on moral grounds. In a letter of March 1796 he observed that the gratuitousness of his wife's pains during pregnancy seemed to contradict Priestley's optimism:

> Other pains are only friendly admonitions that we are not acting as Nature requires – but here are pains most horrible in consequence of having obeyed Nature. Quere – How is it that Dr Priestley is not an atheist? – He asserts in three different Places, that God not only *does,* but *is,* every thing. – But if God *be* every Thing, every Thing is God – : which is all, the Atheists assert.
>
> (*CL* I, 192–93)

The pangs of childbirth were, according to Genesis (3:16), a punishment for the Fall, and by 1798 Coleridge was distancing himself decisively from Priestley's denial of the doctrine of Christ's atonement for mankind's inherent sinfulness: 'I believe most stedfastly in original Sin; that from our mothers' wombs our understandings are darkened [...] that our organization is depraved, & our volitions imperfect' (*CL* I, 396). Having accepted the concept of original sin, Coleridge could no longer adhere to necessitarianism without holding God responsible for the Fall. To admit the existence of evil and the reality of sin was therefore to assume the freedom of the will, an assumption that necessitarianism disallowed. The inexplicability of the death of his infant son Berkeley in 1799 only reinforced Coleridge's discontent with Priestley, as he confided in a letter to his wife (*CL* I, 482); and by 1801 he could inform Thomas Poole that he had 'overthrown the doctrine of Association, as taught by Hartley, and with it all the irreligious metaphysics of modern Infidels – especially, the doctrine of Necessity' (*CL* II, 706). The following year Coleridge repeated this assertion to John Prior

Estlin, adding that he did not now consider 'Christianity to be tenable on the Priestleyan Hypothesis' (*CL* II, 821).

Coleridge's rejection of Priestleyan materialism marks the beginning of what was to be a lifelong challenge of reconciling an attraction to monism, as the solution to the problem of dualism, with an insistence on metaphysical libertarianism – that is, the supposition that humans are capable of choices that are neither causally determined nor random, and that they are therefore responsible for those choices – as the solution to the problem of evil. This challenge certainly conditioned his reception of Spinoza. Coleridge's interest in the Dutch philosopher may have been stimulated in Göttingen by the prolonged furore following the posthumous revelation, in 1785, of the self-professed Spinozism of the much-admired playwright and critic Gotthold Ephraim Lessing, of whom Coleridge considered writing a biography. The revelation was scandalous because Spinoza's radical monism, according to which reality consists of a single, infinite substance that is equally God and nature, was widely regarded as atheistic – a view justified insofar as he rejected the personal God of the Bible, but reductive insofar as he did not (*pace* Pierre Bayle's influential caricature) equate God merely with the totality of the physical world.[11] That Coleridge frequently discussed 'the doctrines of Spinoza' during his months in Göttingen in 1799 was recalled disapprovingly nearly four decades later by Clement Carlyon, an Englishman who had met him there. But the version of those doctrines that Carlyon attributed to Coleridge sounds suspiciously like Priestleyan materialism (even if Priestley himself had explicitly dissociated his philosophy from Spinoza's): 'the great principle of Spinozism is, that there is nothing properly and absolutely existing but matter, and the modifications of matter; among which are even comprehended thought, abstract and general ideas, comparisons, relations, combinations of relations.'[12]

After returning from Germany, Coleridge informed Southey in late September 1799 that he was 'sunk in Spinoza' (*CL* I, 534) and three months later (albeit jokingly) that he was himself a Spinozist (*CL* I, 551). To be sure, it is unclear how much first-hand knowledge Coleridge had of Spinoza's writings before November 1812, when he borrowed his friend Henry Crabb Robinson's set of the *Opera omnia* for a year (returning it heavily annotated: *CM* V, 199–220). But notebook entries of November 1799 and October 1803, in which he sketched the idea for a poem on Spinoza, suggest that Coleridge found in the philosopher's conception of a single substance of which all finite things are 'modes' a compelling explanation of the possibility of 'multeity' in unity, and hence an alternative – though still anti-dualist – to Priestleyan materialism:

I would make a pilgrimage to the burning sands of Arabia, or &c &c to find the Man who could explain to me there can be *oneness*, there being infinite Perceptions – yet there must be a *oneness*, not an intense Union but an Absolute Unity[.]   (*CN* I, 556, also 1561)

By 1810, having in the meantime read Kant's three *Critiques*, Coleridge affirmed Spinoza's monism and Kant's transcendental idealism to be the 'Only two *Systems* of Philosophy – (sibi constantia [self-consistent]) possible' (*CN* III, 3756), the former 'ontological' or realist (proceeding from reflection on existence) and the latter 'anthropological' or idealist (proceeding from reflection on self-consciousness). Subsuming the entire Western philosophical tradition under this distinction, Thomas McFarland argued that Coleridge's spiritual and emotional commitment to Christianity enabled him finally and definitively to reject Spinozism and all other forms of 'pantheism' for Trinitarianism; and this was certainly the impression that Coleridge sought to convey when, for example, he assured Robinson in November 1812 that he believed in the Trinity despite his interest in Spinoza.[13] In the *Biographia*, taking comfort in Kant's 'pre-critical' argument of 1763 that God's existence is necessarily prior to his possibility (since nothing would be possible and nothing could be predicated of him if he did not exist) – an argument in which Kant criticized Spinoza for having conflated God's existence with his essence and effects – Coleridge asserted that a conviction of faith neither provable nor disprovable by rational demonstration had enabled him to resolve the competing claims of Spinoza's infinite substance and Christianity's personal God (*BL* I, 201–2; also *CM* I, 242).[14] Yet his repeated special pleading on Spinoza's behalf, not merely to defend him from the charge of atheism but even to claim his proximity to Christianity, betrays a more complex and less resolute attitude.

Since Coleridge, after rejecting Priestleyan necessitarianism, conceived free will to be the essence of personhood and the foundation of morality, he naturally objected to Spinoza's denial of free will, which followed from his definition of God as necessarily self-caused (*Ethics*, pt. 1, prop. 32): 'Assuredly, the defect in Spinoza's System is the impersonality of God – he makes his only Substance a Thing, not a Will' (*CM* III, 855; also *CM* IV, 226; *SWF* I, 707–8; *CL* IV, 849). This objection ought to have been decisive, but Coleridge sought to mitigate it, claiming variously that Spinoza's philosophy was merely the 'Skeleton' of a system that required elaboration and refinement (*SWF* I, 62; *CM* III, 123; *CL* IV, 548, 775), that it was not '*in itself* and *essentially* [...]' incompatible with religion, natural or revealed' (*BL* I, 152; *SWF* I, 557) despite Spinoza's denial of miracles and inspired prophecy (as Coleridge knew: *CN* I, 1379), that 'it was pantheism, but in the most religious form in which it could appear' (*PLects* II, 578), that its errors were of omission rather than commission (*SWF* I, 609).

Coleridge's dilemma was this: what was most objectionable in Spinoza's metaphysics, the demonstration of the logical necessity of the single substance, was also most appealing, for it seemed to dissolve the dualism of subject and object definitively. Thus he contested, when one might have expected him to endorse, F. H. Jacobi's argument that Spinoza's consistent rationalism, assuming the universal applicability of the principle of sufficient reason, was atheistic by virtue of its determinism.[15] (This was, after all, essentially the same argument that Coleridge himself had directed against Priestley.) In the margin of Robinson's copy of the *Ethics*, Coleridge identified a possible loophole for free will in the principle of finite causality, according to which every finite thing is determined by a series of finite causes:

> If these finite Causes can be said to act at all, then that on which they act has equal power of action – : and even as tho' all in God *essentially*, we are yet each *existentially* individual, so we must have freedom in God in exact proportion to our Individuality. [...] I cannot accord with Jacoby's assertion, that Spinosism as taught by Spinosa, is Atheism [...]. It is true, he contends for Necessity; but then he makes two disparate Classes of Necessity, the one identical with Liberty (even as the Christian Doctrine, 'whose service is perfect Freedom') the other Compulsion = Slavery.　　　　(*CM* v, 207–8)

Referring to part 1, proposition 28, of the *Ethics* (a passage that continues to exercise commentators), Coleridge distinguished between what, as the effect of the infinite cause, could not be otherwise (the *essential*) and what, given a different series of causes, could in theory be otherwise (the *existential* or contingent). If the infinite and eternal actualization of the universe (i.e. God) did not directly determine the temporal and finite actualization of events, then individuals (as finite modes of the universe) would have a kind of freedom to actualize themselves. Still, this interpretation applied only to individuals. And as Coleridge realized, the more fundamental problem was that the *Ethics* denied both free will to God and the existence of evil. In 1815 he lamented to the publisher John Gutch that Spinoza's God was a world with a single pole and no equator: had he proceeded from either the objective pole (nature) or the subjective (mind), he would necessarily have concluded with their identity in 'The Living God [...] the originating Principle of all dependent Existence in his Will and Word' (*CL* IV, 548). However implausible, the belief that Spinoza *might* have arrived at a Coleridgean idea of God was consistent with Coleridge's inability for three decades either fully to accept or fully to reject the Dutch philosopher's monism.[16]

Coleridge was equally, if less explicitly, ambivalent towards the philo-sophical system he considered the only viable alternative to Spinoza's. Given his avowal in the *Biographia* that Kant's works 'took possession of [him] with a giant's hand' and 'invigorated and disciplined [his] understanding' (*BL* I, 153), 'it is surprising how few of Kant's key concepts and ideas he was willing to accept unaltered'.[17] His difficulties, which can be examined only briefly here, had primarily to do with the consequences for metaphysics of Kant's transcendental method – that is, his examination in the *Critique of Pure Reason* (1781, revised 1787) of the possibility of a priori cognition. Because, Kant argued, objects of knowledge must conform to the conditions of knowledge, namely the forms of sensory representation and principles of conceptual organization inherent to the human mind, things as they are in themselves (*Dinge an sich*), reality outside the mind, cannot be known. Thus he excluded traditional metaphysical issues from the realm of knowledge. Although it is rational, Kant maintained, to *assume* the existence of God, the freedom of the will and the immortality of the soul – and hence to act *as if* all are true – these assumptions are incapable of proof.

As with Spinoza, Coleridge sought interpretively to mitigate what he found unpalatable in Kant's critical philosophy, both by extracting hope-ful signals from it and by reinterpreting some of its central concepts. Thus, for example, Kant's argument for the indemonstrability of God's existence was taken to imply also the indemonstrability of God's *non*-existence (*BL* I, 201–2) – an inference Kant allowed (A 641/B 669) – while his insistence on the unknowability of noumena, or things in themselves, was taken to indicate that he must have meant more by them 'than his mere words express' (*BL* I, 155) – a supposition entirely groundless (though shared with Schelling), but permitting Kant's 'doctrines on the limits of our knowing power [to] become a sort of back-door through which the whole of tradi-tional theology is admitted'.[18] Whereas Kant proceeded from the unity of consciousness (without which determinate objects could not be presented to consciousness in an orderly way (A 105–10)), Coleridge thought that the unity of consciousness could itself proceed only from the prior unity of subject and object. He therefore redefined the term *a priori*, which Kant applied to what is not only independent of experience but the condition of the possibility of experience (A 2, 22/B 3–5, 36), to what, having been revealed *through* experience, 'we then know [...] must have pre-existed, or the experience itself would not have been possible' (*BL* I, 293; *Friend* II, 105–6n). In this interpretation, a priori truths perform the same function that Coleridge, looking out the window in April 1805, had sought in natu-ral objects: empirical confirmation of 'something within [him] that already or forever exists' (*CN* II, 2546; *LS* 72). The contrast with Kant, who argued that the mind imposes the unity of nature as it appears to us (A 125)[19], could hardly be greater.

Similarly, Coleridge could not accept Kant's restriction of ideas of speculative reason, or concepts of which no corresponding object is accessible to experience (A 337/B 384), to a purely 'regulative', as opposed to 'constitutive', role (A 509, 616–20, 644/B 537, 644–48, 672). For Kant, concepts such as that of a supreme intelligence have a heuristic value, for example in guiding how we think about nature and pursue the knowledge of it, but they reveal nothing about how the world is really constituted (A 671–74/B 699–702). In the fifth appendix to *The Statesman's Manual* (1816), Coleridge identified as 'the highest *problem* of Philosophy' the question of whether the ideas of reason are indeed regulative (serving an epistemological function) or constitutive (conveying an ontological truth), 'and one with the power and Life of Nature' (*LS* 114; also *CL* V, 14–15). Aligning Kant and Aristotle on one side and Plato and Plotinus on the other, he left little doubt which side he favoured.

To grant ideas constitutive status, Coleridge had to modify another distinction that he clearly appropriated from Kant (even if he claimed otherwise in the *Biographia*: *BL* I, 173), that between reason and understanding. While following Kant closely in defining understanding as 'the faculty by which we generalize and arrange the phænomena of perception: that faculty, the functions of which contain the rules and constitute the possibility of outward Experience' (*Friend* I, 156; *CL* II, 1198; *LS* 59; cf. Kant A 51/B 57), he departed from the German philosopher radically with respect to reason. Of the two functions that Kant assigned to reason, the 'logical' one of systematizing and directing empirical inquiry by means of inferences drawn from the conclusions and judgements of understanding, and the 'pure' one of forming concepts of non-empirical objects (A 299–309/B 355–66), he regarded the second warily on account of its tendency to make unverifiable metaphysical claims (such claims being justified, in Kant's view, only in relation to their 'practical' application in ethics). As G. N. G. Orsini remarked,[20] the distinction between the two mental faculties corresponds to that between traditional metaphysics and Kant's own transcendental idealism, and the purpose of the first *Critique* was precisely to limit the pretensions of reason. Because Coleridge, however, could not accept Kant's argument that the concepts of God, free will and the soul's immortality must be denied to theoretical reason in order to be preserved for practical reason (B xxx), he sought to reverse Kant's separation of reason's metaphysical and moral functions – which he criticized as arbitrary (*CM* V, 756) – by conceiving the faculty to contain within itself the objects it reveals to consciousness.[21] Or to put it another way, 'Practical reason must become cognitive, and noumena or things-in-themselves must be acquaintable through this enhanced practical reason.'[22]

Thus in *The Friend*, contrary to his characteristic desynonimizing practice, Coleridge presented reason – in the passage quoted earlier in this chapter – as essentially coterminous with God, will and being itself. Reinforcing the point in the 'Essays on the Principles of Method' at the end of *The Friend*, he exhorted his readers 'to bear in mind, that all true reality has both its ground and its evidence in the *will*', without which ratiocination is empty (*Friend* I, 519–20). As its own ground, reason offers its own evidence: 'Reason is the Power of universal and necessary Convictions, the Source and Substance of Truths above Sense, and having their evidence in themselves' (*AR*, 216; *LS*, 60–61 n. 1). It is likely (though this is debated in the scholarship) that in elaborating reason in this decidedly un-Kantian way, Coleridge availed himself of the concept of reason that he would have encountered in seventeenth-century Cambridge Platonists such as Henry More, Ralph Cudworth and John Smith: a faculty not only discursive but intuitive, not only formal but substantive, endowed with innate and self-evident principles.[23]

As we saw earlier, Coleridge criticized Spinoza for beginning from neither the objective pole nor the subjective to arrive at his idea of God. One attraction of Schelling's philosophy, as far as overcoming Kantian dualism was concerned, was its argument that these opposed approaches – deriving mind from nature and nature from mind – are actually parallel, in that the goal of either is to establish the fundamental identity of subject and object. So much Coleridge affirmed in Chapter 12 of the *Biographia*, translating without acknowledgement from Schelling's *Treatises on the Elucidation of Idealism* (1796–97) and *System of Transcendental Idealism* (1800) (*BL* I, 254–60 and nn.). Having thus replaced Kant's unknowable thing-in-itself with 'the real and very object' (*BL* I, 263), Coleridge proceeded to elaborate, again through Schelling (and now adding *On the I as a Principle of Philosophy* of 1795 to the mix of sources), ten 'theses' preparatory to a promised 'deduction of the imagination, and with it the principles of production and of genial criticism in the fine arts' (*BL* I, 264). This deduction was theoretically necessary, for Coleridge, as we know from *The Statesman's Manual* – and following Schelling – attributed to imagination the crucial role of mediating between reason and understanding, between the absolute and the finite, thus allowing the ideas of reason to be perceived empirically (if indirectly): 'that reconciling and mediatory power, which incorporating the Reason in Images of Sense [...] gives birth to a system of symbols, harmonious in themselves, and consubstantial with the truths, of which they are the *conductors*' (*LS* 29; also 69, 72–73).[24] It was characteristic of Coleridge that, even while insisting that reason is its own evidence, he sought to assure himself of the possibility that its principles could be manifested empirically in some way: the evidence of things not seen was insufficient.

In the event, the deduction did not materialize, its absence explained away by a fictive exhortation from a friend not to publish it on account of its difficulty (*BL* I, 302–4). Instead, appropriating and compressing Schelling's three *Potenzen* or powers of imagination – unconscious sensory perception; conscious and synthetic perception; and self-conscious and productive perception, used in creating art (III, 350–51, 426, 610–11, 626–27)[25] – Coleridge simply asserted that the imagination consists of a 'primary' and a 'secondary' power. While the former (corresponding roughly to Schelling's second *Potenz*) is the 'prime Agent of all human Perception', the latter, 'co-existing with the conscious will' (and corresponding more closely to Schelling's third *Potenz*), transforms its objects: 'it dissolves, diffuses, dissipates, in order to re-create' (*BL* I, 304). In contrast to Schelling, whose *System* culminates by appealing to art as philosophy's necessary complement, representing objectively what theoretical reason can contemplate only subjectively, the 'original identity' of the subjective and objective,[26] Coleridge broke off at this point without considering art as a product of the secondary imagination. Christoph Bode remarks that, in forgoing his deduction, Coleridge in effect performed what Schelling articulated, 'the ontological gap between the philosophy of art and its object'.[27] But in the succeeding chapters of the *Biographia* Coleridge did address art, more specifically Wordsworth's poetry. Even if he did not affirm, as Schelling did, that art is 'the true and eternal instrument [*Organon*] of philosophy',[28] he perhaps implied as much by declaring Wordsworth capable of producing the 'FIRST GENUINE PHILOSOPHIC POEM' (*BL* II, 156). Adverting to *The Recluse* (which Wordsworth had announced in the preface to *The Excursion* in 1814), Coleridge evidently envisioned the projected poem on nature, mankind and society as the (vicarious) fulfilment of philosophy in a work of imagination, synthesizing thought and feeling (cf. *CL* II, 1034, and IV, 574).

No less significant is what Coleridge *added* to his appropriations from Schelling. In a scholium to his Thesis VI, he argued that individuals can explain their existence by referring to God's existence: 'sum quia deus est' ('I am because God is') and 'sum quia in deo sum' ('I am because I am in God'). Thus incorporating the individual into 'the great eternal I AM', he concluded – in explicit defiance of Schelling[29] – that the grounds of being, knowledge, and ideas are identical (*BL* I, 274–75). And in Thesis X he inferred a divine 'self-conscious will or intelligence' (*BL* I, 285) from Schelling's position that natural philosophy 'places the sole reality in [...]

absolute identity of subject and object'.[30] Where Schelling spoke of self-consciousness as a principle of nature, Coleridge spoke of it as an attribute of the personal God of Trinitarianism.[31] Finally, in Chapter 13 of the *Biographia*, he defined the primary imagination not only as the power of human perception, as quoted above, but 'as a repetition in the finite mind of the eternal act of creation in the infinite I AM' (*BL* I, 304). The kind of repetition that Coleridge meant here is not itself artistic activity, although it is necessarily entailed in that activity. Because he conceived the imagination as mediating between reason and understanding and hence between religion and empirical reality, he was especially concerned to establish, even if by sheer assertion, a connection between the individual mind and God.

These theistic interpolations, incongruous with Schelling but consistent with each other, are as illustrative of Coleridge's relationship to philosophy generally as is his substitution of practical criticism of imaginative works for a deduction of the imagination as such. Critical of a blind faith, he sought to anchor his religion in philosophy; fearful of succumbing to a pantheistic monism, he sought to anchor his philosophy in religion; conscious of the limits of discursive thought, he appealed to the imagination to make the truths of reason intuitable. The unconventional outlets of most of his philosophical writing – letters, notebook entries, marginalia, fragmentary treatises, occasional essays, the 'immethodical miscellany' of the *Biographia* (cf. *BL* I, 88) – are testaments not to a failed systematicity so much as to the conviction that, finally, truth and reality exceed any system by which the mind would seek to contain them. The 'total and undivided philosophy' (*BL* I, 282) that Coleridge sought could not, by its very nature, find total and undivided expression in a conventionally philosophical form, or indeed any form.

Notes

1 Thomas Medwin, *Journal of the Conversations of Lord Byron: Noted during a Residence with His Lordship at Pisa, in the Years 1821 and 1822* (London, 1824), 175–76. Coleridge's knowledge of Byron's comment is confirmed by a letter of 8 April 1825 to his nephew John (*CL* V, 421) and by a notebook entry of 1829 (*CN* V, 6116).

2 On Coleridge's role as a conduit of German philosophy to nineteenth-century anglophone readers, see, for example: René Wellek, *Immanuel Kant in England, 1793–1838* (Princeton University Press, 1931), chap. 3; Rosemary Ashton, *The German Idea: Four English Writers and the Reception of German Thought, 1800–1850* (Cambridge University Press, 1980), chap. 1; and Monika Class, *Coleridge and Kantian Ideas in England, 1796–1817* (London: Bloomsbury, 2012).

3 On which see Raimonda Modiano, *Coleridge and the Concept of Nature* (London: Macmillan, 1985).

4 Letter to William Taylor, 11 July 1808.
5 See also Tim Milnes, 'Through the Looking-Glass: Coleridge and Post-Kantian Philosophy', *Comparative Literature*, 51 (1999), 309–23, at 309, for a valuable interpretation of Coleridge's characterization of his 'system' in the *Table Talk* report.
6 On Hölderlin, Novalis and Schlegel in this context, see Nicholas Halmi, 'Romantic Thinking', in *Thought: A Philosophical History*, eds. Panayiota Vassilopoulou and Daniel Whistler (Abingdon: Routledge, 2021), 60–74.
7 Joseph Priestley, *Hartley's Theory of the Mind, on the Principle of the Association of Ideas; with Essays Relating to the Subject of It* (London, 1775), xix–xxi; *Disquisitions Relating to Matter and Spirit*, 2nd edn. (London, 1782), I, xix–xx. For Coleridge's probable knowledge of these works, see *Lects 1795*, lviii–lix, and *BL* I, 110.
8 Cf. David Hartley, *Observations on Man, His Frame, His Duty, and His Expectations*, 3 vols (London, 1791), I, 114 (chap. 1, prop. 22, cor. 4).
9 On the significance of Darwin to Coleridge in the 1790s, see H. W. Piper, *The Active Universe: Pantheism and the Concept of Imagination in the English Romantic Poets* (London: Athlone Press, 1962), chap. 2; and Ian Wylie, *Coleridge and the Philosophers of Nature* (Oxford: Clarendon Press, 1989), 68–77.
10 See Nicholas Halmi, *The Genealogy of the Romantic Symbol* (Oxford University Press, 2007), chap. 4; and 'Coleridge on Allegory and Symbol', in *The Oxford Handbook of Samuel Taylor Coleridge*, ed. Frederick Burwick (Oxford University Press, 2009), 345–58.
11 Pierre Bayle, *Dictionnaire historique et critique* (Rotterdam, 1697), II, 1090 n. 1. On Spinoza's German reception, see David Bell, *Spinoza in Germany from 1670 to the Age of Goethe* (London: Institute of Germanic Studies, 1984).
12 Clement Carlyon, *Early Years and Late Recollections* (London, 1836), 194; cf. Seamus Perry, *Coleridge and the Uses of Division* (Oxford: Clarendon Press, 1999), 112–16; and Joseph Priestley, *Disquisitions*, I, 42 (a passage added to the second edition).
13 Thomas McFarland, *Coleridge and the Pantheist Tradition* (Oxford: Clarendon Press, 1969), 227, 251; Henry Crabb Robinson, *Henry Crabb Robinson on Books and Their Writers*, ed. E. J. Morley, 3 vols (London: Dent, 1938), I, 112.
14 See Immanuel Kant, 'The Only Possible Argument in Support of a Demonstration of the Existence of God', in *Theoretical Philosophy 1750–1771*, ed. David Walford (Cambridge University Press, 1992), 107–202, esp. 119–20, 134–35.
15 F. H. Jacobi, *Über die Lehre des Spinoza*, ed. Marion Lauschke (Hamburg: Meiner, 2000), 118. For Coleridge's annotations on the 1789 edition of Jacobi's book, see *CM* III, 75–92.
16 For more extended accounts of Coleridge's engagement with Spinoza, see Richard Berkeley, *Coleridge and the Crisis of Reason* (Basingstoke: Palgrave, 2007), chap. 3; and Nicholas Halmi, 'Coleridge's Ecumenical Spinoza', in *Spinoza beyond Philosophy*, ed. Beth Lord (Edinburgh University Press, 2012), 188–207.
17 Christoph Bode, 'Coleridge and Philosophy', in Burwick, *The Oxford Handbook of Coleridge*, 588–619 (594). Bode's chapter and G. N. G. Orsini's *Coleridge and German Idealism* (Carbondale: Southern Illinois University Press, 1969),

chaps 2–5, analyse Coleridge's reception of Kant more fully than is possible here. While his intensive reading of Kant began in 1800 or 1801, Monika Class's *Coleridge and Kantian Ideas in England* establishes that he was almost certainly exposed to the philosopher's ethical and political thought through various intermediaries in the 1790s. The *Critique of Pure Reason* is cited, as is conventional, by the page numbers of the first (= A) and/or second (= B) editions.

18 Wellek, *Immanuel Kant in England*, 115.

19 Quoted by Bode, 'Coleridge and Philosophy', 515.

20 Orsini, *Coleridge and German Idealism*, 84.

21 Cf. Milnes, 'Through the Looking-Glass', 316.

22 Paul Hamilton, *Coleridge and German Philosophy: The Poet in the Land of Logic* (London: Continuum, 2007), 94.

23 See Frederick Beiser, *The Sovereignty of Reason: The Defense of Rationality in the Early English Enlightenment* (Princeton University Press, 1996), 165–68. On Coleridge's reception of the Cambridge Platonists (though not with specific reference to reason), see James Vigus, '"This is not quite fair, Master More!"', in *Revisioning Cambridge Platonism: Sources and Legacy*, eds. Douglas Hedley and David Leech (Cham: Springer, 2019), 191–214.

24 Cf. F. W. J. Schelling, *System des transzendentalen Idealismus*, in *Sämmtliche Werke*, ed. K. F. A. Schelling, 14 vols (Stuttgart, 1856–61), III, 327–634, at 558–59. For a full exposition of Schelling's concept of imagination, see James Engell, *The Creative Imagination* (Cambridge, MA: Harvard University Press, 1981), chap. 20. On Coleridge's use of Schelling more broadly, see Orsini, *Coleridge and German Idealism*, chaps 8–9.

25 Engell, *The Creative Imagination*, 306–8.

26 Schelling, *System des transzendentalen Idealismus*, III, 628.

27 Bode, 'Coleridge and Philosophy', 616–17.

28 Schelling, *System des transzendentalen Idealismus*, III, 627.

29 Schelling, *Vom Ich als Prinzip der Philosophie*, in *Sämmtliche Werke*, I, 149–244, at 164–65, 168–69n.

30 Schelling, *System des transzendentalen Idealismus*, III, 355–56.

31 Friedrich Uehlein, *Die Manifestation des Selbstbewußtseins im konkreten 'Ich bin'* (Hamburg: Meiner, 1982), 110.

15

KAREN SWANN

Coleridge's Later Poetry

When does Coleridge's 'late' poetic career begin, and what works belong within its limits? These questions, which could be asked with respect to the career of any long-lived poet, have special saliency in the case of Coleridge, whose late work, according to accounts that go back to his own day, potentially includes everything on the far side of an early divide, the moment when Coleridge first knew he was 'no poet': everything composed after the 1798 *Lyrical Ballads*, perhaps, or after the 1800 *Lyrical Ballads* and Wordsworth's rejection of 'Christabel' for that volume or after the ensuing psychological crash and descent into opium addiction or after his return from Malta. In this way of thinking of Coleridge's career, there are a handful of great poems, most of them composed in the early years of his friendship with Wordsworth, and then there is everything else – work sporadically produced, occasional or private, carelessly preserved, and 'minor'. As J. C. C. Mays notes, assessments of Coleridge's career have long been dominated by a biographical narrative of 'early brilliance followed by long decline'.[1]

The Bollingen edition of the *Poetical Works* makes clear that at no point was Coleridge 'no poet'. The volumes reveal the richness, depth and continuity throughout his life of his interest in prosody, his experiments in form and metre; they suggest the degree to which he consistently thought in and through verse. They reveal a prodigious and various output, including familiar poems but also translations and adaptations of other writers, epigrams, brief metrical experiments, extemporaneous and improvisational verses intended for ladies' albums and autograph books, and poetic quips, riddles and aphorisms. Some of these Coleridge submitted to annuals and periodicals for publication; others appeared in his own publications. These and other poems ultimately made their way into the *Poetical Works* of 1828 and after. But even these published poems often began as verses written in notebooks, in autograph albums or as oral performances captured by friends. That is, much of the poetry Coleridge produced over the course of his life has a provisional, fugitive quality. His habits of composition produce uncertainty about dating: a poem, or a sketch of a poem, might sometimes sit in a notebook for years, until a few lines are plucked to include in a letter to a friend; repurposed, those lines might later appear in a lady's autograph album; still other lines from the original draft might mutate into a different poem intended for periodical publication. The Bollingen *Poetical Works* thus serves to counter one sort of narrative of Coleridge's poetic career only to present us with new questions. For in these volumes we seem to see not so much discrete poetic 'works' that add up to a corpus as 'work' – ongoing, ceaseless, doubling back on itself and without particular care for producing poetic objects. This work troubles the task of drawing perimeters around late Coleridge and identifying the poems that belong in that category.[2]

I want to pursue these issues by addressing a cluster of poems, some crafted in the mid- to late 1820s, a period that saw Coleridge's revived interest in establishing himself as a published poet, but revisiting poetry of 1802–4 and 1807. These poems, I argue, collectively perform and explore work that understands itself as belated, as coming after the outliving of hope, promise and love. After Coleridge, I call this late work 'work without hope'. My aim is to return to what many readers now argue is a myth or misrepresentation of Coleridge's poetic career as ending with the early loss of his own sense of poetic promise, and to see this myth as a generative fiction that propels his late work, informs a late style and enables his crafting of a public poetic identity as the survivor of the Romantic movement he had been instrumental in shaping.[3]

I

'Work without Hope: Lines Composed 21st. February, 1827' is securely late: the lines comprising its text were composed in 1825 (despite the subtitle's claim) and later revised for inclusion in the 1828 *Poetical Works*. It is thus one of a group of compositions that mark Coleridge's revived interest in his poetic legacy during the late 1820s.[4] Here is the poem in full as it appears in the 1828 *Poetical Works*:

> All Nature seems at work. Slugs leave their lair –
> The bees are stirring – birds are on the wing
> And WINTER slumbering in the open air,
> Wears on his smiling face a dream of Spring!
> And I, the while, the sole unbusy thing,
> Nor honey make, nor pair, nor build, nor sing.
>
> Yet well I ken the banks where Amaranths blow,
> Have traced the fount whence streams of nectar flow.
> Bloom, O ye Amaranths! Bloom for whom ye may,

For me ye bloom not! Glide, rich streams, away!
With lips unbrightened, wreathless brows, I stroll:
And would you learn the spells that drowse my soul?
WORK WITHOUT HOPE draws nectar in a sieve;
And HOPE without an object cannot live.[5]

But for WINTER, who slumbers and dreams, 'All Nature seems at work'. We don't hear how slugs spend their days, but the work of the birds and the bees is predictably productive: making honey, pairing, building and singing, where 'song' is connected and subordinate to reproduction and the laying in of stores. In what initially seems a familiar Romantic gesture, the poet declares his difference from this work: venturing out on a mild winter day, declaring his idleness, he gives himself over to the activities of strolling and composition. *This* work is only described in the negative, however: he is the sole 'unbusy' thing; he does not 'honey make, nor pair, nor build'; he does not 'sing'. His 'unbusiness' does propel and result in the composition of this deft, artful sestet, in which the simple declaratives of the first two lines give way to the longer cadences of the description of winter, and then to the more agitated syntax of the final couplet. Yet his work – non-normative, non-procreative, non-productive – cannot be described as 'song', a claim shored up by the text's foregrounding of its artefactual, printed status by means of its shifting fonts, including the capitalizations of nouns and whole words and, in the manuscript version of the poem, a pedantic gloss appended to the second stanza's allusion to the Amaranth, '*Literally* rendered as Flower Fadeless, or never-fading – from the Greek – a *not* and *maraino* to wither' (*CN* IV, 5192; cited in *CPW* I, ii, 1033).

What initially promises to be an effusion on the coming of spring thus quickly establishes itself as another sort of 'work'. This work's refusal of familiar poetic aspirations becomes more explicit in the octet, with its account of the overtly figurative and archaic landscape that the poet no longer inhabits. The apostrophes to Amaranth and Nectar, along with the draft version's footnote, conjure the Grecian scenes in which the Poet claims to have wandered as one inspired, immortal and wreathed, but as a cancelled environment, while the verse, by virtue of its stilted apostrophes and archaic language, performs the loss it registers. The poem concludes with another sort of apostrophe, this one more modern and familiar, directed to the reader: 'And would you learn the Spells, that drowse my Soul?' The question connects the poet to drowsy Winter, who dreams of spring, but where Winter's dreamwork involves a fulfilment of a wish, the poet's work is 'without hope' and without 'object'. Such 'work' 'draws Nectar in a sieve': capturing nothing, it is fruitless and also, potentially, interminable.

Work without hope emerges from the collapse of other fictions about poetic work: it is post-Greek, post-Romantic, post tropes of poetic inspiration and poetic accomplishment and post a sense of poetry as abundant recompense for the loss of such faith. The style of this work is 'late'. The gestures of earlier poetic modes appear here as deflated, repurposed elements of worlds no longer viable: this is as true of the plain style of the sestet, which evokes the insouciance of early Wordsworth lyrics like 'The Tables Turned' and 'I Wandered Lonely as a Cloud' in a way that registers the exhaustion of that poetic posture, as it is of the more archaic style of the octet, which self-consciously resurrects the poetic devices spurned in the 'Preface' to *Lyrical Ballads*. As readers of Coleridge's late poetry have often pointed out, the distinction – the *surprise* – of this style has to do with this flagging of its post-ness: its reliance, in the wake of the aesthetic movement the principles of which he was instrumental in articulating, on allegorical figures – *'WINTER'*, *'HOPE'* – that function as the personifications of abstract ideas.[6]

With this late style emerges a poetic persona. Morton Paley notes that the popular success of 'Work without Hope' ironically 'had as its by-product the establishment or reconfirmation of the reading public's image of Samuel Taylor Coleridge as a burnt-out case whose poetry declared that he was no longer a poet'.[7] A perverse move, until one remembers that Coleridge is working here with found materials. Mays speculates that the poem's allusion to the Amaranth may respond to Hazlitt's use of the image in his portrait of Coleridge in *Spirit of the Age*, which circulated in print before the volume's official publication date of 1825 (*CPW* I, ii, 1033). The allusion, towards the end of Hazlitt's essay – 'instead of gathering fruits and flowers, immortal fruits and amaranthine flowers' – in fact refers more broadly to a generation of artists and intellectuals whose talents and ambitions were thwarted, he claims, by a repressive political regime and a complicit press. At the close of 'Mr Coleridge', Hazlitt assails Wordsworth's and Southey's capitulation to this regime. In contrast, the nomadic Coleridge pitches his tent on the margins, with 'no abiding place nor city of refuge!' Insular and unproductive, Hazlitt's late Coleridge, a figure of immense but failed promise, leaves no trace behind.[8] If Coleridge is thinking of Hazlitt's essay here, this contribution to the *Poetical Works* offers a public persona that chimes and to an extent falls in with its final reframing of failure as a kind of refusal – unagonized, unvirile and unheroic – and, or indeed any form these reasons possessed of a certain campy piquancy and cultural saliency. Released from the demands of ambition and the trajectory of career, the figure of Coleridge that emerges here adopts the role of a 'has-been', in the words of Jacques Khalip – signalling his lateness, his too-lateness, his survival of the age's great expectations for him, for poetry and for Romanticism itself.[9]

II

Coleridge's late work raises questions about the 'Object': what kind of work has no object and produces no objects? How is it possible to define and circumscribe the poetic 'objects' that make up the late corpus? The text that includes the stanzas ultimately published as 'Work without Hope' presses both kinds of questions. Those stanzas first appear in a Notebook entry of 1825, where they comprise the beginning of a longer draft poem (*CN* IV 5192; *CPW* I, ii, 1030–32). Although this longer poem does not appear as a separate work in the Bollingen *Poetical Works*, there is reason to think of it as such: complex in its own right, the longer composition includes an elaborate framing apparatus reminiscent of those that appear with 'Kubla Khan' and 'Christabel': in this case, a letter addressed to a 'dear Friend' that glosses the poem-to-come points to its literary antecedents in 'Spenser, G. Herbert, and the Poets generally, who wrote before the Restoration (1660)', and bestows on it a title that links it to the Biblical story of Jacob and Rachel: a 'strain in the manner of G. HERBERT – : which might be entitled, THE ALONE MOST DEAR: a complaint of Jacob to Rachel as in the tenth year of his Service he saw in her or *fancied* that he saw Symptoms of Alienation'; it also includes the footnote to 'Amaranth'.

Both the letter and the title it proposes for the poem to come bear primarily on the final stanza of the longer poem, which follows the text published as 'Work without Hope'. Here is the stanza as Mays reconstructs it from Coleridge's drafts:

> I speak in figures, inward thoughts and woes
> Interpreting by Shapes and Outward Shews.
> Where daily nearer me, with magic Ties,
> What time and where (Wove close with
> Line over Line & thickening as they rise)
> The World her spidery thread on all sides spun
> Side answ'ring Side with narrow interspace,
> My Faith (say, I: I and my Faith are one)
> Hung, as a Mirror there! And face to face
> (For nothing else there was, between or near)
> One Sister Mirror hid the dreary Wall.
> But *That* is broke! And with that bright Compeer
> I lost my Object and my inmost All –
> Faith *in* the Faith of THE ALONE MOST DEAR!
>
> JACOB HODIERNUS

At first the poet seems to promise a back story to what has come before. But what in fact follows the poet's declaration that he 'speak[s] in figures' are more figures – the vertiginously redoubled mirrors, the World as thickening web. These in turn could be said to figure the verse itself, with its intricately woven poetic lines, its animated abstractions bound into multiple palindromic constructions ('Line over Line'; 'Side answ'ring Side'; 'My Faith (say I: I and my Faith are one)'; 'face to face'; 'Faith *in* the Faith'). 'I speak in figures' is, simply, a fact about the poet, perhaps the most literal thing that could be said of the creator of this hall of mirrors, the construction of which includes the prefatory letter, or, stepping back, of this riven, refracted poetic 'object' that is two poems, each with its own history, at once.[10]

'THE ALONE MOST DEAR' does not account for the poet's loss of hope in the object: the breaking of the mirror is unmotivated and temporally unlocatable ('but that *is broke*'). But it does dramatize the swerve that follows this breach. 'Love', muses the writer of the poem's letter, 'can outlive all change save a change with regard to itself, and all loss save the loss of it's *Reflex.*' With the cracking of the 'bright Compeer', the poem's Jacob, once a lover, becomes an analyst of love, although he retains a capacity for enchantment. Once caught in the relays of a reflexive mechanism that created the illusion of the object's reciprocity and his own subjective reserves, he transfers his fascination to this image of how Faith and Love *work*: that is, to the mechanism itself. There may be no going back from this position. It is not so much that the Object is now revealed as a projection as that the presumption of its 'constancy', presumed *because* it is a projected version of the 'I', becomes unsustainable; the sister mirror's failure to reflect back reveals an unsettling independence of the Object, as well as the 'drear', claustrophobic and otherwise unpopulated confines within which the illusion lived.

The promise of a love story organized around biographical events, teasingly offered in the beginning of the stanza, gives way to a constellated arrangement of emblematic and allegorical figures. For Mays, the difference between 'Work without Hope' and 'THE ALONE MOST DEAR' is a difference between a text focused on work and one focused on affective life – a difference between what is 'general' and what is 'personal' (*CPW* 1, ii, 1032). I would argue, though, that this final stanza of 'THE ALONE MOST DEAR' exemplifies and performs the poetic work that is 'work without hope'. Forgoing the tropes associated with the Romantic topos of venturing out on a day full of harbingers of spring, this poet gives himself over to the captivating effects of a recursive structure that unravels rather than secures the meaning of affective life. The 'personal' is emptied out, appearing as an illusory effect of a structure of feeling that is itself derivative (of 'Spenser, G. Herbert, and the Poets generally, who wrote before the Restoration (1660)') and dependent on a logic of substitution.[11]

Yet Mays is right to claim that 'THE ALONE MOST DEAR' invites biographical construction. There is evidence that that poem and letter, perhaps originally intended for the feminine readership of an annual such as *The Bijou*, where 'Work without Hope' eventually appeared, may also have been aimed at a particular female reader, Anne Gillman, who assumed the letter was written to herself. ('It was fancy' she wrote on its margins, in response to the writer's 'or fancied he saw'.) Kathleen Coburn accepts Gillman's reading (CN IV, 5192n), as does Mays, who proposes that Coleridge's imagined alienation from Anne Gillman may have plunged him back into memories of Sara Hutchinson (*CPW* I, ii, 1032). Biography hovers at the edges of 'Work without Hope' and 'THE ALONE MOST DEAR': in both, de-natured allegorical figures work to spark in the reader an association of ideas, conjuring biographical information that circulates outside the poem in ways that might vary from reader to reader. In what follows I explore this draft poem's imbrication with earlier biographical and poetic materials, in part to deepen a sense of Coleridge's late 'objects' as porous and unclosed, but also to suggest how they point to ways of reading this work that escape narratives of falling off or failure.

III

'THE ALONE MOST DEAR' belongs to a cluster of poems on the subjects of Hope and Love. Some are contemporaneous with it, while others date back to two earlier moments – 1807, after Coleridge's return from Malta, and 1802–4, the years of his growing attachment to Sara Hutchinson, to which the poetry of 1807 frequently looks back. The set includes published love poems for which Coleridge later became known, along with others that stayed in manuscript until after his death.[12] Mays's dating of these materials suggests both the extent to which they are intertwined and the difficulty of constructing from them a reliable story of the development of a poetic practice or career: some – including 'The Solitary Date Tree' ('[1807–8? 1802–4?]') and 'Recollections of Love' ('[1804? 1806–7?]') – indeterminately belong to one or the other of the two earlier periods, while others suggest the challenge of drawing a boundary around 'late' Coleridge – including 'Constancy to an Ideal Object' ('[1804–1807? 1822?]') 'The Pang More Sharp than All' ('[1807 and later; 1822–25 and later]') and 'A Day Dream' ('[1826–28? Mar 1802?]'). Coleridge's carelessness about preserving and publishing his manuscripts is partly responsible for these challenges: the first known version of 'Constancy' can be dated to 1822, but Mays speculates on thematic grounds that it may have been composed during the earlier period (*CPW* I, ii, 777). As Mays often points out, however, speculating on thematic grounds is tricky given Coleridge's constant reuse of older materials and his recycling of poetic elements. In this group of poems, a limited number of allegorical personifications, emblematic figures, scenarios and biographical persons return again and again, in ways that can make it hard to determine what is a revisiting of what.

The poem Mays has titled 'Imitations of Du Bartas Etc.', after a note Coleridge wrote on the margins of the draft that appears in an 1807 Notebook, belongs in this set of interconnected materials. I have written about it at length in another context: here, I want more briefly to explore its imbrication in a web of associations, poetic and biographical, that connect it to 'THE ALONE MOST DEAR' and speak to the later poem's account of the death of Hope.[13] This earlier poem opens with an evocation of a suspended daydreaming state:

> Fire, That slept in it's Intensity, Life
> Wakeful over all knew no gradations,
> And Bliss in it's excess became a Dream,
> And my visual powers involved such Sense
> all Thought, Sense, Thought & Feeling,
> and Time drew out his subtle
> Threads so quick, That the long
> Summer's Eve was one whole web,
> A space on which I lay commensurate –
> For Memory & all undoubting Hope
> Sang the same note & in the selfsame
> Voice, with each sweet *now* of
> My felicity, and blended momently,
> Like Milk that coming comes & in it's
> easy stream Flows ever in, upon the
> mingling milk, in the Babe's murmuring
> Mouth / or mirrors each reflecting each/—
>
> (CPW I, ii, 830–32)

The web and the mutually reflecting mirrors, tropes central to 'THE ALONE MOST DEAR', appear here but with a more positive valency: a protracted 'sweet *now*' is rendered as a 'space', a 'web' in which the daydreaming 'I' lies suspended, 'commensurate' with the environment that holds him. This 'sweet now' is thick: the environment – 'Fire', 'the long / Summer's Eve' – blends with and sustains the poet's reverie, in which past ('Memory') and future ('all undoubting Hope') coexist with the present. The drift of the passage suggests that the past caught in this web may extend all the way to infancy and the experience of a maternal holding environment, in which the nursing babe's reverie and murmuring song blend with and are sustained by maternal nourishment, song, reverie and a mirroring look.

The passage recalls many moments from Coleridge's early conversation poems and Wordsworth's *Prelude*, in which the present opens to a rich sense of past experience and future promise. But readers of Coleridge may also recognize suspended here elements of a particular scene that resurfaces throughout his writing life: a memory of a summer evening of 1802 at Gallow Hill, home of the Hutchinson sisters, when Coleridge and Sara Hutchinson lay with their heads on Mary's lap on a sofa in front of a fire. In an agonized Notebook entry of 1810 Coleridge returns to this scene as exemplar of the 'association of ideas' (that 'Vulcanian Spider-web Net of Steel' by which his soul is bound up with the memories of Sara Hutchinson that stem from this period (*CN* III, 3708)).[14] Closer to the incident, his draft 'Letter to Sara' and 'The Day Dream', both composed in 1802, refer to this evening. Here are the relevant lines from the 'Letter':

> It was as calm as this, that happy night
> When Mary, thou, & I together were,
> The low decaying Fire our only Light,
> And listen'd to the Stillness of the Air!
> O that affectionate & blameless Maid,
> Dear Mary! On her Lap my head she lay'd –
> Her hand was on my Brow,
> Even as my own is now;
> And on my Cheek I felt thy eye-lash play.   (*CPW* I, ii, 683)

The touch of the poet's own hand conjures another hand, the eyelash that plays on his cheek could be 'thy eye-lash': the boundaries between bodies, between past and present scenes, dissolve. 'The Day Dream' heightens and deepens this 'mingling' of bodies and senses, and, as in the stanza from 'Imitations of Du Bartas', connects the 'touch' of this particular memory to maternal and infantile experience: even as the memory of this evening begins to fade, 'yet still about the *heart* / A dear & playful Tenderness doth linger / Touching my Heart as with a Baby's finger' (*CPW* I, ii, 703). The identifications in this latter poem, published in *The Morning Post* in 1802 with the subtitle 'From an Emigrant to His Absent Wife', are multiple and mobile. The feeling that steals across the poet's lips is, he imagines, like that of a mother dreaming of kissing her babe 'that something more than Babe did seem', conjuring, perhaps, 'an obscure Presence of it's darling Father'; this figurative babe, who stands in for the (absent but longed for) 'Thou'/'Sara', the mother (whom readers not part of the Wordsworth circle might associate with Sara Coleridge) and the father, comes to life at the end of the poem in the form of 'Hartley'/'Frederick', who jolts the daydreaming poet out of his daydream.

Mays's speculation that 'THE ALONE MOST DEAR' turns on an incident with Anne Gillman but opens to Coleridge's experience of Sara Hutchinson draws attention to how, in Coleridge's verse, moments pierce through to and reflect other moments, texts other texts, and, significantly, women stand in for and become superimposed upon other women. These mobile identifications – of biographical persons, of familial and gender roles – reappear in another published poem from 1807, 'To Two Sisters: A Wanderer's Farewell', addressed to Mary Morgan and Charlotte Brent, the two sisters of the Morgan family with whom Coleridge stayed in 1807. (In this setting too, his happiest moment seems to have been curling up on a sofa between the two napping sisters![15]) The first stanza of 'Imitations of Du Bartas' thus suspends in its web these other materials, 'each reflecting each', although in the case of the unpublished and unaddressed poem the associations feel more private and cryptic.

I will come back to these evocative bodies on sofas. For now, I want to pursue this poem's dramatization of the collapse of the protracted 'sweet *now*' that holds this material in its web, sharply registered in its second stanza:

> What never is, but only is to be
> This is not Life: –
> O hopeless Hope, and Death's Hypocrisy!
> And with perpetual promise breaks its promises.

In 1802, Coleridge wrote, hopefully, 'Surely the Hope, that agitates the Mind, / Is not a Thing without an *end* design'd' (*CPW* 1, ii, 677). But at some point, the sense of what 'is to be', a sense of infinitely suspended possibility, gives way from having waited too long. The other face of a protracted 'sweet *now*' is Limbo. Describing that state, Virgil explains to Dante, 'cut off from hope, we live on in desire', as, perhaps, did Jacob, having waited seven years for the promised Rachel, only to receive Leah and seven more years of servitude for his labours. The bleak recognition casts its shadow back over what was, revealing that the impossibility of the fulfilling 'end' was seeded in 'all undoubting hope' all along; the aftermath exposes the 'before' as illusory.

Already in 1807, out of this collapse comes the late style of work without hope. The romantic 'I' of the first stanza, replete with a sense of possibility and depth, empties out; if anguish saturates the tone of the complaint, this is in part because affective life is experienced as alienated, fractured into the masque-like figures of 'Life', 'Hope', 'Hypocrisy'. In the stanza that follows, the 'I' and its dramas give way entirely to the vision of a world and Heaven that are not for us:

> The Stars that wont to start, as on a chase,
> And twinkling insult on Heaven's darkened face,
> Like a conven'd Conspiracy of spies

Wink at each other with confiding eyes,
Turn from the portent, all is blank on high,
No constellations alphabet the sky –
The Heavens one large black Letter only shew,
And as a Child beneath it's master's Blow
Shrills out at once it's Task and it's Affright,
The groaning world now learns to read aright,
And with it's Voice of Voices cries out, O!

The passage dramatizes a scene of revelation, but in a negative mode: the stars, once elements of legible constellations, 'start' from their moorings, signalling to each other a conspiratorial knowledge withheld from the insulted world. Out of this decisive breaking down of 'each mirroring each' comes a modern kind of allegory, pointing to a loss of meaning, and a mode of '[reading] aright', instilled by the violent socialization, that corrects and mocks the child's pleasurable expectation of reciprocal relation.

Like the 'sweet now' that holds Memory in its web, the poetry that emerges on the other side of the death of Hope sutures past and present but with a difference. In the manner of 'THE ALONE MOST DEAR', this poem conjures poets of an earlier period, here Crashaw and Du Bartas, whose conceits presented the world as a book in which we can read God's intentions. Resurrected in the negative mode, these same conceits recall an empty promise and register a modern loss of 'all undoubting Hope', exposing as fiction – as lure – the Romantic fiction of a world that holds us. Mays describes Coleridge as a poet of the affections. But in the late poetry affect tends to slide from recognizably human 'objects' to poetic materials that conjure outmoded belief systems, suggesting a passion melancholically bound to a generalized loss. In the manner of 'Work without Hope', 'Imitation of Du Bartas' dramatizes an exhaustion as much social and poetic as personal, linked to what Thomas Pfau describes as the melancholy of a late Romanticism.[16]

Dramatizing the emptying out of the subject, turning to an impersonal mode, 'Imitations of Du Bartas' retains the biographical as a trace – in the initial scene the poem passes through, in the allusions to the Child receiving the Master's blows and, perhaps most saliently, in its dramatization of the traumatic collapse of Hope.[17] The poem resonates with an early life that was, all agreed, 'full of promise' or, from another perspective, saddled with the burden of a precocity that no achievement could ever fulfil. Hope, Coleridge keeps reminding us, is a reciprocal structure, one that perhaps goes back to infancy: one's sense of being full of promise, of having hope for the future, is connected to another's investment of hope in oneself. This is a perilous reciprocity, as we have seen. Addressing

Wordsworth in 1807, at a moment when his hopes for himself are fragile, Coleridge writes 'thy hopes of me' were 'troublous to me'; 'Limbo',
on the state of living on in desire without hope, was composed in 1811,
after Basil Montagu relayed to Coleridge that Wordsworth had 'no hope
for him'.[18] The collapse of hope and the subsequent emergence of a 'late'
style and persona on the other side of that trauma occur again and again
in Coleridge's biographical and poetic writing. Rather than marking
a datable period of a long career, the 'late' gestures to a moment that
recurs, and with each recurrence halts and undoes a narrative of progress
or development.

If we can piece together this biographical context, and/or if we recast it in
terms of failed hope and love on the part of one who consistently attached
himself to what he couldn't have – Sara Hutchinson, Charlotte Brent, Anne
Gilman or, perhaps more oddly, paired sisters – this is because we are intimates: readers of the conversation poems, of the early love poetry and the
published poetry of 1806–7 and the mid-1820s that revisits those scenes,
and, in the case of Coleridge scholars, of letters and notebooks, of the
Bollingen *Poetical Works*. Or of the *Biographia Literaria, The Friend,* the
reviews of *Sibylline Leaves* and *Christabel* and Hazlitt's 'Mr Coleridge'.
That is, like most nineteenth-century readers, by the time we encounter the
late Coleridge we are likely to know at least some of these things: that he
had left his wife, that he had an opium habit, that he had abandoned poetry
in favour of abstruse research, that his pursuit of the latter was dilatory,
that in his character of the sage of Highgate young men were sitting at his
feet, that he was kept by the Gillmans, that he was a 'mighty heap of hope,
of thought, of learning and humanity' now living 'on the sound of his own
voice', a figure of failure and of a failed historical and aesthetic moment.[19]
If the late verse, however early it appears, abstracts biographical life,
readers come to that verse possessed of a plethora of biographical detail,
gleaned from various sources. Coleridge of course knows this, and it's an
especially salient factor in his efforts to collect and publish his *Works* in
the late 1820s. He presents himself in the late poetry as one who is without
Hope – a peculiarly modern sort of character, perhaps difficult to 'read
aright', although the poetry presents us with models of how we might do
this. One model involves those napping women, intimates caught with the
poet in a porous web of shared memory and allusion, and, once awake
and receiving the poem that comes out of this experience, continuing to
suspend judgements based on norms of productivity and success. Rather,
they recognize and engage with another version of 'work' – unproductive
of discrete monumental objects and allied instead with the occasional, the
fugitive, the intimate, the 'minor', the 'experimental', the open-ended, the

perpetually unfinished.[20] If the late work holds a kind of 'hope' for the future recognition of its resistance to a coming modernity, it might reside in these fashionable readers.

IV

These women reappear in 'The Improvisatore, or, "John Anderson, My Jo, John"', composed for publication in *The Amulet* of 1828. Anya Taylor and Tim Fulford have written extensively on this poem, persuasively seeing in it a response to Letitia Landon's *Improvisatore* (itself influenced by Coleridge's love poems), intended to appeal to the feminine readership of Landon and the annuals.[21] The return to and reworking of earlier materials are a constant feature of Coleridge's habits of composition, but Fulford reminds us that this revisiting was also strategic, as Coleridge worked to reclaim a public identity as a poet in the late 1820s: 'Writing as an aged poet looking back on his youthful love poetry in the light of the new female poetry it had influenced, [Coleridge] found his muse again, and reappeared as a public poet.'[22]

'The Improvisatore' opens with a dramatic prologue, set in a drawing room and consisting of a scripted conversation among three major characters: the 'Friend'/the Improvisatore and two sisters, Eliza and Catherine. The subtitle of the composition, 'Jo Anderson, my Jo', refers to the Burns poem about ageing love. In the framing drama, the two sisters cajole the Improvisatore into sharing his thoughts on love's ability to last. This scripted mini-drama concludes with Eliza's leading question, 'Surely he, who has described [love] so beautifully, must have possessed it?', followed by the Friend's enigmatic answer, also in the third-person hypothetical: 'If he were worthy to have possessed it, and had believingly anticipated and not found it, how bitter the disappointment!' There follows a pause of 'a few minutes', and then the Friend offers the two women an 'Answer, ex improvise', in verse (*CPW* I, ii, 1055–63).

The Improvisatore's poem at once tells a story of loss and performs a loss of investment in the story itself. Fulford points out that the mid-1820s, when Coleridge was reviving a career as a published poet, was a very different moment from the time of his return from Malta.[23] The sense of devastation that marks some of the poems of 1807, including 'Imitations of Du Bartas', gives way here to a retrospective and more detached account of the death of hope: we recognize figures from the earlier poems, but it's as though the tale itself has become old. The answer to the question, 'surely he must have possessed it!' begins with this summary reflection, still in the third person:

> Yes, yes! That boon, life's richest treat,
> He had, or fancied that he had;
> Say, twas but in his own conceit –
>   The fancy made him glad!
> Crown of his cup, and garnish of his dish!
> The boon, prefigured in his earliest wish!
> The fair fulfilment of his poesy,
> When his heart first yearned for sympathy!   (lines 1–8)

Once again, the 'before' of personal narrative quickly erodes. But the Improvisatore shows an odd lack of interest in why the past loses its solidity: perhaps the boon was never in the subject's possession ('he had, or fancied that he had'), but no matter, 'The fancy made him glad!' This past pleasure is strangely effete: the boon was a 'treat', a 'garnish', adding piquancy to something else, something connected to 'poesy'. One gets the sense that the Improvisatore can produce his material so fluently because it's well rehearsed; he can no longer invest in its figures:

> But e'en the meteor offspring of the brain
>   Unnourish'd wane!
> FAITH asks her daily bread,
> And FANCY must be fed!
> And so it chanced – from wet or dry,
> It boots not how – I know not why –
> She missed her wonted food: and quickly
> Poor FANCY stagger'd and grew sickly.
> Then came a restless state, 'twixt yea and nay,
> His faith was fix'd, his heart all ebb and flow;
> Or like a bark, in some half-shelter'd bay,
> Above its anchor driving to and fro.   (lines 9–20)

The situation recalls that of 'Imitations of Du Bartas', where the loss of hope involves the traumatically belated recognition of having already waited too long for promised sustenance: FAITH and FANCY waste for lack of food. Retaining the traces of the sisters of that poem and multiple others, including this poem's Catherine and Eliza, the pair returns in kaleidoscopically mutating forms as the verse proceeds: FANCY and FAITH, HOPE and LOVE, Fancy and Fear; at the poem's conclusion, CONTENTMENT, a 'next to Best' sister, replaces the dead HOPE. Mays's wonderful description of Coleridge's poetry as 'a kind of memory theatre in which a small cast of actors rehearse what is in the end the same plot over and over again in a variety of ways, as if to enact a recurring trauma that can never achieve definitive performance' is germane here: a drama repeats, elements repeat.[24] But ultimately with repetition the affective freight diminishes, not because something is 'worked through' but because of a loss of investment in the trauma. FAITH and FANCY take their place here with other poetic detritus: the figure of a tossed bark ('Constancy', 'The Rime of the Ancyent Marinere archaic formulations ('a peevish mood, a tedious time, I trow!', echoing 'The Rime of the Ancyent Marinere' and 'Christabel'), the Geraldine/Christabel pairing. Already outmoded poetic elements – allegorical figures, personifications of abstract ideas – mix with the flotsam of a life lived in letters. The story of passion and loss, which once received its charge from the surprising re-purposing of allegorical materials, now itself becomes almost wholly derivative and conventional, close to a parody of album verse. Avowedly the product of late-found CONTENTMENT, this work might be more aptly described as work without hope working its way towards its limit point, or as the inevitable wearing away of an analysis interminable that is unsustaining and unsustainable, like nectar gathered in a sieve.

In the frame, the three figures improvise their negotiations with each other: the two sisters draw out the Friend, alternately needling him for going on too long and cajoling him to say more; or perhaps, by a performed reticence – why should a 'grave personage of my years' have anything to say to two young women on the subject of love? (CPW I, ii, 1057) – the Improvisatore incites their encouragement of his speech. If his poetic improvisations – the poem he ultimately offers, his recasting of Moore's poem at the start of the drama – seem tired, his many-faceted improvisational persona, loosely based on the public personage of Samuel Taylor Coleridge, is more inspired: a drawing-room reciter of poetry, a conversationalist who has a hard time stopping, a philosopher of love and the affections, and a favourite with the young ladies with whom his manner is by turns avuncular, flirtatious, fussy, pedantic, affected, campy, a bit queer, a bit outré. Why, the Friend asks his interlocutors, should they trust one who 'obtained the nickname of Improvisatore, by perpetrating charades and extempore verses at Christmas time?' (CPW I, ii, 1057). If there is something a little fallen about this Dr Faustus-like character who deploys his great gifts in the perpetration of party tricks, including these creative manipulations of his own persona, his intransigence about making more of himself nonetheless gives him an odd weight linked to the public character of Coleridge himself.

Hazlitt grants the late Coleridge an eerie posthumousness: 'all that he has done of moment, he had done twenty years ago: since then, he may be said to have lived on the sound of his own voice.' A relic of an earlier period, Hazlitt's Coleridge survives into the present as a thinned-out version of himself, the dilatory, frivolous remainder of what could have

been: where Mr Godwin 'will leave more than one monument to his intellect behind him', Mr Coleridge's faculties, so much greater than Godwin's,
'have gossiped away their time, and gadded from house to house'.[25] One
can understand this exasperation on the part of one who wrote for his living
towards one who did in fact 'live on the sound of his voice' – supported by
the Wedgwoods, kept by the Wordsworths, the Morgans, the Gillmans, on
the basis of the charisma attached to his figure. And yet Hazlitt's essay also
honours Coleridge's intransigence, loyal to the broken promise of an earlier
Romanticism – a refusal, in Khalip's words, 'to make something of itself',
to fall in with 'narratives of modernization, coherence, and social legibility',
narratives to which the other misters of *The Spirit of the Age* conform,
despite their differences.[26] 'And would you know the spells that drowse
my Soul?' asks the non-productive, non-procreative, non-singing poet of
'Work without Hope'. The techniques of abstraction that characterize the
late style make this more than a personal question or complaint, connecting
the poet's lassitude to the endurance, in attenuated form, of a 'promise' that
refuses installation in the narratives we tell about success.

Notes

1 In his writing on Coleridge, to which this essay is much indebted, Mays repeatedly cites and presses back against this story about Coleridge's work. J. C.
C. Mays, 'The Later Poetry', in *The Cambridge Companion to Coleridge*, ed.
Lucy Newlyn (Cambridge University Press, 2002), 89–99; . J. C. C. Mays,
Coleridge's Experimental Poetics (Basingstoke and New York: Palgrave Macmillan, 2013), 1–13.
2 Mays begins *Coleridge's Experimental Poetics* by asking the simple question:
does all this work add up to 'a body of work' (1)? Many critics writing on
Coleridge's late work, myself included, focus on poetry dating back to 1807:
see Morton Paley, *Coleridge's Later Poetry* (Oxford: Clarendon Press, 1996);
Tilottama Rajan, *Dark Interpreter: the Discourse of Romanticism* (Ithaca,
NY, and London: Cornell University Press, 1980), 204–59; 'Coleridge, Wordsworth, and the Texual Abject', *South Atlantic Quarterly*, 95 (1996), 797–820;
and Karen Swann, *Lives of the Dead Poets: Keats, Shelley, Coleridge* (New
York: Fordham University Press, 2019), 92–114. Mays argues persuasively that
in Coleridge's case the category of 'late poetry' is a 'misnomer', since it rests
on a problematically selective account of the style(s) of 'early' Coleridge ('The
Later Poetry', 99).
3 Paley charges Coleridge with 'becloud[ing] the critical issues by frequently disparaging his later work to others and even to himself (*Coleridge's Later Poetry,* 2).
Mays's position is closer to my own: that 'Coleridge's career rests on a sense of
necessary failure' ('The Later Poetry', 92).
4 For a full account of this moment see Tim Fulford, *The Late Poetry of the Lake
Poets: Romanticism Revised* (Cambridge University Press, 2013), 153–96.

5 *Coleridge's Poetry and Prose*, eds. Nicholas Halmi, Paul Magnuson and Raimonda Modiano (New York and London: W. W. Norton, 2004), 207. (I have
substituted 'slugs' for 'stags', the result of a typo in the edition.) In this case I
want to make a distinction between the poem as published in the 1828 *Poetical
Works* and the Notebook version of the poem, which Mays uses in *CPW*. All
other citations from Coleridge's poetry refer to *CPW*.

6 See especially Mays, 'Coleridge's Later Poetry', 94–99; Rajan, *Dark Interpreter*,
236; Paley, *Coleridge's Later Poetry*. Mays and Paley both see in Coleridge's
allegorical mode a return to an earlier pre-Wordsworth style; Paley's discussion
perceptively links Coleridge's use of personified abstractions to his appreciation
for the expressive possibilities of German (7).

7 *Coleridge's Later Poetry*, 80.

8 William Hazlitt, *The Spirit of the Age*, ed. E. D. Mackerness (London and
Glasgow: Collins, 1969), 67.

9 Jacques Khalip, *Last Things* (New York: Fordham University Press, 2018), 11.

10 Mays describes Coleridge's later poems as often 'work[ing] like riddles', 'through
pictures not sound' ('Coleridge's Later Poetry', 94).

11 See Rajan's comment in *Dark Interpreter* that in the late poetry, 'feelings take
the place of other feelings', a logic of substitution connected to allegory (240).

12 In his editorial notes to *CPW*, Mays frequently points out the connections among
this set of poems. See also Fulford, *The Late Poetry of the Lake Poets*, 153–95,
and Paley, *Coleridge's Later Poetry*, especially 91–113.

13 Swann, *Lives of the Dead Poets*, 99–106.

14 Mays's note to the poem in *CPW* makes this connection (*CPW* 1, ii, 1032), as
does Paley, *Coleridge's Later Poetry*, 33–34.

15 Richard Holmes, *Coleridge: Darker Reflections* (New York: Pantheon Books,
1998), 112. See also Anya Taylor, 'Romantic *Improvvisatori*: Coleridge, L.E.L,
and the Difficulties of Loving', for a sensitive account of these connections (*Philological Quarterly*, 79 [Fall 2000], 502).

16 Mays, *Coleridge's Experimental Poetics*, 42; Thomas Pfau, *Romantic Moods:
Paranoia, Trauma, and Melancholy, 1790–1840* (Baltimore: Johns Hopkins
University Press, 2005), 309–78.

17 See Mays's claim in *Coleridge's Experimental Poetics* that the later style 'eschews
personality' but includes 'handles to grasp' (12). See also Fulford on 'The Improvisatore': like other annual poems, 'it raises expectations that it will be confessional, but then avoids confession' (*The Late Poetry of the Lake Poets*, 164).

18 The lines to Wordsworth, from a draft version of 'Dejection: An Ode', are
quoted in Paley, *Coleridge's Later Poetry*, 20. Holmes includes a full account of
this crisis in *Darker Reflections*, 210–20.

19 The quotations are from Hazlitt, *Spirit of the Age*, 62, 56. See Mays's contention in *Coleridge's Experimental Poetics* that 'Coleridge's reputation overtook
and completely subsumed his poetical self' (40). I would argue that Coleridge's
'poetical self' made his reputation his material.

20 Fulford's account of Coleridge's poetic depictions of a female audience of intimates are germane here: that these female readers are adepts in sympathetic
reading and active 'decoding' (*The Late Poetry of the Lake Poets*, 168). One of
the things they may be adept at is, in Mays's terms, the re-evaluation of terms
such as 'failure' and 'success' (*Coleridge's Experimental Poetics*, 10).

21 Anya Taylor, 'Romantic *Improvvisatori:* Coleridge, L.E.L, and the Difficulties of Loving', 501–21; Fulford, *The Late Poetry of the Lake Poets,* 153–95. See also Angela Esterhammer, 'Coleridge's "The Improvisatore": Poetry, Performance, and Remediation', *The Wordsworth Circle,* 42 (2011), 122–28, for an account of the poem that links it to the popularity of the figure of the Improvisatore.

22 Fulford, *The Late Poetry of the Lake Poets,* 159.

23 Fulford, *The Late Poetry of the Lake Poets,* 166.

24 Mays, *Coleridge's Experimental Poetics,* 43. See also Taylor, 'Coleridge, L.E.L, and the Difficulties of Loving', for a perceptive description of the fallen qualities of the verse, 511–12.

25 Hazlitt, *Spirit of the Age,* 56, 64.

26 Khalip, *Last Things,* 12. For this argument about Coleridge's cultural meaning see Swann, *Lives of the Dead Poets,* 115–32.

16

TOM DUGGETT

Coleridge and History

'The line of evolution', Coleridge wrote in *On the Constitution of the Church and State* (1830), 'has still tended to this point' – of a 'harmonious balance' between the two great 'counterpoising ... interests of the state, its permanence, and its progression' (*Church and State*, 29–30). To make this claim was not, Coleridge insisted, to give 'an historical account' of the law and the legislature (30). But it was to suggest that the history of the constitution was something more than its documentation (30, 18). Every historically framed claim on power made a further point. However easily 'the monarch would have had the better' of an 'argument' focused on 'documents and historical records, or even consistent traditions', the common-law constitution was the larger overarching fact (30, 96). 'Nor let it be forgotten', wrote Coleridge, 'that every new growth, every power and privilege, bought or extorted, has uniformly been claimed by an antecedent right; not acknowledged as a boon conferred, but both demanded and received as what had always belonged to them, though withheld by violence and the injury of the times' (30). There was wisdom in this backward-looking kind of argument, Coleridge thought, and not just because what Edmund Burke had called 'men of speculation' could try old customs and discover the 'reasons' they 'involved'.[1] In every claim of every 'alehouse' politician there was implied an 'idea' of 'moral freedom' that 'possesses and modifies their whole practical being' (*Church and State*, 15–18). The orientation back in time was thus actually an orientation *down*, in understanding, towards the 'balance' in the present. The assertion of historical right was 'in truth ... no more than a *practical* way of saying: this or that is contained in the *idea* of our government ... which, in the very first law of state ever promulgated in the land, was pre-supposed as the ground of that first law' (30–31).

Picking up Coleridge's disclaimer about writing history, this chapter sets out to explore the ways in which Coleridge, while not exactly an *historian*, was nevertheless a man *of* history. As Pamela Edwards notes, Coleridge published no major work that could count as 'a history'.[2] A historical way of thinking is nevertheless the ground of his most influential later works. Coleridge's insight into 'permanence' and 'progression' and the dynamic interplay by which societies could grow and persist across time made him important for thinkers of the next generation such as John Stuart Mill. His essential contribution to the history of human culture, said Mill, was a 'philosophy of society, in the only form in which it is yet possible, that of a philosophy of history'.[3] For reasons of space, I will approach the idea of the historical Coleridge in this chapter by first sketching Coleridge's position in relation to historical writers with whom he compared himself. I will also touch briefly on history in Coleridge's early lectures and journalism, as well as in *The Friend* (both 1809–10 and 1818) and *Biographia Literaria* (1817). I will then turn to Coleridge's more explicitly 'historical' works in the two *Lay Sermons* of 1816–17, before returning to *Church and State*. In the process, I hope to suggest specific ways in which history as a mode of thinking and of writing interacts with Coleridge's political and religious positions.

To the Romantic period, Coleridge was comparable perhaps only to Edmund Burke as an avatar of Clio. His presented himself in *The Friend* as a man out of time, cleaving to the 'old Faith' that 'is often modern Heresy' and 'upholding some Principles both of Taste and Philosophy, adopted by the great Men of Europe from the Middle of the fifteenth till towards the Close of the seventeenth Century' (*Friend* II, 17). And it was in this historically withdrawn identity that Coleridge became the model for the historical shipwreck of the Solitary in Wordsworth's *Excursion* (1814), for the time-philosophizing 'Unknown' in Humphry Davy's *Consolations in Travel* (1830) and for the prophetic ghost returning to the 'Cottonian Library' of Greta Hall in Robert Southey's *Sir Thomas More: or, Colloquies on Society* (1829).[4] Coleridge was also a time-ghost of the late 1790s for William Hazlitt, a wasted mind that now 'merely haunts the public imagination with obscure noises' (Howe VII, 114).

Coleridge embraced the image of a Hamlet figure, lapsed in time. But he also defined his own historical character more assertively, through a continual comparison with two other writers with essentially historical gifts and interests: Walter Scott and Robert Southey. In various comments, some private and some published, Coleridge suggested that the contrast was specifically between the man of history, on the one hand, and the industrious antiquarian or chronicler, on the other. 'The statesman who has not learnt … from history' to respect the principles of the 'self-evolving Constitution' has, Coleridge suggests in *Church and State*, 'missed its most valuable result, and might in my opinion as profitably, and far more delightfully have devoted his hours of study to Sir Walter Scott's Novels' (*Church and State* 96, 100). Scott's 'substitute for History' (100) was at least an improvement on eighteenth-century history as represented by David Hume's *History of England* (1754–61). In *The Statesman's Manual* (1816), Coleridge referred to Hume's 'cool systematic attempt to steal away every feeling of reverence' with 'a scheme of *motives*', in which all 'efforts and enterprizes of heroic spirits are attributed to this or that paltry view of the most despicable self-ishness' or written off as the work of 'fanatics and bewildered enthusiasts' (*LS*, 22–23). 'The reading of *histories*, my dear Sir', Coleridge writes at the start of Chapter 3 of *Church and State*, with Hume firmly in mind, 'may dispose a man to satire; but the science of HISTORY, – History studied in the light of philosophy, as the great drama of an ever unfolding Providence, – has a very different effect. It infuses hope' (32). 'Dear Sir Walter Scott and myself were exact, but harmonious, opposites in this', he said in his 'Table Talk' of 4 August 1833, that 'every old ruin or hill or river called up in his mind a host of historical or biographical associations ... whilst ... I should walk over the plain of Marathon without taking more interest in it than in any other plain of similar features' – being less a man living in the past than 'one, who lives not in *time* at all, past, present, or future' (*TT* 1, 412–13).

Southey, still more than Scott, was the man of 'the METHOD of the will' and 'the control over time', which Coleridge contrasted with his own method of 'relations' and 'understanding' in the 'Essays on the Principles of Method' in the 1818 book version of *The Friend* (*Friend* 1, 523, 450–51). 'Of one, by whom' the control of time 'is eminently possessed, we say proverbially, he is like clock-work'; the man of such 'methodical industry and honorable pur-suits' being one who 'realizes' the 'ideal divisions' of time and 'gives a char-acter and individuality to its moments' (*Friend* 1, 449–50). Without naming his brother-in-law, Coleridge surely summons Southey here as his opposite in method: the account of Southey in the *Biographia* having emphasized his 'regular and methodical' and quasi-Burkean 'generous submission' to all his labours and duties, public and domestic (*BL* 1, 65–66). In the *Biographia*, Southey 'stands second to no man, either as an historian or as a bibliogra-pher', and is pre-eminent 'as a popular essayist' (*BL* 1, 63–64).

But this sort of 'always intelligible' writing (*BL* 1, 64) placed Southey as a chronicler rather than an historian with an insight into the relations of things. 'If I compare Robert Southey with an Ideal', Coleridge said in his 'Table Talk' of 19 September 1830, 'then I know nothing in which he excells; but if with the authors of the day, I think he well deserves the rank and reputation which he has; – which is only inferior to Walter Scott's' (*TT* 1, 193). Southey's 'History', Coleridge continued, was on no great classi-cal model, 'neither the Epic of Herodotus, nor the Pragmatic Narrative of Thucydides'. It entirely lacked what the 1818 *Friend* had called 'Method': 'a mere tale of all the striking things to be found in his documents without a single principle or leading intention' (*TT* I, 193). This difference went right back to their early collaboration. Southey's writing ultimately lacked 'wholeness', and 'that *toil* of thinking' which, Coleridge told John Thelwall, 'is necessary in order to plan a *Whole*' (*CL* I, 294). Southey was never shy about returning the compliment, contrasting his own 'perspicacious' manner with Coleridge's 'rambling & inconclusive' way (*CLRS*, 1736). But for Coleridge, Southey's *Life of Wesley* (1820) was the 'unsafe' and unsettling production of a 'bi-partite author', with 'as many as ten different opinions' of its subject 'all asserted dogmatically and even vehemently – and all irreconcilable one with another'.[5] Southey 'may err in his own deductions from facts' but deserved 'honour ... as an historian' to the extent that he never 'conceal[ed] any known part of the grounds and premises on which he had formed his conclusions', and to the extent that his 'statement' was so assembled as frequently to license a completely different interpretation from his own.[6] But even this reflects a failure to grasp history as more than unbiased documentation, requiring – as Coleridge's acquaintance at Rome, Wilhelm von Humboldt, thought – an imaginative reconstruction of the inner 'nexus' of events, with a commitment to pushing beyond the evidence to find the underlying coherence, while never confusing the extent of historical truth with the available documentary trace.[7] 'For example', Coleridge continued in his September 1830 comment (though almost certainly inventing or embellishing the truth), Southey 'told me, he should leave out the Indian Episode in his History of Portugal – as if it were possible to write the history of *Portugal* without that part of *its* history included!' (*TT* I, 193).

A third and more challenging figure with whom Coleridge compared himself was Edmund Burke. In *The Friend*, Burke provided the epigraph to the second number, described as an 'oracular voic[e]' for Coleridge's own handling of political system and party spirit (*Friend* II, 21–22). In issue 9, Burke appeared again in the context of Coleridge statement of the importance of fixed principles. Burke's relative failure to make 'Converts ... during his life time' is the result of a 'perpetual System of Compromise', of his own philosophic 'knowledge of History and the Laws of Spirit ... with the mere Men of Business' (*Friend* II, 123–24). As far as Southey was concerned, however, Coleridge was putting his thumb on the scales. 'You have yourself observed', wrote Southey, in an unused letter that Coleridge had requested 'upon the faults of the Friend', 'that few converts were made by Burke.'[8] But a lack of declared principles 'does not sufficiently explain why'. Was it not rather, Southey suggested, reminding 'Mr Friend' of his own tendency to 'nose out [his] way hound-like in pursuit of truth', because Burke 'neither was, nor could be generally understood? Because instead of endeavouring to make difficult things appear easy of comprehension, he made things which were easy in themselves difficult to be comprehended by the manner in which he presented them, evolving their causes & involving their consequences ... you looked thro the process without arriving at the proof.'

In *Biographia Literaria*, Coleridge renewed the engagement with Burke as part of an attempt specifically to move from mere 'process' towards 'proof'. The example of Burke, and his apparently prophetic reading of the whole course of the French Revolution in his writings of the early 1790s, lends credibility to Coleridge's own claim to real historical insight and a repeatable mode of historical practice. Burke initially appears as an insoluble problem:

> Whence gained [Burke] this superiority of foresight? Whence arose the striking *difference*, and in most instances even the discrepancy between the grounds assigned by *him*, and by those who voted *with* him, on the same questions? How are we to explain the notorious fact, that the speeches and writings of EDMUND BURKE are more interesting at the present day, than they were found at the time of their first publication; while those of his illustrious confederates are either forgotten, or exist only to furnish proofs, that the same conclusion, which one man had deduced scientifically, *may* be brought out by another in consequence of errors that luckily chanced to neutralize each other[?]   (*BL* I, 191)

The final question here, however, suggests the answer. In the near-contemporary 'Essays on Method' in *The Friend* (1818), Burke serves as the prototypical example of the man of true scientific method, in whose discourse 'each integral part, or ... sentence' contains what elsewhere in the *Biographia* Coleridge calls the '*surview*' of the whole (*Friend* I, 449; *BL* II, 58). And Coleridge continues here to suggest that if Burke's writings contain 'indeed the germs of almost all political truths', his own 'merit' is to have 'first explicitly defined and analyzed the nature of Jacobinism; and ... rescued the word from remaining a mere term of abuse' (*BL* I, 217). The reference is to the essay 'Once a Jacobin Always a Jacobin', from his period as leader-writer of the *Morning Post* in 1800–02, as well as to his essays comparing France and Rome, and to his later 'Essays on the Spaniards' in the *Courier* (1809). In these writings, as Coleridge tells the story, he effectively took on the mantle of Burke. But, unlike Burke's, his was at least to some extent a repeatable (scientific) process:

> On every great occurrence I endeavoured to discover in past history the event, that most nearly resembled it. I procured, wherever it was possible, the contemporary historians, memorialists, and pamphleteers. Then fairly subtracting the points of difference from those of likeness, as the balance favored the former or the latter, I conjectured that the result would be the same or different. ... I have mentioned [this] from the full persuasion that, armed with the two-fold knowledge of history and the human mind, a man will scarcely err

in his judgement concerning the sum total of any future national event, if he have been able to procure the original documents of the past together with authentic accounts of the present, and if he have a philosophic tact for what is truly important in facts, and in most instances therefore for such facts as the DIGNITY OF HISTORY has excluded from the volumes of our modern compilers, by the courtesy of the age entitled historians. (BL I, 218–19)

A 'philosophic tact for what is truly important in facts' is cognate with what the 'Essays on Method' call the *'leading Thought'* from apprehension of an anomaly, which overleaps induction with the straightforward propounding of an idea or law.[9] The difference between Burke and Coleridge and the rest was not, then, a matter of 'deficiency of talent ... of experience, or of historical knowledge'. 'The satisfactory solution' was, rather, that the man of history was known by the having 'sedulously sharpened that eye, which sees all things, actions, and events, in relation to the *laws* that determine their existence and circumscribe their possibility' (BL I, 192).

An idea of history as a distinct and fundamental form of knowledge is already present in Coleridge's writings in the 1790s. In 1794, he wrote a fragment on 'The Study of History Preferable to the Study on Natural Philosophy', arguing for history as against metaphysics, logic and science, as a 'mirror' in which 'man [can] contemplate his mental proportions' (SWF I, 26). History was not only interesting but necessary. 'From the actions of beings similar to himself', Coleridge wrote, 'he must infer the operations of his own passions, and by the Analogies of the Past learn to apprehend the Present and anticipate the Future' (SWF I, 26). In his lectures of 1795, Coleridge outlined a residually millenarian view of history associated with Joseph Priestley, imagining an intellectual elite (an early version of the virtual order of 'the learned of all denominations' discussed in *Church and State* (46)), the members of which are able to work changes in the 'vast and various landscape of existence' opening 'around them' (*Lects 1795*, 12).

History is the keynote of the essays in the *Morning Post* from the period 1800–02, including the essay on the character of William Pitt, and the 'Comparison' essays on France and Rome. Plutarch's 'comparative biography of Rome and Greece' was on a wrong model, Coleridge suggested in 'Pitt' (March 1800; EOT I, 219). Rather than connecting similar lives in different ages, the more 'interesting' approach was to discuss 'those ... who had attained to the possession of similar influence, or similar fame, by means, actions, and talents the most dissimilar' (EOT I, 219). The equivalent 'power' of individuals with different inner resources was a way to gauge the spirit and overall disposition of circumstances of each age – a point that Coleridge would later put in terms of a prevailing 'state of the national morals and manners, in which, as constituting a specific susceptibility', it was possible to track 'the true cause both of the Influence itself, and of the Weal or Woe that were its Consequents' (*LS*, 28). In the statesmanship of Pitt, 'the man of words and abstractions', whose eloquence leaves not a single idea behind, the fundamentally hollow and unhistorical character of the age, complete with an 'overbalance of the commercial interest' and a 'panic of property struck by the late revolution', was revealed (*EOT* 1, 223–25).

A similar method of historical mind-reading informs the 'Comparison' essays of 1802. Because France is a modern European nation descended from Rome, and is only *'incrusted'* with the forms of 'political amalgamation' that 'were the very body and limbs of the Roman Empire', Napoleon's closeness in 'the circumstance of *imitation*' actually measures the distance between his thinking and that of 'Caesar, Pompey, and their predecessors', acting 'on the plans of Philip and Alexander' (*EOT* 1, 325, 313). The very first sentence of the first 'Comparison' essay indicates the historical approach to be taken, reading specific actions in relation to norms that are, almost paradoxically, always continuous and always changing: 'As human nature is the same in all ages, similar events will of course take place under similar circumstances; but sometimes names will run parallel, and produce the appearance of a similarity, which does not really exist' (*EOT* 1, 312). A parallel of past and present that actually grasped this tension might be able to turn it towards actual historical knowledge. '[I]t is some little at least in favour of mankind', Coleridge wrote in the second 'Comparison' essay, 'that there has pre-existed a state of things similar to the present state of France': 'We have the example, and warning experience of Rome, familiar to us from our school-days; and we would fain hope, that facts do not accumulate altogether to no purpose – that experience will not be always like the lights in the stern of the vessel, illumining the tract only which we have already passed over' (*EOT* 1, 324).[10]

In the *Lay Sermons* of 1816 and 1817, Coleridge further develops his account of ways of thinking as efficient causes in historical change. A 'hunger-bitten and idea-less' 'mechanical' philosophy, he claims in *The Statesman's Manual* (1816), is the 'true proximate cause' of the current social crisis (*LS*, 30, 13). This perspective put a particular emphasis upon the individual mind as the place where historical facts and experience might 'accumulate'. In language that overlaps with the *Biographia* on the 'tact' for 'facts' normally 'excluded from the volumes of our modern compilers' (*BL* 1, 219), Coleridge in the periodical *Friend* had described the 'great end of Biography' as being 'to fix the attention and to interest the feelings of men, on those qualities and actions which have made a particular Life worthy of being recorded' (*Friend* II, 286). In the words Coleridge adopted from

Francis Bacon: whereas 'Histories do rather set forth the pomp of business than the true and inward resorts thereof ... Lives, if they be well written, *propounding to themselves a Person to represent* in whom actions both greater and smaller, public and private, have a commixture', will tend rather to reveal that 'workmanship of God, that he doth hang the greatest weight upon the smallest wires' (*Friend* ii, 285).

From the outset of *The Statesman's Manual*, Coleridge proposes historical thinking along these more 'inward' lines as nothing less than the 'antidote' for the same national malaise diagnosed in Wordsworth's Preface to *Lyrical Ballads* (1800) and in his own *Morning Post* essays on Britain's historical cringe before Napoleon's new Rome. 'If there be any antidote to that restless craving for the wonders of the day', he writes, or 'means of building up with the very materials of political gloom' a 'stedfast frame of hope', it 'must be sought for in the collation of the present with the past, in the habit of thoughtfully assimilating the events of our own age to those of the time before us' (*LS*, 8–9). Reusing and expanding materials from *The Friend* (ii, 107), Coleridge suggests here that the effort to learn from history has been given up too soon. Scepticism about the possibility of learning the lessons of history is nothing new. '[E]very age has, or imagines it has, its own circumstances which render past experience no longer applicable to the present case.' In specifics, there will always be a need to allow for 'disturbing forces' and to 'modify ... the first projection' (*LS*, 11). But this period is the first to persuade itself that it is a sign of wisdom and maturity to have given up, to decide 'that the history of the past' in total 'is inapplicable to *their* case' (*LS*, 11). Alluding to his own essays in the *Morning Post* and to Burke's *Reflections on the Revolution in France* (1790), Coleridge recalls how efforts to 'adduce' the 'examples of former Jacobins, as Julius Caesar, Cromwell, and the like' were 'ridiculed as pedantry and pedant's ignorance'. To the contrary, 'the magi of the day ... gave us set proofs that similar results were *impossible*, and that it was an insult to so philosophical an age, to so enlightened a nation, to dare direct the public eye towards them as to lights of warning. Alas! like lights in the stern of a vessel they illuminated the path only that had been past over!' (*LS*, 11–12).

As far as Coleridge was concerned, however, the 'enlightened' notion that history had become irrelevant was precisely the opposite of the truth, which was that ways of thinking, or 'the rise and fall of metaphysical systems', were the 'true proximate cause' of actual social ills (*LS*, 13–15). It is a 'paradox only to the unthinking' and 'the unread in history', says Coleridge, that abstraction and violent action go hand in hand (*LS*, 15). This was a truth reflected in the 'almost geometrical abstractions' on 'every tongue' in the early days of the French Revolution, as well as in the works of Shakespeare, where 'profoundest maxims and general truths' are spoken not by 'men at ease' but 'under the influence of passion, when the mighty thoughts over-master and become the tyrants of the mind that has brought them forth' (*LS*, 15–16). Coleridge's point seems to be not that there is anything wrong with abstraction as such – as in Burke's representation of 'Calculation' as 'a sort of crime' (*Friend* ii, 124). Rather, the prevalence of abstract thinking is a surface marker of deep historical change, the return from complex to simple forms simultaneously suspending the efficacy of historical thinking and bringing out its purpose and necessity, as the method of tracking the changing context of norms within which actions can be understood across time. Thus, Coleridge suggests, 'the fearful blunders of the late dread revolution, and all the calamitous mistakes of its opponents' can be traced to 'the neglect of some maxim or other' in the works of historians such as 'Thucydides, Tacitus, Machiavel, Bacon, or Harrington', all 'red-letter names ... in the almanacks of worldly wisdom', as well as the still 'more intelligible, and more comprehensive form' of such knowledge in the Bible (16–17). But on the other hand, it is not surprising that history failed to come in aid at the time of the Revolution, because abstraction was already the order of the day:

> [I]n nothing is Scriptural history more strongly contrasted with the histories of highest note in the present age than in its freedom from the hollowness of abstractions. While the latter present a shadow-fight of Things and Quantities, the former gives us the history of Men, and balances the important influence of individual Minds with the previous state of the national morals and manners, in which, as constituting a specific susceptibility, it presents to us the true cause both of the Influence itself, and of the Weal or Woe that were its Consequents. How should it be otherwise? The histories and political economy of the present and preceding century partake in the general contagion of its mechanic philosophy, and are the *product* of an unenlivened generalizing Understanding. (*LS*, 28)

What was necessary at the present time, Coleridge was suggesting, was a recurrence to a mode of history with the qualities of Biblical narrative, finding a 'medium between *Literal* and *Metaphorical*', and a kind of 'translucent' symbolism in which the representation 'always partakes of the Reality which it renders intelligible', a 'living part' which 'enunciates the whole' (*LS*, 30). Coleridge's thinking here is clearly indebted to German thinkers on history such as Lessing, Schelling and Herder.[11] But Coleridge also sets himself the hard task of actual historical application. Confronting the 'demand' for a 'particular passage from the Bible, that may at once illustrate and exemplify its applicability' to the current case (*LS*, 33, 28), Coleridge rehearses the broadly Burkean standard reading of the Revolution in terms of commerce versus feudalism, and of courtly decadence, atheism and pride in material progress producing delusory notions of 'prophetic power' in government (*LS*, 33–34). This, he then says, is 'revealed' in Isaiah 47.7–13, 'more than two thousand years before it became a sad irrevocable truth of history' (*LS*, 34). But Coleridge also maintains the 'medium' way of symbolic reading as he folds the Biblical text back towards interpretation of present circumstances. He adds a footnote to the lines 'thou hast said in thine heart, I am, and none else besides me. Therefore shall evil come upon thee, thou shalt not know from whence':

> The Reader will scarcely fail to find in this verse a remembrancer of the sudden setting-in of the frost, a fortnight before the usual time ... which caused, and the desolation which accompanied, the flight [of the Grande Armée] from Moscow. The Russians baffled the *physical* forces of the imperial Jacobin, because they were inaccessible to his *imaginary* forces. The faith in St. Nicholas kept off at safe distance the more pernicious superstition of the Destinies of Napoleon the Great. The English in the Peninsula overcame the real, because they *set at defiance*, and had heard only to despise, the imaginary powers of the irresistible Emperor. Thank heaven, the heart of the country was sound at the *core*. (*LS*, 34–35)

In a long note to the *Lay Sermon* of 1817, Coleridge summed up the theme of *The Statesman's Manual*: a 'tame acquiescence in things as they are' and an approaching 'moral *necrosis*' are only to be 'counteracted by the philosophy of history, that is, by history read in the spirit of prophecy!' (*LS*, 123–24). History is the vital stock from which religion may grow as the crown. 'What insight might not our statesmen acquire from the study of the Bible merely as history, if only they had been previously accustomed to study history in the same spirit, as that in which good men read the Bible!' (*LS*, 124). As it was of the first, the argument of the second 'Lay Sermon' is concerned most immediately with religion and the Bible. But again the underlying subject and method is history. Coleridge's concern, he says explicitly, is 'with the requisite correctives of the commercial spirit, and with Religion therefore no otherwise, than as a counter-charm' (*LS*, 199). Religion is indeed only the third of the weak or absent counter-weights proposed, after 'the ancient feeling of rank and ancestry, compared with our present self-complacent triumph over these supposed prejudices' and 'the general neglect of all the austerer studies' (*LS*, 170).

The point is complex because in Coleridge's thinking religion also has an importance of its own, quite apart from the realm of social 'correctives'. Indeed, Coleridge's powerfully counter-intuitive point – anticipating *Church and State* and the account of an ideally non-denominational and primarily educational 'National Church' co-equal with the legislature and needing to be fully withdrawn 'at last' from the interference of all 'parliamentary Religions' (44, 103) – the point is that, unless this non-instrumental importance of religion is recognized, even as a mere 'counter-charm' it will fail. A counterbalancing effect was not to be looked for from a religion (typified here by Quakerism and also by Unitarianism), which 'holds all the truths of Scripture and all the doctrines of Christianity so very transcendent, or so very easy, as to make study and research either vain or needless', leaving 'the understanding vacant and at leisure for a thorough insight into present and temporal interests' (*LS*, 194). It was in effect only by preoccupying the mind with history, as a social feeling and a discipline basic to religious thinking and all the 'austerer studies', that hopes of a more than merely commercial society might still live.

Church and State represents the culmination of Coleridge's analysis of the social efficacy of ideas and of historical thinking. The full title encapsulates the animating tension between these motives in the work: *On the Constitution of the Church and State, According to the Idea of Each; with Aids towards a Right Judgment on the Late Catholic Bill*. This emphasis on ideas and institutional 'evolution' – rather than on past or present alliances or separations between church and state – was still clearer in the alternative title contained in an unused advertisement Coleridge wrote for the volume: 'The Volume might have been entitled Epistolary Disquisitions, or Extracts from a series of Letters on the word, <Idea; and on the> Constitution, the State, the Church, according to the Idea' (*Church and State*, lvi). The history of the constitution was in this sense secondary to ideas, which Coleridge lastingly redefined here (including for T. S. Eliot) in terms of 'that conception of a thing, which is not abstracted from any particular state, form, or mode, in which the thing may happen to exist at this or at that time; nor yet generalized from any number or succession of such forms or modes; but which is given by the knowledge of *its ultimate aim*' (*Church and State*, 12).[12] But as I discussed at the start of this chapter, such 'aim' could only be known historically – the backward look being the 'practical way' to understand the present.

Within *Church and State*, Coleridge includes a sort of miniature potted history, or what he calls a 'chapter of contents of the moral history of the last 130 years', tracing the effects of the revolution of 1688 and the associated rise of 'the Mechanic Philosophy' (*Church and State*, 64). This 'history' combines reworked materials from earlier works, including above all *The Friend* and *The Statesman's Manual*.[13] But what is new in *Church and State* is a specification of these 'contents' in terms of a 'contrast', and a living part enunciating the whole:

Result illustrated, in the remarkable contrast between the acceptation of the word, Idea, *before* the Restoration, and the *present* use of the same word. *Before* 1660 ... Algernon [SIDNEY] – Soldier, Patriot, and Statesman – [communed] with HARRINGTON, MILTON, and NEVIL on the IDEA of the STATE ... [*Now* a metaphysician] explodes all *ideas* but those of sensation ... [with] no *idea* of a better flavored haunch of venison, than he dined off at the London Tavern last week.   (*Church and State*, 64–66)

Here the contrast between past and present is measured not in time so much as in a coarsening or fundamental lack of continuity in thinking and the tools of thinking. The word 'idea' having lost almost all of what it used to mean, Coleridge suggests, the very possibility of historical knowledge as he and Burke had (ostensibly) produced it is at risk. The list of 'contents' of the present indicates the problem of resuming continuity through its own straining to achieve a narrative voice:

Idealess facts, misnamed proofs from history, grounds of experience, &c., substituted for principles and the insight derived from them. State-policy, a Cyclops with one eye, and that in the back of the head! Our measures of policy, either a series of anachronisms, or a truckling to events substituted for the science, that should command them; for all true insight is foresight. ... Mean time, the true historical feeling, the immortal life of an historical Nation, generation linked to generation by faith, freedom, heraldry, and ancestral fame, languishing, and giving place to the superstitions of wealth, and newspaper reputation.   (*Church and State*, 66–67)

Perhaps the thing that seems most contemporary about Coleridge is his apparent comfort in invoking 'history'. Second only to that might be his apparent pessimism about the idea that experience has any lessons to teach. 'If men could learn from history', Coleridge said in another moment of historical 'Table Talk' on 17 December 1831, 'what lessons it might teach us! But Passion and Party blind our eyes, and the light which Experience gives is a lantern on the stern which shines only on the waves behind us!' (*TT* 1, 260). The 'lantern on the stern' was one of Coleridge's favourite images of historical blindness. It was there in the 'Comparison' essays of 1802 and (carried over from *The Friend*) in *The Statesman's Manual* of 1816. Becoming more conservative or 'Burkean' with each repetition, the image itself reflects a permanent change in Coleridge's view of history around 1800. In *Aids to Reflection* (1825), Coleridge developed an aphorism from the seventeenth-century divine Archbishop Robert Leighton into the suggestion that it was 'at once the disgrace and the misery of men, that they live without fore-thought' (*AR*, 12). 'Suppose yourself fronting a mirror', Coleridge continued: 'Now what the objects behind you are to their images at the same apparent distance before you, such is Reflection to Fore-thought' (*AR*, 12). But there was no suggestion here that to fore-think was in any sense reliably to fore-know. It was rather a matter of human dignity and possession of reason requiring at least the effort: 'As a man without Fore-thought scarcely deserves the name of a man, so Fore-thought without Reflection is but a metaphorical phrase for the *instinct* of a beast' (12–13). Historical thinking had seemed much more certain and predictive in *A Moral and Political Lecture* of 1795 – where the 'thinking and disinterested Patriots' who 'regard all the affairs of man as a process' had inhabited a fully illuminated intellectual landscape, and 'not that twilight of political knowledge which gives us just light enough to place one foot before the other' (*Lects 1795*, 12).

In the change from early to late, the mirror has effectively replaced the lamp. Coleridge's pessimistic-seeming 'lantern on the stern' has, nevertheless, taken on a life and a strangely hopeful energy of its own. In recent times the image has come in aid of efforts at historical thinking in such salient places as the leader column in the *Journal of Public Health* and in contributor segments on political television programmes such as *The Last Word* – uses which themselves probably track back to the quotation of Coleridge in the 'Epilogue' to Barbara Tuchman's classic discussion of political 'wooden-headedness' in *The March of Folly* (1984).[14] 'Leaders in government', wrote Tuchman, 'do not learn beyond the convictions they bring with them', and '[l]earning from experience is a faculty almost never practiced'. Tuchman then quotes Coleridge's 'lament' about the lantern on the stern in the version from his 'Table Talk', and adds: 'The image is beautiful but the message misleading, for the light on the waves we have passed through should enable us to infer the nature of the waves ahead.' At all stages of his career, Coleridge would probably have agreed.

Notes

1 Edmund Burke, *Reflections on the Revolution in France*, ed. J. G. A. Pocock (Indianapolis and Cambridge: Hackett Publishing Company, 1987), 76.
2 Pamela Edwards, 'Coleridge on Politics and Religion: *The Statesman's Manual, Aids to Reflection, On the Constitution of Church and State*', in *The Oxford Handbook of Samuel Taylor Coleridge*, ed. Fred Burwick (Oxford University Press, 2009), 235–53 (239).
3 See John Stuart Mill, *On Bentham and Coleridge*, ed. F. R. Leavis (Cambridge University Press, 1959), 129.
4 See Nicholas Roe, *Wordsworth and Coleridge: The Radical Years* (Oxford University Press, 1988), 27; Molly Lefebure, 'Consolations in Opium: The Expanding Universe of Coleridge, Humphry Davy and "The Recluse"', *The Wordsworth Circle*, 17 (1986), 51–60; and Robert Southey, *Sir Thomas More: or, Colloquies on the Progress and Prospects of Society*, ed. Tom Duggett, 2 vols (London and New York: Routledge, 2018), I, 10.

5 See Coleridge's marginalia, as reproduced in Robert Southey, *The Life of Wesley; and the Rise and Progress of Methodism ... Third Edition, with Notes by the Late Samuel Taylor Coleridge, Esq.* [etc.], ed. Charles Cuthbert Southey, 2 vols (London: Longman, 1846), I, 186; and see *TT* I, 195–96.

6 See Robert Southey, *The Life of Wesley; and the Rise and Progress of Methodism ... Third Edition, with Notes by the Late Samuel Taylor Coleridge, Esq.* [etc.], ed. Charles Cuthbert Southey, 2 vols (London: Longman, 1846), I, 307.

7 See Wilhelm von Humboldt, 'On the Historian's Task', in *The Modern Historiography Reader: Western Sources*, ed. Adam Budd (London: Routledge, 2008): 'The manifestations of an event are scattered, disjointed, isolated; what it is that gives unity to this patchwork, puts the isolated fragment into its proper perspective, and gives shape to the whole, remains removed from direct observation' (167). For the 'historian's mind' to restore this withdrawn 'causal nexus' involves 'merely' learning 'to understand better the genuinely intelligible material by making its own the structure of all occurrences; thus it must learn to perceive more in that material than could be achieved by the mere operation of the intellect' (167–68).

8 *CLRS*, 1704; and see *Friend* II, 498–99.

9 See *Friend* I, 455; and for a helpful account of Method and the 'anomaly', see Jeffrey Hipolito, 'Coleridge's Lectures 1818–1819: On the History of Philosophy', in *The Oxford Handbook of Samuel Taylor Coleridge*, ed. Burwick, 257–58.

10 See the important discussions of the 'Comparison' essays in Stephen Cheeke, 'The Sword "Which eats into itself": Romanticism, Napoleon, and the Roman Parallel', *Romanticism*, 10.2 (2004), 209–27; and in Jonathan Sachs, *The Poetics of Decline in British Romanticism* (Cambridge University Press, 2018), 144–57.

11 See Douglas Hedley, 'Coleridge as a Theologian', in *The Oxford Handbook of Samuel Taylor Coleridge*, ed. Burwick, 491–92.

12 John Colmer notes that Eliot's *The Idea of a Christian Society* (1939) takes its title from Coleridge, and that 'Eliot includes a note in which he states explicitly that his definition of the word "Idea" comes from *Church and State*' (*Church and State*, lxvii).

13 See *Church and State*, 64–68; *Friend* I, 446–47; and *LS*, 100–03.

14 See the Editorial in *Journal of Public Health*, 42 (2020), 1–2; available at: doi:10.1093/pubmed/fdaa023; and see the exchange between the historian John Meacham and Ali Velshi on MSNBC's *The Last Word* on 25 September 2020; transcript available at: www.msnbc.com/transcripts/transcript-last-word-lawrence-o-donnell-september-25-2020-n1260187; and see also Barbara Tuchman, *The March of Folly: From Troy to Vietnam* (New York: Random House, 1984), 383.

FURTHER READING

Abrams, M. H., *The Correspondent Breeze: Essays on English Romanticism* (Cambridge University Press, 1984).

Allsop, Thomas, ed., *Letters, Conversation and Recollections of S. T. Coleridge*, 2 vols (New York: Harper and Brothers, 1836).

Armour, Richard W., and Raymond F. Howes, eds., *Coleridge the Talker* (1940; rev. edn. London: Johnson Reprints, 1969).

Ashton, Rosemary, *The Life of Samuel Taylor Coleridge: A Critical Biography* (Oxford: Basil Blackwell, 1997).

Barbeau, Jeffrey W., *Sara Coleridge: Her Life and Thought* (Basingstoke: Palgrave Macmillan, 2014).

Barfield, Owen, *What Coleridge Thought* (Middletown: Wesleyan University Press, 1971).

Bate, Walter Jackson, *Coleridge* (Toronto: Macmillan, 1968).

Beer, John, *Coleridge the Visionary* (London: Chatto and Windus, 1959).
  Coleridge's Poetic Intelligence (London: Macmillan, 1977).

Brett, R. L., *S. T. Coleridge*, Writers and their Background series (London: Bell, 1971)

Budge, Gavin, *Romanticism, Medicine and the Natural Supernatural: Transcendent Vision and Bodily Spectres, 1789–1852* (Houndmills: Palgrave, 2013).

Bygrave, Stephen, *Coleridge and the Self: Romantic Egotism* (Basingstoke and London: Macmillan, 1986).

Carlson, Julie A., *In the Theatre of Romanticism: Coleridge, Nationalism, Women* (Cambridge University Press, 1994).

Christensen, Jerome, *Coleridge's Blessed Machine of Language* (Ithaca, NY, and London: Cornell University Press, 1981).

Christie, William, 'Res Theatralis Histrionica: Acting Coleridge in the Lecture Theater', *Studies in Romanticism*, 52.4 (2013), 485–509.

Coburn, Kathleen, *The Self-Conscious Imagination: A Study of the Coleridge Notebooks in Celebration of his Birth 21 October 1772* (London: Oxford University Press, 1974).
  Experience into Thought: Perspectives in the Coleridge Notebooks (Toronto: Toronto University Press, 1979).

Coleridge, Samuel Taylor, *The Fall of Robespierre*, ed. Daniel E. White. Romantic Circles Electronic Editions. https://romantic-circles.org/editions/robespierre/index.html

Corbin, Christopher W., *The Evangelical Party and Samuel Taylor Coleridge's Return to the Church of England* (New York: Routledge, 2019).

Cornwell, John, *Coleridge: Poet and Revolutionary, 1772–1804* (London: Allen Lane, 1973).

Corrigan, Timothy J., *Coleridge, Language, and Criticism* (Athens, GA: University of Georgia Press, 1982).

Cox, Jeffrey N., 'Spots of Time: The Structure of the Dramatic Evening in the Theater of Romanticism', *Texas Studies in Language and Literature*, 41.4 (1999), 403–25.

De Quincey, Thomas, 'Samuel Taylor Coleridge', *Tait's Magazine* (September 1834–January 1835).

Edwards, Pamela, *The Statesman's Science: History, Nature, and Law in the Political Thought of Samuel Taylor Coleridge* (New York: Columbia University Press, 2004).

Eilenberg, Susan, *Strange Power of Speech: Wordsworth, Coleridge, and Literary Possession* (Oxford University Press, 1992).

Everest, Kelvin, *Coleridge's Secret Ministry: The Context of the Conversation Poems, 1795–1798* (Brighton: Harvester, 1979).

Fairer, David, *Organising Poetry: The Coleridge Circle, 1790–1798* (Oxford University Press, 2009).

Fulford, Tim, 'Coleridge and the Oriental Tale', in *The Arabian Nights in Historical Context: Between East and West*, eds. Saree Makdisi and Felicity Nussbaum (Oxford University Press, 2008), 213–34.

  The Late Poetry of the Lake Poets: Romanticism Revised (Cambridge University Press, 2013).

  'The Self-Experiment Narrative, the Aeriform Effusion, and the Greater Romantic Lyric', *English Literary History*, 85 (2018), 85–117.

Ford, Jennifer, *Coleridge on Dreaming: Romanticism, Dreams and the Medical Imagination* (Cambridge University Press, 1998).

Gamer, Michael, *Romanticism and the Gothic: Genre, Reception, and Canon Formation* (Cambridge University Press, 2000).

Gillman, James, *The Life of Samuel Taylor Coleridge* (London: W. Pickering, 1838).

Goodson, A. C., *Verbal Imagination: Coleridge and the Language of Modern Criticism* (Oxford University Press, 1988).

Halmi, Nicholas, *The Genealogy of the Romantic Symbol* (Oxford University Press, 2007).

Hamilton, Paul, *Coleridge's Poetics* (Oxford: Basil Blackwell, 1983).

Harding, A. J., *Coleridge and the Inspired Word* (Kingston and Montreal: McGill-Queen's University Press, 1985).

Harter, Joel, *Coleridge's Philosophy of Faith*. Religion in Philosophy and Theology, 55 (Tübingen: Mohr Siebeck, 2011).

Hayter, Alethea, *Opium and the Romantic Imagination* (London: Faber and Faber, 1968).

Hedley, Douglas, *Coleridge, Philosophy and Religion: 'Aids to Reflection' and the Mirror of the Spirit* (Cambridge University Press, 2000).

Hill, Geoffrey, 'Redeeming the Time' and 'Poetry and Value', *Collected Critical Writings*, ed. Kenneth Haynes (Oxford University Press, 2008).

Hipolito, Jeffrey, 'Coleridge's Lectures 1818–1819: On the History of Philosophy', in *The Oxford Handbook of Samuel Taylor Coleridge*, ed. Frederick Burwick (Oxford University Press, 2009), pp. 254–70.

Holmes, Richard, *Coleridge: Early Visions* (London: Hodder and Stoughton, 1989). *Coleridge: Darker Reflections* (London: Harper Collins, 1998).

House, Humphry, *Coleridge, The Clark Lectures, 1951–2* (London: Rupert Hart-Davis, 1953).

Jackson, J. R. de J., *Samuel Taylor Coleridge: The Critical Heritage, Volume 1, 1794–1834* (London: Routledge and Kegan Paul, 1971).

James, Felicity, *Charles Lamb, Coleridge and Wordsworth: Reading Friendship in the 1790s* (Houndmills: Palgrave Macmillan, 2008).

Jasper, David, ed., *The Interpretation of Belief: Coleridge, Schleiermacher and Romanticism* (London: Macmillan, 1986).

Jones, Ewan James, *Coleridge and the Philosophy of Poetic Form* (Cambridge University Press, 2014).

Kessler, Edward, *Coleridge's Metaphors of Being* (Princeton University Press, 1979).

Kitson, Peter, 'The Whore of Babylon and the Woman in White: Coleridge's Radical Unitarian Language', in *Coleridge's Visionary Languages: Essays in Honour of John Beer*, eds. T. Fulford and M. D. Paley (Cambridge: D. S. Brewer, 1993). 'Coleridge, the French Revolution and The Ancient Mariner: A Reassessment', *Coleridge Bulletin*, n.s. 7 (Spring 1996), 30–48.

Klancher, Jon, *Transfiguring the Arts and Sciences: Knowledge and Cultural Institutions in the Romantic Age* (Cambridge University Press, 2013).

Kooy, Michael John, 'Romanticism and Coleridge's Idea of History', *Journal of the History of Ideas*, 60.4 (1999), 717–35.

Kuiken, Kir, *Imagined Sovereignties: Toward a New Political Romanticism* (New York: Fordham University Press, 2014).

Leadbetter, Gregory, *Coleridge and the Daemonic Imagination* (Houndmills: Palgrave Macmillan, 2011).

Leask, Nigel, *The Politics of Imagination in Coleridge's Critical Thought* (Basingstoke: Macmillan, 1988).

Levere, Trevor, *Poetry Realized in Nature: Samuel Taylor Coleridge and Early Nineteenth-Century Science* (Cambridge University Press, 1981).

Levinson, Marjorie, *The Romantic Fragment Poem* (Chapel Hill, NC, and London: University of North Carolina Press, 1986).

Lowes, John Livingston, *The Road to Xanadu* (London: Picador, 1978).

Magnuson, Paul, *Coleridge and Wordsworth: A Lyrical Dialogue* (Princeton University Press, 1988).

Mahoney, Charles, *Romantics and Renegades: The Poetics of Political Reaction* (Basingstoke and New York: Palgrave Macmillan, 2003).

Manning, Peter J., 'Manufacturing the Romantic Image: Hazlitt and Coleridge Lecturing', in *Romantic Metropolis: The Urban Scene of British Culture, 1780–1840*, ed. James Chandler and Kevin Gilmartin (Cambridge University Press, 2005), 227–45.

McFarland, Thomas, *Coleridge and the Pantheist Tradition* (Oxford: Clarendon Press, 1969).

McGann, Jerome J., 'The Meaning of "The Ancient Mariner"', *Critical Inquiry*, 8 (1981), 35–66.

'Coleridge and the Economy of Nature', *Studies in Romanticism*, 35 (1996), 375–92.

McKusick, James C., '"Wisely forgetful": Coleridge and the Politics of Pantisocracy', in *Romanticism and Colonialism: Writing and Empire, 1780–1830*, eds. Tim Fulford and Peter J. Kitson (Cambridge University Press, 1998).

Modiano, Raimonda, *Coleridge and the Concept of Nature* (London and Basingstoke: Macmillan, 1985).

Morrow, John, *Coleridge's Political Thought: Property, Morality and the Limits of Traditional Discourse* (Basingstoke: Macmillan, 1990).

Murray, Chris, *Tragic Coleridge* (London: Routledge, 2013).

Newlyn, Lucy, *Coleridge, Wordsworth and the Language of Allusion* (Oxford: Clarendon Press, 1986; repr. 2000).

Reading, Writing, and Romanticism: The Anxiety of Reception (Oxford University Press, 2000).

Owens, Tom, 'Coleridge, Nitric Acid and the Spectre of Syphilis', *Romanticism*, 20 (2014), 282–93.

Paley, Morton D., *Coleridge's Later Poetry* (Oxford: Clarendon Press, 1996).

Portraits of Coleridge (Oxford: Clarendon Press, 1999).

Perry, Seamus, *Coleridge and the Uses of Division* (Oxford: Clarendon Press, 1999).

ed., *S. T. Coleridge Interviews and Recollections* (Houndmills: Palgrave, 2000).

'Coleridge's Desultoriness', *Studies in Romanticism*, 59 (2020), 15–34.

Piper, H. W., *The Active Universe: Pantheism and the Concept of the Imagination in the English Romantic Poets* (London: Athlone Press, 1962).

Porter, Dahlia, *Science, Form, and the Problem of Induction in British Romanticism* (Cambridge University Press, 2018).

Prickett, Stephen, *Coleridge and Wordsworth: The Poetry of Growth* (Cambridge University Press, 1970).

Romanticism and Religion: The Tradition of Coleridge and Wordsworth in the Victorian Church (Cambridge University Press, 1976).

Reed, Arden, *Romantic Weather: The Climates of Coleridge and Baudelaire* (Providence, RI: Brown University Press, 1983).

Roe, Nicholas, *Wordsworth and Coleridge: The Radical Years* (Oxford University Press, 1988, rev. edn. 2018).

Ruoff, Gene, *Wordsworth and Coleridge: The Making of the Major Lyrics, 1802–1804* (New Brunswick, NJ: Harvester Wheatsheaf, 1989).

Russett, Margaret, *Fictions and Fakes: Forging Romantic Authenticity, 1760–1845* (Cambridge University Press, 2006).

Sachs, Jonathan, 'Coleridge's Slow Time', in *The Poetics of Decline in British Romanticism* (Cambridge University Press, 2018), 142–60.

Schneider, Elisabeth, *Coleridge, Opium, and 'Kubla Khan'* (University of Chicago Press, 1953).

Stillinger, Jack, *Coleridge and Textual Stability: The Multiple Versions of the Major Poems* (New York: Oxford University Press, 1994).

Swann, Karen, 'Christabel: The Wandering Mother and the Enigma of Form', *Studies in Romanticism*, 23 (1984), 533–53.

'Literary Gentlemen and Lovely Ladies: The Debate on the Character of Christa-bel', *English Literary History*, 52 (1985), 397–418.

Lives of the Dead Poets: Keats, Shelley, Coleridge (New York: Fordham University Press, 2019).

Taussig, Gurion, *Coleridge and the Idea of Friendship, 1789–1804* (Newark: Delaware University Press, 2002).

Taylor, Anya, 'Coleridge, Wollstonecraft, and the Rights of Woman', in *Coleridge's Visionary Languages*, eds. Tim Fulford and Morton D. Paley (Cambridge: D. S. Brewer; 1993), 83–99.

Bacchus in Romantic England: Writers and Drink, 1780–1830 (London: Macmillan, 1999).

Erotic Coleridge: Women, Love, and the Law against Divorce (New York: Palgrave Macmillan, 2005).

Taylor, Joanna, 'Mighty Poets: Hartley Coleridge and William Wordsworth', *Essays in Romanticism*, 25 (2018), 141–59.

Thompson, E. P., 'Disenchantment or Default: A Lay Sermon', in *Power and Consciousness*, eds. C. C. O'Brien and D. Vanech (London and New York: University of London Press, 1969), 149–81.

Vardy, Alan, *Constructing Coleridge: The Posthumous Life of the Author* (Houndmills: Palgrave Macmillan, 2010).

Ware, Malcolm, 'Coleridge's "Spectre Bark": A Slave Ship?', *Philological Quarterly*, 40 (1961), 589–93.

Whalley, George, *Coleridge and Sara Hutchinson and the Asra Poems* (London: Routledge and Kegan Paul, 1955).

Woodring, Carl, *Politics in the Poetry of Coleridge* (Madison: University of Wisconsin Press, 1961).

Wylie, Ian, *Young Coleridge and the Philosophers of Nature* (Oxford: Clarendon Press, 1989).

Zimmerman, Sara, *The Romantic Literary Lecture in Britain* (Oxford University Press, 2019).

INDEX

Abernethy, John, 171–72

Baillie, Joanna, 121
ballads *see also* supernatural poems
  'Christabel', 86–90
  enchanted recitation, 88–89
  expressions of trauma, 87–88
  'Love', 82
  metrical irregularities, 90–91
  Percy's *Reliques*, 87
  'The Dark Ladie', 86–87
  'The Rime of the Ancyent Marinere', 86
  traumatic repetition, 89–90
Beddoes, Thomas, 163, 165–66
Berkeley, George, 180, 209, 213
Biographia Literaria
  Coleridge on Edmund Burke, 247
  Coleridge on Southey as a historian, 245
  Coleridge's engagement with Kant, 218
  Coleridge's Jacobinism, 15
  Coleridge's philosophical thought, 210
  as a collaborative project, 40–43
  critical dicta, 1, 192–93
  definition of a poem, 201, 221
  discussions of Wordsworth, 199–203, 221
  language of poetry, 202
  link between Coleridge the lecturer and
    Coleridge the critic, 192–94
  on the *Lyrical Ballads*, 37
  on metre, 104–105
  philosophical critic of the imagination, 71,
    199–202
  poetic style, 84
  Sara Coleridge's editing of, 42–43
  on scholarly legacy, 192
  Shakespeare, William, 201–202
  writing of, 7
Blumenbach, J.F., 11–12

Böhme, Jakob, 161, 173, 210
Bowles, William, 41, 48
Bowyer, James, 41
Boyer, James, 104
Burke, Edmund
  Coleridge's engagement with, 246–48
  on the constitution, 27
  criticism of natural philosophy, 163
  criticism of the French Revolution, 21–22,
    250
  on Government, 21
  as a historian, 243, 244
  in 'Monody on the Death of Chatterton',
    34
  'To Burke', 22
Byron, Lord, 88–90, 209

Cambridge Platonists, 183
cancel culture, 3–4
Chester, John, 130
'Christabel'
  ballad form, 86–90
  collaborative aspects of, 38
  framing apparatus, 229
  omission from *Lyrical Ballads*, 37–38
  'one red leaf' reference, 38, 132
  rhythm and verse form, 90–91, 96, 97, 99,
    100, 103–104
  as a supernatural poem, 86–90, 113
  writing of, 7
Coleridge, George, 15
Coleridge, Hartley, 30, 38, 42, 64, 100
Coleridge, Sara
  on Coleridge as a religious thinker, 178,
    189
  on Coleridge's abstraction, 66
  editing of Coleridge, 42–43
  lessons in prosody, 100

on metre, 96
collaboration *see also Lyrical Ballads; Poems
    on Various Subjects*
    and the 'The Rime of the Ancyent
        Marinere', 36, 37
    appropriation and, 39, 41, 43, 210, 220
    Biographia Literaria as, 40–43
    in 'Christabel', 38
    Coleridge's dialogue with himself, 33–34
    Coleridge's forms of, 30–31, 33, 43–44
    Coleridge's tendencies to over-writing, 32,
        35, 42
    failed collaboration, 36–39, 181
    as imaginative involvement with the
        experience of another, 30
    political collaboration, 34
    role of the reader, 33, 34, 40–41
    in Romanticism, 32–33
    Sara Coleridge's editing as, 42–43
    the Southey/Coleridge household at Greta
        Hall, 39–40, 42
    use of organic metaphors, 31–32, 38–39, 41
    of Wordsworth and Coleridge on *Lyrical
        Ballads*, 36–37, 40, 42, 43, 48, 59, 80
    writer-reader-friends of Coleridge, 6–7, 33
Conciones ad Populum, 16, 25–26
conversation poems *see also* 'Dejection:
        an Ode'; 'Frost at Midnight'; 'The
        Nightingale'
    ecopoetics, 63
    'Effusion xxxv', 35, 132, 166
    experimental language, 48–50
    'Fears in Solitude', 49, 50, 56, 115, 116,
        127, 128
    figures of alienation and existential
        differentiation, 57–58
    'France: An Ode', 16, 116
    lived experience in, 50–51
    'Meditative Poems in Blank Verse', 49
    metre in, 56, 105–109
    non-human/preverbal communication, 50
    'Ode to the Departing Year', 116
    political elements, 56–57, 126–28
    'Reflections on Having Left a Place of
        Retirement', 49–50, 115, 132
    relationship between poetry, the natural
        world and human life, 47–48, 51–54,
        59–60
    rhyme in, 106
    role of friendship, 49
    'The Eolian Harp', 49, 57, 127, 132, 180
    'This Lime-Tree Bower my Prison', 30–32,
        49–51, 115, 128, 132

'To William Wordsworth', 49, 56, 59–60
Cowper, William, 115, 131
Critical Review, 97–98
criticism *see also Biographia Literaria*;
        essays; lectures
    attacks on mass culture, 91–92
    Coleridge's legacy, 206–207
    Coleridge's Shakespeare criticism, 2,
        192–93, 195–98, 204–205
    *Essays on the Principles of Genial
        Criticism*, 193, 198–99
    genial criticism, concept, 199
    link between Coleridge the lecturer and
        Coleridge the critic, 192–94
    marginalia, 205–206
    philosophical criticism, 194, 198–202,
        207
    principles of criticism, 192–99
    in *The Friend*, 196
    theoretical/practical relationship in,
        203–204, 207
    theory of organic unity, 197–99, 207
    of Wordsworth, 199–203

Darwin, Erasmus, 162, 164–65, 213
Davy, Humphry
    as a chemist, 161, 166, 173–75
    Coleridge's estimation of, 161, 166–68,
        173–74
    Consolations in Travel, 244
    editorial work, 36
    the poet-philosopher figure, 194
    'The Spinosist', 167–68
De Quincey, Thomas, 83, 84, 92
'Dejection: an Ode'
    as a catalyst for ecopoetics, 62, 73
    Coleridge's disconnection and isolation,
        73–75
    Coleridge's personal circumstances, 59, 73
    as a conversation poem, 49, 128
    failed collaboration in, 3, 38–39
    interconnectedness of nature, 75–77
    'A Letter to [Asra]', 38
    as a letter to Sara Hutchinson, 7–8, 38,
        74
    mental anguish and self-therapy in, 7–8
    nature as a redemptive force, 58–59, 75
    religion and, 185
dreams
    in the notebooks, 152–53
    prosody of, 109
    the state of mind, 81
    'The Pains of Sleep', 8–10

ecocriticism *see also* nature
  'Dejection: an Ode' as a catalyst for, 62,
    73
  material ecocriticism, 67–68
  role of literature, 67
  Wordsworth's centrality to the field,
    66–67
ecology *see also* nature
  Coleridge's thought on, 62–63
  difference between Coleridge and
    Wordsworth's thought on, 63–64, 66,
    73
  ecological crisis in 'The Rime of the
    Ancyent Marinere', 2–3
ecomimesis, 67
ecopoetics *see also* nature
  abstraction, 65–66, 70–72, 75
  central doubt, 62
  disconnection of the human from the
    nonhuman, 64–66, 69–70
  enmeshment between thought and thing,
    70–72
  interconnectedness of nature, 62–63,
    68–72
  relationship between the self and the
    nonhuman world, 46, 50–52, 54, 58,
    60, 65–66, 69–72
  Wordsworthian, 63, 64, 66–67
Emerson, Ralph Waldo, 189
empiricism, 27
essays
  'Essay on Fasts', 180
  *Essays on the Principles of Genial
    Criticism*, 193, 198–99
  Essays on the Principles of Method, 193,
    204, 220, 245, 247–48
  'Essays on the Spaniards', 247
  on history, 248–49
  'Once a Jacobin Always a Jacobin', 247

Fenwick, Isabella, 36, 42
Finch, Anne, 115
'Fire, Famine, and Slaughter: A War
  Eclogue', 14, 16
'France: An Ode', 16, 56, 116
French Revolution
  Burke's condemnation of, 21–22
  Coleridge's writings on, 16, 21, 180
  The Fall of Robespierre, 111, 114–16
  on the London stage, 114, 116–17
Frend, William, 15, 179–80
Freud, Sigmund, 84, 85, 109
Friend, The

Coleridge on Edmund Burke, 246
Coleridge's political thought, 14, 19, 20,
  24, 26
distinction between reason and
  understanding, 20–22, 25, 220
enmeshment between thought and thing,
  71
Essays on the Principles of Method, 204,
  220, 245, 247–48
history in, 249–50
'Method' applied to science, 172–73
as an outlet for Coleridge's criticism, 196
scientific writings, 170, 173
'Frost at Midnight'
  careful observation in, 53, 115
  as a conversation poem, 49, 128
  interplay of thought and feeling, 54, 58,
    166
  lived experience, 50
  metre and rhyme, 106–109
  nature and creative energy, 64
  religious readings of, 180, 213–14

Gillman, Anne, 231, 233–34, 236
Gillman, James, 100, 142, 186, 236
Godwin, William, 25, 27, 92–93
gothic genre *see also* supernatural poems
  The Castle Spectre, 117, 119
  role of shock tactics, 89–90
  suspension of disbelief, 81
gothic novels, 80, 81, 86, 92
Greater Romantic Lyric, 166

Hartley, David
  associationism, 164, 183, 210, 211
  Coleridge's engagement with, 180, 209,
    211–13
Hazlitt, William
  on 'Christabel', 89–90
  on Coleridge, 1, 18, 145–46, 239–40, 244
  confrontation with Wordsworth, 63
  description of walking with Coleridge,
    130–31, 135–36, 142
  on 'Kubla Khan', 85
  Spirit of the Age, 228
history
  assertion of historical rights, 243
  in *Biographia Literaria*, 245, 247
  Coleridge as a man of history, 244
  Coleridge on Edmund Burke, 243, 244,
    246–48
  Coleridge on Southey as a historian,
    245–46

Coleridge on Walter Scott, 244–45
Coleridge's early writings, 248–49
Coleridge's engagement with, 243–44
essays on, 248–49
in *The Friend*, 249–50
the 'lantern on the stern' image, 254–55
in the *Lay Sermons*, 249–53
in the lectures, 248
On the Constitution of the Church and State, 244, 253–54
religion and, 252–53
in *The Statesman's Manual*, 245, 249–53
Hobbes, Thomas, 20, 26
Horsley, Samuel, 97–98, 183–84
Hume, David, 244–45
Hutchinson, Mary, 6, 8, 38, 233
Hutchinson, Sara
the 'Dejection' verses as a letter for, 7–8, 38, 74
Coleridge's love for, 6, 59, 183, 185, 231
in Coleridge's notebooks, 150–51
letter to from the Lake District, 138, 139
memories of summer evening from 1802, 232–33

imagination
nature and, 30, 46, 50, 52–53, 56
philosophical criticism of the imagination, 199–202, 207
in Schelling's thought, 220–21
self-altering action of, 48
self-therapy and the role of the imagination, 7–8

Jacobi, F. H., 217
Johnson, Samuel, 81

Kant, Immanuel
a priori cognition, 218–19
Coleridge's engagement with, 20, 183, 199, 210, 217–20
ideas of speculative reason, 219
transcendental philosophy, 209, 216
Keats, John
description of walking with Coleridge, 142
La Belle Dame Sans Merci, 69, 120
'Kubla Khan'
disconnection of the human from the nonhuman, 64
framing apparatus, 229
narrations of shifting subjectivities, 166
prosody, 85, 91

as a supernatural poem, 58
writing of, 7

Lamb, Charles
on Coleridge's notebook-writing, 149
on Coleridge's temperament, 1
on collaboration with Coleridge, 32, 35, 41–42
friendship with Coleridge, 41
Pantisocracy, 34
poems in *Poems on Various Subjects*, 34–35
stay at Nether Stowey, 51
on suspension of disbelief, 93
in 'This Lime-Tree Bower my Prison', 31
Landon, Letitia, 237
language
in 'The Rime of the Ancyent Marinere', 84–85
artfulness and naturalness in poetic language, 48–50, 55–56
ecomimesis, 67
evocation of the natural world, 53
non-human/preverbal communication, 50
of the notebooks, 136–40, 144–45
poetic style, 46–47, 84–85, 202
late works
'A Day Dream', 231, 233
biographical elements, 230–31, 235–37
categorisation of, 225–26
Coleridge's love for Sara Hutchinson, 231
Coleridge's public persona and, 228
'Constancy to an Ideal Object', 231
draft 'Letter to Sara', 233
examination of poetic work, 227–28
Hope in, 226–28, 231, 234–38, 240
'Imitations of Du Bartas Etc', 232–35, 237, 238
interconnected memories and associations in, 231–35
Love in, 231–34
memories of summer evening from 1802, 232–33
the 'Object' of work, 227
Poetical Works, 225–26
'Recollections of Love', 231
re-worked material, 231–32, 237
'THE ALONE MOST DEAR', 228–34
'The Improvisatore, or, "John Anderson, My Jo, John"'. 237–39
'The Pang More Sharp than All', 231
'The Solitary Date Tree', 231
'To Two Sisters: A Wanderer's Farewell', 234, 240

Lavoisier, Antoine, 169, 170, 174
Lawrence, William, 171–72
Lay Sermons, 14, 18–20, 23, 26, 28, 154, 249–53
lectures
  Bristol lectures, 10–11, 14, 16–19, 23–24, 194, 195
  Coleridge's lecture style, 84, 193
  Coleridge's legacy and, 192
  criticism of Schlegel, 197–98
  denunciation of the established church, 180–81
  history in, 248
  'Lectures on Revealed Religion', 213
  link between Coleridge the lecturer and Coleridge the critic, 192–94
  marginalia, 205–206
  motivations for, 193–94, 206
  on the principles of poetry, 193–95
  records of, 193
  Shakespeare lectures, 192–93, 195–98, 204–205
Lessing, Gotthold Ephraim, 181, 215, 251
Lewis, Matthew, 80, 82, 86, 117, 119
'Life is a vision shadowy of Truth', 180
life of Coleridge
  domestic circle with the Wordsworths, 6, 8
  epitaph, 178
  European tour with Wordsworth, 154
  genius of, 1
  Hazlitt's figure of, 228
  love for Sara Hutchinson, 6, 59, 183, 185, 231
  in Malta, 6, 53, 54, 70, 141–42, 183–84, 225, 231, 237
  mental health struggles, 6–10, 65–66, 183
  opium addiction, 6–10, 73, 183, 186
  personal life, 6–7, 73, 183, 236
  racial hierarchy beliefs, 11–13
  the Southey/Coleridge household at Greta Hall, 39–40, 42
  'suspension of disbelief' phrase, 81, 192
Lloyd, Charles, 36
Locke, John, 209
love
  Coleridge's love for Sara Hutchinson, 6, 59, 183, 185, 231
  in the later poems, 231–34
  'Love', 82
  love and the object of imaginings, 7–8
  love of life in 'The Rime of the Ancyent Mariner', 5–6

'The Improvisatore, or, "John Anderson, My Jo, John"'. 237–39
  in and through nature, 47
  within theology of the symbol, 185
Lovell, Robert, 6
Lyrical Ballads see also 'The Rime of the Ancyent Marinere'
  'Christabel's omission from, 37–38
  myth of within Romanticism, 35–36
  Preface, 37, 40, 199, 202, 250
  the supernatural in, 80, 113
  'The Dungeon', 52
  'The Foster Mother's Tale, a Dramatic Fragment', 36, 57–58
  wider collaborative network of, 36
  Wordsworth's and Coleridge's collaboration, 36–37, 40, 42, 43, 48, 59, 80

Mackenzie, Henry, 112
mental health
  Coleridge's struggles with, 6–10, 65–66, 183
  self-therapy and the role of the imagination, 7–8
  'The Pains of Sleep', 8–10
  writing and poetry's therapeutic effects, 7–8, 10
metre *see also* prosody
  centrality of for Sara Coleridge, 96
  'Christabel', 90–91, 96, 97, 99, 100, 103–104
  classical metres and modern vernacular, 98–100
  in Coleridge's work, 96–97
  within contemporary literary criticism, 96
  in the conversation poems, 56, 105–109
  foot-based metrics in Coleridge, 99–100
  four-beat system, 99, 100, 102, 103
  'Frost at Midnight', 106–109
  'Metrical Feet', 101–103
  metrical irregularity of the ballad form, 90–91
  metrical surprise and variation, 103–105
  'The Nightingale', 106–109
  treatment of in *Biographia Literaria*, 104–105
Mill, J. S., 28, 244
Mitford, Mary Russell, 193
Morgan, John, 6–7, 40
Morning Post, The, 14, 16, 17, 21, 233, 247, 248, 250

nature *see also* ecocriticism; ecopoetics
  in Dorothy Wordsworth's journals,
    31–32
  educative role of poetry, 52, 54–56
  feeling and responsiveness to, 54–55
  healing properties, 51–52
  human/nature/divine relationship in
    scientific thought, 161, 163–65
  organic metaphors for collaboration,
    31–32, 38–39, 41
  poetry and human epistemic, empathetic
    and creative powers, 52
  poetry and meditation, 49, 50, 54, 56
  poetry and will, 52, 54, 59
  poetry as psychoactive, 60
  relationship between poetry, the natural
    world and human life, 47–48, 51–54,
    59–60
  tension between artfulness and naturalness
    in poetic language, 48–50, 55–56
  'The Nightingale', 46–47, 50, 53
  as a transformative space, 46–47, 51–52
  in Wordsworth's thought, 63, 64
Newton, Isaac, 165, 167
notebooks
  the act of writing and the process of
    thinking, 148–49
  entries on children, 152–53
  entries on dreams, 152–53
  entries on religion, 186
  entries on the lectures, 193
  'Fly-catcher' trope, 156–58
  language of, 136–40, 144–45
  from the later years, 154
  literary value of, 1–2
  materiality, 150
  memories of a summer evening from
    1802, 232–33
  readership, 151–52
  re-visited entries and self-knowledge,
    154–57
  Sara Hutchinson in, 150–51
  unity/diversity dialectic, 145–48, 153
  ways of seeing, 148–49
  wide-ranging contents of, 148–50
  as a window into Coleridge's intellect,
    145–48, 153–54, 156–58

'Ode on the Departing Year', 14, 16, 24
*On the Constitution of the Church and
  State*, 14, 17, 18, 25, 27–28, 188–89,
  243, 244, 253–54
Opus Maximum, 2, 185, 210

Osorio
  drama of emotional stasis, 117–21
  hoped for production of, 111
  influences, 120
  narrative, 117
  rejection of, 117
  'The Dungeon', 52
  'The Foster Mother's Tale, a Dramatic
    Fragment', 36, 57–58
  transformation into *Remorse*, 111, 112,
    121–23
  writing of, 7

Paine, Thomas, 22
pantheism, 60, 180, 183–85, 210, 216
Pantisocracy, 6, 15, 18, 31, 114, 183
Percy, Thomas, 87
philosophy
  assessments of Coleridge's thought,
    209–210
  associationism, 164, 183, 210, 211
  Coleridge's engagement with Hartley, 209,
    211–13
  Coleridge's engagement with Kant,
    217–20
  Coleridge's engagement with Priestley,
    180, 210, 212–15
  Coleridge's engagement with Schelling, 71,
    184, 210, 220–22
  Coleridge's engagement with Spinoza,
    215–17
  Coleridge's philosophical thought, 209, 222
  Coleridge's religious concerns, 209, 211,
    216, 222
  distinction between reason and
    understanding, 20–22, 25, 219–20
  Kant's a priori cognition, 218–19
  materialism, 211–14
  monism, 167–68, 215–16
  organic unity, 197–99, 207
  philosophical critic of the imagination,
    199–202, 207
  philosophical criticism, 194, 198–99, 207
  philosophical theology, 182–85
  the poet-philosopher figure, 194, 209
  reflective self-consciousness, 210–11
  science's integration with metaphysics,
    170–71
  speculative reason, 219
  Spinoza's denial of free will, 216–17
  value of personhood, 10, 24–25
plays *see also Osorio*
  Coleridge's admiration for Schiller, 112–14

plays (cont.)
  The Fall of Robespierre, 111, 114–16
  financial rewards for, 111–12
  hybrid dramas, 112
  Remorse, 111, 112, 121–23
  Schiller's influence on, 112–14, 117–18,
    123
  within London theatre culture, 112,
    116–17
  Zapolya, 111, 121–28
Poems on Various Subjects
  in *Biographia Literaria*, 41
  Coleridge's dialogue with himself, 33–34
  Lamb's poems, 34–35
  'Monody on the Death of Chatterton', 34
  Pantisocracy in, 33, 34
  political collaboration, 34
  'Religious Musings', 19, 23–24, 33,
    146–47, 162–64, 180, 212–13
  sonnet to Friedrich Schiller, 112
poetry
  definition of a poem, 201
  educative role of, 52, 54–55, 56
  great poetry as a form of possession,
    85–86
  as knowledge, 59
  language of poetry, 202
  nature and poetic composition, 46–47
  poetic style, 46–47, 84–85, 202
  poetry and human epistemic, empathetic
    and creative powers, 52
  poetry and meditation, 49, 50, 54, 56
  poetry and will, 52, 54, 59
  poetry as psychoactive, 60
  tension between artfulness and naturalness
    in poetic language, 48–50, 55–56
Polidori, John, 88
political economy, 26–27
politics
  assertions of historical rights, 243
  Coleridge's changing views on, 16–18
  Coleridge's early radicalism, 14–18, 34,
    168
  Coleridge's political legacy, 28
  Coleridge's political writings, 14
  constitutional framework, 27–28
  in the conversation poems, 56–57, 126–28
  dissenting Unitarianism, 33, 34, 179–82
  elitism, 23–24
  Greater Romantic Lyric, 166
  of Humphry Davy, 168, 173–74
  Jacobinism, 14–16, 21, 26, 27
  monarchism, 16–17

moral obligations in, 25–26
political collaboration, 34
political theology, 188–89
religion and, 17, 22–23
of *Remorse*, 121–23
revisions in the political writings, 16
role of property, 18–20, 22, 26, 34,
  163–64
role of Reason and Understanding in,
  20–22, 25
role of taxation and commerce, 19–20,
  26–27
in *Zapolya*, 125–27
Poole, Thomas, 30, 179, 194
post-traumatic stress disorder
  definition, 85, 86
  experiences of trauma, 85, 86
  'The Rime of the Ancyent Marinere' as an
    expression of, 3–6, 85–86
  trauma and the ballad form and, 87–88
  traumatic repetition, 89–90
Priestley, Joseph
  Coleridge's engagement with the
    philosophy of, 180, 210, 212–15
  Coleridge's later rejection of, 165
  debates with Samuel Horsley, 183–84
  as a Dissenter, 162, 179, 181
  on the immortal soul, 211–12
  materialism, 211–14
  in 'Religious Musings', 162, 164
  science's threat to the state, 162, 168
  scientific studies, 170
  Socinian theology, 165, 179
  Unitarianism, 183
prosody *see also* metre
  in 'Christabel', 90–91, 96, 97, 99, 100,
    103–104
  classical metres and modern vernacular,
    98–100
  Coleridge's prosodic lessons, 100–103
  Coleridge's review of Samuel Horsley,
    97–98
  Coleridge's shifting views on Greek
    prosody, 97–98
  dolnik style, 99, 102
  Greek prosody, 97
  and the individual experience of poetry,
    109
  in 'Kubla Khan', 85, 91
psychoanalysis, 80–81, 84
psychology
  belief in the supernatural, 80–81
  illusion/delusion distinction, 81–82

infant development, 152–53
suspension of disbelief, 81, 92–93

Radcliffe, Ann, 80–83, 90
religion
    Aids to Reflection, 188
    Catholic Emancipation, 27
    Coleridge as a religious thinker, 178, 189
    Coleridge as a theologian and biblical
        scholar, 179, 181, 185–89
    in Coleridge's childhood, 179
    Coleridge's Christian organicism, 11–13
    Coleridge's early radicalism, 14–18
    Coleridge's model of the Clerisy, 27–28
    in Coleridge's philosophical thought, 209,
        211, 216, 222
    Coleridge's religious legacy, 189–90
    Coleridge's Unitarianism, 14, 17, 22, 165,
        179–82
    Coleridge's writings on prayer, 186–87
    collaboration on a poem about
        Muhammad, 181–82
    epitaph, 178
    history and, 252–53
    human/nature/divine relationship in
        scientific thought, 161, 163–65
    'Letters on the Inspiration of the
        Scriptures', 187
    in the notebooks, 186
    *On the Constitution of the Church and
        State*, 27–28, 188–89, 243, 244,
        253–54
    pantheism, 60, 180, 183–85, 210, 216
    participation in the established church,
        17, 186
    political theology, 188–89
    role in politics, 17, 22–23
    role of faith, 146–47
    role of Reason and Understanding, 183
    in 'The Rime of the Ancyent Marinere',
        147, 181
    theology of the symbol, 185
    Trinitarian Anglicanism, 165, 179,
        182–85, 216
'Religious Musings', 19, 23–24, 33, 146–47,
    162–64, 180, 212–13
Robinson, Henry Crabb, 62, 193, 198,
    215–17
Romanticism *see also* plays
    creative collaboration in, 32–33
    Romantic Drama, 111
    Romantic sociability, 33
Rousseau, Jean-Jacques, 20

Schelling, F. W. J.
    Coleridge's engagement with the
        philosophy of, 71, 184, 210, 220–22
    Coleridge's plagiarism of, 43, 184
Schiller, Friedrich, 112–14, 117–18, 123
Schlegel, August Wilhelm, 197–98
Schlegel, Friedrich, 211
science *see also* Priestley, Joseph
    'Method' applied to, 172–73
    chemical elements, 169
    Coleridge's engagement with, 161,
        169–70, 174–75
    Coleridge's estimation of Humphry Davy,
        161, 166–68, 173–74
    French science, 163
    human/nature/divine relationship, 161,
        163–65
    integration with Coleridge's metaphysics,
        170–71
    nature of life debates, 171–72
    nineteenth-century disciplinary
        framework, 161, 168–74
    pneumatic research, 165–66
    political reform and, 168
    role of Reason and Understanding in,
        170–71
Scott, Walter, 38, 88–89, 90, 120, 244–45
Shakespeare, William
    in the *Biographia Literaria*, 201–202
    Coleridge's criticism, 2
    Hamlet, 197, 198
    as the ideal poet, 201–202
    influence on *Zapolya*, 123
    King Lear, 85–86
    reading of Method in *Hamlet*, 172
    Shakespeare lectures, 192–93, 195–98,
        204–205
    The Tempest, 197
Shelley, Percy, 88
slavery
    addressed in 'The Rime of the Ancyent
        Marinere', 3–4, 24
    Coleridge's anti-slavery writings, 10–11,
        14, 24–25, 180–81
    racial hierarchy beliefs, 11–13
    'The Sailor who Served in the Slave
        Trade', 3–4
Sotheby, William, 104
Southey, Robert
    on Coleridge, 15–16, 41, 111, 206, 210
    Coleridge on necessitarianism, 211
    Coleridge on Southey as a historian,
        245–46

Southey (cont.)
  collaboration with Coleridge, 42, 181–82
  The Fall of Robespierre, 114–16
  Joan of Arc, 117, 165, 213
  Life of Wesley, 246
  Pantisocracy, 6, 15, 31, 34, 114, 183
  *Sir Thomas More: or, Colloquies on
    Society*, 244
  Southey/Coleridge household at Greta
    Hall, 39–40, 42
  'The Sailor who Served in the Slave
    Trade', 3–4
Spinoza, Benedict de
  Coleridge's affinity with, 148, 182
  Coleridge's engagement with the
    philosophy of, 210, 215–17
  denial of free will, 216–17
  monism, 167–68, 215–16
  pantheism, 183
  'The Spinosist' (Davy), 167–68
Statesman's Manual, The
  Coleridge's elitism, 24
  history in, 245, 249–53
  role of Reason and Understanding, 219
  role of religion in political thought, 23,
    187
  theology of the symbol, 185
Steele, Joshua, 99
supernatural poems
  'Christabel', 86–90, 113
  Coleridge's goals for, 80–81, 112–13
  enchantment/disenchantment dialectic,
    88–91
  illusion/delusion distinction, 81–82
  in *Lyrical Ballads*, 80, 113
  rhythm and verse form, 90–91
  suspension of disbelief, 81, 92–93
  'The Dark Ladie', 86–87
  'The Rime of the Ancyent Marinere' as,
    82–85, 113
  white magic in, 82
Swinburne, Algernon Charles, 85
Sybilline Leaves, 16, 40, 49, 73, 83

Table Talk, 98
Tennyson, Alfred, 70–71, 120
'The Nightingale'
  as a conversation poem, 36
  metre, 106–109
  non-human communication, 53
  poetry and nature relationship, 46–47,
    50, 53
  the value of walking, 133

'The Pains of Sleep', 8–10
'The Rime of the Ancyent Marinere'
  anti-slavery themes, 3–4, 24
  ballad form, 86
  Coleridge's recitation of, 83, 92
  Coleridge-as-Mariner, 84
  collaborative aspects, 36, 37
  disconnection of the human from the
    nonhuman, 64–65, 69, 74–75
  emotions of guilt and shame, 4
  as an expression of post-traumatic stress
    disorder, 3–6, 85–86
  language, 84–85
  love of life, 5–6
  marginal glosses, 83–84
  as a parable of ecological crisis, 2–3
  religious readings of, 147, 181
  the supernatural in, 82–83, 113
'The Spinosist' (Davy), 167–68
'The Wanderings of Cain', 181
Thelwall, John, 15–16, 36, 246
'To Burke', 22

Unitarianism, 14, 17, 22, 165, 179–82

verse
  metre, 56
  short blank verse poems, 49, 56

walking
  aesthetic pleasures, 130–31, 135
  Coleridge Way footpath, 130–31, 135–36
  discourse during, 130, 131, 142
  on Hampstead Heath, 142
  with Hazlitt, 130–31, 135–36, 142
  journal of the solo walk through the Lake
    District, 136–40
  in Malta, 140–42
  physical and mental pleasures, 51, 60,
    130, 133–34, 139–40
  in Scotland with Wordsworth, 8, 9
  shared walks with Dorothy Wordsworth,
    31–32, 131–35, 136
  ways of seeing, 131–32, 135
Walpole, Horace, 80, 86, 92
Watchman, The, 14, 15, 24, 163
Wordsworth, Dora, 154
Wordsworth, Dorothy
  Coleridge's admiration for, 132–33
  Lyrical Ballads and, 36
  shared walks with Coleridge, 31–32,
    131–36
  the 'side peep', 134–35

'The Nightingale' and, 47
Wordsworth/Coleridge domestic circle, 6, 8
Wordsworth, William *see also Lyrical Ballads*
in *Biographia Literaria*, 199–203, 221
The Borderers, 111
in Coleridge's criticism, 199–203
collaboration with Coleridge on *Lyrical Ballads*, 36–37, 40, 42, 43, 48, 59, 62, 80
difference in his ecological thought from Coleridge, 63–64, 66, 73
domestic circle with Coleridge, 6, 8
ecopoetics, 63, 64, 66–67

European tour, 154
'Evening Voluntaries', 42
failed collaboration on 'The Wanderings of Cain', 181
marriage to Mary Hutchinson, 38
'Ode: Intimations of Immortality', 39, 43, 73
'Peter Bell', 74–75
Sara Coleridge and, 42, 43
The Excursion, 244
'The Nightingale' and, 47
thoughts on nature, 63, 64
'To William Wordsworth', 49, 56, 59–60

Cambridge Companions To ...

AUTHORS

Edward Albee edited by Stephen J. Bottoms

Margaret Atwood edited by Coral Ann Howells (second edition)

W. H. Auden edited by Stan Smith

Jane Austen edited by Edward Copeland and Juliet McMaster (second edition)

Balzac edited by Owen Heathcote and Andrew Watts

Beckett edited by John Pilling

Bede edited by Scott DeGregorio

Aphra Behn edited by Derek Hughes and Janet Todd

Saul Bellow edited by Victoria Aarons

Walter Benjamin edited by David S. Ferris

William Blake edited by Morris Eaves

James Baldwin edited by Michele Elam

Boccaccio edited by Guyda Armstrong, Rhiannon Daniels, and Stephen J. Milner

Jorge Luis Borges edited by Edwin Williamson

Brecht edited by Peter Thomson and Glendyr Sacks (second edition)

The Brontës edited by Heather Glen

Bunyan edited by Anne Dunan-Page

Frances Burney edited by Peter Sabor

Byron edited by Drummond Bone

Albert Camus edited by Edward J. Hughes

Willa Cather edited by Marilee Lindemann

Catullus edited by Ian Du Quesnay and Tony Woodman

Cervantes edited by Anthony J. Cascardi

Chaucer edited by Piero Boitani and Jill Mann (second edition)

Chekhov edited by Vera Gottlieb and Paul Allain

Kate Chopin edited by Janet Beer

Caryl Churchill edited by Elaine Aston and Elin Diamond

Cicero edited by Catherine Steel

J. M. Coetzee edited by Jarad Zimbler

Coleridge edited by Lucy Newlyn

Coleridge edited by Tim Fulford (new edition)

Wilkie Collins edited by Jenny Bourne Taylor

Joseph Conrad edited by J. H. Stape

H. D. edited by Nephie J. Christodoulides and Polina Mackay

Dante edited by Rachel Jacoff (second edition)

Daniel Defoe edited by John Richetti

Don DeLillo edited by John N. Duvall

Charles Dickens edited by John O. Jordan

Emily Dickinson edited by Wendy Martin

John Donne edited by Achsah Guibbory

Dostoevskii edited by W. J. Leatherbarrow

Theodore Dreiser edited by Leonard Cassuto and Claire Virginia Eby

John Dryden edited by Steven N. Zwicker

W. E. B. Du Bois edited by Shamoon Zamir

George Eliot edited by George Levine and Nancy Henry (second edition)

T. S. Eliot edited by A. David Moody

Ralph Ellison edited by Ross Posnock

Ralph Waldo Emerson edited by Joel Porte and Saundra Morris

William Faulkner edited by Philip M. Weinstein

Henry Fielding edited by Claude Rawson

F. Scott Fitzgerald edited by Ruth Prigozy

Flaubert edited by Timothy Unwin

E. M. Forster edited by David Bradshaw

Benjamin Franklin edited by Carla Mulford

Brian Friel edited by Anthony Roche

Robert Frost edited by Robert Faggen

Gabriel García Márquez edited by Philip Swanson

Elizabeth Gaskell edited by Jill L. Matus

Edward Gibbon edited by Karen O'Brien and Brian Young

Goethe edited by Lesley Sharpe

Günter Grass edited by Stuart Taberner

Thomas Hardy edited by Dale Kramer

David Hare edited by Richard Boon

Nathaniel Hawthorne edited by Richard Millington

Seamus Heaney edited by Bernard O'Donoghue

Ernest Hemingway edited by Scott Donaldson

Hildegard of Bingen edited by Jennifer Bain

Homer edited by Robert Fowler

Horace edited by Stephen Harrison

Ted Hughes edited by Terry Gifford

Ibsen edited by James McFarlane

Henry James edited by Jonathan Freedman

Samuel Johnson edited by Greg Clingham

Ben Jonson edited by Richard Harp and Stanley Stewart

James Joyce edited by Derek Attridge (second edition)

Kafka edited by Julian Preece

Keats edited by Susan J. Wolfson

Rudyard Kipling edited by Howard J. Booth

Lacan edited by Jean-Michel Rabaté

D. H. Lawrence edited by Anne Fernihough

Primo Levi edited by Robert Gordon

Lucretius edited by Stuart Gillespie and Philip Hardie

Machiavelli edited by John M. Najemy

David Mamet edited by Christopher Bigsby

Thomas Mann edited by Ritchie Robertson

Christopher Marlowe edited by Patrick Cheney

Andrew Marvell edited by Derek Hirst and Steven N. Zwicker

Ian McEwan edited by Dominic Head

Herman Melville edited by Robert S. Levine

Arthur Miller edited by Christopher Bigsby (second edition)

Milton edited by Dennis Danielson (second edition)

Molière edited by David Bradby and Andrew Calder

Toni Morrison edited by Justine Tally

Alice Munro edited by David Staines

Nabokov edited by Julian W. Connolly

Eugene O'Neill edited by Michael Manheim

George Orwell edited by John Rodden

Ovid edited by Philip Hardie

Petrarch edited by Albert Russell Ascoli and Unn Falkeid

Harold Pinter edited by Peter Raby (second edition)

Sylvia Plath edited by Jo Gill

Plutarch edited by Frances B. Titchener and Alexei Zadorojnyi

Edgar Allan Poe edited by Kevin J. Hayes

Alexander Pope edited by Pat Rogers

Ezra Pound edited by Ira B. Nadel

Proust edited by Richard Bales

Pushkin edited by Andrew Kahn

Thomas Pynchon edited by Inger H. Dalsgaard, Luc Herman and Brian McHale

Rabelais edited by John O'Brien

Rilke edited by Karen Leeder and Robert Vilain

Philip Roth edited by Timothy Parrish

Salman Rushdie edited by Abdulrazak Gurnah

John Ruskin edited by Francis O'Gorman

Sappho edited by P. J. Finglass and Adrian Kelly

Seneca edited by Shadi Bartsch and Alessandro Schiesaro

Shakespeare edited by Margareta de Grazia and Stanley Wells (second edition)

George Bernard Shaw edited by Christopher Innes

Shelley edited by Timothy Morton

Mary Shelley edited by Esther Schor

Sam Shepard edited by Matthew C. Roudané

Spenser edited by Andrew Hadfield

Laurence Sterne edited by Thomas Keymer

Wallace Stevens edited by John N. Serio

Tom Stoppard edited by Katherine E. Kelly

Harriet Beecher Stowe edited by Cindy Weinstein

August Strindberg edited by Michael Robinson

Jonathan Swift edited by Christopher Fox

J. M. Synge edited by P. J. Mathews

Tacitus edited by A. J. Woodman

Henry David Thoreau edited by Joel Myerson

Tolstoy edited by Donna Tussing Orwin

Anthony Trollope edited by Carolyn Dever and Lisa Niles

Mark Twain edited by Forrest G. Robinson

John Updike edited by Stacey Olster

Mario Vargas Llosa edited by Efrain Kristal and John King

Virgil edited by Fiachra Mac Góráin and Charles Martindale (second edition)

Voltaire edited by Nicholas Cronk

David Foster Wallace edited by Ralph Clare

Edith Wharton edited by Millicent Bell

Walt Whitman edited by Ezra Greenspan

Oscar Wilde edited by Peter Raby

Tennessee Williams edited by Matthew C. Roudané

William Carlos Williams edited by Christopher MacGowan

August Wilson edited by Christopher Bigsby

Mary Wollstonecraft edited by Claudia L. Johnson

Virginia Woolf edited by Susan Sellers (second edition)

Wordsworth edited by Stephen Gill

Richard Wright edited by Glenda R. Carpio

W. B. Yeats edited by Marjorie Howes and John Kelly

Xenophon edited by Michael A. Flower

Zola edited by Brian Nelson

TOPICS

The Actress edited by Maggie B. Gale and John Stokes

The African American Novel edited by Mary-emma Graham

The African American Slave Narrative edited by Audrey A. Fisch

African American Theatre by Harvey Young

Allegory edited by Rita Copeland and Peter Struck

American Crime Fiction edited by Catherine Ross Nickerson

American Gothic edited by Jeffrey Andrew Weinstock

American Horror edited by Stephen Shapiro and Mark Storey

American Literature and the Body by Travis M. Foster

American Literature and the Environment edited by Sarah Ensor and Susan Scott Parrish

American Literature of the 1930s edited by William Solomon

American Modernism edited by Walter Kalaidjian

American Poetry since 1945 edited by Jennifer Ashton

American Realism and Naturalism edited by Donald Pizer

American Travel Writing edited by Alfred Bendixen and Judith Hamera

American Women Playwrights edited by Brenda Murphy

Ancient Rhetoric edited by Erik Gunderson

Arthurian Legend edited by Elizabeth Archibald and Ad Putter

Australian Literature edited by Elizabeth Webby

The Beats edited by Stephen Belletto

Boxing edited by Gerald Early

British Black and Asian Literature (1945–2010) edited by Deirdre Osborne

British Fiction: 1980–2018 edited by Peter Boxall

British Fiction since 1945 edited by David James

British Literature of the 1930s edited by James Smith

British Literature of the French Revolution edited by Pamela Clemit

British Romantic Poetry edited by James Chandler and Maureen N. McLane

British Romanticism edited by Stuart Curran (second edition)

British Romanticism and Religion edited by Jeffrey Barbeau

British Theatre, 1730–1830, edited by Jane Moody and Daniel O'Quinn

Canadian Literature edited by Eva-Marie Kröller (second edition)

The Canterbury Tales edited by Frank Grady

Children's Literature edited by M. O. Grenby and Andrea Immel

The Classic Russian Novel edited by Malcolm V. Jones and Robin Feuer Miller

Contemporary Irish Poetry edited by Matthew Campbell

Creative Writing edited by David Morley and Philip Neilsen

Crime Fiction edited by Martin Priestman

Dante's 'Commedia' edited by Zygmunt G. Barański and Simon Gilson

Dracula edited by Roger Luckhurst

Early American Literature edited by Bryce Traister

Early Modern Women's Writing edited by Laura Lunger Knoppers

The Eighteenth-Century Novel edited by John Richetti

Eighteenth-Century Poetry edited by John Sitter

Eighteenth-Century Thought edited by Frans De Bruyn

Emma edited by Peter Sabor

English Dictionaries edited by Sarah Ogilvie

English Literature, 1500–1600 edited by Arthur F. Kinney

English Literature, 1650–1740 edited by Steven N. Zwicker

English Literature, 1740–1830 edited by Thomas Keymer and Jon Mee

English Literature, 1830–1914 edited by Joanne Shattock

English Melodrama edited by Carolyn Williams

English Novelists edited by Adrian Poole

English Poetry, Donne to Marvell edited by Thomas N. Corns

English Poets edited by Claude Rawson

English Renaissance Drama edited by A. R. Braunmuller and Michael Hattaway, (second edition)

English Renaissance Tragedy edited by Emma Smith and Garrett A. Sullivan Jr.

English Restoration Theatre edited by Deborah C. Payne Fisk

Environmental Humanities edited by Jeffrey Cohen and Stephanie Foote

The Epic edited by Catherine Bates

Erotic Literature edited by Bradford Mudge

The Essay edited by Kara Wittman and Evan Kindley

European Modernism edited by Pericles Lewis

European Novelists edited by Michael Bell

Fairy Tales edited by Maria Tatar

Fantasy Literature edited by Edward James and Farah Mendlesohn

Feminist Literary Theory edited by Ellen Rooney

Fiction in the Romantic Period edited by Richard Maxwell and Katie Trumpener

The Fin de Siècle edited by Gail Marshall

Frankenstein edited by Andrew Smith

The French Enlightenment edited by Daniel Brewer

French Literature edited by John D. Lyons

The French Novel: from 1800 to the Present edited by Timothy Unwin

Gay and Lesbian Writing edited by Hugh Stevens

German Romanticism edited by Nicholas Saul

Global Literature and Slavery edited by Laura T. Murphy

Gothic Fiction edited by Jerrold E. Hogle

The Graphic Novel edited by Stephen Tabachnick

The Greek and Roman Novel edited by Tim Whitmarsh

Greek and Roman Theatre edited by Marianne McDonald and J. Michael Walton

Greek Comedy edited by Martin Revermann

Greek Lyric edited by Felix Budelmann

Greek Mythology edited by Roger D. Woodard

Greek Tragedy edited by P. E. Easterling

The Harlem Renaissance edited by George Hutchinson

The History of the Book edited by Leslie Howsam

Human Rights and Literature edited by Crystal Parikh

The Irish Novel edited by John Wilson Foster

Irish Poets edited by Gerald Dawe

The Italian Novel edited by Peter Bondanella and Andrea Ciccarelli

The Italian Renaissance edited by Michael Wyatt

Jewish American Literature edited by Hana Wirth-Nesher and Michael P. Kramer

The Latin American Novel edited by Efraín Kristal

Latin American Poetry edited by Stephen Hart

Latina/o American Literature edited by John Morán González

Latin Love Elegy edited by Thea S. Thorsen

Literature and the Anthropocene edited by John Parham

Literature and Climate edited by Adeline Johns-Putra and Kelly Sultzbach

Literature and Disability edited by Clare Barker and Stuart Murray

Literature and Food edited by J. Michelle Coghlan

Literature and the Posthuman edited by Bruce Clarke and Manuela Rossini

Literature and Religion edited by Susan M. Felch

Literature and Science edited by Steven Meyer

The Literature of the American Civil War and Reconstruction edited by Kathleen Diffley and Coleman Hutchison

The Literature of the American Renaissance edited by Christopher N. Phillips

The Literature of Berlin edited by Andrew J. Webber

The Literature of the Crusades edited by Anthony Bale

The Literature of the First World War edited by Vincent Sherry

The Literature of London edited by Lawrence Manley

The Literature of Los Angeles edited by Kevin R. McNamara

The Literature of New York edited by Cyrus Patell and Bryan Waterman

The Literature of Paris edited by Anna-Louise Milne

The Literature of World War II edited by Marina MacKay

Literature on Screen edited by Deborah Cartmell and Imelda Whelehan

Lyrical Ballads edited by Sally Bushell

Medieval British Manuscripts edited by Orietta Da Rold and Elaine Treharne

Medieval English Culture edited by Andrew Galloway

Medieval English Law and Literature edited by Candace Barrington and Sebastian Sobecki

Medieval English Literature edited by Larry Scanlon

Medieval English Mysticism edited by Samuel Fanous and Vincent Gillespie

Medieval English Theatre edited by Richard Beadle and Alan J. Fletcher (second edition)

Medieval French Literature edited by Simon Gaunt and Sarah Kay

Medieval Romance edited by Roberta L. Krueger

Medieval Women's Writing edited by Carolyn Dinshaw and David Wallace

Modern American Culture edited by Christopher Bigsby

Modern British Women Playwrights edited by Elaine Aston and Janelle Reinelt

Modern French Culture edited by Nicholas Hewitt

Modern German Culture edited by Eva Kolinsky and Wilfried van der Will

The Modern German Novel edited by Graham Bartram

The Modern Gothic edited by Jerrold E. Hogle

Modern Irish Culture edited by Joe Cleary and Claire Connolly

Modern Italian Culture edited by Zygmunt G. Baranski and Rebecca J. West

Modern Latin American Culture edited by John King

Modern Russian Culture edited by Nicholas Rzhevsky

Modern Spanish Culture edited by David T. Gies

Modernism edited by Michael Levenson (second edition)

The Modernist Novel edited by Morag Shiach

Modernist Poetry edited by Alex Davis and Lee M. Jenkins

Modernist Women Writers edited by Maren Tova Linett

Narrative edited by David Herman

Narrative Theory edited by Matthew Garrett

Native American Literature edited by Joy Porter and Kenneth M. Roemer

Nineteen Eighty-Four edited by Nathan Waddell

Nineteenth-Century American Poetry edited by Kerry Larson

Nineteenth-Century American Women's Writing edited by Dale M. Bauer and Philip Gould

Nineteenth-Century Thought edited by Gregory Claeys

The Novel edited by Eric Bulson

Old English Literature edited by Malcolm Godden and Michael Lapidge (second edition)

Performance Studies edited by Tracy C. Davis

Piers Plowman by Andrew Cole and Andrew Galloway

The Poetry of the First World War edited by Santanu Das

Popular Fiction edited by David Glover and Scott McCracken

Postcolonial Literary Studies edited by Neil Lazarus

Postcolonial Poetry edited by Jahan Ramazani

Postcolonial Travel Writing edited by Robert Clarke

Postmodern American Fiction edited by Paula Geyh

Postmodernism edited by Steven Connor

Prose edited by Daniel Tyler

The Pre-Raphaelites edited by Elizabeth Prettejohn

Pride and Prejudice edited by Janet Todd

Queer Studies edited by Siobhan B. Somerville

Renaissance Humanism edited by Jill Kraye

Robinson Crusoe edited by John Richetti

Roman Comedy edited by Martin T. Dinter

The Roman Historians edited by Andrew Feldherr

Roman Satire edited by Kirk Freudenburg

Science Fiction edited by Edward James and Farah Mendlesohn

Scottish Literature edited by Gerald Carruthers and Liam McIlvanney

Sensation Fiction edited by Andrew Mangham

Shakespeare and Contemporary Dramatists edited by Ton Hoenselaars

Shakespeare and Popular Culture edited by Robert Shaughnessy

Shakespeare and Race edited by Ayanna Thompson

Shakespeare and Religion edited by Hannibal Hamlin

Shakespeare and War edited by David Loewenstein and Paul Stevens

Shakespeare on Film edited by Russell Jackson (second edition)

Shakespeare on Screen edited by Russell Jackson

Shakespeare on Stage edited by Stanley Wells and Sarah Stanton

Shakespearean Comedy edited by Alexander Leggatt

Shakespearean Tragedy edited by Claire McEachern (second edition)

Shakespeare's First Folio edited by Emma Smith

Shakespeare's History Plays edited by Michael Hattaway

Shakespeare's Language edited by Lynne Magnusson with David Schalkwyk

Shakespeare's Last Plays edited by Catherine M. S. Alexander

Shakespeare's Poetry edited by Patrick Cheney

Sherlock Holmes edited by Janice M. Allan and Christopher Pittard

The Sonnet edited by A. D. Cousins and Peter Howarth

The Spanish Novel: from 1600 to the Present edited by Harriet Turner and Adelaida López de Martínez

Textual Scholarship edited by Neil Fraistat and Julia Flanders

Theatre and Science edited by Kristen E. Shepherd-Barr

Theatre History by David Wiles and Christine Dymkowski

Transnational American Literature edited by Yogita Goyal

Travel Writing edited by Peter Hulme and Tim Youngs

Twentieth-Century British and Irish Women's Poetry edited by Jane Dowson

The Twentieth-Century English Novel edited by Robert L. Caserio

Twentieth-Century English Poetry edited by Neil Corcoran

Twentieth-Century Irish Drama edited by Shaun Richards

Twentieth-Century Russian Literature edited by Marina Balina and Evgeny Dobrenko

Utopian Literature edited by Gregory Claeys

Victorian and Edwardian Theatre edited by Kerry Powell

The Victorian Novel edited by Deirdre David (second edition)

Victorian Poetry edited by Joseph Bristow

Victorian Women's Poetry edited by Linda K. Hughes

Victorian Women's Writing edited by Linda H. Peterson

War Writing edited by Kate McLoughlin

Women's Writing in Britain, 1660–1789 edited by Catherine Ingrassia

Women's Writing in the Romantic Period edited by Devoney Looser

World Literature edited by Ben Etherington and Jarad Zimbler

World Crime Fiction edited by Jesper Gulddal, Stewart King and Alistair Rolls

Writing of the English Revolution edited by N. H. Keeble

The Writings of Julius Caesar edited by Christopher Krebs and Luca Grillo

CPSIA information can be obtained
at www.ICGtesting.com
Printed in the USA
LVHW022025041222
734570LV00002B/207